Agile Network Businesses

Agile Network Businesses
Collaboration, Coordination, and Competitive Advantage

Vivek Kale

CRC Press
Taylor & Francis Group
Boca Raton London New York

CRC Press is an imprint of the
Taylor & Francis Group, an **informa** business

AN AUERBACH BOOK

CRC Press
Taylor & Francis Group
6000 Broken Sound Parkway NW, Suite 300
Boca Raton, FL 33487-2742

First issued in hardback 2019

First issued in paperback 2022

© 2018 by Vivek Kale
CRC Press is an imprint of Taylor & Francis Group, an Informa business

No claim to original U.S. Government works

ISBN 13: 978-1-03-247675-9 (pbk)
ISBN 13: 978-1-4987-4832-2 (hbk)

DOI: 10.4324/9781315368559

Library of Congress Cataloging-in-Publication Data

Names: Kale, Vivek, author.
Title: Agile network businesses : collaboration, coordination, and
competitive advantage / Vivek Kale.
Description: New York : CRC Press, 2017.
Identifiers: LCCN 2016056575| ISBN 9781498748322 (hb : alk. paper) | ISBN
9781315368559 (eISBN)
Subjects: LCSH: Business networks. | Knowledge management. | Information
technology--Management.
Classification: LCC HD69.S8 K353 2017 | DDC 658.4/038028546--dc23
LC record available at https://lccn.loc.gov/2016056575

Visit the Taylor & Francis Web site at
http://www.taylorandfrancis.com

and the CRC Press Web site at
http://www.crcpress.com

L. G. Joshi and his highly successful entrepreneurial ventures that sparked my interest, imagination, and insight into the power of networks.

Contents

SECTION I GENESIS OF NETWORK BUSINESSES

SECTION II ROAD TO NETWORK BUSINESSES

SECTION III   NETWORK BUSINESSES

SECTION IV   NETWORK BUSINESSES EXAMPLES

List of Figures

List of Tables

Preface

In the last couple of decades, the business environment has changed with unprecedented speed. Firms structured along tight hierarchies first started to cooperate in tightly coupled strategic networks with stable interorganizational ties, then moved into more loosely coupled configurations of legally independent firms in order to create competitive advantages. The networked enterprise that emerged represents an organizational form that is vastly better at managing unpredictable environments and conditions of uncertainty.

These changes in the competitive environment have had a profound effect on the way organizations compete and cooperate today. Whereas vertically integrated firms are reconfiguring their value chain and focusing on added-value activities, small firms aggregated into industrial districts are growing globally, creating loosely coupled networks of firms.

Customers in geographically dispersed, emerging, and established global markets nowadays demand higher quality products in a greater variety, at lower cost, and in a shorter time. As a result, enterprises have moved from centralized, vertically integrated, single-site manufacturing facilities to geographically dispersed networks of capabilities, competencies, and resources, namely, network enterprises. Enterprises are now constructing more fluid "network businesses" in which each member focuses on its differentiation and relies increasingly on its partners, suppliers, and customers to provide the rest. This book shifts focus from the traditional network of *real* businesses to such *virtual* IT-enabled network businesses or enterprises, because their operations and dynamics as such represent the market more closely. Network businesses have emerged as an organizational paradigm for collaboration and coordination across loosely connected individual organizations.

A network enterprise needs to be differentiated from the traditional focal firm acting as an orchestrator or systems integrator: the traditional focal firm seldom plays simultaneous differing roles in different network of enterprises. In contrast, the focal firm within a network enterprise may participate simultaneously in differing roles to differing degrees in more than one but disparate network enterprises.

There may be an impression that managing the network enterprise will entail frightening proportions of issues in the areas of leadership, human resources, and so on. The author would hasten to allay any sense of alarm by pointing out that the network enterprise is not as far fetched as it may seem at the first blush. All project-oriented businesses, ranging from small engineering and construction firms to engineering procurement construction (EPC) behemoths like Bachtel, have been routinely enacting this very business model for decades while undertaking projects across the whole world.

Network businesses or enterprises are a realization of the vision of IT/IS-enabled virtual network enterprises that reform and reconfigure automatically to address the opportunities available in the market. They have especially become viable and governable after the advent of cloud computing and big data computing. Big data computing systems and environments combine the power of elastic infrastructure (via cloud computing) and information management with the ability to analyze and discern recurring patterns in the colossal pools of operational and transactions data (via big data computing) to leverage and transform them into success patterns for an enterprise's business. These extremes of requirements for storage and processing arose primarily from developments of the past decade in the areas of e-business networks, social networks, wireless networks, and so on.

What Makes This Book Different?

This book interprets the 1990s phenomenon of network enterprises from the point of view of business and technology. It enables IT managers and business decision makers to get a clear understanding of what network businesses or enterprises really means, what it might do for them, and how it can be realized.

The characteristic features of this book are as follows:

- Introduces the network solutions and distributed systems that were a first step toward enabling a network enterprise. It also gives a detailed description of network of enterprises and agent systems related solutions that paved the road to network enterprises.
- Describes the basics of service oriented architecture (SOA), cloud computing, and big data computing that were essential prerequisites to the latest network enterprises.
- Details the distinguishing aspects of network enterprises, namely, virtual enterprises, taxonomy and management of network enterprises, and collaborative enterprises.
- Covers major application areas of interest in network enterprises, namely, supplier, manufacturing, e-business, platform, social, and wireless sensor networks.
- Introduces new *decision networks* in the context of supply chain networks.

In the final analysis, network enterprise is a realization of the vision of the *internetworked virtual enterprise* that reforms and reconfigures automatically to address the opportunities available in the market and which falls within the gambit of the market mandated by the stakeholders. It also reinterprets the traditional supply chain (SC) in terms of the flow of decisions, information, and materials, leading to the trifurcation of SC networks into mutually separable decision networks (like fourth-party logistics [4PLs]), information networks (like wireless sensor networks [WSN] and Sensor Farms), and logistics networks (like third-party logistics [3PLs]). I wanted to write a book presenting network enterprises from this novel perspective; the outcome is the book that you are reading now. Thank you!

Notwithstanding the worldwide protectionist tide against globalization, the separation of decision networks envisaged in this book will lead to a worldwide renewed interest in supply chain management businesses and SCM systems. In their new avatar of the trifurcated SC networks, SCM will chart *blue ocean* opportunities powered by artificial intelligence (AI) solutions for the decision networks, and big data and data fusion solutions for the information networks.

How Is This Book Organized?

This book traces the genesis and the road to network businesses, the detailed features and characteristics of network businesses, and, in the last part of the book, the high-potential examples of network businesses.

Chapter 1 provides an overview of agile enterprises. Chapter 2 explores the various types of business networks and describes the taxonomy of alliances between organizations.

Section I presents the genesis of network businesses. Chapters 3 and 4 provide an overview of computer networks and distributed systems respectively.

Section II presents the road that led to network businesses. Chapter 5 introduces the basic concepts of systems theory, complexity, and networks. Networks of enterprises and agent-based systems are described in Chapters 6 and 7, respectively. Chapter 8 discusses the nature and characteristics of cloud computing, service-oriented architecture, and business processes. Big data computing, NoSQL, and the graph database Neo4j are presented in Chapter 9.

Section III deals with network businesses. Chapter 10 introduces the characteristics of virtual organization and explores brands as a virtual organization, that is, a network enterprise. Chapter 11 deals with the management of network enterprises. Collaborative network enterprises are covered in Chapter 12.

Section IV deals with examples of network enterprises. Chapters 13 and 14 present the supplier and manufacturing network enterprises, respectively. Chapters 15 and 16 describe e-business and platform network enterprises, respectively. Chapter 17 is on popular social network enterprise applications such as Facebook and Twitter. Chapter 18 introduces sensor network enterprises.

Who Should Read This Book?

All stakeholders of a network enterprise can read this book. All those who are involved in any aspect of a IT/IS-enabled network enterprise project will profit by using this book as a road map to make a more meaningful contribution to the success of their network enterprise initiatives.

The minimal recommendations for different categories of stakeholders are as follows:

- Executives and business managers should read Chapters 1, 2, 5, and 10–17.
- Operational managers should read Chapters 1, 2, 5, 6, and 10–18.
- Project managers and module leaders should read Chapters 1, 3–9, and 13–18.
- Technology managers should read Chapters 1–18.
- Professionals interested in network enterprises should read Chapters 1, 2, and 5–17.
- Students of computer courses should read Chapters 1–10 and 13–18.
- Students of management courses should read Chapters 1, 2, 5, 6, and 10–18.
- General readers interested in the phenomenon of network enterprises should read Chapters 1–6 and 10–18.

Vivek Kale
Mumbai, India

Acknowledgments

I would like to thank all those who have helped me with their clarifications, criticism, and valuable information during the writing of this book.

Thanks again to John Wyzalek for making this book happen and guiding it through to completion.

My wife, Girija, and my daughters, Tanaya and Atmaja, patiently tolerated my mental and physical absences during the writing (and rewritings) of this book. Ultimately, it is their cheerful support that make these book projects possible and worthwhile.

Vivek Kale
Mumbai, India

Author

Vivek Kale has more than two decades of professional IT experience, during which he has handled and consulted on various aspects of enterprise-wide information modeling, enterprise architectures, business process redesign, and e-business architectures. He has been CIO of both the Essar Group, the steel, oil, and gas major of India, and Raymond Ltd., the textile and apparel major of India. He is a seasoned practitioner in transforming the business of IT, facilitating business agility, and enhancing IT-enabled enterprise intelligence. He is the author of *Inverting the Paradox of Excellence: How Companies Use Variations for Business Excellence and How Enterprise Variations Are Enabled by SAP* (CRC Press, 2014).

Other Books by Vivek Kale

Big Data Computing: A Guide Business and Technology Managers (CRC Press, 2017)

Enhancing Enterprise Intelligence: Leveraging ERP, CRM, SCM, PLM, BPM, and BI (CRC Press, 2016)

Guide to Cloud Computing for Business and Technology Managers: From Distributed Computing to Cloudware Applications (CRC Press, 2015)

Inverting the Paradox of Excellence: How Companies Use Variations for Business Excellence and How Enterprise Variations Are Enabled by SAP (CRC Press, 2015)

Implementing SAP® CRM: The Guide for Business and Technology Managers (CRC Press, 2015)

Chapter 1

Smart Enterprises

1.1 Agile Enterprises

The difficult challenges facing businesses today require enterprises to be transitioned into flexible, agile structures that can respond to new market opportunities quickly with minimal new investment and risk. As enterprises have experienced the need to be simultaneously efficient, flexible, responsive, and adaptive, they have transitioned themselves into agile enterprises with small, autonomous teams that work concurrently, reconfigure quickly, and adopt highly decentralized management that recognizes its knowledge base and manages it effectively.

Enterprise agility is the ability to be

1. Responsive: Adaptability is enabled by the concept of loosely coupled interacting components reconfigurable within a unified framework. This is essential for ensuring opportunity management to sustain viability.

   The ability to be responsive involves the following aspects:
   - An organizational structure that enables change is based on reusable elements that are reconfigurable in a scalable framework. Reusability and reconfigurability are generic concepts that are applicable to work procedures, manufacturing cells, production teams, or information automation systems.
   - An organizational culture that facilitates change and focuses on change proficiency.

2. Intelligence intensive: An enterprise should have the ability to manage and apply knowledge effectively, whether it is knowledge of a customer, a market opportunity, a competitor's threat, a production process, a business practice,

a product technology, or an individual's competency. This is essential for ensuring innovation management to sustain leadership.

The ability to be intelligence intensive involves the following aspects:

- Enterprise knowledge management
- Enterprise collaborative learning

 When confronted with a competitive opportunity, a smaller company is able to act more quickly, whereas a larger company has access to more comprehensive knowledge (options, resources, etc.) and can decide to act sooner and more thoroughly.

Agility is the ability to respond to (and ideally benefit from) unexpected change. Agility is unplanned and unscheduled adaptation to unforeseen and unexpected external circumstances. However, we must differentiate between agility and flexibility. Flexibility is scheduled or planned adaptation to unforeseen yet expected external circumstances.

One of the foremost abilities of an agile enterprise is its ability to quickly react to change and adapt to new opportunities. This ability to change works along two dimensions:

1. The *number* or *types of changes* an enterprise is able to undergo
2. The *degree of change* an enterprise is able to undergo

The former is termed as *range*, and the latter is termed as *response ability*. The more response able an enterprise is, the more radical a change it can gracefully address. Range refers to how large a domain is covered by the agile response system—in other words, how far from the expected set of events one can go and still have the system respond well. However, given a specific range, how well the system responds is a measure of response or change ability.

 Enterprises primarily aim progressively for efficiency, flexibility, and innovation in that order. The Model Builder's kit, Erector Set kit, and Lego kit are illustrations of enterprises targeting for efficiency, flexibility, and innovation (i.e., agility), respectively.

Construction toys offer a useful metaphor because the enterprise systems we are concerned with must be configured and reconfigured constantly, precisely the objective of most construction toys. An enterprise system architecture and structure consisting of reusable components reconfigurable in a scalable framework can be an effective base model for creating variable (or built-for-change) systems. For achieving this, the nature of the framework appears to be a critical factor. We can introduce the framework/component concept by looking at three types of construction toys and observe how they are used in practice—namely, the Model Builder's kit, Erector Set kit, and Lego kit.

You can build virtually anything over and over again with either of these toys, but fundamental differences in their architectures give each system unique dynamic characteristics. All consist of a basic set of core construction components and also have an architectural and structural framework that enables builders to connect the components into an unbounded variety of configurations. Nevertheless, the Model Builder's kit is not as reusable in practice as the Erector Set, the Erector Set is not as reusable or reconfigurable or scalable in practice as Lego, and Lego is more reusable, reconfigurable, and scalable than either of them. Lego is the dominant construction toy of choice among preteen builders, who appear to value experimentation and innovation.

The Model Builder's kit can be used to construct an object, such as an airplane, of an intended size. A highly integrated system, this construction kit offers maximum esthetic appeal for one-time construction use, but the parts are not reusable, the construction cannot be reconfigured, and one intended size precludes any scalability. But it will remain what it is for all time—there is zero variability here.

Erector Set kits can be purchased for constructing specific models, such as a small airplane, that can be assembled in many different configurations. With the Erector Set kit, the first model built is likely to remain as originally configured in any particular play session. Erector Set, for all its modular structure, is just not as reconfigurable in practice as Lego. The Erector Set connectivity framework employs a special-purpose intermediate subsystem used solely to attach one part to another—a nut-and-bolt pair and a 90° elbow. The components in the system all have holes through which the bolts may pass to connect one component with another. When a nut is lost, a bolt is useless and vice versa; when all the nuts and bolts remaining in a set have been used, any remaining construction components are useless and vice versa. All the parts in a Lego set can always be used and reused, but the Erector Set, for all its modularity, is not as reusable in practice.

Lego offers similar kits, and both toys include a few necessary special parts, such as wheels and cowlings, to augment the core construction components. Watch a child work with either and you'll see the Lego construction undergoes constant metamorphosis; the child may start with one of the pictured configurations but then reconfigure the pieces into all manner of other imagined styles. Lego components are plug compatible with each other, containing the connectivity framework as an integral feature of the component. A standard grid of bumps and cavities on component surfaces allow them to snap together into a larger configuration, without limit.

The Model Builder's kit has a tight framework: a precise construction sequence, no part interchangeability, and high integration. Erector Set has a loose framework that doesn't encourage interaction among parts and insufficiently discriminates among compatible parts. In contrast, each component in the Lego system carries all it needs to interact with other components (the interaction framework rejects most unintended parts) and can grow without end.

1.1.1 Stability versus Agility

Most large-scale change efforts in established enterprises fail to meet expectations because nearly all models of organization design, effectiveness, and change assume stability is not only desirable but also attainable. The theory and practice in organization design explicitly encourage organizations to seek alignment, stability, and equilibrium. The predominant logic of organizational effectiveness has been that an organization's fit with its environment, its execution, and its predictability are the keys to its success. Organizations are encouraged to institutionalize best practices, freeze them into place, focus on execution, stick to their knitting, increase predictability, and get processes under control. These ideas establish stability as the key to performance.

The stability of a distinctive competitive advantage is a strong driver for organization design because of its expected link to excellence and effectiveness. Leveraging an advantage requires commitments that focus attention, resources, and investments onto the chosen alternatives. In other words, competitive advantage results when enterprises finely hone their operations to perform in a particular way. This leads to large investments in operating technologies, structures, and ways of doing things. If such commitments are successful, they lead to a period of high performance and a considerable amount of positive reinforcement. Financial markets reward stable competitive advantages and predictable streams of earnings: a commitment to alignment reflects a commitment to stability.

Consequently, enterprises are built to support stable strategies, organizational structures, and enduring value creations, not to vary. For example, the often-used strengths, weaknesses, opportunities, and threats (SWOT) analysis encourages firms to leverage opportunities while avoiding weaknesses and threats. This alignment of positive and negative forces is implicitly assumed to remain constant, and there is no built-in assumption of agility. When environments are stable or at least predictable, enterprises are characterized by rules, norms, and systems that limit experimentation, control variation, and reward consistent performance. There are many checks and balances in place to ensure that the organization operates in the prescribed manner. Thus, to get the high performance they want, enterprises put in place practices they see as a good fit, without considering whether they can be changed and whether they will support changes in future; that is, by aligning themselves to achieve high performance today, enterprises often make it difficult to vary so that they can have high performance tomorrow.

When the environment is changing slowly or predictably, these models are adequate. However, as the rate of change increases with increasing globalization, technological breakthroughs, associative alliances, and regulatory changes, enterprises have to look for greater agility, flexibility, and innovation from their companies. Instead of pursuing strategies, structures, and cultures that are designed to create long-term competitive advantages, companies must seek a string of temporary competitive advantages through an approach to organization design that assumes change is normal. With the advent of the Internet and the accompanying extended "virtual" market spaces, enterprises are now competing based on intangible assets such as identity, intellectual property, ability to attract and stick to customers, and their ability to organize, reorganize frequently, or organize differently in different areas, depending on the need. Thus, the need for changes in management and organization is much more frequent, and excellence is much more a function of possessing the ability for changes. Enterprises need to be built around practices that encourage change, not thwart it. Instead of having to create change efforts, disrupt the status quo, or adapt to change, enterprises should be built for change.

To meet the conflicting objectives of performing well against the current set of environmental demands and changing themselves to face future business environments, enterprises must engender two types of changes: the natural process of evolution, or what we will call *strategic adjustments*, and *strategic reorientations*.

1. Strategic adjustments involve the day-to-day tactical changes required to bring in new customers, make incremental improvements in products and services, and comply with regulatory requirements. This type of change helps fine-tune current strategies and structures to achieve short-term results; it is steady, incremental, and natural. This basic capability to evolve is essential if an enterprise is to survive to thrive.
2. Strategic reorientations involve altering an existing strategy and, in some cases, adopting a new strategy. When the environment evolves or changes sufficiently, an enterprise must significantly adjust some elements of its strategy and the way it executes that strategy. More often than not, enterprises have to face a transformational change that involves not just a new strategy but a transformation of the business model that leads to new products, services, and customers, and requires markedly new competencies and capabilities. However, operationally, all these changes can be seen as manifestations of the basic changes, only differing in degrees and multiple dimensions.

Maintaining an agile enterprise is not a matter of searching for the strategy but continuously strategizing; it is not a matter of specifying an organization design but committing to a process of organizing; and it is not generating value but continuously improving the efficiency and effectiveness of the value generation process. It is a search for a series of temporary configurations that create short-term advantages. In turbulent environments, enterprises that string together a series of temporary but adequate competitive advantages will outperform enterprises that stick with one advantage for an extended period of time. The key issue for the built-for-change enterprise is orchestration, or coordinating the multiple changing subsystems to produce high levels of current enterprise performance.

1.1.2 Aspects of Agility

This section addresses the analytical side of agility or the change proficiency of the enterprise. It highlights the fundamental principles that underlie an enterprise's ability to change and indicates how to apply these principles in real situations. It illustrates what it is that makes a business and any of its constituting systems easy to change.

Agility or change proficiency enables both efficiency programs (e.g., lean production) and transformation programs; if the enterprise is proficient at change, it can adapt to take advantage of an unpredictable opportunity and can also counter the unpredictable threat. Agility can embrace semantics across the whole spectrum: it can capture cycle time reduction, with everything happening faster; it can build on lean production, with high resource productivity; it can encompass mass customization, with customer-responsive product variation; it can embrace virtual enterprise, with streamlined supplier networks and opportunistic partnerships; it can echo reengineering, with a process and transformation focus; it can demand a learning organization, with systemic training and education. Being agile means being proficient at change. Agility allows an enterprise to do anything it wants to do whenever it wants to—or has to—do it. Thus, an agile enterprise can employ *business process reengineering* (BPR) as a core competency when transformation is called for; it can hasten its conversion to lean production when greater efficiencies are useful; it can continue to succeed when constant innovation becomes the dominant competitive strategy. Agility can be wielded overtly as a business strategy as well as inherently as a sustainable-existence competency.

Agility derives from both the physical ability to act (*change ability*) and the intellectual ability to find appropriate things to act on (*knowledge management*). Agility can be expressed as the ability to manage and apply knowledge effectively, so that an enterprise has the potential to thrive in a continuously changing and unpredictable business environment. Agility derives from two sources: an enterprise architecture that enables change and an organizational culture that facilitates change. The enterprise architecture that enables change is based on reusable elements that are reconfigurable in a scalable framework.

Agility is a core fundamental requirement of all enterprises. It was not an area of interest when environmental change was relatively slow and predictable. Now there is virtually no choice; enterprises must develop a conscious competency. Practically all enterprises now need some method to assess their agility and determine whether it is sufficient or needs improvement. This section introduces techniques for characterizing, measuring, and comparing variability in all aspects of business and among different businesses.

1.1.3 Principles of Built-for-Change Systems

Christopher Alexander introduced the concept of *patterns* in the late 1970s in the field of architecture. A pattern describes a commonly occurring solution that generates decidedly successful outcomes.

A list of success patterns for agile enterprises (and systems) in terms of their constituent elements, functions, or components is as follows:

1. Reusable

   Agility pattern 1: Self-contained units (components). The components of agile enterprises are autonomous units cooperating toward a shared goal.

   Agility pattern 2: Plug compatibility. The components of agile enterprises are reusable and multiply replicable; that is, depending on requirements, multiple instances of the same component can be invoked concurrently.

   Agility pattern 3: Facilitated reuse. The components of agile enterprises share well-defined interaction and interface standards and can be inserted, removed, and replaced easily and noninvasively.

2. Reconfigurable

   Agility pattern 4: Flat interaction. The components of agile enterprises communicate, coordinate, and cooperate with other components concurrently and in real-term sharing of current, complete, and consistent information on interactions with individual customers.

   Agility pattern 5: Deferred commitment. The components of agile enterprises establish relationships with other components in real terms to enable the deferment of customer commitment to as late a stage as possible within the sales cycle, coupled with the corresponding ability to postpone the point of product differentiation as close as possible to the point of purchase by the customer.

   Agility pattern 6: Distributed control and information. The components of agile enterprises are defined declaratively rather than procedurally; the network of components display the defining characteristics of any *small world* network—namely, local robustness and global accessibility.

   Agility pattern 7: Self-organization. The components of agile enterprises are self-aware and interact with other components via on-the-fly integration, adjustment, or negotiation.

3. Scalable

   Agility pattern 8: Evolving standards (frameworks). The components of agile enterprises operate within predefined frameworks that standardize inter-component communication and interaction, determine component compatibility, and evolve to accommodate old, current, and new components.

   Agility pattern 9: Redundancy and diversity. The components of agile enterprises replicate components to provide the desired capacity, load-balancing and performance, and fault-tolerance as well as variations on the basic component functionality and behavior.

Agility pattern 10: Elastic capacity. The components of agile enterprises enable the dynamic utilization of additional or a reduced number of resources, depending on the requirements.

1.1.4 Framework for Change Proficiency

How do we measure enterprise agility? This section establishes a metric framework for proficiency at change. An enterprise's change proficiency may exist in one or more dimensions of changes, and these dimensions can form a structural framework for understanding current capabilities and setting strategic priorities for improvement. How does the agile enterprise know when it is improving its changeability or losing ground? How does it know if it is less changeable than its competition? How does it set improvement targets? Thus, a practical measure of change proficiency is needed before we can talk meaningfully about getting more, or even some, of it.

It must be highlighted that measuring change competency is generally not unidimensional, nor is it likely to result in an absolute and unequivocal comparative metric. Change proficiency has both reactive and proactive modes. Reactive change is opportunistic and responds to a situation that threatens viability. Proactive change is innovative and responds to a possibility for leadership. An enterprise sufficiently proficient at reactive change, when prodded, should be able to use that competency proactively and let others do the reacting.

Would it be proficient if a short-notice change was completed in the time required but at a cost that eventually bankrupted the company, or if the changed environment thereafter required the special wizardry and constant attention of a specific employee to keep it operational? Is it proficient if the change is virtually free and painless but out of synch with market opportunity timing? Is it proficient if it can readily accommodate a broad latitude of change that is no longer needed or too narrow for the latest challenges thrown at it by the business environment? Are we change proficient if we can accommodate any change that comes our way as long as it is within a narrow 10% of where we already are?

Therefore, change proficiency can be understood to be co-determined by four parameters.

- Time: A measure of elapsed time to complete a change (fairly objective)
- Cost: A measure of monetary cost incurred in a change (somewhat objective)
- Quality: A measure of prediction quality in meeting change time, cost, and specification targets robustly (somewhat subjective)
- Range: A measure of the latitude of possible change, typically defined and determined by a mission or charter (fairly subjective)

1.2 Enhancing Enterprise Agility

1.2.1 E-Business Strategy

The term *e-business* refers to an enterprise that has reengineered itself to conduct its business via the Internet. Successful enterprises need to reconceptualize the very nature of their business.

As customers begin to buy via the Internet and enterprises rush to use the Internet to create new operational efficiencies, most enterprises seek to update their business strategies. Enterprises survey the changing environment and then modify their company strategies to accommodate these changes. This involves major changes in the way companies do business, including changes in marketing, sales, service, product delivery, and even manufacturing and inventory. Changed strategies will entail changed business processes that, in turn, imply changed software systems, or better still, software systems that are changeable!

1.2.2 Business Process Reengineering

Although BPR has its roots in information technology (IT) management, it is basically a business initiative that has a major impact on the satisfaction of both the internal and external customer. Michael Hammer, who triggered the BPR revolution in 1990, considers BPR a "radical change," for which IT is the key enabler. BPR can be broadly described as the rethinking and changing of business processes to achieve dramatic improvements in measures of performances such as cost, quality, service, and speed.

Some of the principals advocated by Hammer are as follows:

■ Organize around outputs, not tasks.
■ Put the decisions and control, and hence all relevant information, into the hands of the performer.
■ Have those who use the outputs of a process perform the process, including the creation and processing of the relevant information.
■ The location of user data and process information should be immaterial; it should function as if all were in a centralized place.

The most important outcome of BPR has been viewing business activities as more than a collection of individual or even functional tasks; it has engendered a process-oriented view of business. However, BPR is different from quality management efforts such as TQM, ISO 9000, and so on, which refer to programs and initiatives that emphasize bottom-up incremental improvements in existing work processes and outputs on a continuous basis. In contrast, BPR usually refers to top-down dramatic improvements through redesigned or completely new processes on a discrete basis. In the continuum of methodologies ranging from ISO 9000,

TQM, ABM, and so on at one end and BPR on the other, Siebel implementation definitely lies on the BPR side of the spectrum when it comes to corporate change management efforts.

1.2.3 Mobilizing Enterprise Processes

This strategy entails replacing the process or process segment under consideration with a mobile-enabled link. In the next subsection, we discuss an overview of business processes before discussing the characteristics of mobilized processes.

Mobility offers new opportunities to dramatically improve business models and processes and will ultimately provide new, streamlined business processes that never would have existed if not for this new phenomenon.

1.2.3.1 Extending Web to Wireless

The first step in the evolution of mobility is to extend the Web to wireless; this is also known as *webifying*. For the most part, business processes are minimally affected in this phase. The goal is to provide value-added services through mobility with minimal disruption to existing processes. An example might be creating a new company website accessible through Apple iOS or Google Android–based smartphones. Firms attain immediate value through realizing additional exposure and market presence, and customers realize value through additional services.

1.2.3.2 Extending Business Processes with Mobility

The next step in the evolution of mobility is to extend existing business processes. New opportunities to streamline company business processes emerge and evolve to produce new revenue opportunities. One example is the way that mobility extends business processes through a supply chain optimization model. New business processes emerge through these new mechanisms that ultimately shorten the supply chain cycle, thus minimizing error and maximizing efficiency and realizing the utmost customer satisfaction. Real-time tracking and alert mechanisms provide supply chain monitors with the capability to monitor shipments and product line quality in ways that traditional business models are not capable of doing.

1.2.3.3 Enabling a Dynamic Business Model

The final phase in the evolution of mobility is the one that has only been touched on in today's world. The unique attributes of mobility will provide new and exciting ways of managing processes and allow for efficiencies never before attainable. The convergence of wireless technologies with existing business models will result in fully dynamic business processes.

1.3 Customer Responsiveness

It comes as a revelation that customers are neither necessarily looking for more products and services, nor are they looking for a wider range of choices. Customers simply want solutions to their individual needs—when, where, and how they want them. The goal of a responsive enterprise is the cost-effective delivery of an interactively defined need of a customer.

In traditional mass marketing, the primary focus is on the offering, and the goal is the sales transaction (Table 1.1). It is the offering (whether tangible or intangible), that must be defined, produced, and distributed. All measures of activity—namely, cost, revenue, and profits—are based on the offering. Mass marketing enterprises emphasize deterministic planning—for example, the best offering, the best way to produce and deliver the offering, the best way to inform potential customers about the offering, and so on. The "best" method is typically based on the anticipated need of a prototypical customer who represents the needs of the target market. And success depends on how many customers buy the offering. In customized marketing, the focus is on flexibility—the flexibility to obtain the capability and capacity needed to respond quickly to a wide variety of

Table 1.1 Customer Satisfaction Orientation of Traditional Mass Marketing vs. Value Orientation of Customized Relationship Marketing

Traditional Mass Marketing's Customer Satisfaction Orientation	*Customized Relationship Marketing's Customer Value Orientation*
Focuses on the product—emphasizes the firm's offering or tactical solution.	Focuses on the customer/product interaction—emphasizes fundamental needs of customer
Emphasizes product attributes and features.	Considers all aspects of the customer/product interaction, viz., attributes, values, and consequences
This is inherently more short term and unstable, leads to incremental or marginal product/service change and improvement, and results in historical orientation.	Is inherently more long term and stable, leads to innovation and radical improvements, and has a future orientation
Typically fails to measure trade-offs that determine customer value.	Measures the trade-offs that determine customer value
Often difficult to assess in the absence of consequence-level information.	Helpful to assess because of available interaction-level information and actionability

individual customer requests. Customer-responsive activities are used to find the best way to solve individual customer needs. In customized relationship marketing (or, in short, customized marketing), the emphasis is on delivered solution effectiveness (i.e., how well the individual problems are communicated, diagnosed, and solved) and delivered solution efficiency (i.e., how few resources are required to solve the problems).

While mass marketing enterprises try to sell a single product to as many customers as possible, customized marketing enterprises try to sell to a single customer as many products across as many different product lines over as long a period of time as possible. Customer relationship management (CRM) systems such as SAP CRM give enterprises the ability to interact *one-to-one* with individual customers and the ability to produce in response to individual customer requests.

The mass marketing and customized marketing approaches are organized very differently. The mass marketing approach anticipates customer needs and defines solutions before interacting with the customers, while the customized marketing approach involves developing a process that allows interaction with each individual customer one-to-one to define his or her need and then to customize the delivered solution in response to that need. Each type of marketing requires a different type of enterprise.

When the inflexibilities are because of natural causes beyond the control of the enterprise, competitors will not be able to gain a responsive edge and, hence, a competitive advantage. However, to the degree that inflexibilities are institutionally caused by organizational structure, processes, or strategies, the inflexibility is self-inflicted, and the enterprise should definitely be liberated from such inflexibilities to make it customer responsive. True customer centricity is reflected in the enterprise transitioning from providing customers a range of choice offerings to providing solutions to the specific needs of the customers; until the enterprise becomes customer-centric, the emphasis will be on the offering, not on the responsiveness. In the offering-based approach, when the range of offerings is small and demand is relatively stable, enterprises can focus on producing and mass marketing more new offerings and rely on the customer attending to the best of these offerings. As against this, in the customer responsiveness–based or customized marketing approach, rather than merely proliferating the number of offerings, enterprises focus on meeting the individual needs of the customers.

 It must be emphasized that, contrary to the common perception, responsiveness as an alternative approach to management has applications not only for services but also for production activities.

Whereas offering-based enterprises are characterized by *top-down management*, customer-responsive enterprises are oriented toward *bottom-up management*. As the response is guided by the prior organizational experience that is embodied in the *best-practice* guidelines readily available to all the frontline workers, the delivery is necessarily effective and efficient. Customer-responsive enterprises are knowledge based rather than plan based. This knowledge base consists of knowing how to divide the envisaged work into tasks, identify individual delivery units capable of performing it, assigning the work/tasks, and monitoring activities to ensure that the tasks are completed as per the agreed requirements. Unless the knowledge is captured, it will only be available to those who have experienced it or learned about it. Because it is modifiable, unlike a plan, the captured knowledge becomes a list of best practices to guide responses to requests in the future. Conditional best-practice guidelines specify the processes required for diagnosing needs and developing customized delivery plans. We discuss the development of best practices in "Best-practice guidelines management" in Section 1.3.1.

1. Advantages of customer responsiveness
   The various advantages of customer responsiveness are as follows:
   - Improves the fit between the customer's need and what the enterprise delivers
   - Increases profits through customer retention
   - Increases profits by reducing costs
   - Makes the enterprise more change capable

   Responsiveness reduces costs for the providers by reducing capital costs, making planning activities more efficient and effective, and increasing capacity utilization. Section 1.3.2.3, "Economics of Customer Responsiveness," looks at several aspects of costs associated with customer responsiveness.

2. Responsiveness reduces costs
   But can an enterprise be more responsive at reduced cost? Yes! In a career spanning about four decades, Taiichi Ohno spent years fine-tuning the principles for controlling costs that became the foundations of the world-famous Toyota Production System. He surprisingly discovered that not only the best way for increasing revenue but also the best way to reduce cost of automobile production was to make the system more flexible and responsive! This is akin to the situation in the 1960s and 1970s, when manufacturing quality and costs were mistakenly believed to be in opposition to each other; however, by the early 1990s, it was clearly established that not only can an enterprise achieve excellent quality at reduced costs, but it was also imperative for its success.

   Ohno discovered that the best way to reduce cost was also the best way to make the enterprise more responsive: customer-responsive management (crm) was the most cost-effective way to solve customer needs. Toyota found that to control costs, they had to separate capacity scheduling (*capacity management*) from work dispatching (*task assignments*): the responsiveness was not necessarily limited because of the constraints, inflexibilities, or limitations of the infrastructure but primarily because of the inflexible way the deliveries were scheduled and assigned (i.e., coordinated, monitored, and, if delayed, expedited).

3. Customer responsiveness is activity based

Customer responsiveness is activity based, where every activity is constituted of four parts.

- The first is an event (whether internal, external, regular, or dramatic) that triggers the response.
- The second defines the actions or tasks (guided by existing or customized best-practice guidelines) that need to be taken in response to the event.
- Third is the assignment (i.e., JIT coordination) of the identified actions to resources, with appropriate capability and capacity, in response to the event. Assignment minimizes lead time and thus contributes to enhancing the flexibility.
- Lastly, the desired benefits are delivered to the customer.

1.3.1 Salient Aspects of Customer Responsiveness

A major part of the following sections has been inspired by the insightful book *Customer-Responsive Management: The Flexible Advantage*, authored by Frank W. Davis and Karl B. Manrodt. The literature on enterprise responsiveness is rather limited, but this book is an exception and has had a lasting impression on the author in that it ignited an abiding interest in the nature of responsiveness and the characteristics of responsive enterprises.

The salient aspects involved with CRM are as follows:

1. Needs diagnosis management

This involves activities related to identifying, discovering, or understanding the needs of prospects or the newer needs of existing customers. Traditional offering-based or mass marketing enterprises typically achieve this through product catalogues, demonstrations, or even product data sheets. However, responsive enterprises achieve this through dialog with the customer regarding their operational or design issues problems, inefficiencies, and so on.

2. Best-practice guidelines management

Best-practice guidelines management is to response-based enterprises what strategic and tactical planning is to offering-based or mass marketing enterprises. It is the management of the enterprise's knowledge base by collecting newer needs encountered, solutions proposed and delivered by the frontline workers, and disseminating to all frontline workforce on a continual basis. It involves activities like development of new guidelines when new resources become available; dynamic modification of existing guidelines when new situations are encountered; and the periodic review of existing guidelines for continuous improvement.

There are two major categories of best-practice guidelines.
- Needs diagnosis
- Defining work, identifying resources/capacity, assigning work, and coordinating deliveries

The guideline should identify each task required, the skill needed to perform that task, the timing of the task, the conditions under which the task needs to be performed, and the capacity required to perform the task.

Processes are under continual review to verify the result and assess the delivered solution effectiveness and the efficiency of adopting the best-practice guidelines.

3. Responsive task management

Responsive task management is not unlike project management except that
- Customer requirements are often more similar than different, but never completely identical.
- Instead of a single big project, it is a series of smaller projects or tasks.
- Lead time is typically shorter.

It deals with the prioritized assignment list that is used to determine, plan, assign, and coordinate the work steps composing the deliveries to the individual customers. It also deals with the best-practice guidelines that must be developed to oversee the assigning, tracking, and delivery process.

4. Responsive capacity management

Responsive capacity management is the process of maximizing capacity utilization to deliver benefits to customers. It is the process of minimizing unutilized capacity; whereas delivered capacity generates revenue, unutilized capacity creates only additional cost, as this wasted capacity cannot be inventoried. As discussed in the following paragraphs, capacity is scheduled in the short term but sold only in the real term.

The various methods utilized to maintain high utilization are as follows:
- Forecasting needs so that access capacity is not scheduled in the short term: The ideal situation being the matching of capacity scheduling to the capacity utilization.
- The cross-training of employees so that the same capacity can be used for a wider variety of tasks: This is counter to the tendency of specialization in mass production or offering-based enterprises.
- Developing cooperative networks for real-term flexibility: The main driver for this method is the fact that the cost of transactions coupled with the cost of interfacing, collaboration, coordination, and communication between enterprises maybe be lower than the cost of those transactions being undertaken by a vertically integrated enterprise. Mass production or offering-based enterprises are more amenable to

"cooperative partnerships" that are oriented toward long-term, steady-state, and continuous relationships. Typically, a customer will have a limited number of cooperative partnerships; while it ensures the customer a consistent and reliable supply of know-how and offerings, it also ensures steady business for the provider. However, customer-responsive enterprises, rather than limiting the number of partners, place more emphasis on developing a large network of providers (each having their own special core competency) to increase the range of capabilities that they can access to meet their customers' needs. Instead of emphasizing steady-state relationships, customer-responsive enterprises focus more on obtaining a greater diversity of capabilities by enabling ready access to a broader network of solution-delivering units (i.e., resources) that are available for assigning on an as-need basis at any instant, at a lower cost, seamlessly, and with minimal friction.

Please also see Section 1.3.2.3, "Economics of Customer Responsiveness."

5. Resource interface management

Interface management is not unlike channel management, whose prime objective is to minimize the number of interfaces and to continuously optimize the performance of the existing interfaces in line with the business objectives and strategies of the enterprise. The more diverse are the final customer needs, the broader is the network necessary to provide access to more core competencies (i.e., capabilities); the greater is the variation in capacity needs, the greater is the depth of the network required to ensure the capacity required for each core competency. For enterprises to be flexible, they need access and the ability to integrate, assign, and coordinate the delivered solution at a very low cost. Whereas efficient network interface management enables network members to actually become additional solution-delivering units for the response-based enterprise, just as in-house delivery units do, inefficient interface management forces the enterprises to integrate vertically. Thus, its options for access solely to the capabilities (i.e., core competencies) of its in-house delivery units are limited.

With successful interface management, an enterprise has the following advantages:

- Virtually all enterprises can become part of the delivery network.
- Thus, the enterprise has virtually unlimited capability and capacity at its disposal to serve the needs of its customers.
- Thus, the enterprise can focus on meeting the needs of the customers unfettered by the need to find a revenue-generating use for the existing unused in-house capacity.

6. Customer service management

Products are rapidly being equated as the cost of doing business rather than as sales items; they are becoming more in the nature of *containers* or *platforms* for all sorts of upgrades and value-added services. This allows the enterprise to initiate and maintain a long-term relationship with the customer. For this reason, platforms are often sold at cost, or even given away free, in the expectation of selling even more lucrative services to the customer over the lifetime of the product, or rather, more correctly, the lifetime of the customer!

In these times of rapid product obsolescence and the continual onslaught of superior competitors, a sustainable competitive advantage can only be obtained through services such as

- Tailor-made designs
- Just-in-time logistics
- Installation of the equipment
- Customer training
- Documentation of goods
- Maintenance and spare part service
- Service recovery and complaints management
- Handling of enquiries
- Customer-oriented invoicing
- Pricing below the market standard

In the servicized economy, defined by shortening product life cycles and an ever-expanding flow of competitive goods and services, it is the customer's attention rather than resources that is becoming scarce. Giving away products is increasingly being used as a marketing strategy to capture the attention of potential customers. A growing number of enterprises are giving away their products for free to attract customers and then charging them for managing, upgrading, and servicing for the uninterrupted availability and usage of the products. Microsoft, after initially missing the Internet wave, invested massively to come up with the reasonably competitive Internet Explorer (IE) Web browser, but decided to give this away free to its customers.

Especially in the case of software companies, the cost of producing and delivering individual product orders is almost zero; hence, if enough customers "hook on" to the company's product and if the enterprise can set its product as an industry standard, it can sell upgrades and services at significant margins. The greater the number of customers linked together through an enterprise's program (see "Metcalfe's Law and Network Effects"), the greater the benefits to each of the participating customers and, consequently, more valuable are

- The services provided by the enterprise (at much lower cost, because the costs are spread across a much larger installed base of customers)
- The attendant long-term relationships with the customer

1.3.2 Customer-Responsive Management

The traditional philosophy of management focused on mass production was developed during the twentieth century. The foundation of mass production is based on

- Eli Whitney's concept of interchangeable parts
- Ford's development of the production line
- Frederick W. Taylor's scientific management
- GM and Dupont's cost-accounting methods

Mass production management focused on large-scale production and the mass marketing of standardized, low-cost products produced for homogenous markets. Customers' needs are researched so that the right product is offered to the marketplace. This approach results in centralized product planning, process planning, production scheduling, and market planning that is separated from the daily operations. When the change is gradual and incremental, the traditional make-and-sell enterprises focus on optimizing the efficiency of execution in terms of the following:

- Predicting, forecasting, or projecting the market demand
- Minimizing the cost of making and selling the corresponding offering

In contrast, when the customer-driven change becomes rapid and essentially unpredictable, adaptiveness takes precedence over efficiency: the enterprises need to sense the needs of the customer early and respond in the real term, individual customer by individual customer. The sense-and-respond enterprise becomes a pool of modular capabilities that can be dynamically configured and reconfigured to respond to the customer's latest requirements. Therefore, in make-and-sell enterprises the plan comes first, while in the sense-and-respond enterprises the customer comes first; make-and-sell enterprises primarily focus on what is common among many customers rather than what is different about individual ones. The customer commitment rather than the command-and-control structure defines the dynamic interactions between the modular capabilities.

Customer-responsive management (*crm*) enables enterprises to be more adaptable to changing conditions and responsive to smaller markets. The responsiveness could be in terms of

1. Timeliness (e.g., a schedule)
2. Time window (i.e., by a specified time range)
3. Priority (e.g., a dynamic dispatch list)

It recognizes that forecasting and planning become more difficult as the marketplace and environment become more turbulent. The detailed planning of work is done at the front line. The purpose of flexible planning is not to plan all the details of the work but to plan the infrastructure that is necessary to enable and facilitate individual-level changes. The emphasis in crm is to take steps that minimize the time and cost required to recognize and respond to changes. Whereas mass production is based on defining a product and designing the most efficient means of producing large quantities of a product, crm designs flexible processes that could make it easier to respond to changing conditions.

Thus, *crm* consists of two major relationships: one relationship is with the customers to identify and diagnose needs, and the second relationship is with the network of suppliers who make the delivery. For offering-based enterprises, the former corresponds to the marketing function (e.g., market research, product planning, advertising, sales, and customer service) and the later corresponds to the operations function (e.g., purchasing, production, supply chain logistics, and human resources). For traditional offering-based enterprises, logistics is generally understood as the process of managing the efficient flow and storage of raw materials, in-process inventory, finished goods, and information for conformance with the customer requirements. But within the crm framework, this logistics concept transforms to the coordination of deliveries that are responsive to individual customer requests using a network of resources and integrated by flexible processes and communications.

As emphasized brilliantly by Frank Davis, the separation of assignment and delivery is critical to achieving responsiveness. It is the frontline worker that interacts with the individual customer to determine individual needs. These individual needs are then used in conjunction with the conditional best-practice guidelines to develop the individual delivery plan. The individual delivery plan, which itemizes each task, schedule, and the responsible person, becomes the prioritized assignment list or *kanban*. This list is used to assign each task dynamically to the resource network as also for recording the results.

The offering-based deterministic enterprise uses highly structured systems or channels to develop a plan that not only includes the product design but also the channels that will be used to deliver the product to the customer. When enterprises do not have the flexibility to respond to a wide variety of needs, a different system must be established to meet each type of need. This makes it very expensive to respond to new markets. In contrast, the customer-responsive enterprise tends to build and use networks of resources that it can call on to respond to a wide range of needs. The customer-responsive enterprise is able to put together a large combination of resources to respond according to initial conditions–determined best-practice guidelines to a wide range of needs.

The role of the responsive enterprise is to develop an infrastructure that facilitates the integration of the provider network into the solution process and the assigning and monitoring of each delivery. When the infrastructure works, the relationship is effective and hassle free; otherwise, it is frustrating and unresponsive.

Similarly, when the infrastructure works, the delivery is efficient and the coordination cost is low; otherwise, the delivery is late and ineffective, and special recovery mechanisms such as expediting, inspection, signoffs, and approvals must be implemented to work around these shortcomings of the infrastructure. These recovery mechanisms unduly increase expense, slow delivery, and make the enterprise inflexible and unresponsive.

Thus, to be able to respond, the enterprise must create an enterprise infrastructure that includes

- Best-practice guideline development, to maintain a repertoire of delivery practices
- Resource network development that identifies resources, interfaces, and builds relationships to ensure that the resources are available when needed
- Information infrastructure development that integrates and coordinates individual deliveries

 Surely, the Internet is the classic illustration of a *neural network* on a large scale that displays a top-down oversight combined with a bottom-up cooperative delivery of digital content.

It displays the characteristic features of

- Network effects
- Small-world networks (SWNs)
- Cooperative patterns, etc.

We touch on these topics briefly in the following sections.

1.3.2.1 Networks of Resources

The customer-responsive enterprise is not aware of the exact needs of the customer until the customer calls them. Therefore, the enterprise cannot ever be more responsive to its customers than are its delivery units. The enterprise's ability to respond is determined by the capability and capacity available for assignment. Consequently, customer-responsive enterprises constantly seek to expand the core competencies—that is, the capability and capacity for assignment to serve customers. The more capability and capacity that is available, the more customers that can be served.

Because responsive enterprises typically deliver benefits to customers in the form of products, information, or even money, an enterprise utilizes a wide range of resources. Resources typically provide functions (or services) such as transport, storage, security, or processing. The range of resources includes

- Transportation network resources such as satellites (for communication movement), datacom (for data movement), truck lines (for products movement), and airlines (for people movement)
- Storage resources such as computer hard-disk storage banks (for e-data or e-content), voice mails (for messages), e-mails (for information messages), warehouses (for products), and hotels (for people)
- Security resources such as PINs and e-passports (for computer authentication), vaults or refrigeration units (for products), and escort services, smart cards, or identity cards (for people).
- Processing resources such as data-processing centers (for data and information), fulfillment centers (for products), janitorial services (for facilities), and health-care providers (for people)

Each of these resources would have a core competency. An enterprise cannot be more responsive than their resources enable them to be. To make responsive deliveries, the enterprise must be able to build a network of resources, develop guidelines that allow the integration of the resources into the delivery task, and information systems that allow the coordination and assigning of work to these resources. The resource units may either be owned by the responsive enterprise or may have a relationship with the responsive enterprise. Notwithstanding the legal nature of these collaborative relationships, which could either be collaborative exclusive partnerships or intermittently used networks, these resources have to be "always on"—that is, available when needed—and have the capability and capacity to respond to the responsive enterprise's dynamic assigning and monitoring requirements.

Infrastructure development is not a one-time effort but must evolve continually to allow the enterprise to stay ahead of competition and keep pace with technology and environmental changes. For instance:

- As new customer needs evolve, the infrastructure must enable these needs to be satisfied.
- As new resources become available, the infrastructure must integrate the new resource into the delivery process readily.
- As new technology becomes available, the infrastructure must allow newer options for communicating, coordinating deliveries, and relating with customers.
- As new measurement techniques become available, the infrastructure must incorporate them to enhance delivery coordination and monitoring.

The network of resources achieves two apparently contradictory goals: a greater ability to respond to customer needs and a reduction in the cost of the response.

In fact, by analogy with Sun's vision that "the network is the computer" one can say that "the network is the resource provider"! (Kale 2015).

1.3.2.2 Business Webs

Don Tapscott introduced the concept of a *business Web* (B-Web) as a cluster of businesses coming together, particularly over the Internet. B-Webs are the mechanisms for the accumulation of digital capital, consisting of three parts:

1. Human capital is the sum of the capabilities of individuals in the enterprise, including skills, knowledge, intellect, creativity, and know-how.
2. Customer capital is the wealth contained in an enterprise's relationships with its customers.
3. Structural capital is the knowledge embodied in enterprise procedures and processes.

The rise in affiliate marketing and the existence of Internet-based *extranets* or *exchanges* are examples of the rise of B-Webs.

1.3.2.3 Economics of Customer Responsiveness

Unlike mass production enterprises, which define the average cost per unit in terms of the constituent fixed and variable costs, customer-responsive enterprises classify costs into three components.

- Fixed-capacity costs are incurred to acquire or develop facilities, tools, and skills.
- Scheduled-capacity costs are incurred when the acquired facilities, tools, and skills are scheduled so that they become available to serve customers.
- Service delivery costs are the costs incurred when the benefits are actually delivered to the individual customer.

Consequently,

1. The total capacity costs are the combination of both fixed- and scheduled-capacity costs.
2. The total service delivery costs are the sum of the total capacity costs and the service delivery costs.

While fixed-capacity costs remain unchanged even in the long term, scheduled-capacity costs are variable costs in the short term and service delivery costs are variable costs even in the real term.

For responsive enterprises, revenues are determined in real time when the enterprise interacts with the customer. Therefore, for responsive activities capacity acquisitions, modifications or abdications are decided on a long-term basis, capacity is scheduled on a short-term basis, and capacity is committed on a real-term (or real-time or immediate-term) basis. While the capacity acquisition costs are based on the long-term trends analysis, the capacity is usually scheduled on a periodic basis, such as accounting periods, because of the availability of the relevant information on sales, production, costs, revenue, and inventory on which the schedule is based. As against this, the capacity is committed on the basis of real-term operational data available in CRM systems such as SAP CRM.

Moreover, the role of inventory changes radically in the process of the enterprise becoming more customer responsive. In the mass production (i.e., mass marketing) approach, inventory greatly simplifies the task of managing an offering-based enterprise because it allows the enterprise to manufacture products and ship finished goods to the marketplace in anticipation of market demand. It is the key for enabling various functions like purchasing, production, distribution, and sales to function independently and also seek optimal performance independently. There is no major emphasis on extensive coordination, planning, or scheduling, as inventory is used to buffer purchasing, planning, and scheduling. In times of market uncertainty and turbulence, inventory

- Desensitizes decision making
- Enables longer lead times
- Reduces flexibility
- Reduces the complexity of coordination

Thus, in offering-based enterprises, the local functional efficiencies and strategies are truly at the cost of increased inventory and inventory-carrying costs at the enterprise level. However, in the mass customization (i.e., customized marketing) approach, enterprises seek to minimize inventory because this not only reduces the costs but also enhances the enterprise's flexibility—that is, its ability to respond to changing conditions. But increases in flexibility also increase the complexity of coordination; the enterprise has to shift from the deterministic planning and scheduling management approach to the protocol and assignment method of coordination.

> However, inventory could change from a large user of capital (because inventory turns slower than payment terms) to a source of capital for financing retail outlets by dramatically increasing the normal inventory turns to much more rapid inventory churns. An inventory churning 24 times per year generates cash flow fast enough to provide its value in working capital to help finance the building of a new store.

As pointed out by Frank Davis, a customer-responsive enterprise does not have the luxury of inventory to buffer real-term variations and reduce management complexity. Although capacity has to be scheduled in anticipation of customer requests, the use of capacity can only be scheduled after receiving such a customer request. If the provider schedules too much capacity, the excess capacity gets wasted because capacity cannot be preserved in an inventory. But, on the other hand, if inadequate capacity is scheduled, some users are likely to go unserved. As the service delivery costs are typically less than 10% of the total delivery costs explained earlier, the profitability of the enterprise depends on reducing the fixed- and scheduled-capacity costs and maximizing the percent utilization.

To minimize wasted capacity, responsive enterprises have to enable more flexible scheduling in the short term and higher utilization in the real term. This can be achieved through the following:

- Economies of scope: An approach that allows the provider to increase capacity utilization (e.g., percentage billable hours, load factors, occupancy rates etc.) through the cross-training of the workforce.
- Economies of use: An approach that seeks to utilize every unit of scheduled capacity to generate revenue to minimize the amount of nonrevenue generation and wasted capacity.
- Economies of modularity: An approach that seeks greater flexibility to schedule capacity by developing modules so that less capacity can be scheduled when the demand is expected to be low. The more modular the organizational structure, the more efficiently the enterprise can respond to variations in expected capacity utilization. One way of increasing modularity is through networking.
- Economies of networking: An approach that seeks to allow enterprises the flexibility to focus on the changing customer needs rather than to be burdened with finding a revenue-generating use for the inflexible resources. Resources can either be acquired or networked: responsive enterprises will typically acquire resources where expected demand is continual and stable; whereas, if there is a greater variation in the expected capability and capacity needs, the enterprise will network with resources on an as-needed basis. Acquired resources become fixed-capacity costs, whereas networked resources become variable service delivery costs because they are paid on a per-use basis. It may be more efficient to have the resource in-house on a per-hour basis, but on a per-use basis it is more efficient to network for the resources. Thus, the network approach not only enhances the flexibility to respond to the customer needs but also makes this possible at a much lower cost!

The purpose of a network is to provide the enterprise with the range of capabilities and capacities it needs to serve its customers' diverse needs while at the same time maintaining the cost of the resource as a service delivery cost (which is a variable cost in the real term) rather than as a capacity cost (which is a fixed cost in the real term).

1.4 Network of Enterprises

Agile companies produce the right product, at the right place, at the right time, at the right price, and for the right customer. As pointed out by Jagdish Sheth, in these times of market change and turbulence, the half-life of customer knowledge (i.e., the time within which it loses currency by 50%) is getting shorter and shorter. The difficult challenges facing businesses today require organizations to transition into flexible, agile structures that can respond to new market opportunities quickly with a minimum of new investment and risk.

As enterprises have experienced the need to be simultaneously efficient, flexible, responsive, and adaptive, they have turned increasingly to the network form of organization, which has the following characteristics:

- Networks rely more on market mechanisms rather than on administrative processes to manage resource flows. These mechanisms are not the simple arm's-length relationships usually associated with independently owned economic entities. Instead, to maintain the position within the network, members recognize their interdependence and are willing to share information, cooperate with each other, and customize their product or service.
- While networks of subcontractors have been common for many years, recently formed networks expect members to play a much more proactive role in improving the final product or service.
- Instead of holding all the assets required to produce a given product or service in-house, networks use the collective assets of several firms located along the value chain.

The agile enterprise is composed of small, autonomous teams or subcontractors who work concurrently and reconfigure quickly to thrive in an unpredictable and rapidly changing customer environment. Each constituent has the full resources of the company or the value chain at its disposal and has a seamless information exchange between the lead enterprise and the virtual partners.

Thus, an enterprise network is a coalition of enterprises that work collectively and collaboratively to create value for the customers of a focal enterprise. Sometimes, the coalition is loosely connected; at other times, it is tightly defined, as in the relationship between Dell and its component suppliers. An enterprise network consists of a wide range of companies—suppliers, joint venture partners, contractors, distributors, franchisees, licensees, and so on—that contribute to the focal enterprise's creation and delivery of value to its customers. Each of these enterprises in turn will have their own enterprise networks focused around themselves. Thus, the relationships between enterprises in the network both enable and constrain the focal companies in the achievement of their goals.

Though they appear similar, there are fundamental differences between the agile and lean approaches to running a business. Lean production is at heart simply an enhancement of mass production methods, whereas agility implies breaking out of the mass production mold and into mass customization. Agility focuses on economies of scope rather than economies of scale, ideally serving ever-smaller niche markets—even in quantities of one—without the high cost traditionally associated with customization. A key element of agility is an enterprise-wide view, whereas lean production is usually associated with the efficient use of resources on the operations floor.

1.5 Summary

This chapter discussed the needs and characteristics of agile enterprises. It presents various strategies adopted for enabling enterprise agility ranging from e-Business transformations to mobilizing business processes. In the last part, the chapter introduced the concept of network of enterprises or, in other words, enterprise network.

Chapter 2

Business Networks

Any analysis of network enterprises puts emphasis on three aspects—the "nodes" (identified as the actors, agents, or network members, that is, firms, managers, individual entrepreneurs, or institutions), the ties and relations (identified as the links that facilitate transitivity, reciprocity, directionality, and multiplexity of content), and the overall network configuration, or network structure. This chapter discusses various types of network of enterprises; each type presents the particular network as a structure of relationships between heterogeneous actors. The heterogeneity of actors refers to business organizations, the individuals within them, institutions, technologies, and other artifacts that participate in the relational dynamics.

2.1 Network of Enterprises Taxonomy

2.1.1 Family Network Businesses

In the household economy, other motivations besides economic gain operate. Family business networks are based on family employment, with all subsequent aspects of risk taking, flexibility, self-financing, and control. Family businesses embedded in the web of family relationships absorb higher risk in response to uncertain employment and income opportunities. This is particularly useful for absorbing the shocks of economic restructuring and to assist in economic development via self-employment. Households not only can provide for themselves but can support family members in other social and economic activities through the internal redistribution of wealth.

People in the household base their actions on traditional or patriarchal reasoning and may run their own business as a source of identity, as well as for the preservation of dignity and independence. This different rationality is based on the concepts of *risk* and *insecurity* within the family, which contrasts with the conventional presumption of maximizing benefits from entrepreneurial activity. The most important factors that determine the scope of the family business are

- Inheritance law
- The passing of ownership rights from one generation to another
- The separation of the household and the family from the firm

2.1.2 Entrepreneurial Small Network Businesses

Entrepreneurial and small business networks usually represent dispersed and heterogeneous networks with fuzzy boundaries and resource-based and role-based divisions of labor. They comprise autonomous agents that are linked to each other via various formal and informal contracts and who share information and design collective strategies. Small firms mostly subcontract their services to some large firm, either in the region or nationally.

Small firms use networks primarily to complement their own limited resources. The growth orientation of the small business is determined by the embedded entrepreneurial attitudes toward exploring business opportunities, the perceived benefits and expected profits, and the participation of the firm in the redistribution of resources in the local community. Small businesses are more likely to choose to remain small and flexible in network configurations, where the collective results go far beyond the abilities of any single company. Together, these networks of small entrepreneurial firms generate higher profits for all by gaining access to larger markets, by benefiting from economies of scale, and by competing with larger firms without merging or being acquired.

The behavior of small entrepreneurial firms and their strategic decisions and choices to interlink with other business partners depends on a number of environmental factors. Among these are

- The demographic specificities of the region
- The local culture and the support from local institutions
- The regional structure of the economy in terms of leading companies that build the local pool of skills
- Professional and business links with leading employers in the region
- The level of entrepreneurial education
- The number of years running a business of their own
- The industry sector

■ The size of the firm
■ The growth orientation of the firm

Entrepreneurs develop contacts not only in their neighborhood but also with firms located at a distance and across multiple borders and boundaries. Relationships of resource sharing dominate the dynamics of interfirm exchanges and transactions. Entrepreneurial firms exist only because they satisfy certain market demands, even though they actively construct their market space with their innovations. By emerging in a certain market space, entrepreneurial firms connect to other firms, organizations, or individual customers.

What makes entrepreneurial small business networks different from family business networks is that they rely much more on resources outside of the family. Entrepreneurial networks are similar to family business networks and represent a dispersed type of structural network configuration. What distinguishes them from supply networks is that they are much closer to customers and therefore much more vulnerable to changes in customer needs.

2.1.3 Guanxi: Chinese Family and Community Network Businesses

Guanxi networks are based on the reciprocity of favors, which facilitates social exchanges supported by a mutual belief in reciprocity. Guanxi resemble a set of affective ties between people, linked through kinship, native place, dialect, school, workmates, or sworn brotherhood. Guanxi are established to facilitate the exchange of personal and knowledge-based resources, for mutual benefit and protection.

Guanxi refers to the relationships that bind people through the exchange of favors. It also refers to a reliance on informal business agreements. While some authors attempt to link the strength of the Chinese business networks to some fundamental religious attitudes, others argue that the normative basis of guanxi does not come from Confucianism. The values of interpersonal trust and affinal reciprocity are universal, and many other people and nations have recognized the practical advantage of reciprocal obligations against fears of reprisal and of losing functional ties. The merchant class in China itself has adopted Confucian rhetoric only as part of its flexible adaptation and search for legitimacy.

Guanxi networks have most of the features described for the previous category of family business networks. A main distinction is their ability to grow beyond the family and to expand into economic activities within the wider community. Although known as guanxi networks in the literature, the Chinese family and community business networks encompass a number of different social practices. Very often these different practices, which are based on different institutional formations, are bundled together as Chinese business networks or guanxi.

Usually, Chinese family and community business networks are homogeneous and have clear boundaries. There is no formal division of labor and different individuals are collectively entrusted to do different things and engage in different operations. The network develops its own rules and norms that generate normative interdependence. These networks use family representation and develop informal institutions that coordinate the collective efforts.

2.1.4 Keiretsu: Japanese Corporate Network Businesses

Keiretsu represent close, long-term business relationships established by large corporations with selected groups of smaller firms and financial and trading institutions. They represent a web of overlapping financial, commercial, and governance relationships, initiated from a central core. Keiretsu relationships are considered in terms of three different attributes: corporate groups, financial centrality, and industrial interdependency. These groups are linked through cross-shareholding investments, the exchange of personnel, shared debt and equity, and mutual strategic plans. Share ownership is a symbol of commitment and mutual obligation, rather than being motivated by expectations of dividends and returns on investment. A typical keiretsu core company will have 20%–40% of its stock owned by other companies within the keiretsu. Long-term shareholding agreements with other corporations create a situation whereby 60%–80% of the keiretsu stock is never traded.

Keiretsu groups exhibit a complex business network that has a multilevel structure with clear hierarchical orientation and core-periphery components. As a network, it has a governance structure and employs a complex resources- and capabilities-based division of labor. The firms within are characterized by shared ownership and coordinated interdependence. The strategic leadership resides within the presidents' club, *shacho-kai*, where implicit rules and shared understandings in unstated gentlemen's agreements lead to coordination and general cooperation between firms for mutual benefits. Shacho-kai is a regularly convening association that comprises the presidents of the core keiretsu member firms. It represents the inner circle of the keiretsu as a clique of firms whose reciprocal commitments stem from shared ownership and from long associations and strong collective identity. These councils hold monthly meetings to discuss group strategy. They support group solidarity, mediate intragroup activities, and settle intragroup disagreements.

Other direct linkages within the keiretsu are represented by the stable corporate cross-shareholdings, the dispatch of managers to insider director positions, and *director interlocking*, when directors of one keiretsu member sit on the board of another member firm. These arrangements as control relations are superimposed on the network of regular business transactions. Keiretsu groupings are also held to be an effective system of minimizing transaction costs and maximizing efficiency gains by economizing on information and control through regularized communication and exchange.

Keiretsu equalize the fortunes of their members, smoothing inequality in financial returns across participating firms. Members are not able to maximize their benefits, that is, extraction of profits and rents, but instead are obliged to optimize output measures. Keiretsu networks are seen as clusters of large firms charging each other efficient prices (i.e., prices in line with their respective opportunity costs) while extracting other market benefits through collective action to maximize the joint welfare of all member firms. Keiretsu members experience lower risk than independent companies in Japan because the entire group shares individual risks.

2.1.5 Chaebol: Korean Circular Shareholding Networks

Korean *chaebol* are family-controlled business groups or cross-industry conglomerates that include a large number of affiliated firms as independent legal entities, interlocked by circular shareholdings. The chaebol simultaneously represents a family-centered and distributed network that crosses multi-industry boundaries through asset ownership. It is based on circular shareholding governance and an asset-based division of labor. The member firms experience controlled and negotiated interdependence.

The main driving force behind the growth of the chaebol business network, however, is the Korean government, which has created the main financial and market conditions: a protected domestic market, a state-controlled banking sector, active industrial policy, and subsidized export credits. As a result of these policies, the families merely utilize the available resources, such as cheap loans and subsidized export credits, and diversify the business portfolio accordingly. The expansion of these cross-industry conglomerates is financed by the government through preferential loans below the cost of capital and through almost unconstrained borrowing by the member firms from government-owned banks. The circular shareholdings within the chaebol enable the families to exercise control with a minority stake only.

2.1.6 Research and Development Alliance Networks and Project Networks

Managing research and development (R&D) and innovation across firms is one of the most challenging tasks and requires wide intrafirm and interfirm cooperation.

Managing R&D fundamentally depends on the management of diverse formalized and tacit knowledge that is scattered between specialized units and scientific fields, embodied in current products, processes and technologies, and carried out by scientists and researchers, employed by a wide range of business organizations.

The complex nature of R&D in industry is associated with many different activities. These include

- Innovation in concepts and ideas and the joint creation of knowledge
- Sharing knowledge between specialized knowledge fields
- The definition of new scientific questions and hypotheses and seeking their answers in partnerships
- The emergence of new solutions to problems and their market realization
- Novelty in processes and the cross-border integration of operations
- Enhancing new patterns and routines in market behavior, in lifestyle, and at the workplace

An R&D network is a safeguard against market redundancy. It may explore multiple alternative technologies without knowing what might be successfully selected at the final stage. Some explorations in R&D lead to a dead end both in terms of a technological breakthrough or a successful realization on the market. These are discontinued at an early stage before they are challenged in the marketplace, and the costs are shared by the network.

R&D networks are usually project based and resemble project networks involved in research and the business application of scientific knowledge. The project itself is an institution that has specific aims and limited resources (including knowledge). It bundles together a variety of economic, social, and scientific agents such as firms, consumer associations, laboratories, government bodies, technologies, physical artifacts, and documentation. These heterogeneous agents are of a different kind: individual experts carrying specific knowledge, institutions that represent different interests, or nonhuman elements that are employed for a particular utility function. The particular institutional form and the specific bundle of interests of all stakeholders establish the project boundaries. A distinctive feature of R&D and project networks is that they have clear boundaries between members and nonmembers.

The government plays a central role in R&D networks—both by shaping and framing the environment for R&D networks and by acting as an active participant in them. Specific policies aim to build the comparative advantage of key industrial sectors in the economies, to facilitate and coordinate intense knowledge sharing between the public and the private sector, to provide stability and funding for the coevolution of complex research strategies and new markets, and to develop relational research capacities within leading firms and industrial sectors. The major forms of government intervention in building R&D networks are procurement contracts and leadership in R&D consortium formation.

2.1.7 Value Chain Supply Networks: Global Sourcing and Global Commodity Chains

Each product or service of the corporation has its own value chain and hence multiple supply chains cross through a corporation. The corporation makes strategic choices and decisions as to which parts of the value chain are to be performed in-house and which parts of the chain are to be controlled. The uncontrolled part is outsourced to suppliers (and forms the supply chain) or to distributors (and forms the distribution chain).

Once these decisions are made, the corporation develops internal capabilities to service these value chains both internally and externally. The corporation also develops control mechanisms in order to manage the input from its supply chains. Outsourcing and subcontracting are specific forms of business relationships used by the corporation in order to externalize costs and to appropriate value-added from different parts of the value chain.

There are two trends, particularly since the 1980s, that changed the processes in the value chain:

Large corporations started international expansion, which involved the transfer of low value-added activities to foreign units, while building a high value-added capacity at home. In this way the value chain of the corporation stretched across borders.

Large corporations started downsizing, which involved *externalizing* costs by outsourcing and subcontracting business operations to other firms. This led to a wave of new business start-ups and spin-offs from the main corporation and a flow of resources from the corporation to its partners externally, enhancing the business opportunities for the constellation of supplier and subcontractors situated at the periphery of the focal corporate network.

2.1.8 Network-Based Businesses: Utilities, Public Services, and Infrastructure Networks

Network-based businesses exist in many industries: telecommunications, transportation, airlines and railroads, banks and financial institutions, and even public services such as health-care organizations and education establishments. Bank branches and automated machines, for example, transport funds so customers can make transactions at any point in the network. The health-care system facilitates the flow of medical knowledge about disease and medical practices for diagnosis and treatment. Network-based businesses deliver services and are structured along geographical and technological boundaries. These are heterogeneous networks with a certain degree of connectivity, which evolves into various zone and lane concentration areas. The boundaries of the network are usually clear, as these are determined by ownership of the peripheral units. The governance mechanism is determined by ownership, hierarchy, and connectivity principles, and the individual actors and units are exposed to hub dependence, while the hubs themselves are subject to hierarchical and connectivity control.

These networks transport people, goods, information, or resources as a service to customers, not just for distribution purposes. The flow of resources is, hence, the objective of the network and not an outcome of building business relationships or expanding the network. The transport effect constitutes a substantial portion of the added value to customers and to companies, and derives from the value inherent in connectivity or linking an entry point in the network to a desired exit point. As such, infrastructure networks enable customers to achieve personal objectives, and this enabling function generates the value added for which these networks receive payments.

Although the transport effect accounts for a great deal of the value in a network, much of its costs tend to be concentrated in the individual outlets of entry and exit points. This asymmetry can obscure the relationship between value and cost, making it hard to determine what constitutes a natural business unit in an infrastructure network, and, hence, which nodes can be expressed both as the cost centers and the value-added parts, which usually do not coincide.

2.1.9 International Corporate Networks

One of the distinctive features of international business organizations is that they resemble a complex net of business units that are integrated within a number of value chains and spread across different industries and different countries. The most distinctive example of an international corporate network is the multinational corporation (MNC), where the business headquarters and individual subsidiary units represent the *nodes* in the network. The structure of the MNC has been described in terms of the concepts of the multidivisional corporation, and more recently as a heterarchy and a network. It represents a simultaneously hierarchical and distributed network with fuzzy boundaries. The governance mechanisms are a combination of ownership and contract arrangements. The division of labor is based on resource location and prescribed roles in the value chain. The firms are bound by a complex hierarchical and semiautonomous relationship that results in various levels of interdependence.

MNCs are highly differentiated organizations that comprise multiple units located in different countries and are embedded in different business systems and sociopolitical contexts. The growth of MNCs can be analyzed both from the perspective of the firm, with its integrated units, assets, resources, and processes, and from the perspective of the foreign market entry, or the expansion of the firm beyond the home market. There is also a distinction between the internal growth of the corporation, emphasizing the cumulative expansion of business activities within the firm versus external growth, and the expansion through foreign direct investment (FDI) and mergers and acquisitions (M&A) of other organizational entities with their own business operations.

The evolution of the national firm to a multinational corporation includes a progressive vertical integration of downstream and upstream operations within individual product value chains and the managed diversification of the initial product/service lines. Part of this evolution is the internal structuring of units and operations and the external positioning of these units in relation to suppliers, customers, and competitors.

In a multinational context, the growth pattern of MNCs can be understood in terms of global integration, global strategic coordination, and local responsiveness. The aim of the combination of these strategies is to attain a balance between pulling out localized resources into the global network and relocating global resources into local clusters of firms. Integration is related to the degree of subsidiary autonomy, and it is operationalized as the intensity of flows of resources between parent and subsidiaries and between the subsidiaries themselves. Responsiveness is the adaptation of the MNC to the local market and regulatory forces in its many locations; these put constraints on the standardization of products and operations and require additional coordination.

2.1.10 Spatial Clusters, Industry Clusters, and Cluster–Network Relationships

A *cluster* is an agglomeration of firms that form either geographic or other types of product- and technology-based clusters in which intense collaboration takes place. Clusters are agglomerations of firms colocated in a geographic area, connected by value-adding activities, and with access to benefits from input/output markets, from infrastructure, and from environmental coordination via institutions and policies. The clustering phenomena emerge with the beginning of economic transactions where buyers and sellers congregate together in a marketplace to enhance their individual chances for a transaction.

The foundations of the linkages between firms within a cluster—namely, skills, shared infrastructure, and knowledge—are because of

- The existence of a pooled market for specialized workers
- The provision of specialized inputs from suppliers and service providers
- The relatively rapid flow of business-related knowledge between firms, which results in technological spillovers

The clustering of firms is a process that is driven by firm-specific, industry-specific, and location-specific factors such as the nature of technology; specialization and differentiation within the value chain (or production chain); product and process innovations; the emergence of niche markets; competitive pressures from suppliers, buyers, and new market entries; environmental changes; and the impact of government policies.

Clusters are composed of interlinked firms and the relationships in business clusters involve multiple resource exchanges based on collaborative agreements. The main distinction between business clusters and business networks is in the level of coordination, where clusters are loose agglomerations combining collaborative and competitive relationships, while networks are predominantly collaborative and include business relationships that involve some form of resource sharing. In addition, clusters comprise firms that share vertical and horizontal linkages, which suggests that clusters incorporate networks of firms.

 MNCs locate subsidiaries in selected industrial clusters as scanning units that tap selectively into sources of advantage in other national innovation systems.

2.2 Alliances

Companies in many industries become connected in large networks of *alliances*. Alliances (or *partnerships* or *joint ventures*) are important tools for building and reinforcing the collective competitive advantage or *network power*. Alliances can be defined as enduring and formalized collaborative relationships between two or more firms that involve significant exchanges of information, resources, and *influence* or *decision power*; alliance networks are conduits across which information, resources, and decisions flow, reflecting the company's network power (NP). The traffic between partners includes the exchange of ideas, technologies, resources, people, and power. All of the alliances a company has with its partners represent the company's alliance portfolio.

Companies have different positions in alliance networks. A firm's network power and, hence, success is majorly dependent on the configuration of the alliance networks and the company's situational position within any of these networks. For example:

■ Some companies are found in dense clusters of companies that all have ties to each other.
■ Some companies exist at the center of a spider web of companies that connect to them but not to each other.
■ Some companies are at the edge of the web.
■ Some companies are isolated.

Most alliances are routinely judged as failures; the primary cause is the singular focus on individual alliances to the exclusion of the collective context of all other alliances. A company's network power is simply not a summation of the network advantages resulting from individual alliances in isolation. The benefits reaped from an individual alliance depend on the other alliances surrounding the firm—its alliances with other partners, its partners' alliances with other partners, and the overall network of alliances. So, despite a firm's best efforts to form a cooperative and mutually beneficial alliance, it may still not result in an affirmative outcome. By understanding how each individual alliance fits into the broader context of the network of alliances, a company can reduce the failure rate of its individual alliances.

A company can unlock three key advantages from its alliance network(s):

1. Information: Coordination with partners in the network via the exchange of information to provide the company, based on priority and competencies, with ideas for product or service innovation, sources of operational efficiencies, or opportunities for finding new customers
2. Competencies: Cooperation with partners in the network via the pooling of competencies—that is, the capabilities, resources, or knowledge to achieve resource-sharing synergies or joint learning opportunities that enable the company to benefit, based on priority, from the assets and expertise of others
3. Decisions: Collaboration with partners in the network to influence and structure the activities of the alliance partners as well as the allocation of priorities and, hence, capabilities, resources or knowledge, and rewards

Most companies are unaware of the huge collective competitive advantages or *network power* available in the alliance networks and are instead preoccupied with capitalizing on the advantages gained from singular alliances, one alliance at a time.

2.2.1 Types of Network Power

2.2.1.1 First-Degree Network Power: Coordination

First-degree network power (FDNP) is the unique ability to get timely access to information, secure commitment, and gain network power by using the connections among your firm's alliance partners. The extent to which your partners have alliances with one another determines the power, types of information, and coordination flowing across the network.

Patterns of connections can be of three types:

1. *Hub-and-spoke* corresponds to a configuration in which the company operates at the center (the hub) and is connected like spokes in a wheel to partners that are mostly not connected to each other; being at the center of a hub-and-spoke configuration provides your firm with access to new information from each partner. It also helps your firm to engage in *brokerage*—combining ideas and resources from one partner with the ideas and resources of another partner. This configuration is great for making breakthrough innovations.
2. *Integrated* corresponds to a configuration in which the company is connected to partners that are also mostly connected to each other. An integrated configuration connects your firm to interconnected alliance partners who share the same types of information and are more likely to develop common norms around extensive exchanges of information. This facilitates coordination and the execution of complex projects as well as incremental innovation.
3. *Hybrid* corresponds to a configuration in which the company has an assortment of connected and unconnected partners. Sometimes a company may need to innovate and at other times it may need to coordinate and execute. A hybrid pattern of connections combines the benefits of both the configurations in the following ways:
   a. The more unconnected partners there are in a hybrid configuration, the more this pattern resembles a hub-and-spoke configuration and the better it is for developing breakthrough innovations.
   b. The more connected partners there are in a hybrid configuration, the more this pattern resembles an integrated configuration and the better it is for incremental innovations and the execution of improvement projects.

 Traditional leaders tend to focus on generating and monitoring the specific benefits expected from each individual relationship, and this is where they usually stop. Investing in relationships with individual partners is necessary, but it is not sufficient to extract maximum network power. Working just at this level delivers only a small amount of network power in terms of achieving coordination and power benefits. To get the biggest network advantage, a company must broaden the field of vision to incorporate the second- and third-degree perspectives on their alliance network.

2.2.1.2 Second-Degree Network Power: Cooperation

Second-degree network power (SDNP) comes from the unique ability to combine a company's competencies—that is, capabilities, resources, or knowledge—with the competencies of each individual alliance partner.

The factors contributing to SDNP are as follows:

1. Partner complementarity: Complementary partners have different skills and knowledge, which they combine in order to achieve their objective. Most companies form successful alliances with complementary partners.
2. Partner compatibility: Compatible partners have similar skills and routines, which makes it easier to work with each other and to achieve mutual trust. Most alliances fail because they lack compatibility between partners. Successful partners need to be comfortable with working together, which necessitates the ability to form joint routines around the operations of the alliance, whether this involves doing research, developing products, or producing a good or service. Cooperation entails knowledge of what the other company requires and willingness to supply it, as well as the inherent trust that this will be reciprocated.

2.2.1.3 Third-Degree Network Power: Collaboration

Third-degree network power (TDNP) comes from the unique ability to determine priority and, hence, define the aggregate mix of individual partner's competency capabilities or resources or knowledge, and rewards. If a company's partners are connected to other well-connected partners, the company would be perceived as a *status* player with significant influence and leadership within its areas of operations.

The most obvious strategy for increasing company status would be to form alliances with other high-status firms. Measures to make a company attractive to a high-status partner involves investing in brand awareness, thought leadership campaigns, and increased visibility in the industry. The company needs to be smart about how and when it communicates with the public about its alliances with high-status partners and about its experiences as an alliance partner. The company also needs to establish a strong track record as a good collaborator and make it known. High-status companies will want to partner with a company if they know that the company works well with partners and collaborates with them to create value.

2.2.2 Alliances for Enhancing Network Power

A network of enterprises consists of distinct enterprises, each working for their own benefit. If they cooperate, the external integration brings benefits that can be shared among all members of the enterprise network. When an enterprise pays money to its suppliers, it is assumed that it can only benefit at the expense of the other. This adversarial attitude has major drawbacks. Suppliers set rigid conditions and, as they have no guarantee of repeat business, see no point in cooperation, thus trying to make as much profit from each sale as possible. At the same time, enterprises have no loyalty, and they shop around to get the best deal and remind suppliers of the competition. Each is concerned only with their own objectives and will—when convenient to themselves—change specifications and conditions at short notice.

The results include

- Constantly changing suppliers and customers
- Uncertainty about the number and size of orders
- Changing products and conditions
- Irregular gaps between orders
- No guarantee of repeat orders
- Variable costs

Thus, enterprises come to recognize that it is in their own long-term interest to replace conflict with agreement. Table 2.1 presents a comparison of the competitive versus cooperative views of relationships between enterprises.

If an enterprise has a good experience with a supplier, it will continue to use them and over a period will develop a valuable working relationship (Figure 2.1). Sometimes the cooperation is more positive, such as small companies making joint purchases to get the same quantity discounts as larger companies, forming EDI links to share information, combining loads to reduce transport costs, agreeing package sizes to ease material handling, making lists of preferred suppliers, and so on. But the key point with these informal arrangements is that there is no commitment.

 Japanese companies take the informal approach further forming *Keiretsu*—which are groups that work together without actually forming partnerships (see Section 10.1.4).

Table 2.1   Competitive vs. Cooperation Views

Factor	Competitive View	Cooperation View
Profit	One organization profits at the expense of the other	Both share profits
Relationship	One is dominant	Equal partners
Trust	Little	Considerable
Communication	Limited and formal	Widespread and open
Information	Secretive	Open and shared
Control	Intensive policing	Delegation and empowerment
Quality	Blame for faults	Solving shared problems
Contract	Rigid	Flexible
Focus on	Own operations	Customers

	Cooperative approach	Noncooperative approach
Common ownership	Vertically integrated company Shared goals	Bureaucracy Frequently adversarial relationships
No common ownership	Virtual corporation Belief that "we are stronger together"	Market Arm's length relationships

Figure 2.1   Ownership patterns and cooperative versus competitive approach.

An informal arrangement has the advantage of being flexible and non-binding. On the other hand, it has the disadvantage that either party can end the cooperation without warning and at any time that suits them. This is why many enterprises prefer a more formal arrangement, with a written contract setting out the obligations of each party. More formal agreements have the advantage of showing the details of the commitment, so that each side knows exactly what it has to do. On the other hand, they have the disadvantage of losing flexibility and imposing rigid conditions. But such contracts are common when companies see themselves as working together for some time.

This is the basis of a strategic alliances or partnerships. An alliance or partnership can be defined as an ongoing relationship between firms that involves a commitment over an extended time period and a mutual sharing of information and the risks and rewards of the relationship.

The characteristic features of alliances are as follows:

- Partners work closely together at all levels.
- Openness and mutual trust.
- Senior managers and everyone in the organizations support the alliance.
- Shared business culture, goals, and objectives.
- Long-term commitment.
- Shared information, expertise, planning, and systems.
- Flexibility and willingness to solve shared problems.
- Continuous improvements in all aspects of operations.
- The joint development of products and processes.
- Guaranteed reliable and high-quality goods and services.
- An agreement on costs and profits to give fair and competitive pricing.
- Increasing business between partners.

Partnerships can lead to changes in operations. For instance, the stability of a partnership might encourage suppliers to specialize in a restricted type or subset of products. They give a commitment to the alliance that they will reduce their product range, make these as efficiently as possible, and concentrate on giving a small number of customers a very high-quality service. They share such information with customers without the threat that this will be used in turn to gain some form of trading advantage. On the other hand, customers reduce the number of their suppliers, as they no longer need to look around to get the best deals. Japanese companies were among the first to develop strategic alliances, and at a time when Toyota had formed partnerships with its 250 suppliers, General Motors was still working separately with 4000 suppliers (Figure 2.2).

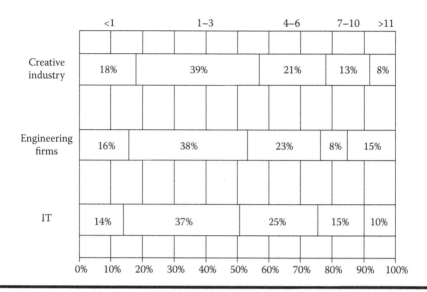

Figure 2.2 Alliance lifetime in years.

2.2.2.1 Types of Alliances

The term *alliance* covers a wide range of collaborations, ranging from simple and informal handshake agreements to complex outsourcing subcontract agreements, technology transfer contracts, or joint venture investment agreements.

Table 2.2 lists the reasons for collaborations between companies. Figure 2.3 shows the whole range of relationships.

Alliances can be categorized as follows:

1. Informal alliances
   a. Family ties
      All over the world, family clans form alliances for mutual defense or support. For instance, in South Korea, family members keep track of each other in *family books* dating back multiple generations. Korean society expects the eldest son to provide family leadership and support; he is the one who is responsible for taking care of others in the family, especially the infirm or elderly.
   b. Social networks
      Numerous social networks exist—alumni associations, religious organizations, charities, philanthropies, and other types of nongovernmental organizations (NGOs), such as those working toward social causes such as bettering the environment, furthering world peace, and defending

Table 2.2   Motives for Collaborations

Market Development	Cost Advantages	Knowledge Development	External Pressure
Developing joint market power	Realizing advantages of scale	Organizing joint innovation	Political pressure: "one face to citizens"
Improving and increasing distribution power	Overcoming investment impediments	Gaining access to new technology	Legal obligation of consultation
Gaining access to new markets	Establishing joint supporting services	Using partner complimentary competencies	Moral appeals from society or politics
Protection against competition	More efficient and rationalized production	Learning from partners' skills and knowledge	
Chain integration through better chain coordination		Learning from partners' cultures	
		New patents as well as access to patented knowledge	

human rights. In business, social networks help to build up an entrepreneur company's social capital (i.e., reputation and credibility). Social networks are powerful and long lasting, and provide solidarity and support to the respective members of the network or business association, who have banded together for mutual advantage in a trust-based relationship. Entrepreneurial companies employ various networks to obtain information, resources, and knowledge to help them get started in their businesses. For instance, in Chinese society, *guanxi* (one's personal network) is a central cultural precept for the giving and receiving of favors and influence. There is also a dark side to networks and networking. Mafias and their powerful equivalents exist all over the world; they are not limited to Italy.

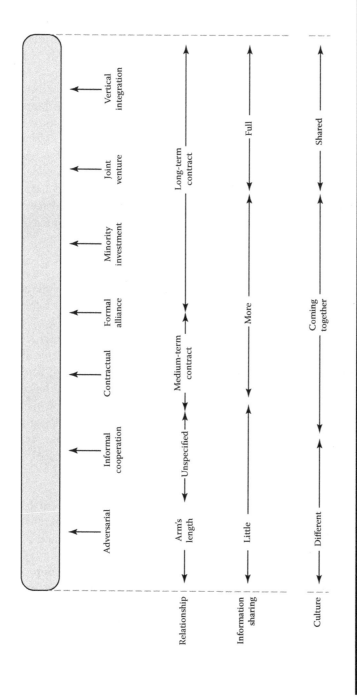

Figure 2.3 Range of relationships.

c. Opportunistic alliances

Opportunistic alliances spring up spontaneously around particular business or social ventures. They are quite common in academic research circles, where two or three doctoral students might band together to do a field study, or company researchers decide to pursue a particular development project. They may quickly dissipate or evolve into something more structured and permanent, depending on the personal chemistry of the teams involved and the importance of the project or venture.

Consortia are temporary partnerships or associations. Although we classify them under opportunistic alliances, they fit into a number of the other categories as well, as their form and nature vary widely. Some consortia operate like loose umbrella organizations and have ad hoc membership rules. Other consortia are more formal and may require members to join a foundation. Basic research consortia consist of groups formed to carry out complex, large, and multidisciplinary research efforts, sometimes over long periods of time. Networks of academic institutions, NGOs, privately funded research centers, government-sponsored research laboratories, or corporate members may decide to partner and to collectively accomplish what no one member could do in isolation.

Normally, research consortia are bound by contractual agreements, such as a memorandum of understanding (or letter of intent) and basic confidentiality agreements. The allocation of intellectual property (IP) rights must be decided ahead of time by the consortia partners, to reduce the potential for later conflicts on who keeps which IP rights. The decisions and agreements on IP rights for a research consortium may be incorporated into the master memorandum of understanding or documented in a series of separate agreements.

2. Formal alliances

Formal contractual agreements can be short-term contracts (perhaps a single transaction) or long-term contracts that may involve a series of multiple and repeated transactions over a defined period of time. For instance, a contract for buying or selling foreign exchange or some other commodity is a short-term contract. Similarly, when a major engineering construction company puts out a single tender request to procure a quantity of high-pressure valves for a utility project, it is an order that may be satisfied by a number of qualified vendors or suppliers. The engineering company will award the contract to the vendor offering the lowest bid that still meets the specified product quality and delivery conditions. The terms are easily specified, and the competitive bids comparable. Both of these sample contracts would be relatively straightforward procurement contracts, and neither would be particularly strategic in nature. These contracts involve no long-term exchange of core competencies or proprietary know-how; therefore, they are considered to be ordinary collaborations, not strategic alliances.

Long-term contracts are often used when closer supplier and customer relationships are needed. A long-term contract helps reduce opportunistic behavior (where one party takes advantage of the other), provides more security, and lowers risk, particularly if the parties must make transaction-specific or project-specific investments that are not reusable elsewhere. On the other hand, long-term contracts may prove to be too inflexible, since it is nearly impossible to foresee all the circumstances that may arise during the course of a project. Most contracts allow for the management of change orders, which enables changes to be effected to the original scope or the terms of reference of the work specified in the contract.

a. Subcontracting agreements

The use of subcontracting to complete major projects is common in many industries; a contractor chooses to award parts of a particular service or process to a third party. For instance, top-tier companies fork out parts of major contracts to lower-tier companies. The principal contractor is fully liable for the work of any subcontractors while they are undertaking or delivering any part of the primary contract. Not all subcontracting is strategic in nature; it depends on how critical it is to the contractor's competitive advantage and strategic capabilities development. In some subcontracting or outsourcing contracts, the processed work is returned to the contractor. In other cases, it may also be passed on to another partner in the supply chain for further processing.

Such a sub-subcontracting assignment may also entail hiring temporary staff to undertake programming work, help do the inventory audit at the end of the fiscal year, or do some seasonal assembly work.

b. Nonequity joint ventures

In a nonequity joint venture, no equity investment is involved; instead, the two parties sign a long-term contractual agreement to collaborate with a specified time horizon, after which the contract is renewed or expires. This is the simplest form of association for joint ventures, under which the parties agree to associate as independent contractors for a limited period rather than as shareholders in a company or partners in a legal partnership. Such an association is purely a contractual cooperation agreement. This mode of collaboration is suitable where the parties want to signal commitment without the formality and permanence of a corporate vehicle. For instance, IKEA, the giant Swedish-based furniture retailer, operates a series of nonequity buyer–supplier alliances around the world that are structured as non-equity joint ventures. IKEA provides component suppliers with product design, technical assistance, leased equipment, and even loans. IKEA's suppliers get new skills, direct access to a large and growing retailer, and steadier sales. The benefit for both sides is a sense of partnership and loyalty from IKEA to its suppliers and from the suppliers toward IKEA. The customers ultimately benefit from the volume procurement of lower-cost but higher-quality furniture, designed to IKEA's specifications.

c. Technology transfer agreements

Technology transfer agreements are a very common form of strategic alliance in technology-intensive and science-driven industries such as biotechnology, nanotechnology, medical devices, semiconductors, and telecommunications, and many other industries where brands and registered designs are valuable (e.g., fashionable clothes, luxury accessories, and consumer electronics). These are licensing agreements to transfer protectable intellectual property rights from, for example, a start-up high-tech venture to a third party, such as another strategic partner involved in a different part of the value chain or an investor group placing funds into the venture. The license agreement allows the licensor to transfer the rights to use its various kinds of intellectual property either in isolation or bundled together with other systems. The IP would be its patents, trademarks, designs, copyrights, trade secrets, or proprietary technological know-how. Once the IP is identified and the rights specified, the agreement also defines the time frame and geographical territory where these rights may be exercised. The firm that buys the rights usually gives in exchange a combination of lump-sum advances, royalties, and milestone payments.

d. Franchising

Franchising is a booming trend in both developed and emerging markets, particularly in fast food, retailing, auto parts, quick copy shops, and various service businesses—especially professional services such as accounting, tax, and real estate brokerage. Franchising is a business system used by companies to execute their growth strategy, penetrate markets, and extend their geographical reach by leveraging other interested parties' money, labor, and energy. The franchisor is the owner of a trademarked product, brand, business format, or service that grants the exclusive right to market, sell, or distribute a product or provide a service in a designated territory to the franchisee. In return, for the use of these rights, brand, and business concept, the owner receives payment of a franchise fee, royalties (typically on net sales), and the franchisee's promise to conform to the quality standards of the franchise and comply with any other specifications in the contract. With all franchising and licensing arrangements, the owner must consider the capabilities, reliability, and trustworthiness of the counterparties. This is particularly crucial when licensing high-profile luxury brand names; the owner of the brand trademark must carefully protect the brand's reputation and use by the licensees so as not to dilute the value of the brand. The McDonald's Corporation, based in Oakbrook, Illinois, and Yum! Brands, Inc., based in Louisville, Kentucky (owner of Pizza Hut and Taco Bell), are rapidly and successfully expanding their franchises in China, South Korea, other parts of Asia, and the rest of the world.

3. Equity alliances

In an equity joint venture, two parties remain independent but jointly set up a newly created company as a sign of both parties' commitment to a long-term collaboration. Equity ownership changes the nature of the alliance collaboration in important ways by lengthening the possible time of collaboration (unlimited) and changing the risk and reward profile of the joint endeavor. When a joint venture is formed, generally one party contributes a combination of cash, resources, and capabilities to fund the joint venture; the other party, usually the start-up company, contributes its *sweat equity* into the new joint venture, meaning its intellectual property assets (patent portfolio and associated rights), technological know-how, and so forth. Both firms will choose key people from their respective firms to join the new joint venture, which then has its own independent identity.

Some joint ventures are fully vertically integrated and perform many activities in a business's value chain. Other joint ventures are focused on only one small part of the overall value chain. A focused joint venture may be set up specifically for research, development, manufacturing, sales, or customer relationship management support. For instance, Sony Corporation and Ericsson teamed up in 2001 to form a 50/50 equity joint venture with the goal of becoming a global leading provider of mobile multimedia devices. The joint venture, Sony Ericsson, carries out product research, design, and development, as well as manufacturing, marketing, sales, distribution, and customer services. The global management is based in London, whereas R&D is done in Sweden, the United Kingdom, France, the Netherlands, India, Japan, China, and the United States.

Companies try to discourage opportunistic behavior in their alliance partners by carefully considering the allocation of risks and rewards when negotiating joint ventures and *minority investments*. By becoming equity partners, economic interests and the risks of the venture are better aligned, as both upside rewards and downside losses are shared in accordance with the ownership percentage in the company.

> ✎ In the automotive industry, there has been a major shift away from arm's-length supplier contracts to long-term collaborations with a handful of key global suppliers. In many instances, competitive tenders and the requirement for multiple bidders are being replaced by single-supplier arrangements. All the automotive majors have a host of international alliances and joint ventures, ranging from minority stakes to equity joint ventures with a variety of suppliers and other automotive rivals. The difficulty in specifying complete contracts for long-term supplier agreements enhances the attractiveness of long-term partnership arrangements that involve minority investments.

2.2.3 Multinational Network of British Petroleum

Today, British Petroleum (BP) is one of the largest MNCs in the world and the second largest British company with revenues of US$390 billion in 2013, more than 80,000 employees, and operations in 80 countries. With a stake of 19.75% in the Russian giant Rosneft, it maintains an extensive network of exploration, production, refining and sales operations worldwide.

On April 20, 2010, a gas release and subsequent explosion occurred on the Deepwater Horizon oil rig working for BP in the Gulf of Mexico. Eleven people died as a result of the accident. For 3 months, the oil well spilled enormous amounts in the sea. It is now estimated that more than 3 million barrels of oil were released; the accident was one of the largest environmental disasters ever. The company had to compensate and participate in measures to limit the environmental impact, including fighting the spill, removing and dispersing the oil offshore, protecting the shoreline, and clean-up activities of the oil that came ashore. Legitimate claims by local businesses (e.g., fishermen), individuals, government agencies, etc., had to be fulfilled. A trust has been set up with a value of US$20 billion to make sure that the funds are available in the long-run. This dramatic event changed the future of BP and put its existence at risk. Within less than 5 years, BP drastically downsized and carried out a divestment of almost US$50 billion.

BP has operations in all stages of the oil and gas value chain:

1. Upstream
    a. The exploration and extraction of crude oil and gas
    b. The transportation and trade in oil and gas.
        The configuration of upstream activities is strongly determined by where the natural resources are found and where they can be exploited most profitably. The locations are often in developing countries and in politically unstable environments. Concerning the external partners, these are often state-owned or at least with close relationships to the

respective governments who tend to keep a strong influence on their energy reserves.

The accident in the Gulf of Mexico has led to a substantial reorganization and reconfiguration of BP's upstream business. The recent strategy of BP in this respect is "value over volume." For example, this meant divesting many non-core assets in the upstream portfolio and maintaining in particular those in which BP has particular capabilities, for example, in deepwater oil reserves. Since 2010, BP has reduced its operated installations worldwide by more than half and the operated wells by 35%. This means reducing the exposure to low-margin assets and keeping the more profitable ones. The investment focus of BP in its upstream projects and operations is now on four key regions: Angola, Azerbaijan, the Gulf of Mexico, and the North Sea. BP has divested many of its smaller upstream operations, for example, those in Vietnam or Colombia.

2. Downstream:
   a. The manufacturing stage, including refining of fuels, lubricants, and petrochemicals
   b. Marketing and sales activities which involve selling the refined petrol through almost 18,000 service stations.

   The configuration is strongly influenced by demand patterns. For fuel, for example, the countries of Europe and the United States are important sales markets. Since these activities need to be carried out close to the market (e.g., via networks of service stations), they are often also done in partnerships, for example, via franchising. Similarly, petrochemicals which are used as inputs for other products are mainly sold in the industrialised countries.

   A major move in BPs downstream business is the divestment of refineries. Since 2000, BP has sold 13 refineries, reducing its capacity by almost 40%. It now only operates nine refineries and five joint venture refineries, which are operated by remaining partners.

BP has a global network of subsidiaries with different roles for the company, often focusing on one part of the value chain. Some of them are for oil or gas exploration, some of them are dedicated to refining or transporting oil or gas, and some focus on the sale of fuels via gas service stations. Many of these activities are carried out in partnerships with are institutionalized in different modes. Ranging from consortiums with other oil companies (for example, the BTC pipeline) to a minority stake in one of the largest companies in the world, Rosneft, to many joint ventures which are operated by BP or by other partners and other contractual relationships for the production or refinery of hydrocarbons , the case of BP clearly demonstrates how the activities of a modern MNC are carried out within a network of wholly owned subsidiaries, partly owned subsidiaries, and external partnerships.

2.3 Summary

This chapter focused on the various taxonomies for the network enterprises. The first half of the chapter described various types of networks ranging from the now familiar Chinese Guanxi, Japanese Keiretsu, and Korean Chaebol, to the more contemporary value chain supply networks, corporate networks, and industry clusters. After introducing the concept of network power (coordination, cooperation, and collaboration), the latter of the chapter discussed various types of alliances ranging from informal (family, social, opportunistic) to formal (subcontracting, nonequity, technology, franchising) and equity.

GENESIS OF NETWORK BUSINESSES

This section introduces the genesis of network businesses. Chapter 3 traces the genesis of the cloud to the networking and internetworking technologies of the 1980s. Chapter 4 describes the concepts of distributed systems.

Chapter 3

Computer Networks

The merging of computers and communications has had a profound influence on the way computer systems are organized. Although data centers holding thousands of Internet servers are becoming common, the once-dominant concept of the computer center as a room with a large computer to which users bring their work for processing is now totally obsolete. The old model of a single computer serving all of the organization's computational needs has been replaced by one in which a large number of separate but interconnected computers do the job. These systems are called *computer networks*.

Two computers are said to be networked if they are able to exchange information. The connection need not be via a copper wire; fiber optics, microwaves, infrared, and communication satellites can also be used. Networks come in many sizes, shapes, and forms, as we will see later. They are usually connected together to make larger networks, with the Internet being the most well-known example of a network of networks.

The key distinction between a *computer network* and a *distributed system* is that in the latter, a collection of independent computers appears to its users as a single coherent system. Usually, it has a single model or paradigm that it presents to the users. Often, a layer of software on top of the operating system, called *middleware*, is responsible for implementing this model. A well-known example of a distributed system is the World Wide Web (WWW). It runs on top of the Internet and presents a model in which everything looks like a document (Web page). On the other hand, in a computer network, coherence, a model, and software are absent. Users are exposed to the actual machines, without any attempt by the system to make the machines look and act in a coherent way. If the machines have different hardware and different operating systems, it is fully visible to the users. If a user wants to run a program on a remote machine, it entails logging on to that machine and running it there.

In effect, a distributed system is a software system built on top of a network. The software gives it a high degree of cohesiveness and transparency. Thus, the distinction between a network and a distributed system lies with the software (especially the opeTrating system), rather than with the hardware. Nevertheless, there is considerable overlap between the two subjects. For example, both distributed systems and computer networks need to move files around. The difference lies in who invokes the movement: the system or the user.

3.1 Network Principles

3.1.1 Protocol

The term *protocol* is used to refer to a well-known set of rules and formats to be used for communication between processes in order to perform a given task. The definition of a protocol has two important parts to it:

1. A specification of the sequence of messages that must be exchanged
2. A specification of the format of the data in the messages

The existence of well-known protocols enables the separate software components of distributed systems to be developed independently and implemented in different programming languages on computers that may have different order codes and data representations. A protocol is implemented by a pair of software modules located in the sending and receiving computers. For example, a transport protocol transmits messages of any length from a sending process to a receiving process. A process wishing to transmit a message to another process issues a call to a transport protocol module, passing it a message in the specified format. The transport software then concerns itself with the transmission of the message to its destination, subdividing it into packets of some specified size and format that can be transmitted to the destination via the network protocol—another, lower-level protocol. The corresponding transport protocol module in the receiving computer receives the packet via the network-level protocol module and performs inverse transformations to regenerate the message before passing it to a receiving process.

3.1.2 Protocol Layers

Network software is arranged in a hierarchy of layers. Each layer presents an interface to the layers above it that extends the properties of the underlying communication system. A layer is represented by a module in every computer connected to the network. Each module appears to communicate directly with a module at the same level in another computer in the network, but in reality, data are not transmitted directly between the protocol modules at each level. Instead, each layer of network software communicates by local procedure calls with the layers above and below it. On the sending side, each layer (except the topmost or application layer) accepts items of data in a specified format from the layer above it and applies transformations to encapsulate the data in the format specified for that layer before passing it to the layer below for further processing. On the receiving side, the converse transformations are applied to data items received from the layer below before they are passed to the layer above. The protocol type of the layer above is included in the header of each layer, to enable the protocol stack at the receiver to select the correct software components to unpack the packets. The data items are received and passed upward through the hierarchy of software modules, being transformed at each stage until they are in a form that can be passed to the intended recipient process.

3.1.3 Protocol Suite

A complete set of protocol layers is referred to as a *protocol suite* or a *protocol stack*, reflecting the layered structure. Figure 3.1 shows a protocol stack that conforms to the seven-layer reference model for Open Systems Interconnection (OSI) adopted by the International Organization for Standardization (ISO). The OSI reference model was adopted in order to encourage the development of protocol standards that would meet the requirements of open systems. The purpose of each level in the OSI reference model is summarized in Table 3.1. As its name implies, it is a framework for the definition of protocols and not a definition for a specific suite of protocols.

Protocol suites that conform to the OSI model must include at least one specific protocol at each of the seven levels that the model defines (Table 3.1).

3.1.4 Datagram

Datagram is essentially another name for *data packet*. The term refers to the similarity of this delivery mode to the way in which letters and telegrams are delivered. The essential feature of datagram networks is that the delivery of each packet is a one-shot process; no setup is required, and once the packet is delivered, the network retains no information about it.

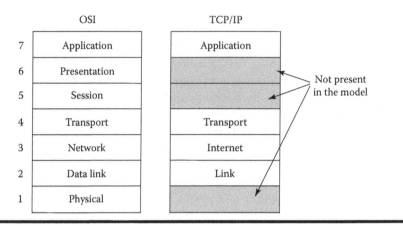

Figure 3.1   OSI vs. TCP/IP network reference models.

3.2 Types of Networks

There is no generally accepted taxonomy into which all computer networks fit, but two dimensions stand out as important: transmission technology and scale. We will now examine each of these in turn. Broadly speaking, there are two types of transmission technology that are in widespread use: broadcast links and point-to-point links.

Point-to-point links connect individual pairs of machines. To go from the source to the destination on a network made up of point-to-point links, short messages, called *packets* in certain contexts, may have to first visit one or more intermediate machines. Often, multiple routes of different lengths are possible, so finding good ones is important in point-to-point networks. Point-to-point transmission with exactly one sender and exactly one receiver is sometimes called *unicasting*. In contrast, on a broadcast network, the communication channel is shared by all the machines on the network; packets sent by any machine are received by all the others. An address field within each packet specifies the intended recipient. Upon receiving a packet, a machine checks the address field. If the packet is intended for the receiving machine, that machine processes the packet; if the packet is intended for some other machine, the packet is just ignored.

Broadcast systems usually also allow the possibility of addressing a packet to all destinations by using a special code in the address field. When a packet with this code is transmitted, it is received and processed by every machine on the network. This mode of operation is called *broadcasting*. Some broadcast systems also support transmission to a subset of the machines, which is known as *multicasting*. An alternative criterion for classifying networks is by scale. Distance is important as a classification metric because different technologies are used at different scales. At the top are personal area networks (PANs), networks that are meant for one person. Beyond these come longer-range networks. These can be divided into local,

Table 3.1 OSI Layers or Stack

Layer	Description	Examples
Application	Protocols at this level are designed to meet the communication requirements of specific applications, often defining the interface to a service.	HTTP, FTP, SMTP, CORBA HOP
Presentation	Protocols at this level transmit data in a network representation that is independent of the representations used in individual computers, which may differ. Encryption is also performed in this layer, if required.	TLS security, CORBA data representation
Session	At this level, reliability and adaptation measures are performed, such as detection of failures and automatic recovery.	SIP
Transport	This is the lowest level at which messages (rather than packets) are handled. Messages are addressed to communication ports attached to processes. Protocols in this layer may be connection oriented or connectionless.	TCP, LDP
Network	Transfers data packets between computers in a specific network. In a WAN or an internetwork, this involves the generation of a route passing through routers. In a single LAN, no routing is required.	IP, ATM virtual circuits
Data link	Responsible for transmission of packets between nodes that are directly connected by a physical link. In a WAN, transmission is between pairs of routers or between routers and hosts. In a LAN, it is between any pair of hosts.	Ethernet MAC, ATC cell transfer, PPP
Physical	The circuits and hardware that drive the network. It transmits sequences of binary data by analogue signaling, using amplitude or frequency modulation of electrical signals (on cable circuits), light signals (on fiber optic circuits), or other electromagnetic signals (on radio and microwave circuits).	Ethernet baseband signaling, ISDN

metropolitan, and wide area networks, each with increasing scale. Finally, the connection of two or more networks is called an internetwork. The worldwide Internet is certainly the best-known (but not the only) example of an internetwork.

3.2.1 Personal Area Networks

PANs let devices communicate over the range of a person. A common example is a wireless network that connects a computer with its peripherals. Almost every computer has an attached monitor, keyboard, mouse, and printer. Without using wireless, this connection must be done with cables. So many new users have a hard time finding the right cables and plugging them into the right little holes (even though they are usually color coded) that most computer vendors offer the option of sending a technician to the user's home to do it. To help these users, some companies came together to design a short-range wireless network called *Bluetooth* to connect these components without wires. The idea is that if your devices have Bluetooth, then you need no cables. You just put them down, turn them on, and they work together. For many people, this ease of operation is a big plus. PANs can also be built with other technologies that communicate over short ranges, such as RFID on smartcards and library books.

3.2.2 Local Area Networks

Wireless Local Area Networks (LANs) are very popular these days, especially in homes, older office buildings, cafeterias, and other places where it is too much trouble to install cables. An LAN is a privately owned network that operates within and nearby a single building such as a home, office, or factory. LANs are widely used to connect personal computers and consumer electronics to let them share resources (e.g., printers) and exchange information. When LANs are used by companies, they are called *enterprise networks*.

In these systems, every computer has a radio modem and an antenna that it uses to communicate with other computers. In most cases, each computer talks to a device in the ceiling called an *access point* (AP), *wireless router*, or *base station*, which relays packets between wireless computers and also between them and the Internet. However, if other computers are close enough, they can communicate directly with one another in a peer-to-peer configuration.

There is a standard for wireless LANs called IEEE 802.11, popularly known as Wi-Fi, which has become very widespread. It runs at speeds anywhere from 11 to hundreds of megabytes per second. Wired LANs use a range of different transmission technologies. Most of them use copper wires, but some use optical fiber. LANs are restricted in size, which means that the worst-case transmission time is bounded and known in advance. Knowing these bounds helps with the task of designing network protocols. Typically, wired LANs run at speeds of 100 Mbps to 1 Gbps, have low delay (microseconds or nanoseconds), and make very few errors.

Newer LANs can operate at up to 10 Gbps. Compared with wireless networks, wired LANs exceed them in all dimensions of performance. It is just easier to send signals over a wire or a fiber than through the air.

The topology of many wired LANs is built from point-to-point links. IEEE 802.3, popularly called *Ethernet*, is by far the most common type of wired LAN. In *switched Ethernet*, each computer speaks the Ethernet protocol and, using a point-to-point link, connects to a box called a *switch*, hence the name. A switch has multiple ports, each of which can connect to one computer. The job of the switch is to relay packets between computers that are attached to it, using the address in each packet to determine which computer to send it to. Switched Ethernet is a modern version of the original classic Ethernet design that broadcasts all the packets over a single linear cable. Only one machine could successfully transmit at a time, and a distributed arbitration mechanism was used to resolve conflicts. It used a simple algorithm: computers could transmit whenever the cable was idle. If two or more packets collided, each computer just waited a random time and tried later. To build larger LANs, switches can be plugged into each other using their ports.

Both wireless and wired broadcast networks can be divided into static and dynamic designs, depending on how the channel is allocated. A typical static allocation would be to divide time into discrete intervals and use a round-robin algorithm, allowing each machine to broadcast only when its time slot comes up. Static allocation wastes channel capacity when a machine has nothing to say during its allocated slot, so most systems attempt to allocate the channel dynamically (i.e., on demand). Dynamic allocation methods for a common channel are either centralized or decentralized. In the centralized channel allocation method, there is a single entity (e.g., the base station in a cellular network) that determines who goes next. It might do this by accepting multiple packets and prioritizing them according to some internal algorithm. In the decentralized channel allocation method, there is no central entity; each machine must decide for itself whether to transmit. You might think that this approach would lead to chaos, but it does not. Later, we will study many algorithms designed to bring order out of the potential chaos.

3.2.3 Metropolitan Area Networks

A metropolitan area network (MAN) covers a city. The best-known examples of MANs are the cable television networks available in many cities. These systems grew from the earlier community antenna systems used in areas with poor over-the-air television reception. In those early systems, a large antenna was placed on top of a nearby hill and a signal was then piped to subscribers' houses. However, cable television is not the only MAN. Recent developments in high-speed wireless Internet access have resulted in another MAN; this has been standardized as IEEE 802.16 and is popularly known as WiMAX.

3.2.4 Wide Area Networks

A wide area network (WAN) spans a large geographical area, often a country or continent. Each of the offices within the network contains computers intended for running user (i.e., application) programs. The rest of the network that connects these hosts is then called the *communication subnet*, or just *subnet* for short. The job of the subnet is to carry messages from host to host. In most WANs, the subnet consists of two distinct components: transmission lines and switching elements. Transmission lines move bits between machines. They can be made of copper wire, optical fiber, or even radio links. Most companies do not have transmission lines lying about, so instead, they lease the lines from a telecommunications company. *Switching elements*, or just *switches* or *routers*, are specialized computers that connect two or more transmission lines. When data arrive on an incoming line, the switching element must choose an outgoing line on which to forward them.

A WAN, as we have described it, looks similar to a large wired LAN, but there are some important differences that go beyond long wires. First, in a WAN, the hosts and subnet are usually owned and operated by different people. Second, the routers will usually connect different kinds of networking technology. Lastly, subnet(s) can be entire LANs themselves. This means that many WANs will in fact be internetworks or composite networks that are made up of more than one network.

Rather than lease dedicated transmission lines, a company might connect its offices to the Internet. A virtual private network (VPN) allows connections to be made between offices as virtual links that use the underlying capacity of the Internet. Compared with the dedicated arrangement, a VPN has the usual advantage of virtualization, which is that it provides the flexible reuse of a resource (Internet connectivity), and the usual disadvantage of virtualization, which is a lack of control over the underlying resources.

3.3 Network Models

Now that we have discussed layered networks in the abstract, it is time to look at some examples. We will discuss two important network architectures: the OSI reference model and the TCP/IP reference model. Although the protocols associated with the OSI model are not used any more, the model itself is actually quite general and still valid, and the features discussed at each layer are still very important.

The TCP/IP model has the opposite properties: the model itself is not of much use, but the protocols are widely used.

3.3.1 OSI Reference Model

The OSI model (minus the physical medium) is shown in Figure 3.1. This model is based on a proposal developed by the International Organization for Standardization (ISO) as a first step toward international standardization of the protocols used in the various layers. The model is called the ISO Open Systems Interconnection (OSI) reference model because it deals with connecting open systems—that is, systems that are open for communication with other systems. We will just call it the *OSI model* for short.

The OSI model has seven layers. The principles that were applied to arrive at the seven layers can be briefly summarized as follows:

1. A layer should be created where a different abstraction is needed.
2. Each layer should perform a well-defined function.
3. The function of each layer should be chosen with an eye toward defining internationally standardized protocols.
4. The layer boundaries should be chosen to minimize the information flow across the interfaces.
5. The number of layers should be large enough that distinct functions need not be thrown together in the same layer out of necessity and small enough that the architecture does not become unwieldy.

We describe each layer of the model in turn, starting at the bottom layer. Note that the OSI model itself is not a network architecture because it does not specify the exact services and protocols to be used in each layer. It just describes what each layer should do. However, ISO has also produced standards for all the layers, although these are not part of the reference model itself. Each one has been published as a separate international standard. The model (in part) is widely used, although the associated protocols have long been forgotten.

3.3.1.1 Physical Layer

The physical layer is concerned with transmitting raw bits over a communication channel. The design issues have to do with making sure that when one side sends a 1 bit, it is received by the other side as a 1 bit, not as a 0 bit. Typical questions here are what electrical signals should be used to represent a 1 and a 0, how many nanoseconds a bit lasts, whether transmission may proceed simultaneously in both directions, how the initial connection is established, how it is torn down when both sides are finished, how many pins the network connector has, and what each pin is used for. These design issues largely deal with mechanical, electrical, and timing interfaces, as well as the physical transmission medium, which lies below the physical layer.

3.3.1.2 Data Link Layer

The main task of the data link layer is to transform a raw transmission facility into a line that appears free of undetected transmission errors. It does so by masking the real errors so the network layer does not see them. It accomplishes this task by having the sender break up the input data into data frames (typically a few hundred or a few thousand bytes) and transmit the frames sequentially. If the service is reliable, the receiver confirms correct receipt of each frame by sending back an acknowledgment frame.

Another issue that arises in the data link layer (and most of the higher layers as well) is how to keep a fast transmitter from drowning a slow receiver in data. Some traffic regulation mechanism may be needed to let the transmitter know when the receiver can accept more data.

Broadcast networks have an additional issue in the data link layer: how to control access to the shared channel. A special sublayer of the data link layer, the medium access control sublayer, deals with this problem.

3.3.1.3 Network Layer

The network layer controls the operation of the subnet. A key design issue is determining how packets are routed from source to destination. Routes can be based on static tables that are wired into the network and rarely changed, or more often, they can be updated automatically to avoid failed components. They can also be determined at the start of each conversation—for example, a terminal session, such as a log-in to a remote machine. Finally, they can be highly dynamic, being determined anew for each packet to reflect the current network load. If too many packets are present in the subnet at the same time, they will get in one another's way, forming bottlenecks. Handling congestion is also a responsibility of the network layer, in conjunction with higher layers that adapt the load they place on the network. More generally, the quality of service provided (delay, transit time, jitter, etc.) is also a network layer issue.

When a packet has to travel from one network to another to get to its destination, many problems can arise. The addressing used by the second network may be different from that used by the first one, the second one may not accept the packet at all because it is too large, the protocols may differ, and so on. It is up to the network layer to overcome all these problems to allow heterogeneous networks to be interconnected. In broadcast networks, the routing problem is simple, so the network layer is often thin or even nonexistent.

3.3.1.4 Transport Layer

The basic function of the transport layer is to accept data from above it, split them up into smaller units if need be, pass these to the network layer, and ensure that the pieces all arrive correctly at the other end. Furthermore, all this must be done efficiently and in a way that isolates the upper layers from the inevitable changes in the hardware technology over the course of time. The transport layer also determines what type of service to provide to the session layer and, ultimately, to the users of the network. The most popular type of transport connection is an error-free point-to-point channel that delivers messages or bytes in the order in which they were sent. However, other possible kinds of transport service exist, such as the transporting of isolated messages with no guarantee about the order of delivery and the broadcasting of messages to multiple destinations. The type of service is determined when the connection is established.

> As an aside, an error-free channel is completely impossible to achieve; what people really mean by this term is that the error rate is low enough to ignore in practice.
>
> The transport layer is a true end-to-end layer; it carries data all the way from the source to the destination. In other words, a program on the source machine carries on a conversation with a similar program on the destination machine, using the message headers and control messages. In the lower layers, each protocol is between a machine and its immediate neighbors, and not between the ultimate source and destination machines, which may be separated by many routers. The difference between layers 1–3, which are chained, and layers 4–7, which are end to end, is illustrated in Figure 3.1.

3.3.1.5 Session Layer

The session layer allows users on different machines to establish sessions between them. Sessions offer various services, including dialog control (keeping track of whose turn it is to transmit), token management (preventing two parties from attempting the same critical operation simultaneously), and synchronization (checkpointing long transmissions to allow them to pick up from where they left off in the event of a crash and subsequent recovery).

3.3.1.6 Presentation Layer

Unlike the lower layers, which are mostly concerned with moving bits around, the presentation layer is concerned with the syntax and semantics of the information transmitted. In order to make it possible for computers with different internal data representations to communicate, the data structures to be exchanged can be defined in an abstract way, along with a standard encoding to be used on the wire. The presentation layer manages these abstract data structures and allows higher-level data structures (e.g., banking records) to be defined and exchanged.

3.3.1.7 Application Layer

The application layer contains a variety of protocols that are commonly needed by users. One widely used application protocol is the Hypertext Transfer Protocol (HTTP), which is the basis for the WWW. When a browser wants a Web page, it sends the name of the page it wants to the server hosting the page using HTTP. The server then sends the page back. Other application protocols are used for file transfer, electronic mail, and network news.

3.3.2 TCP/IP Reference Model

Let us now turn from the OSI reference model to the reference model used in the grandparent of all wide area computer networks, the ARPANET, and its successor, the worldwide Internet. Although we will give a brief history of the ARPANET later, it is useful to mention a few key aspects of it now. The ARPANET was a research network sponsored by the U.S. Department of Defense (DoD). It eventually connected hundreds of universities and government installations using leased telephone lines. When satellite and radio networks were added later, the existing protocols had trouble interworking with them, so a new reference architecture was needed. Thus, from nearly the beginning, the ability to connect multiple networks in a seamless way was one of the major design goals. This architecture later became known as the TCP/IP reference model, after its two primary protocols. Given the DoD's worry that some of its precious hosts, routers, and internetwork gateways might get blown to pieces at a moment's notice by an attack from the Soviet Union, another major goal was that the network be able to survive the loss of subnet hardware, without existing conversations being broken off. In other words, the DoD wanted connections to remain intact as long as the source and destination machines were functioning, even if some of the machines or transmission lines in between were suddenly put out of operation. Furthermore, since applications with divergent requirements were envisioned, ranging from transferring files to real-time speech transmission, a flexible architecture was needed.

3.3.2.1 Link Layer

All these requirements led to the choice of a packet-switching network based on a connectionless layer that runs across different networks. The lowest layer in the model, the link layer, describes what links such as serial lines and classic Ethernet must do to meet the needs of this connectionless Internet layer. It is not really a layer at all, in the normal sense of the term, but rather an interface between hosts and transmission links. Early material on the TCP/IP model has little to say about it.

3.3.2.2 Internet Layer

The Internet layer is the linchpin that holds the whole architecture together. Its job is to permit hosts to inject packets into any network and have them travel independently to the destination (potentially on a different network). They may even arrive in a completely different order than they were sent, in which case, it is the job of the higher layers to rearrange them, if in-order delivery is desired. Note that *Internet* is used here in a generic sense, even though this layer is present in the Internet.

An analogy here is the (snail) mail system. A person can drop a sequence of international letters into a mailbox in one country, and with a little luck, most of them will be delivered to the correct address in the destination country. The letters will probably travel through one or more international mail gateways along the way, but this is transparent to the users. Furthermore, that each country (i.e., each network) has its own stamps, preferred envelope sizes, and delivery rules is hidden from the users. The Internet layer defines an official packet format and protocol called the Internet Protocol (IP), plus a companion protocol called the Internet Control Message Protocol (ICMP), which help it function. The job of the Internet layer is to deliver IP packets where they are supposed to go. Packet routing is clearly a major issue here, as is congestion (though IP has not proven effective at avoiding congestion).

3.3.2.3 Transport Layer

The layer above the Internet layer in the TCP/IP model is now usually called the *transport layer*. It is designed to allow peer entities on the source and destination hosts to carry on a conversation, just as in the OSI transport layer. Two end-to-end transport protocols have been defined here. The first one, the Transmission Control Protocol (TCP), is a reliable connection-oriented protocol that allows a byte stream originating on one machine to be delivered without error to any other machine in the Internet. It segments the incoming byte stream into discrete messages and passes each one on to the Internet layer. At the destination, the receiving TCP process reassembles the received messages into the output stream. TCP also handles flow control to make sure a fast sender cannot swamp a slow receiver with more messages than it can handle.

The second protocol in this layer, the User Datagram Protocol (UDP), is an unreliable, connectionless protocol for applications that do not want TCP's sequencing or flow control and wish to provide their own. It is also widely used for one-shot, client–server-type request–reply queries and applications in which prompt delivery is more important than accurate delivery, such as transmitting speech or video. Since the model was developed, IP has been implemented on many other networks.

3.3.2.4 Application Layer

The TCP/IP model does not have session or presentation layers; no need for them was perceived. Instead, applications simply include any session and presentation functions that they require. Experience with the OSI model has proven this view correct: these layers are of little use to most applications.

On top of the transport layer is the application layer, which contains all the higher-level protocols. The early ones included virtual terminal (Telnet), file transfer (FTP), and electronic mail (Simple Mail Transfer Protocol or SMTP). Many other protocols have been added to these over the years. Some important ones include the Domain Name System (DNS), for mapping host names onto their network addresses; HTTP, the protocol for fetching pages on the WWW; and Real-Time Transport Protocol (RTP), the protocol for delivering real-time media such as voices or movies.

OSI versus TCP/IP: The OSI reference model was devised before the corresponding protocols were invented. This ordering meant that the model was not biased toward one particular set of protocols, a fact that made it quite general. The downside of this ordering was that the designers did not have much experience with the subject and did not have a good idea of which functionality to put in which layer. For example, the data link layer originally dealt only with point-to-point networks. When broadcast networks came around, a new sublayer had to be hacked into the model. Furthermore, no thought was given to internetworking. With TCP/IP, the reverse was true: the protocols came first, and the model was really just a description of the existing protocols. There was no problem with the protocols fitting the model. They fit perfectly. The only trouble was that the model did not fit any other protocol stacks. Consequently, it was not especially useful for describing other non-TCP/IP networks.

3.4 Internet

The origins of the Internet can be traced to the U.S. government's support of the ARPANET project. Computers in several U.S. universities were linked via packet switching, and this allowed messages to be sent between the universities that were part of the network. The use of ARPANET was limited initially to academia and to the U.S. military, and in the early years, there was little interest from industrial companies.

However, by the mid-1980s, there were over 2000 hosts on the TCP/IP-enabled network, and the ARPANET was becoming more heavily used and congested. It was decided to shut down the network by the late 1980s, and the National Science Foundation (NSF) in the United States commenced work on the NSFNET. This work commenced in the mid-1980s, and the network consisted of multiple regional networks connected to a major backbone. The original links in NSFNET were 56 Kbps, but these were later updated to the faster T1 (1.544 Mbps) links. The NSFNET T1 backbone initially connected 13 sites, but this increased due to a growing interest from academic and industrial sites in the United States and from around the world. The NSF began to realize from the mid-1980s onward that the Internet had significant commercial potential.

The NSFNET backbone was upgraded with T1 links in 1988, and the Internet began to become more international. Sites in Canada and several European countries were connected to the Internet. The Defense Advanced Research Projects Agency (DARPA) formed the Computer Emergency Response Team (CERT) to deal with any emergency incidents arising during the operation of the network. Advanced Network Services (ANS) was founded in 1991. This was an independent not-for-profit company, and it installed a new network that replaced the NSFNET T1 network. The ANSNET backbone operated over T3 (45 Mbps) links, and it was different from previous networks such as ARPANET and NSFNET in that it was owned and operated by a private company rather than the U.S. government. The NSF decided to focus on the research aspects of networks rather than the operational side. The ANSNET network was a move away from a core network such as NSFNET to a distributive network architecture operated by commercial providers such as Sprint, MCI, and BBN. The network was connected by major network exchange points, termed *Network Access Points* (NAPs). There were over 160,000 hosts connected to the Internet by the late 1980s.

3.4.1 Internet Services

3.4.1.1 Electronic Mail

Electronic mail, or *e-mail*, is the computerized version of writing a letter and mailing it at the local post office. Many people are so committed to using e-mail that if it were taken away tomorrow, some serious social and economic repercussions would be felt throughout the United States and the rest of the world. Many commercial e-mail programs are in existence, as well as a number of free ones that can be downloaded from the Internet. Although each e-mail program has its own unique feel and options, most offer the following services:

- Creating an e-mail message
- Sending an e-mail message to one recipient, multiple recipients, or a mailing list
- Receiving, storing, replying to, and forwarding e-mail messages
- Attaching a file, such as a word-processing document, a spreadsheet, an image, or a program, to an outgoing e-mail message

3.4.1.2 File Transfer Protocol

The File Transfer Protocol (FTP) was one of the first services offered on the Internet. Its primary functions are to allow a user to download a file from a remote site to the user's computer and to upload a file from the user's computer to a remote site. These files could contain data, such as numbers, text, or images, or executable computer programs. Although the WWW has become the major vehicle for retrieving text- and image-based documents, many organizations still find it useful to create an FTP repository of data and program files.

3.4.1.3 Remote Log-In (Telnet)

Remote log-in, or Telnet, is a terminal emulation program for TCP/IP networks, such as the Internet, that allows users to log in to a remote computer. The Telnet program runs on your computer and connects your workstation to a remote server on the Internet. Once you are connected to the remote server or host, you can enter commands through the Telnet program, and those commands will be executed as if you were entering them directly at the terminal of the remote computer.

3.4.1.4 Voice over IP

One of the newer services that is attracting the interest of companies and home users alike is the sending of voice signals over an IP-based network such as the Internet. The practice of making telephone calls over the Internet has had a number of different names, including *packet voice, voice over packet, voice over the Internet,* and *Internet telephony*. But it appears the industry has settled on the term *voice over IP* (VoIP), in reference to the Internet Protocol (IP), which controls the transfer of data over the Internet. Whatever its title, VoIP has emerged as one of the hottest Internet services and has certainly drawn the attention of many companies.

3.4.1.5 Listservs

A *listserv* is a popular software program used to create and manage Internet mailing lists. Listserv software maintains a table of e-mail addresses that reflects the current members of the listserv. When an individual sends an e-mail to the listserv address, the listserv sends a copy of this e-mail message to every e-mail address stored in the listserv table. Thus, every member of the listserv receives the e-mail message.

3.4.1.6 Streaming Audio and Video

Streaming audio and video involves the continuous download of a compressed audio or video file, which can then be heard or viewed on the user's workstation. Typical examples of streaming audio are popular and classical music, live radio broadcasts, and historical or archived lectures, music, and radio broadcasts. Typical examples of streaming video include prerecorded television shows and other video productions, lectures, and live video productions. Businesses can use streaming audio and video to provide training videos, product samples, and live feeds from corporate offices, to name a few examples.

3.4.1.7 Instant Messages, Tweets, and Blogs

Instant messaging (IM) allows a user to see if people are currently logged in on the network and, if they are, to send them short messages in real time. Many users, especially those in the corporate environment, are turning away from e-mail and using IM as a means of communicating. The advantages of IM include real-time conversations, server storage savings (because you are not storing and forwarding instant messages, as you would e-mails), and the capability of carrying on a silent conversation between multiple parties. Service providers such as AOL, Microsoft's MSN, and Yahoo!, as well as a number of other software companies, incorporate IM into their products.

3.5 World Wide Web

The WWW was invented by Tim Berners-Lee in 1990 at CERN in Geneva, Switzerland. CERN is a key European and international center for research in the nuclear field, and several thousand physicists and scientists work there. Berners-Lee first came to CERN in 1980 for a short contract programming assignment. He came from a strong scientific background, as both his parents had been involved in the programming of the Mark I computer at Manchester University in the 1950s. He graduated in physics in the mid-1970s at Oxford University in England. Berners-Lee's invention of the WWW was a revolutionary milestone in computing. It has transformed the way that businesses operate as well as transforming the use of the Internet from mainly academic (with some commercial use) to an integral part of peoples' lives.

One of the problems that scientists at CERN faced was that of keeping track of people, computers, documents, databases, and so on. This problem was more acute due to the international nature of CERN, as the center had many visiting scientists from overseas who would spend several months there. It also had a large pool of permanent staff. Visiting scientists used to come and go, and in the late 1980s, there was no efficient and effective way to share information among scientists. It was often desirable for a visiting scientist to obtain information or data from the CERN computers. In other cases, the scientists wished to make results of their research available to CERN in an easy manner. Berners-Lee developed a program called Enquire to assist with information sharing, and the program also assisted in keeping track of the work of visiting scientists. He returned to CERN in the mid-1980s to work on other projects, and he devoted part of his free time to considering solutions to the information-sharing problem. This was eventually to lead to his breakthrough and his invention of the WWW in 1990.

His vision and its subsequent realization was beneficial to both CERN and the wider world. He envisioned that all information stored on computers everywhere could be linked and computers could be programmed to create a space where everything is linked to everything. Berners-Lee essentially created a system to give every page on a computer a standard address. This standard address is called the *uniform resource locator* and is better known by its acronym URL. Each page is accessible via the Hypertext Transfer Protocol (HTTP), and the page is formatted with the Hypertext Markup Language (HTML). Each page is visible using a Web browser.

The characteristic features of the WWW are as follows:

1. A uniform resource locator (URL) (previously known as a *uniform resource identifier*) provides a unique address code for each Web page. Browsers decode the URL location to access the Web page. For example, www.amazon.com uniquely identifies the Amazon host website in the United States.
2. Hypertext Markup Language (HTML) is used for designing the layout of Web pages. It allows the formatting of pages containing hypertext links. HTML is standardized and controlled by the World Wide Web Consortium (W3C) (http://www.w3.org).
3. The Hypertext Transfer Protocol (HTTP) allows a new Web page to be accessed from the current page.
4. A *browser* is a client program that allows a user to interact with pages and information on the WWW. It uses HTTP to make requests of Web servers throughout the Internet on behalf of the browser's user.

Inventors tend to be influenced by existing inventions, especially inventions that are relevant to their areas of expertise. The Internet was a key existing invention, and it allowed worldwide communication via electronic e-mail, the transfer of files electronically via FTP, and newsgroups that allowed users to make postings on various topics. Another key invention that was relevant to Berners-Lee was that of hypertext. This was invented by Ted Nelson in the 1960s, and it allows links to be present in text. For example, a document such as a book contains a table of contents, an index, and a bibliography. These are all links to material that is either within the book itself or external to the book. The reader of a book is able to follow the link to obtain the internal or external information. The other key invention that was relevant to Berners-Lee was that of the mouse. This was invented by Doug Engelbart in the 1960s, and it allowed the cursor to be steered around the screen.

The major leap that Berners-Lee made was essentially a marriage of the Internet, hypertext, and the mouse into what has become the World Wide Web. He was especially concerned with allowing communication across computers and software of different types. He also wanted to avoid the structure of most databases, which forced people to put information into categories before they knew if such classifications were appropriate or not. To these ends, he devised a uniform resource identifier (later called a uniform resource locator or URL) that could point to any document (or any other type of resource) in the universe of information. In place of the File Transfer Protocol then in use, he created the more sophisticated Hypertext Transfer Protocol (HTTP), which was faster and had more features. Finally, he defined Hypertext Markup Language (HTML) for the movement of hypertext across the network. Within a few years, these abbreviations, along with WWW for the World Wide Web itself, would be as common as RAM, K, or any other jargon in the computer field.

In order to create and display Web pages, some type of markup language is necessary. While there are many types of markup languages, we will briefly introduce three common types here: Hypertext Markup Language (HTML), dynamic Hypertext Markup Language (dynamic HTML), and Extensible Markup Language (XML). HTML, D-HTML, and XML are members of a family of markup languages called Standard Generalized Markup Language (SGML). Despite the name, SGML itself is not a markup language but a description of how to create a markup language. To put it another way, SGML is a metalanguage. HTML is a set of codes inserted into a document that is intended for display on a Web browser. The codes, or markup symbols, instruct the browser how to display a Web page's text, images, and other elements. The individual markup codes are often referred to as *tags* and are surrounded by brackets (< >). Most HTML tags consist of an opening tag, followed by one or more attributes, and a closing tag. Closing tags are preceded by a forward slash (/). Attributes are parameters that specify various qualities that an HTML tag can take on. For example, a common attribute is HREF, which specifies the URL of a file in an anchor tag (<A>).

3.5.1 Origin of the World Wide Web Browser

The invention of the WWW by Berners-Lee was a revolution in the use of the Internet. Users could now "surf the Web"—that is, hyperlink among the millions of computers in the world and obtain information easily. The WWW creates a space in which users can access information easily in any part of the world. This is done using only a Web browser and simple Web addresses. Browsers are used to connect to remote computers over the Internet to request, retrieve, and display the Web pages on the local machine. The user can then click on hyperlinks on Web pages to access further relevant information that may be on an entirely different continent. Berners-Lee developed the first Web browser, called the World Wide Web browser. He also wrote the first browser program, and this allowed users to access Web pages throughout the world.

Early browsers included Gopher, developed at the University of Minnesota, and Mosaic, developed at the University of Illinois. These were replaced in later years by Netscape, and the objective of its design was to create a graphical user interface browser that would be easy to use and would gain widespread acceptance in the Internet community. Initially, the Netscape browser dominated the market, and this remained so until Microsoft developed its own browser, called Internet Explorer. Microsoft's browser would eventually come to dominate the market, after what became known as the *browser wars*. The eventual dominance of Internet Explorer was controversial, and it was subject to legal investigations in the United States. The development of the graphical browsers led to the commercialization of the WWW.

The WWW got off to a slow start. Its distinctive feature, the ability to jump to different resources through hyperlinks, was of little use until there were at least a few other places besides CERN that supported it. Until editing software was written, users had to construct the links in a document by hand, a very tedious process. To view Web materials, one used a browser (the term may have originated with Apple's HyperCard). Early Web browsers (including two called Lynx and Viola) presented screens that were similar to Gopher's, with a list of menu selections.

Around the fall of 1992, Marc Andreessen and Eric Bina began discussing ways of making it easier to navigate the Web. While still a student at the University of Illinois, Andreessen took a job programming for the National Center for Supercomputing Applications (NCSA), a center set up with NSF that was also the impetus for the original ARPANET. By January 1993, Andreessen and Bina had written an early version of a browser they would later call Mosaic, and they released a version of it over the Internet. Mosaic married the ease of use of HyperCard with the full hypertext capabilities of the WWW. To select items, one used a mouse (thus circling back to Doug Engelbart, who invented it for that purpose). One knew an item had a hyperlink by its distinct color. A second feature of Mosaic, the one that most impressed the people who first used it, was its seamless integration of text and images. With the help of others at NCSA, Mosaic was rewritten to run on Windows-based machines and Macintoshes as well as workstations. As a product of a government-funded laboratory, Mosaic was made available free or for a nominal charge.

Andreessen managed to commercialize his invention quickly. In early 1994, he was approached by Jim Clark, the founder of Silicon Graphics, who suggested that they commercialize the invention. Andreessen agreed, but apparently the University of Illinois objected to this idea. Like the University of Pennsylvania a half-century before it, Illinois saw the value of the work done on its campus, but it failed to see the much greater value of the people who did that work. Clark left Silicon Graphics and with Andreessen founded Mosaic Communications that spring. The University of Illinois asserted its claim to the name Mosaic, so the company changed its name to Netscape Communications Corporation. Clark and Andreessen visited Champaign–Urbana and quickly hired many of the programmers who had worked on the software. Netscape introduced its version of the browser in September 1994. The University of Illinois continued to offer Mosaic in a licensing agreement with another company, but Netscape's software quickly supplanted Mosaic as the most popular version of the program.

3.5.2 Applications of the World Wide Web

Berners-Lee used the analogy of the market economy to describe the commercial potential of the WWW. He realized that the WWW offered the potential to conduct business in cyberspace without human interaction, rather than the traditional way of buyers and sellers coming together to do business in the market place. Anyone can trade with anyone else, except that they do not have to go to the market square to do so. The invention of the WWW was announced in August 1991, and the growth of the Web has been phenomenal since then. The growth has often been exponential, and exponential growth rate curves became a feature of newly formed Internet companies and their business plans.

The WWW is revolutionary in that

- No single organization is controlling the Web.
- No single computer is controlling the Web.
- Millions of computers are interconnected.
- It is an enormous marketplace of millions (if not billions) of users.
- The Web is not located in one physical location.
- The Web is a space and not a physical thing.

The WWW has been applied to many areas, including

- The travel industry (booking flights, train tickets, and hotels)
- e-Marketing
- Portal sites (such as Yahoo! and Hotmail)
- Ordering books and CDs over the Web (e.g., www.amazon.com)

- Recruitment services (e.g., www.jobserve.com)
- Internet banking
- Online casinos (for gambling)
- Newspapers and news channels
- Online shopping and shopping malls

Berners-Lee invented the well-known terms URL, HTML, and WWW, and these terms are ubiquitous today. Berners-Lee is now the director of the World Wide Web Consortium, and this MIT-based organization sets the software standards for the Web.

3.6 Semantic Web

While the Web keeps growing at an astounding pace, most Web pages are still designed for human consumption and cannot be processed by machines. Similarly, while Web search engines help retrieve Web pages, they do not offer support to interpret the results—for that, human intervention is still required. As the size of search results is often just too big for humans to interpret, finding relevant information on the Web is not as easy as we would desire. The existing Web has evolved as a medium for information exchange among people, rather than machines. As a consequence, the semantic content—that is, the meaning of the information on a Web page—is coded in a way that is accessible to human beings only. Today's Web may be defined as the Syntactic Web, where information presentation is carried out by computers, and the interpretation and identification of relevant information is delegated to human beings. With the volume of available digital data growing at an exponential rate, it is becoming virtually impossible for human beings to manage the complexity and volume of the available information. This phenomenon, often referred to as *information overload*, poses a serious threat to the continued usefulness of today's Web.

As the volume of Web resources grows exponentially, researchers from industry, government, and academia are now exploring the possibility of creating a Semantic Web in which meaning is made explicit, allowing machines to process and integrate Web resources intelligently. Biologists use a well-defined taxonomy, the Linnaean taxonomy, adopted and shared by most of the scientific community worldwide. Likewise, computer scientists are looking for a similar model to help structure Web content. In 2001, T. Berners-Lee, J. Hendler, and O. Lassila published a revolutionary article in *Scientific American* titled "The Semantic Web: A New Form of Web Content That Is Meaningful to Computers Will Unleash a Revolution of New Possibilities."[*]

---

[*] Berners-Lee, T.; Lassila, O.; Hendler, J. (2001) The semantic web: A new form of Web content that is meaningful to computers will unleash a revolution of new possibilities. *Scientific American*, 284(5), pp. 34–43.

The Semantic Web is an extension of the current Web in which information is given well-defined meaning, enabling computers and people to work in cooperation. In the lower part of the architecture, we find three building blocks that can be used to encode text (Unicode), to identify resources on the Web (URLs), and to structure and exchange information (XML). The Resource Description Framework (RDF) is a simple yet powerful data model and language for describing Web resources. The SPARQL Protocol and RDF Query Language (SPARQL) is the de facto standard used to query RDF data. While RDF and RDF Schema provide a model for representing Semantic Web data and for structuring semantic data using simple hierarchies of classes and properties, respectively, the SPARQL language and protocol provide the means to express queries and retrieve information from across diverse Semantic Web data sources. The need for a new language is motivated by the different data models and semantics at the level of XML and RDF, respectively.

Ontology is the formal, explicit specification of a shared conceptualization of a particular domain—concepts are the core elements of the conceptualization, corresponding to the entities of the domain being described, and properties and relations are used to describe interconnections between such concepts. Web Ontology Language (OWL) is the standard language for representing knowledge on the Web. This language was designed to be used by applications that need to process the content of information on the Web instead of just presenting information to human users. Using OWL, one can explicitly represent the meaning of terms in vocabularies and the relationships between those terms. The Rule Interchange Format (RIF) is the W3C recommendation that defines a framework to exchange rule-based languages on the Web. Like OWL, RIF defines a set of languages covering various aspects of the rule layer of the Semantic Web.

3.7 Internet of Things

Just as the Internet and the Web connect humans, the Internet of Things (IoT) is a revolutionary way of architecting and implementing systems and services based on evolutionary changes. The Internet as we know it is transforming radically, from an academic network in the 1980s and early 1990s to a mass market, consumer-oriented network. Now it is set to become fully pervasive, connected, interactive, and intelligent. Real-time communication is possible not only by humans but also by things at any time and from anywhere.

It is quite likely that sooner or later the majority of items connected to the Internet will not be humans but things. The IoT will primarily expand communication from the 7 billion people around the world to the estimated 50–70 billion machines. This would result in a world where everything is connected and can be accessed from anywhere—this has the potential to connect the 100 trillion things that are deemed to exist on Earth. With the advent of the IoT, the physical world itself will become a connected information system. In the world of the IoT, sensors and actuators embedded in physical objects are linked through wired and wireless networks that connect the Internet. These information systems churn out huge volumes of data that flow to computers for analysis. When objects can both sense the environment and communicate, they become tools for understanding the complexity of the real world and responding to it swiftly.

 This would also mean significant opportunities for the telecom industry to develop new IoT subscribers that would easily overtake the number of current subscribers based on population.

The Internet of Things (IoT) can be defined as the network formed by things or objects having identities and virtual personalities that interact using intelligent interfaces to connect and communicate with the users' social and environmental contexts. IoT is also referred to as *pervasive* or *ubiquitous computing systems*. The goal of the IoT is to achieve pervasive IoT connectivity and grand integration and to provide secure, fast, and personalized functionalities and services such as monitoring, sensing, tracking, locating, alerting, scheduling, controlling, protecting, logging, auditing, planning, maintenance, upgrading, data mining, trending, reporting, decision support, dashboard, back-office applications, and so on.

The IoT would be closely associated with environmental, societal, and economic issues such as climate change, environment protection, energy saving, and globalization. For these reasons the IoT would be increasingly used in a large number of sectors such as health care, energy and environment, safety and security, transportation, logistics, and manufacturing.

Major IoT applications in various sectors are as follows:

- *Energy and power*: Supply/alternatives/demand. Turbines, generators, meters, substations, switches
- *Health care*: Care/personal/research. Medical devices, imaging, diagnostics, monitor, surgical equipment
- *Buildings*: Institutional/commercial/industrial/home. HVAC, fire and safety, security, elevators, access control systems, lighting
- *Industrial*: Process industries/forming/converting/discrete assembly/distribution/supply chain. Pumps, valves, vessels, tanks, automation and control equipment, capital equipment, pipelines
- *Retail*: Stores/hospitality/services. Point-of-sale terminals, vending machines, RFID tags, scanners and registers, lighting and refrigeration systems
- *Security and infrastructure*: Homeland security/emergency services/national and regional defense. GPS systems, radar systems, environmental sensors, vehicles, weaponry, fencing

- *Transportation*: On-road vehicles/off-road vehicles/nonvehicular/transport infrastructure. Commercial vehicles, airplanes, trains, ships, signage, tolls, RF tags, parking meters, surveillance cameras, tracking systems
- *Information technology and network infrastructure*: Enterprise/data centers. Switches, servers, storage
- *Resources*: Agriculture/mining/oil/gas/water. Mining equipment, drilling equipment, pipelines, agricultural equipment
- *Consumer/professional*: Appliances/white goods/office equipment/home electronics. M2M devices, gadgets, smartphones, tablet PCs, home gateways

In terms of the type of technological artifacts involved, IoT applications can be subdivided into four categories:

1. The Internet of Devices: machine to machine (M2M)
   M2M refers to technologies that allow both wireless and wired devices to communicate with each other or, in most cases, a centralized server. An M2M system uses devices (e.g., sensors or meters) to capture events (e.g., temperature or inventory level), which are relayed through a network (wireless, wired, or hybrid) to an application (software program) that translates the captured events into meaningful information. M2M communication is a relatively new business concept, born from the original telemetry technology, utilizing similar technologies but modern versions.
2. The Internet of Objects: radio frequency identification (RFID)
   RFID uses radio waves to transfer data from an electronic tag attached to an object to a central system through a reader for the purpose of identifying and tracking the object.
3. The Internet of Transducers: wireless sensor networks WSN
   WSNs consist of spatially distributed autonomous sensors that monitor physical or environmental conditions, such as temperature, sound, vibration, pressure, motion, or pollutants, and cooperatively pass their data through the network to a main location. More modern networks are bidirectional, becoming wireless sensor and actuator networks (WSANs), enabling the control of sensor activities.
4. The Internet of Controllers: supervisory control and data acquisition (SCADA)
   SCADA is an autonomous system based on closed-loop control theory or a smart system or cyber-physical system (CPS) that connects, monitors, and controls equipment via the network (mostly wired short-range networks, sometimes wireless or hybrid) in a facility such as a plant or a building.

3.8 From Physical to Logical Networks

In the Internet, a client-server (software) architecture was put in use to support such popular applications of WWW as FTP and email. This is a logical network overlaying the physical one. The main idea was that many users access a centrally hosted server and exchange their information over this central mediator. Local code and functional roles were more and more shifted to servers in the Internet, leading to weak and simple clients on the user side. This logic network approach allows the operation of specialized machines for certain tasks to buy and sell computation services in the Internet and to increase both efficiency and productivity.

The concept of service-oriented architectures (SOA) was introduced in the late 1990s as an approach to organize software architectures, that is, logic networks. Its main idea is to map business processes to workflows, which are decomposable into smaller service units. Individual services may then be either programmed by the user himself or bought in a (not-yet-existing) global marketplace for services. Through the clear separation and specification of single services, a marketplace may be born, leading to professional and well-tested service components as well as flexibility in the design of system architectures. An extension of the SOA idea from software services to platform and infrastructure services has recently had a large impact under the term *cloud computing* (see Chapter 8, "Cloud Computing," Subsection 8.6.2). While SOA is limited to the hosting and execution of remote code, cloud computing offers a wider set of services.

3.9 Summary

This chapter described the genesis of computer networks at ARPANET, the natures and types of networks, and the standard network models. It recounted briefly the history of the invention of the Internet and the WWW, ending with some practical applications of the WWW.

Chapter 4

Distributed Systems

The origins of big data technologies come from database systems and distributed systems, as well as data-mining and machine-learning algorithms that can process these vast amounts of data to extract knowledge. Several distributed database prototype systems were developed in the 1980s and 1990s to address the issues of data distribution, data replication, distributed query and transaction processing, distributed database metadata management, and other topics. More recently, many new technologies have emerged that combine database and distributed technologies. These technologies and systems are being developed for dealing with the storage, analysis, and mining of the vast amounts of data that are being produced and collected, and they are referred to generally as *big data* (see Chapter 9).

The centralized approach to processing data, in which users access a central database on a central computer through personal computers (PCs) and workstations, dominated organizations from the late 1960s through the mid-1980s because there was no alternative approach to compete with it. The introduction of reasonably priced PCs during the 1980s, however, facilitated the placement of computers at various locations within an organization; users could access a database directly at those locations. Networks connected these computers, so users could access not only data located on their local computers but also data located anywhere across the entire network.

This chapter addresses the issues involved in distributed databases, where a database is stored on more than one computer.

Distributed systems consist of a collection of heterogeneous but fully autonomous components that can execute on different computers. While each of these components has full control over its constituent subparts, there is no master component that possesses control over all the components of a distributed system. Thus, for each of these systems to appear as a single and integrated whole, the various components need to be able to interact with each other via predefined interfaces through a computer network.

The characteristic global features of a successful distributed system are as follows:

■ Distributed systems are heterogeneous, arising from the need to, say, integrate components on a legacy IBM mainframe, with the components newly created to operate on a UNIX workstation or Windows NT machine.

■ Distributed systems are scalable in that, when a component becomes overloaded with too many requests or users, another replica of the same component can be instantiated and added to the distributed system to share the load among them. Moreover, these instantiated components can be located closer to the local users and other interacting components to improve the performance of the overall distributed system.

■ Distributed systems execute components concurrently in a multithreaded mode via multiply invoked components corresponding to the number of simultaneously invoked processes.

■ Distributed systems are fault tolerant in that they duplicate components on different computers so that if one computer fails another can take over without affecting the availability of the overall system.

■ Distributed systems are more resilient in that, whereas distributed systems have multiple points of failure, the unaffected components are fully operational even though some of the components are not functional or are malfunctioning. Moreover, the distributed system could invoke another instance of the failed components along with the corresponding state of the process (characterized by the program counter, the register variable contents, and the state of the virtual memory used by the process) to continue with the process.

■ Distributed systems demonstrate invariance or transparency with reference to characteristics such as
   – Accessibility, either locally or across networks to the components
   – The physical location of the components
   – The migration of components from one host to another
   – The replication of components, including their states
   – The concurrency of components requesting services from shared components
   – Scalability, in terms of the actual number of requests or users at any instance
   – Performance, in terms of the number and types of available resources
   – Points of failure, be it a failure of the component, network, or response

The terms *parallel system* and *distributed system* are often used interchangeably; however, the term *distributed* refers to a wider class of systems, while the term *parallel* implies a subclass of tightly coupled systems.

Distributed systems encompass any architecture or system that allows the computation to be broken down into units and executed concurrently on different computing elements, whether these are processors on different nodes, processors on the same computer, or cores within the same processor. *Distributed* often implies that the locations of all the constituting computing elements are not the same, and such elements might be heterogeneous in terms of hardware and software features. Classic examples of distributed computing systems are computing grids or Internet computing systems, which combine the biggest variety of architectures, systems, and applications in the world.

Parallel refers to a model in which the computation is divided among several processors sharing the same memory. The architecture of a parallel computing system is often characterized by the homogeneity of components: each processor is of the same type and it has the same capability as the others. The shared memory has a single address space that is accessible to all the processors. Parallel programs are then broken down into several units of execution that can be allocated to different processors and can communicate with each other by means of the shared memory.

Originally, parallel systems used to include only those architectures that featured multiple processors sharing the same physical memory and computer. However, parallel systems are now considered to include all those architectures that are based on the concept of shared memory, regardless of whether this is physically colocated or created with the support of libraries, specific hardware, and a highly efficient networking infrastructure. For example, a cluster in which the nodes are connected through an InfiniBand network and configured with a distributed shared memory system can also be considered a parallel system.

4.1 Parallel Computing

Parallel computing involves architecture that is capable of allowing multiple machines to work together. In 1966, Michael J. Flynn created a taxonomy of computer architectures that support parallelism, based on the number of concurrent control and data streams the architecture can handle. This classification is used extensively to characterize parallel computing architectures (Figure 4.1a).

They are briefly described as follows:

1. Single instruction, single data stream (SISD): This is a sequential computer that exploits no parallelism, such as a PC (single core).
2. Single instruction, multiple data stream (SIMD): This architecture supports multiple data streams to be processed simultaneously by replicating the

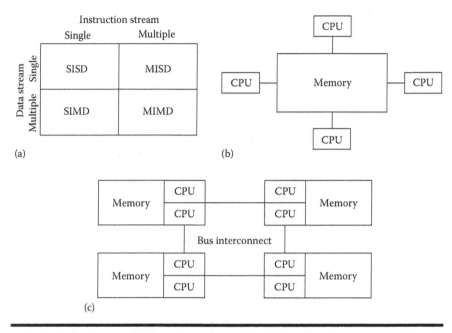

Figure 4.1   Parallel computing architectures: (a) Flynn's taxonomy, (b) a shared-memory system, and (c) a distributed system.

computing hardware. Single Instruction means that all the data streams are processed using the same compute logic. Examples of parallel architectures that support this model are array processors or graphics processing unit (GPU).

3. Multiple instruction, single data stream (MISD): This architecture operates on a single data stream but has multiple computing engines using the same data stream. This is not a very common architecture and is sometimes used to provide fault tolerance with heterogeneous systems operating on the same data to provide independent results that are compared with each other.

4. Multiple instruction, multiple data stream (MIMD): This is the most generic parallel processing architecture where any type of distributed application can be programmed. Multiple autonomous processors executing in parallel work on independent streams of data. The application logic running on these processors can also be very different. All distributed systems are recognized to be MIMD architectures.

A variant of SIMD is the single program, multiple data (SPMD) model, where the same program executes on multiple computer processes. While SIMD can achieve the same result as SPMD, SIMD systems typically execute in lockstep with a central controlling authority for program execution. As can be seen, when multiple instances of the *map* function are executed in parallel, they work on different data streams using the same function.

Parallelism within an application can operate at several levels.

■ Large grain (or task level)
■ Medium grain (or data level)
■ Fine grain (or instruction level)
■ Very fine grain (bit level)

Thus, Flynn's taxonomy is representative of the hardware architecture at many different levels.

1. Task-level parallelism in a multiprocessor system is synonymous with Flynn's MIMD architecture, which occurs when each CPU executes a different process on the same or different data. The varying threads can execute the same or completely different code. In any case, however, varying threads must communicate with one another as they work. Communication takes place usually to pass data from one thread to the next as part of a workflow. Task parallelism emphasizes the distributed (parallelized) nature of the processing (i.e., threads), as opposed to the data (data parallelism). Most real programs fall somewhere on a continuum between task parallelism and data parallelism. Most supercomputers fall into this category.

2. Data-level parallelism is synonymous with Flynn's SIMD architecture: single instruction (all processing units perform identical instruction) and multiple data (each processing unit can operate on varying data elements). Data-level parallelism is accomplished when each processor performs the same task on different data inputs. In some circumstances, one thread may control operations on several different pieces of data. In other situations, threads may control the operation, however they may execute the same code. Data-level parallelism emphasizes the distributed (parallelized) nature of the data, as opposed to the processing (task parallelism). Most modern computers, particularly those with graphics processor units (GPUs), employ SIMD instructions and execution units.

3. Instruction-level parallelism performs many concurrent operations in a single computer program. For instance:
   a. $R3 \leftarrow R1 + R2$
   b. $R6 \leftarrow R4 + R5$
   c. $R7 \leftarrow R3 + R6$

   The third operation is dependent on the prior two operations being complete. However, the first two operations are independent, so they can be calculated at the same time. The most efficient compiler and processor design would identify and take advantage of as much of this parallelism as possible. Ordinary programs are typically written under a sequential execution model in which instructions execute one after the other and in the order specified by the programmer.

4. Bit-level parallelism is a form of parallel computing based on increasing processor word size. It is done by performing the arithmetic on two numbers, bit by bit. The addition, for example, of two 32-bit numbers was performed in 32 machine cycles, by very simple circuitry capable only of adding one bit to another. Quite possibly the earliest use of parallelism in computers was to perform the operations on all bits simultaneously in parallel.

Instruction-level parallelism allows the compiler and the processor to overlap the execution of multiple instructions or even to change the order in which instructions are executed. *Pipelining* is an excellent example of this form of parallel processing. The idea of pipelining is that as each instruction completes a step, the following instruction moves into the stage just vacated. Thus, when the first instruction is completed, the next one is already one stage short of completion. Data hazards occur when the processor fetches data (say) c and f. Since c and f have not been written back, the fetch may access the wrong data (previously stored in c and f, not the current ones). This is called *read after write* (RAW).

Memory can either be shared or distributed (Figure 4.1b). Shared memory typically is comprised of one of the following two architectures: uniform memory access (or UMA) or non-uniform memory access (or NUMA). Regardless of the specific architecture, shared memory is generally accessible to all the processors in the system and multiple processors may operate independently and continue to share the same memory. Figure 4.1b illustrates the UMA architecture. Multiple CPUs are capable of accessing one memory resource. This is also referred to as a *symmetric multiprocessor* (SMP). In contrast, NUMA is often made by physically linking two or more SMPs. One SMP is capable of directly accessing the memory of another SMP.

Like shared-memory systems, distributed memory systems (Figure 4.1c) vary widely but share a common characteristic: they require a communication network to connect the interprocessor memory. In this type of architecture, processors have access to their own memory and do not share memory with another SMP. If a processor needs information from another data store, it has to communicate how and when it is to be accessed. This sharing generally comes about through a simple Ethernet connection. Hybrids of this technology have also been developed and are referred to as *distributed shared-memory architecture*. However, this type of architecture is generally used in supercomputers.

Within parallel computing, there are devices that provide a niche market because of its capabilities. As previously discussed, a system may have multiple cores, but may continue to be limited because of the amount of memory available to those cores. General-purpose computing on graphics processing units (GPGPU) is an inexpensive means of adding additional processing ability to a computer. A very beneficial and generous amount of memory is attached to video cards that are only accessible to its GPU. GPGPU addresses the multiple cores and memory limitations as an add-on card to a single computer system. As long as a motherboard has an available PCI-Express x16 slot, it will be capable of hosting a very powerful GPGPU.

4.2 Distributed Computing

Distributed computing studies the models, architectures, and algorithms used for building and managing distributed systems. A distributed system is a collection of independent computers that appears to its users as a single coherent system. Distributed systems are primarily focused on the aggregation of distributed resources and unified usage. This is accomplished by communicating with other computers only by exchanging messages.

A distributed system is the result of the interaction of several components across the entire computing stack from hardware to software. The hardware and operating system layers make up the bare-bones infrastructure of one or more data centers, where racks of servers are deployed and connected together through high-speed connectivity. This infrastructure is managed by the operating system, which provides the basic capabilities of machine and network management. The core logic is then implemented in the middleware that manages the virtualization layer, which is deployed on the physical infrastructure in order to maximize its utilization and provide a customizable runtime environment for applications. The middleware provides different facilities and functionalities per the requirement of the end customers and users. These facilities range from virtual infrastructure building and deployment to application development and runtime environments.

The different layers constituting the distributed system stack are as follows:

1. Hardware layer: At the very bottom layer, computer and network hardware constitute the physical infrastructure; these components are directly managed by the operating system, which provides the basic services for interprocess communication (IPC), process scheduling and management, and resource management in terms of the file system and local devices. Taken together, these two layers become the platform on top of which specialized software is deployed to turn a set of networked computers into a distributed system.

2. Operating system layer: The use of well-known standards at the operating system level and even more at the hardware and network levels facilitates the harnessing of heterogeneous components and their organization into a coherent and uniform system. For example, network connectivity between different devices is controlled by standards, which allow them to interact

seamlessly. At the operating system level, IPC services are implemented on top of standardized communication protocols such as the Transmission Control Protocol/Internet Protocol (TCP/IP), User Datagram Protocol (UDP), and others.

3. Middleware layer: The middleware layer leverages such services to build a uniform environment for the development and deployment of distributed applications. This layer supports the programming paradigms for distributed systems. By relying on the services offered by the operating system, the middleware develops its own protocols, data formats, and programming language or frameworks for the development of distributed applications. All of them constitute a uniform interface to distributed application developers that is completely independent from the underlying operating system and hides all the heterogeneities of the bottom layers.

4. Application layer: The topmost layer is represented by the applications and services designed and developed to use the middleware. These can serve several purposes and often expose their features in the form of graphical user interfaces (GUIs) accessible locally or through the Internet via a Web browser.

Architectural styles for distributed systems are helpful in understanding the different roles of components in the system and how they are distributed across multiple computers.

Architectural styles are of two types:

- System architectural styles
- Software architectural styles

4.2.1 System Architectural Styles

System architectural styles cover the physical organization of components and processes over a distributed infrastructure. They provide a set of reference models for the deployment of such systems and help engineers to not only have a common vocabulary in describing the physical layout of systems but also quickly identify the major advantages and drawbacks of a given deployment and whether it is applicable for a specific class of applications.

These reference models can be further enhanced or diversified according to the specific needs of the application to be designed and implemented.

4.2.1.1 N-Tier Architecture

In the 1980s, the prior monolithic architecture began to be replaced by the client–server architecture, which split applications into two pieces in an attempt to leverage new inexpensive desktop machines. Distributing the processing loads across many inexpensive clients allowed client–server applications to scale more linearly than single-host/single-process applications could, and the use of off-the-shelf software such as relational database management systems (RDBMS) greatly reduced application development time. While the client could handle the user interface and data display tasks of the application, and the server could handle all the data management tasks, there was no clear solution for storing the logic corresponding to the business processes being automated. Consequently, the business logic tended to split between the client and the server; typically, the rules for displaying data became embedded inside the user interface, and the rules for integrating several different data sources became stored procedures inside the database. Whereas this division of logic made it difficult to reuse the user interface code with a different data source, it also made it equally difficult to use the logic stored in the database with a different front-end user interface (e.g., an ATM or a cell phone) without being required to redevelop the logic implemented in the earlier interface. Thus, a customer service system developed for a particular client system (e.g., a 3270 terminal, a PC, or a workstation) would have great difficulty in providing telephony and Internet interfaces with the same business functionality.

The client–server architecture failed to recognize the importance of managing the business rules applicable to an enterprise independently of both the user interface and the storage and management of enterprise data. The three-tiered application architecture of the 1990s resolved this problem by subdividing the application into three distinct layers:

1. Data management, which stores and manages data independently of how they are processed and displayed by the other layers
2. Business logic, which implements the business logic to process data independent of how they are stored or displayed by the other two layers
3. Presentation, which formats and displays the data independent of the way they are interpreted/processed and stored by the other two layers

With the advent of the Internet, in the past few years, the three tiers were split even further to accommodate the heterogeneity in terms of the user interfaces, processing systems, or databases existing in various parts of an enterprise.

The power of the *n*-tier architecture derives from the fact that, instead of treating them as integral parts of systems, components are treated as stand-alone entities that can provide services for applications.

Applications exist only as cooperating constellations of components, and each component in turn can simultaneously be part of many different applications.

4.2.1.2 Peer-to-Peer

The peer-to-peer model introduces a symmetric architecture in which all the components, called *peers*, play the same role and incorporate both the client and server capabilities of the client–server model. More precisely, each peer acts as a server when it processes requests from other peers and as a client when it issues requests to other peers. With respect to the client–server model that partitions the responsibilities of the IPC between server and clients, the peer-to-peer model attributes the same responsibilities to each component. Therefore, this model is quite suitable for highly decentralized architecture, which can scale better along the dimension of the number of peers. The disadvantage of this approach is that the management of the implementation of algorithms is more complex than in the client–server model.

4.2.2 Software Architectural Styles

Software architectural styles are based on the logical arrangement of software components. They are helpful because they provide an intuitive view of the whole system, despite its physical deployment.

4.2.2.1 Data-Centered Architectures

The repository architectural style is the most relevant reference model in this category. It is characterized by two main components: the central data structure, which represents the current state of the system, and a collection of independent components, which operate on the central data. The ways in which the independent components interact with the central data structure can be very heterogeneous. In particular, repository-based architectures differentiate and specialize further into subcategories according to the choice of control discipline to apply to the shared data structure.

Data-centered architectures are of two types:

1. Databases systems: In this case the dynamic of the system is controlled by the independent components, which, by issuing an operation on the central repository, trigger the selection of specific processes that operate on data.
2. Blackboard systems: In this case, the central data structure itself is the main trigger for selecting the processes to execute; knowledge sources representing the intelligent agents sharing the blackboard react opportunistically to changes in the knowledge base—almost in the same way that a group of specialists brainstorm in a room in front of a blackboard.

The blackboard architectural style is characterized by three main components:

1. Knowledge sources: These are the entities that update the knowledge base that is maintained on the blackboard.
2. Blackboard: This represents the data structure that is shared among the knowledge sources and stores the knowledge base of the application.
3. Control: The control is the collection of triggers and procedures that govern the interaction with the blackboard and update the status of the knowledge base.

Blackboard models have become popular and widely used for artificial intelligence applications, in which the blackboard maintains the knowledge about a domain in the form of assertions and rules, which are entered by domain experts. These operate through a control shell that controls the problem-solving activity of the system. Particular and successful applications of this model can be found in the domains of speech recognition and signal processing.

4.2.2.2 Data Flow Architectures

In the case of data flow architectures, it is the availability of data that controls the computation. With respect to the data-centered styles, in which access to data is the core feature, data flow styles explicitly incorporate the pattern of data flow, since their design is determined by an orderly motion of data from component to component, which is the form of communication between them. Styles within this category differ in one of the following ways: how the control is exerted, the degree of concurrency among components, and the topology that describes the flow of data.

Data flow architectures are optimal when the system to be designed embodies a multistage process, which can be clearly identified into a collection of separate components that need to be orchestrated together. Within this reference scenario, components have well-defined interfaces exposing input and output ports, and the connectors are represented by the data streams between these ports.

1. Batch sequential style: The batch sequential style is characterized by an ordered sequence of separate programs executing one after the other. These programs are chained together by providing as input for the next program the output generated by the last program after its completion, which is most likely in the form of a file. This design was very popular in the mainframe era of computing and still finds applications today. For example, many distributed applications for scientific computing are defined by jobs expressed as sequences of programs that, for example, prefilter, analyze, and postprocess data. It is very common to compose these phases using the batch sequential style.
2. Pipe-and-filter style: The pipe-and-filter style is a variation of the previous style for expressing the activity of a software system as sequence of data

transformations. Each component of the processing chain is called a *filter*, and the connection between one filter and the next is represented by a data stream. With respect to the batch sequential style, data is processed incrementally and each filter processes the data as soon as it is available on the input stream. As soon as one filter produces a consumable amount of data, the next filter can start its processing. Filters generally do not have state, know the identity of neither the previous nor the next filter, and they are connected with in-memory data structures such as first-in/first-out (FIFO) buffers or other structures. This particular sequencing is called *pipelining* and introduces concurrency in the execution of the filters.

A classic example of this architecture is the microprocessor pipeline, whereby multiple instructions are executed at the same time by completing a different phase of each of them. We can identify the phases of the instructions as the filters, whereas the data streams are represented by the registries that are shared within the processors. Unix shell pipes (i.e., cat <file-name>| grep<pattern>| wc –l) are another example, where the filters are the single shell programs composed together and the connections are their input and output streams that are chained together. Applications of this architecture can also be found in compiler design (e.g., the lex/yacc model is based on a pipe of the following phases: scanning | parsing | semantic analysis | code generation), image and signal processing, and voice and video streaming.

4.2.2.3 Call and Return Architectures

This category identifies all systems that are organized into components mostly connected together by method calls. The activity of systems modeled in this way is characterized by a chain of method calls whose overall execution and composition identify the execution of one or more operations. The internal organization of components and their connections may vary. Nonetheless, it is possible to identify three major subcategories, which differentiate by the way the system is structured and how methods are invoked: top-down style, layered style, and object-oriented style.

1. Top-down style: This architectural style is quite representative of systems developed with imperative programming, which leads to a divide-and-conquer approach to problem resolution. Systems developed according to this style are composed of one large main program that accomplishes its tasks by invoking subprograms or procedures. The components in this style are procedures and subprograms, and connections are method calls or invocation. The calling program passes information with parameters and receives data from return values or parameters. Method calls can also extend beyond

the boundary of a single process by leveraging techniques for remote method invocation, such as remote procedure call (RPC) and all its descendants. The overall structure of the program execution at any point in time is characterized by a tree, the root of which constitutes the main function of the principal program. This architectural style is quite intuitive from a design point of view but hard to maintain and manage in large systems.

2. Layered style: The layered system style allows the design and implementation of software systems in terms of layers, which provide a different level of abstraction of the system. Each layer generally operates with, at most, two layers: one that provides a lower abstraction level and one that provides a higher abstraction layer. Specific protocols and interfaces define how adjacent layers interact. It is possible to model such systems as a stack of layers, one for each level of abstraction. Therefore, the components are the layers and the connectors are the interfaces and protocols used between adjacent layers. A user or client generally interacts with the layer at the highest abstraction, which, in order to carry out its activity, interacts and uses the services of the lower layer. This process is repeated (if necessary) until the lowest layer is reached. It is also possible to have the opposite behavior: events and callbacks from the lower layers can trigger the activity of the higher layer and propagate information up through the stack.

The advantages of the layered style are that

- It supports a modular design of systems and allows us to decompose the system according to different levels of abstractions by encapsulating together all the operations that belong to a specific level.
- It enables layers to be replaced as long as they are compliant with the expected protocols and interfaces, thus making the system flexible.

The main disadvantage is constituted by the lack of extensibility, since it is not possible to add layers without changing the protocols and the interfaces between layers. This also makes it complex to add operations. Examples of layered architectures are the modern operating system kernels and the International Standards Organization/Open Systems Interconnection (ISO/OSI) or the TCP/IP stack.

3. Object-oriented style: This architectural style encompasses a wide range of systems that have been designed and implemented by leveraging the abstractions of object-oriented programming (OOP). Systems are specified in terms of classes and implemented in terms of objects. Classes define the types of components by specifying the data that represent their state and the operations that can be done over these data. One of the main advantages over the top-down style is that there is a coupling between the data and the operations used to manipulate them. Object instances become responsible for hiding their internal state representation and for protecting its integrity while providing operations to other components. This leads to a better decomposition process and more manageable systems. The disadvantages of this

style are mainly two: each object needs to know the identity of an object if it wants to invoke operations on it, and shared objects need to be carefully designed in order to ensure the consistency of their state.

4.2.2.4 Virtual Architectures

The virtual machine class of architectural styles is characterized by the presence of an abstract execution environment (generally referred to as a *virtual machine*) that simulates features that are not available in the hardware or software. Applications and systems are implemented on top of this layer and become portable over different hardware and software environments as long as there is an implementation of the virtual machine they interface with. The general interaction flow for systems implementing this pattern is the following: the program (or the application) defines its operations and state in an abstract format, which is interpreted by the virtual machine engine. The interpretation of a program constitutes its execution. It is quite common in this scenario for the engine to maintain an internal representation of the program state. Very popular examples within this category are rule-based systems, interpreters, and command language processors.

Virtual machine architectural styles are characterized by an indirection layer between the applications and the hosting environment. This design has the major advantage of decoupling applications from the underlying hardware and software environment, but at the same time it introduces some disadvantages, such as a slowdown in performance. Other issues might be related to the fact that, by providing a virtual execution environment, specific features of the underlying system might not be accessible.

1. Rule-based style: This architecture is characterized by representing the abstract execution environment as an inference engine. Programs are expressed in the form of rules or predicates that hold true. The input data for applications are generally represented by a set of assertions or facts that the inference engine uses to activate rules or to apply predicates, thus transforming data. The output can either be the product of the rule activation or a set of assertions that holds true for the given input data. The set of rules or predicates identifies the knowledge base that can be queried to infer properties about the system. This approach is quite peculiar, since it allows the expression of a system or a domain in terms of its behavior rather than in terms of the components. Rule-based systems are very popular in the field of artificial intelligence. Practical applications can be found in the field of process control, where rule-based systems are used to monitor the status of physical devices by being fed from the sensory data collected and processed by PLCs1 and by activating alarms when specific conditions on the sensory data apply. Another interesting use of rule-based systems can be found in the networking domain: network intrusion detection systems (NIDS) often rely

on a set of rules to identify abnormal behaviors connected to possible intrusions in computing systems.

2. Interpreter style: The core feature of the interpreter style is the presence of an engine that is used to interpret a pseudo-program expressed in a format acceptable for the interpreter. The interpretation of the pseudo-program constitutes the execution of the program itself. Systems modeled according to this style exhibit four main components: the interpretation engine that executes the core activity of this style, an internal memory that contains the pseudo-code to be interpreted, a representation of the current state of the engine, and a representation of the current state of the program being executed. This model is quite useful in designing virtual machines for high-level programming (e.g., Java, C#) and scripting languages (e.g., Awk, PERL, and so on). Within this scenario, the virtual machine closes the gap between the end-user abstractions and the software/hardware environment in which such abstractions are executed.

4.2.2.5 Independent Components

This class of architectural style models systems in terms of independent components that have their own life cycles, which interact with each other to perform their activities. There are two major categories within this class: communicating processes and event systems, which differentiate in the way the interaction among components is managed.

1. Communicating processes: In this architectural style, components are represented by independent processes that leverage IPC facilities for coordination management. This is an abstraction that is quite suitable to modeling distributed systems that, being distributed over a network of computing nodes, are necessarily composed of several concurrent processes. Each of the processes provides other processes with services and can leverage the services exposed by the other processes. The conceptual organization of these processes and the way in which the communication happens vary according to the specific model used: either peer-to-peer or client–server. Connectors are identified by the IPC facilities used by these processes to communicate.

2. Event systems: In this architectural style, the components of the system are loosely coupled and connected. In addition to exposing operations for data and state manipulation, each component also publishes (or announces) a collection of events with which other components can register. In general, other components provide a callback that will be executed when the event is activated. During the activity of a component, a specific runtime condition can activate one of the exposed events, thus triggering the execution of the callbacks registered with it. Event activation may be accompanied by contextual information that can be used in the callback to handle the event. This

information can be passed as an argument to the callback or by using some shared repository between components. Event-based systems have become quite popular, and support for their implementation is provided either at the Application Programming Interface (API) level or the programming language level.

The main advantage of such an architectural style is that it fosters the development of open systems: new modules can be added and easily integrated into the system as long as they have compliant interfaces for registering to the events. This architectural style solves some of the limitations observed for the top-down and object-oriented styles.

- The invocation pattern is implicit, and the connection between the caller and the callee is not hard coded; this provides a lot of flexibility, since the addition or removal of a handler to events can be done without changes in the source code of applications.
- The event source does not need to know the identity of the event handler in order to invoke the callback.

The disadvantage of such a style is that it relinquishes control over system computation. When a component triggers an event, it does not know how many event handlers will be invoked and whether there are any registered handlers. This information is available only at runtime and, from a static design point of view, becomes more complex to identify the connections among components and to reason about the correctness of the interactions.

4.2.3 Technologies for Distributed Computing

Middleware is system services software that executes between the operating system layer and the application layer and provides services. It connects two or more applications, thus providing connectivity and interoperability to the applications. Middleware is not a silver bullet that will solve all integration problems. Due to overhyping in the 1980s and early 1990s, the term *middleware* has lost popularity but has been coming back in the last few years. The middleware concept, however, is today even more important for integration, and all integration projects will have to use one or many different middleware solutions. Middleware is mainly used to denote products that provide glue between applications, which is distinct from simple data import and export functions that might be built into the applications themselves.

All forms of middleware are helpful in easing the communication between different software applications. The selection of middleware influences the application architecture, because middleware centralizes the software infrastructure and its deployment. Middleware introduces an abstraction layer in the system architecture and thus reduces the complexity considerably. On the other hand, each middleware product introduces a certain communication overhead into the system, which can influence performance, scalability, throughput, and other efficiency factors. This is important to consider when designing the integration architecture, particularly if our systems are mission critical and are used by a large number of concurrent clients.

Middleware is connectivity software that is designed to help manage the complexity and heterogeneity inherent in distributed systems by building a bridge between different systems, thereby enabling communication and the transfer of data. Middleware could be defined as a layer of enabling software services that allow application elements to interoperate across network links, despite differences in the underlying communications protocols, system architectures, operating systems, databases, and other application services. The role of middleware is to ease the task of designing, programming, and managing distributed applications by providing a simple, consistent, and integrated distributed programming environment. Essentially, middleware is a distributed software layer, or *platform*, that lives above the operating system and abstracts over the complexity and heterogeneity of the underlying distributed environment with its multitude of network technologies, machine architectures, operating systems, and programming languages.

The middleware layers are interposed between applications and Internet transport protocols. The middleware abstraction comprises two layers. The bottom layer is concerned with the characteristics of protocols for communicating between processes in a distributed system and how the data objects (e.g., a customer order) and data structures used in application programs can be translated into a suitable form for sending messages over a communications network, taking into account that different computers may rely on heterogeneous representations for simple data items. The layer above is concerned with IPC mechanisms, while the layer above that is concerned with non-message- and message-based forms of middleware. Message-based forms of middleware provide asynchronous messaging and event notification mechanisms to exchange messages or react to events over electronic networks. Non-message-based forms of middleware provide synchronous communication mechanisms designed to support client–server communication.

Middleware uses two basic modes of message communication:

1. Synchronous or time dependent: The defining characteristic of a synchronous form of execution is that message communication is synchronized between two communicating application systems, which must both be up and running, and that execution flow at the client's side is interrupted to execute the call. Both sending and receiving applications must be ready to communicate with each other at all times. A sending application initiates a request (sends a message) to a receiving application. The sending application then blocks its processing until it receives a response from the receiving application. The receiving application continues its processing after it receives the response.

2. Asynchronous or time independent: With asynchronous communication, an application (requestor or sender) sends a request to another while it continues its own processing activities. The sending application does not have to wait for the receiving application to complete and for its reply to come back. Instead, it can continue processing other requests. Unlike the synchronous mode, both application systems (sender and receiver) do not have to be active at the same time for processing to occur.

The basic messaging processes inherently utilize asynchronous communication. There are several benefits to asynchronous messaging:

1. Asynchronous messaging clients can proceed with application processing independently of other applications. Loose coupling of senders and receivers optimizes system processing by not having to block sending client processing while waiting for the receiving client to complete the request.
2. Asynchronous messaging allows the batch and parallel processing of messages. The sending client can send as many messages to receiving client without having to wait for the receiving clients to process previously sent messages. On the receiving end, different receiving clients can process the messages at their own speed and timing.
3. There is less demand on the communication network because the messaging clients do not have to be connected to each other or the message-oriented middleware (MOM) while messages are processed. Connections are active only to put messages to and get messages from the MOM.
4. The network does not have to be available at all times because of the timing independence of client processing. Messages can wait in the queue of the receiving client if the network is not available. MOM implements asynchronous message queues at its core. It can concurrently service many sending and receiving applications.

Despite the performance drawbacks, synchronous messaging has several benefits over asynchronous messaging. The tightly coupled nature of synchronous messaging means the sending client can better handle application errors in the receiving client. If an error occurs in the receiving client, the sending client can try to compensate for the error. This is especially important when the sending client requests a transaction to be performed in the receiving client. The better error handling ability of synchronous messaging means it is easier for programmers to develop synchronous messaging solutions. Since both the sending and receiving clients are online and connected, it is easier for programmers to debug errors that might occur during the development stage. Since most developers are also more familiar with programming using synchronous processing, this also facilities the development of synchronous messaging solutions over asynchronous messaging solutions.

When speaking of middleware products, we encompass a large variety of technologies. The most common forms of middleware are as follows:

1. Database access technologies
    a. Microsoft Open Database Connectivity (ODBC)
    b. Java Database Connectivity (JDBC)
2. Asynchronous middleware
    a. Store and forward messaging
    b. Publish/subscribe messaging
    c. Point-to-point queuing
    d. Event-driven processing mechanism
3. Synchronous middleware
    a. Remote Procedure Call (RPC)
    b. Remote Method Invocation (RMI)
4. Message-oriented middleware (MOM)
    a. Integration brokers
    b. Java Messaging Service (JMS)
5. Request/reply messaging middleware
6. Transaction processing monitors (TPMs)
7. Object request brokers (ORBs)
    a. OMG CORBA ORB compliant
    b. Java RMI and RMI Internet Inter-ORB Protocol (IIOP)
    c. Microsoft COM/DCOM/COM+/.NET Remoting/WCF
8. Application servers
9. Service-oriented architecture
    a. Web services using WSDL, UDDI, SOAP, and XML
    b. RESTful services
10. Enterprise service buses (ESBs)
11. Enterprise systems

For a detailed discussion on the preceding technologies, refer to the companion volume *Guide to Cloud Computing for Business and Technology Managers* (Kale 2015).

4.3 Distributed Databases

A distributed database is a logically interrelated collection of shared data (and a description of this data) physically distributed over a computer network. A distributed database management system (DDBMS) is the software that transparently manages the distributed database.

A DDBMS is distinct from distributed processing, where a centralized DBMS is accessed over a network. It is also distinct from a parallel DBMS, which is a DBMS running across multiple processors and disks and which has been designed to evaluate operations in parallel, whenever possible, in order to improve performance. The advantages of a DDBMS are that it is enabled to reflect the organizational structure; it makes remote data more shareable; it improves reliability, availability, and performance; it may be more economical; it provides for modular growth, facilitates integration, and helps organizations remain competitive. The major disadvantages are cost, complexity, a lack of standards, and the need for experience.

A DDBMS may be classified as homogeneous or heterogeneous. In a homogeneous system, all sites use the same DBMS product. In a heterogeneous system, sites may run different DBMS products, which need not be based on the same underlying data model, and so the system may be composed of relational, network, hierarchical, and object-oriented DBMSs. A multidatabase system (MDBS) is a distributed DBMS in which each site maintains complete autonomy. An MDBS resides transparently on top of existing databases and file systems and presents a single database to its users. It maintains a global schema against which users issue queries and updates; an MDBS maintains only the global schema and the local DBMSs themselves maintain all user data.

Communication takes place over a network, which may be a local area network (LAN) or a wide area network (WAN). LANs are intended for short distances and provide faster communication than WANs. A special case of the WAN is a metropolitan area network (MAN), which generally covers a city or suburb. As well as having the standard functionality expected of a centralized DBMS, a DDBMS needs extended communication services, an extended system catalog, distributed query processing, and extended security, concurrency, and recovery services.

> Network design and performance issues are critical for the efficient operation of a distributed database management system (DDBMS) and are an integral part of the overall solution. The nodes may all be located in the same campus and connected via a local area network, or they may be geographically distributed over large distances and connected via a long-haul or wide area network. Local area networks typically use wireless hubs or cables, whereas long-haul networks use telephone lines, cables, wireless communication infrastructures, or satellites.

The DDBMS appears as a centralized DBMS by providing a series of transparencies. With distribution transparency, users should not know that the data have been fragmented/replicated. With transaction transparency, the consistency of the global database should be maintained when multiple users are accessing the database concurrently and when failures occur. With performance transparency, the system should be able to efficiently handle queries that reference data at more than one site.

A relation may be divided into a number of subrelations called *fragments*, which are allocated to one or more sites. Fragments may be replicated to provide improved availability and performance. There are two main types of fragmentation: horizontal and vertical. Horizontal fragments are subsets of tuples and vertical fragments are subsets of attributes. The definition and allocation of fragments are carried out strategically to achieve the locality of reference, improved reliability and availability, acceptable performance, balanced storage capacities and costs, and minimal communication costs.

4.3.1 Characteristics of Distributed Databases

4.3.1.1 Transparency

A highly transparent system offers a lot of flexibility to the end user and application developer since it implies being oblivious of the underlying details on their part. The concept of transparency extends the general idea of hiding implementation details from end users. In the case of a traditional centralized database, transparency simply pertains to logical and physical data independence for application developers. However, in a distributed database scenario, the data and software are distributed over multiple nodes connected by a computer network, so additional types of transparencies are introduced.

1. Distribution or network transparency: This refers to freedom for the user from the operational details of the network and the placement of the data in the distributed system. Distribution transparency can be of two types:
   a. Naming transparency implies that once a name is associated with an object, the named objects can be accessed unambiguously without additional specification as to where the data are located.
   b. Location transparency refers to the fact that the command used to perform a task is independent of the location of the data and the location of the node where the command was issued.
2. Fragmentation transparency: Fragmentation transparency can be of two types:
   a. Horizontal fragmentation distributes a relation (table) into subrelations that are subsets of the tuples (rows) in the original relation, which is also known as *sharding* in the newer big data and cloud computing systems.
   b. Vertical fragmentation distributes a relation into subrelations where each subrelation is defined by a subset of the columns of the original relation. Fragmentation transparency makes the user unaware of the existence of fragments.
3. Replication transparency implies that copies of the same data objects may be stored at multiple sites for better availability, performance, and reliability. Replication transparency makes the user unaware of the existence of these copies.

4.3.1.2 Availability and Reliability

Reliability and availability are two of the most common potential advantages cited for distributed databases. *Reliability* is broadly defined as the probability that a system is running (not down) at a certain time point, whereas *availability* is the probability that the system is continuously available during a time interval. Reliability and availability of the database are directly related to the faults, errors, and failures associated with it. Fault is the cause of an error. Errors constitute the subset of system states that causes the failure. A failure can be described as a deviation of a system's behavior from that which is specified in order to ensure the correct execution of operations.

A reliable DDBMS tolerates the failures of underlying components, and it processes user requests as long as database consistency is not violated.

A DDBMS system can adopt several strategies to achieve the objective of system reliability:

1. A cure-oriented fault tolerance strategy recognizes that faults will occur, and it designs mechanisms that can detect and remove faults before they can result in a system failure.
2. A prevention-oriented strategy attempts to ensure that the final system does not contain any faults. This is achieved through an exhaustive design process followed by extensive quality control and testing.

A DDBMS recovery manager deals with failures arising from transactions, hardware, and communication networks. Hardware failures can either be those that result in the loss of main memory contents or the loss of secondary storage contents. Network failures occur due to errors associated with messages and line failures. Message errors can include their loss, corruption, or out-of-order arrival at destination.

4.3.1.3 Scalability and Partition Tolerance

Scalability determines the extent to which the system can expand its capacity while continuing to operate without interruption.

Scalability can be of two types:

1. Horizontal scalability: This refers to expanding the number of nodes in the distributed system. As nodes are added to the system, some of the data and processing loads are distributed from existing nodes to the new nodes.
2. Vertical scalability: This refers to expanding the capacity of the individual nodes in the system, such as expanding the storage capacity or the processing power of a node.

The concept of partition tolerance states that the system should have the capacity to continue operating while the network is partitioned. As the system expands its number of nodes, it is possible that the network, which connects the nodes, may have faults that cause the nodes to be partitioned into groups of nodes. The nodes within each partition are still connected by a subnetwork, but communication among the partitions is lost.

4.3.1.4 Autonomy

Autonomy determines the extent to which individual nodes or databases in a connected DDB can operate independently. A high degree of autonomy is desirable for the increased flexibility and customized maintenance of an individual node.

Autonomy can be of three types:

1. *Design autonomy* refers to the independence of data model usage and transaction management techniques among nodes.
2. *Communication autonomy* determines the extent to which each node can decide on the sharing of information with other nodes.
3. *Execution autonomy* refers to the independence of users to act as they please.

4.4 Advantages and Disadvantages of Distributed Databases

The advantages of distributed databases are as follows:

1. Improved ease and flexibility of application development: Developing and maintaining applications at the geographically distributed sites of an organization is facilitated due to the transparency of data distribution and control.
2. Increased availability: This is achieved by the isolation of faults to their site of origin without affecting the other database nodes connected to the network. When the data and DDBMS software are distributed over many sites, one site may fail while other sites continue to operate. Only the data and software that exist at the failed site cannot be accessed. Further improvement is achieved by judiciously replicating data and software at more than one site. In a centralized system, failure at a single site makes the whole system unavailable to all users. In a distributed database, some of the data may be unreachable, but users may still be able to access other parts of the database. If the data in the failed site have been replicated at another site prior to the failure, then the user will not be affected at all. The ability of the system to survive network partitioning also contributes to high availability.
3. Improved performance: A DDBMS fragments the database by keeping the data closer to where it is needed most. Data localization reduces the contention for CPU and I/O services and simultaneously reduces access delays in

wide area networks. When a large database is distributed over multiple sites, smaller databases exist at each site. As a result, local queries and transactions accessing data at a single site have better performance because of the smaller local databases. In addition, each site has a smaller number of transactions executing than if all transactions are submitted to a single centralized database. Moreover, interquery and intraquery parallelism can be achieved by executing multiple queries at different sites, or by breaking up a query into a number of subqueries that execute in parallel. This contributes to improved performance.

4. Easier expansion via scalability: In a distributed environment, expanding the system in terms of adding more data, increasing database sizes, or adding more nodes is much easier than in a centralized (nondistributed) system.

The disadvantages of distributed databases are as follows:

1. More complex treatment of concurrent update
2. Update of replicated data
3. More complex query processing
4. More complex recovery measures
5. More complicated security and backup requirements
6. More difficult management of the data dictionary
7. More complex database design

4.5 Summary

In this chapter, we provided an introduction to parallel and distributed computing as a foundation for the better understanding of cloud and big data computing. Parallelism is achieved by leveraging hardware capable of processing multiple instructions in parallel. Different architectures exploit parallelism to increase the performance of a computing system, depending on whether parallelism is realized on data, instructions, or both. The development of parallel applications often requires specific environments and compilers that provide transparent access to the advanced capabilities of the underlying architectures.

Distributed systems constitute a large umbrella under which several different software systems are classified. The unification of parallel and distributed computing allows one to harness a set of networked and heterogeneous computers and present them as a unified resource. Architectural styles help categorize and provide reference models for distributed systems. More precisely, system architectural styles are more concerned with the physical deployment of such systems, whereas software architectural styles define the logical organization of components and their roles. These two styles are the fundamental deployment blocks of any distributed system. Message-based communication is the most relevant abstraction for interprocess communication (IPC) and forms the basis for several techniques of IPC, which is a fundamental element in distributed systems; it is the element that ties together separate processes and allows them to be seen as a unified whole. The last part of the chapter introduced the concepts, characteristics, and issues related to distributed databases.

ROAD TO NETWORK BUSINESSES

This section presents the road that led to network businesses. Chapter 5 introduces the basic concepts of systems theory, complexity, and networks. Networks of enterprises and agent-based systems are described in Chapters 6 and 7, respectively. Chapter 8 discusses the nature and characteristics of cloud computing, service-oriented architecture (SOA), and business processes. Big data computing, NoSQL, and graph database Neo4j are presented in Chapter 9.

Chapter 5

Systems Science, Complexity, and Networks

The attempt to apply reductionism, and the natural scientific method generally, to social and organizational problems has not been a happy one and has yielded only limited success. Systems thinking can be seen as a reaction to the failure of natural science when confronted with complex, real-world problems set in social systems. Systems thinkers advocate using *holism* rather than reductionism in such situations. Holism does not seek to break down complex problem situations into their parts in order to study them and intervene in them. Rather, it respects the profound interconnectedness of the parts and concentrates on the relationships between them and how these often give rise to surprising outcomes—the emergent properties. Systems thinking uses models rather than laboratory experiments to try to learn about the behavior of the world and even then does not take for granted or impose any arbitrary boundary between the *whole* that is the subject of its attention, in the model, and the environment in which it is located. Instead, it reflects upon and questions where the boundary has been drawn and how this impacts on the kind of improvements that can be made. Contemporary systems thinking also respects the different *appreciative systems* that individuals bring to bear in viewing the world and making value judgments about particular situations. In order to contribute to a *holistic* appreciation of the problem situation at hand, different perspectives on its nature and possible resolution should be encouraged. Greater creativity will result and mutual understanding might be achieved about a way forward as appreciative systems become more shared.

5.1 Systems Science

When scientific knowledge advances to the extent that there is a discrepancy between theory and practice, there is a paradigm shift, according to the eminent scientific historian Thomas Kuhn (1962). Such paradigm shifts have also occurred with systems thinking. The four paradigms of systems thinking described in this chapter are

1. Hard systems thinking (HST)
2. Soft systems thinking (SST)
3. Critical systems thinking (CST)
4. Multimodal systems thinking (MST)

HST or functionalist approaches: Though there is wide diversity in the techniques embraced by HST, they all have certain common characteristics. First, they are essentially goal-seeking strategies using quantitative tools to achieve an optimal or near-optimal solution. Second, they need a clear definition of ends and the optimal means for achieving those ends. This characteristic is a handicap when a messy and complex situation has to be dealt with, which is inevitable in nearly all engineering and planning projects. And third, they are best suited for tackling problems that don't involve human activity systems.

SST or interpretive approaches: This is a form of systemic thinking that understands reality as the creative thinking of human beings. It takes into consideration social reality as the construction of people's interpretation of their experiences and works with the aspirations of people's views, interpretations, and intentions. Although there are quite a number of soft systems methodologies that have been employed since the 1970s, we describe four that have been extensively used.

1. Ackoff's Interpretive Planning
2. Checkland's Soft Systems Methodology (SSM)
3. Senge's Fifth Discipline
4. Strategic Options Development and Analysis (SODA)

CST or emancipatory approaches: While many practitioners have hung on to and made good use of both HST and SST, it became obvious to practitioners that emancipatory interests for dealing with inequalities, such as power and economic differences in society, were not being adequately considered by SST. As a result, CST emerged in the 1990s to address these inequalities. Werner Ulrich, a Swiss planner inspired by Churchman, made a breakthrough by operationally addressing this problem.

MST: The most recent addition to the family of systems thinking is MST, and it has recently been adopted in Europe. Developed by J. D. R. de Raadt and his colleagues in Sweden, MST uses as many as 15 performance indicators to question the validity of decisions made by planners and policy makers. Many of these performance indicators cover the issues of sustainability and environmental and ethical issues.

5.1.1 Principles of Systems Science

The principles of systems science include the following:

1. *Systemness*: Bounded networks of relations among parts constitute a holistic unit. Systems interact with other systems, forming yet larger systems. The universe is composed of systems of systems.
2. Systems are processes organized in structural and functional hierarchies.
3. Systems are themselves, and can be represented abstractly as, networks of relations between components.
4. Systems are dynamic on multiple timescales.
5. Systems exhibit various kinds and levels of complexity.
6. Systems evolve.
7. Systems encode knowledge and receive and send information.
8. Systems have regulation subsystems to achieve stability.
9. Systems contain models of other systems (e.g., protocols for interaction with anticipatory models).
10. Sufficiently complex adaptive systems can contain models of themselves (e.g., brains and mental models).
11. Systems can be understood (a corollary of 9)—science.
12. Systems can be improved (a corollary of 6)—engineering.

5.2 Enterprise Offerings

The products of an enterprise are exposed to external complexity and cause internal complexity; products must be designed to cope with the implications of both external and internal complexity because they are very important instruments for achieving sustained profits and assuring long-term survival.

The benefits created by product variants and the costs they cause must be weighed against each other in order to find the optimum combination. The purpose of product variety is to match products with customers' requirements as closely as possible and to acquire new customers, which increases sales, and retain existing ones. On the cost side, introducing product variants entails additional complexity costs that are effective initially (when the product is launched) as well as continuously over the product's life cycle. As the product variety benefits cannot be harvested without a rise in complexity costs, the goal is not to reduce product complexity as far as possible but to find the optimum level of complexity that takes into account the benefits as well as the costs generated by product variety.

A successful product must satisfy customer requirements and preferences. As this bundle of market needs has many facets and is highly complex in its nature, it is called *external complexity* here. The way in which the enterprise-internal value chain is formed largely depends on the external complexity. For instance, the production process might boast fully automated manufacturing equipment geared to an output of a large number of standardized goods or, alternatively, could be based on highly skilled workers manufacturing and assembling customized products in small lot sizes.

To cater to the envisaged diversity of demands, companies design their product portfolios accordingly; that is, they introduce variety to their products. This, in turn, not only increases the product's complexity but also affects the complexity within the entire company. This enterprise-internal complexity spreads to all functional areas (product development, logistics, production, and sales, to name a few) and is called *internal complexity*.

External complexity also affects the way in which the product's architecture is designed—that is, what modules it consists of, how much variety it offers, which components are standardized, and so on. This cluster describing the translation of market requirements into a physical product is the manifestation of internal complexity.

There is a set of complexity drivers that determine the degree of internal complexity.

■ Organizational complexity: Enterprise processes become highly fragmented due to a strong orientation along functional lines and due to specialization. The interface density and fragmented responsibilities generate a high degree of organizational complexity.
■ Production complexity: The production is based on the philosophy of producing a considerable number of components and piece parts in-house and is characterized by an order penetration point (OPP) at a very early stage of the value chain.

As the product portfolio grows and variants proliferate, complexity costs do not spread equally among all product variants. Due to a lack of economies of scale, low-sales variants generate more per-unit costs than the high-sales variants, which are produced in larger numbers. A problem of traditional cost-accounting systems lies in their insufficient capability of transparently tracing back all costs to the respective variants. As a result, low-sales variants are priced too low, effectively being subsidized by the high-sales variants. The economies of scale expected when introducing new variants are overestimated and the diseconomies of scope are underestimated.

5.2.1 *Product Complexity*

The product architecture inherently determines the nature of the complexity costs generated by all the variants of that product. It is a very important element in defining the internal complexity necessary to respond to the external (market) complexity. Depending on how the architectures of its products are structured, an enterprise can take advantage of a high degree of commonality, which keeps costs low, while still maintaining a sufficiently high level of distinctiveness—what customers care about. Bearing in mind that complexity costs affect virtually all enterprise functions over the entire product life cycle, one can appreciate the importance of well-founded decisions concerning the product architecture.

A product as a system can be described as an assembly of elements related in an organized whole. Elements can be thought of as components, building blocks, piece parts, or ingredients, while relationships take the form of interfaces, functional dependencies, communication channels, or interactions of any kind. Interaction can be of four types—namely, spatial, energy, information, and material. Any characteristic quality or property ascribed to an element is termed an *attribute* of that element (e.g., color, size, strength, or shape). The way in which the elements are related to each other is called the *structure* of a system. It is important to distinguish a system from its environment, which necessarily entails the definition of a system boundary. The elements of a closed system do not engage in relationships with anything outside the system, while open systems share spatial relationships or exchange material, information, or energy with their environment across the boundary.

As an attribute, complexity has two aspects; namely, connectivity describes the number and diversity of relationships, and variety is determined by the number and diversity of elements. Complexity is characterized by the following dimensions:

1. The number of elements constituting a system
2. The number of different kinds of elements constituting a system
3. The number of relationships between the elements of a system
4. The number of different kinds of relationships between the elements of a system

A system with a large number of varying elements and relationships is complex. A simple three-element system consists of a maximum of three relationships. Assuming the elements are fixed and the relationships are bidirectional, do not vary in fashion and intensity, and, as an oversimplification, can take on only two states—*present* and *absent*—the system can take on eight different state structures. By merely increasing the number of elements to six, the same calculation leads to a total number of 32,768 possible structures.

Many complex systems have a nearly decomposable, hierarchic structure, defined as follows:

- A nearly decomposable system is composed of subsystems among which the interactions are weak but not negligible; that is, intracomponent linkages are generally stronger than intercomponent linkages.
- A hierarchic system consists of interrelated subsystems, each of which is hierarchic in structure until the lowest level of elementary subsystem is reached. Hierarchic systems have the property of near-decomposability.

A modular system architecture as being characterized by the property of near-decomposability (i.e., consisting of relatively autonomous subsystems). A module, therefore, can be defined as a special subsystem whose internal relationships are much stronger than the relationships with other subsystems (e.g., to other modules). On the other end of the scale, in integral system architectures, the relationships among subsystems are more pronounced. As a result, subsystems are more dependent on each other and less easily distinguished; they lose their autonomy.

5.2.2 Product Architecture

Product architecture decisions have profound implications on several issues of fundamental importance to the entire enterprise, ranging from product performance, product change, product variety, component standardization, manufacturability, and product development management. Product architecture dictates the way in which the product balances commonality (i.e., reducing costs through economies of scale) and distinctiveness (which enhances the competitive edge).

Applying the theory of systems architecture to products leads to the concept of product architecture, which can be defined as the scheme by which the function of a product is allocated to physical components. Product architecture is constituted by three distinct aspects:

1. The structure of functionality determines the arrangement of the overall function, subfunctions, and functional elements. The structure of functionality describes what the product does. It is characterized by the fact that the higher its level of detail, the more assumptions about how the product physically works are embodied. It is readily seen that the structure of functionality defines the requirements of what the product must be able to do—that is, the needs and expectations of customers or the external complexity.
2. The structure of physical components identifies the individual components—the physical elements of the product—and their organization into subassemblies. The collection of components implements the functions of the product. The specification of the interfaces among interacting components is

often part of the structure of physical components, as is information about product variety (e.g., the variants of one particular component). While the structure of functionality is concerned with what the product does, the structure of physical components describes how it is done.

The structure of physical components, which describes how the required functionality is translated into a physical product, may be viewed as a representation of the cost effects that, for instance, product variety, optional product features, and nonstandardized interfaces exert on the enterprise's value chain. Thus, the structure of physical components is an important indicator of internal complexity.

3. Mapping from the structure of functionality to the structure of physical components is determined by functional elements implemented by physical components. The mapping can be one-to-one, many-to-one, or one-to-many, depending on the type of product architecture.

Figure 5.1 shows the classification of product architectures in terms of the functional and physical independence.

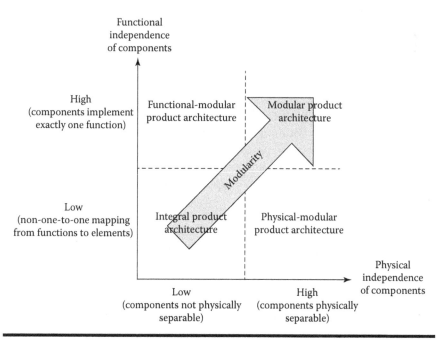

Figure 5.1 Product architectures in terms of their functional and physical independence.

5.2.2.1 Integrated Product Architecture

An integral architecture includes a complex (non-one-to-one) mapping of functional elements to the components and coupled interfaces between components. A modular product architecture comprises a number of modules, which can be described as relatively autonomous subassemblies.

5.2.2.2 Modular Product Architecture

A modular architecture includes a one-to-one mapping of functional elements to the physical components and specifies the decoupled interfaces between components.

Modular product architecture can be further subdivided into two categories:

■ *Functional-modular* product architecture is defined by functionally independent components that are connected through physical interfaces that are difficult to separate.
■ *Physical-modular* product architecture, on the other hand, consists of physically independent components (i.e., easily separable) that share strong functional dependencies. Such products can readily be disassembled into their components but only provide their functionality when their constituent components are connected.

5.3 Modularity

Modularity is a structural property of systems that arises when a system is composed of self-contained groups of elements that behave as a single unit. Complex systems often contain modules, which increase predictability and simplify control. Modules can usually be identified by the pattern of connections, which are stronger and more numerous within modules than between them. Modularity has the effect of isolating elements and processes from one another and constraining their interactions. Modules isolate functionality into units that are both reliable and reusable. Complicated problems can be approached by dividing them into smaller problems to reduce the combinatorial complexity.

Modules are the most common mechanism for dealing with complexity, not only in natural systems but also in artificial systems as diverse as organizational structures and the design of electronic products. A television is a complex system of electronic components. Such consumer products are now manufactured in modules using subsystems or circuit boards that can be easily replaced. Modularity simplifies the tasks of design and repair. The use of modules allows a reduction in complexity in almost any context where a system is composed of many interacting parts. Of course, the organization of a system into modules involves the cost of implementing an increased infrastructure. For example, an effort is required to change the known working design of a nonmodular computer to the modular version.

Modularity plays a key role in complex adaptive systems. In a system that is changing, the ability to form modules conveys several advantages:

1. Modules simplify the process of adaptation by reducing the range of connections. This makes the outcome of any change more predictable and less prone to errors. In a complex structure, the richness of connections means that changes often lead to unexpected and sometimes disastrous results. Complex adaptive systems can avoid such problems by forming modules.
2. Modules tend to be stable structures. So, forming modules provides a way of fixing adaptations, thus ensuring that desirable features are retained.
3. Modules provide convenient building blocks, so making it possible to create large robust systems quickly and easily.

The human body provides an example of a natural complex system that contains a hierarchy of modules. Each cell in the body is a module; the cell's internal component parts and processes are isolated from those of other cells. The cells themselves are not a homogenous collection. Instead, groups of cells are specialized and clustered together to form modules. These modules are recognizable as organs, such as the liver, the heart, and the lungs, as well as muscles, nerves, and so on. Each organ, or module, can be identified with a particular function. The interaction between these modules is well defined.

5.3.1 Hierarchy

Hierarchy is a structural property of systems that arises when a system is composed of modules that are themselves composed of smaller modules. A hierarchy can have any number of such levels. The human body has a hierarchy beginning with modules such as the heart, lungs, and kidneys. These modules are composed of smaller structures; for example, the kidney is composed of nephrons, these are in turn composed of cells, and cells are composed of organelles. So, hierarchies appear in organizational structures; there are hierarchies in knowledge (e.g., the Dewey catalogue system) and hierarchical structures in manufactured systems. Another example is a power distribution system comprising power stations, local distribution switchyards, suburban transformers, and residential dwellings. The unifying principle is efficiency and the reduction of complexity.

The study of modularity in natural systems gives many insights that can be applied in artificial systems. Like modularity, hierarchical structure seems to be an integral feature of biological systems.

5.4 Networks

Networks occupy a central position in complexity theory because they underlie both the structure and behavior of every complex system. In formal terms, we can obtain a network from the structure of any system by mapping its elements to network nodes and the relationships (or interactions) between elements to edges of the network. Likewise, we can obtain a network from the behavior of a system by representing all possible states of the system as network nodes and representing transitions between states as the edges of the network. These mappings provide a rigorous way of representing complex structures and behaviors as networks. The implication is that certain properties of complex systems (e.g., criticality) emerge as consequences of the underlying network.

Networks and graphs are commonly used to represent the structure of complex systems. A *network* is a system of interconnected entities. An example is a social network where people are the entities, and they are connected to each other by relationships such as family relationships or friendships. More generally, a network is usually described in terms of nodes, which are the entities, and *links*, which are the relationships between entities. A *graph* is a simple mathematical structure that consists of *vertices*, or *points*, to represent the nodes and uses edges to represent the links that join pairs of nodes. A *network* is a graph in which the nodes and/or edges have attributes.

Some basic properties of a graph are as follows:

- The degree of a vertex is the number of edges meeting at that vertex.
- A sparse graph has relatively few edges.
- A directed graph has connections that apply in one direction only.
- A path is a sequence of consecutive edges. A pair of consecutive edges shares one vertex.
- The length of a path is the number of consecutive edges in the path.
- The diameter of a graph is the maximum length that can be found by considering the shortest path between every pair of vertices. The diameter is finite only for connected graphs.
- A connected graph is one in which every vertex is connected to every other by at least one path. A connected graph with n nodes has at least $n - 1$ edges, and its largest possible diameter is also $n - 1$.
- A fully connected graph is one in which every vertex is connected directly to every other. The diameter of a fully connected graph is 1. In a fully connected graph with n vertices, the number of edges is $\dfrac{n(n-1)}{2}$.
- A cycle is a closed path; that is, any pair of edges in a cycle shares a vertex.

Graph theory provides a useful tool for analyzing modular and hierarchical structures in complex systems (Figure 5.2).

1. Figure 5.2a represents a system with seven components. Such a graph could represent a system of interconnected components in many diverse contexts—for example, cities connected by roads or manufacturing workstations connected by the flow of products and raw materials.

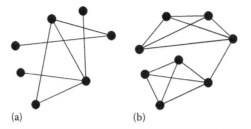

Figure 5.2 (a) Asimple graph, (b) a modular graph.

2. Figure 5.2b is clearly divided into two sections or modules. The number of connections within each module is relatively high, whereas the number of connections between the modules is low.

Some vertices are highly connected, while others have only one connection. The distribution of the degree of vertices in a graph will determine its properties.

5.4.1 Random Graphs and Networks

A random graph is a graph in which the edges are distributed at random among pairs of vertices. This type of graph is least likely to contain modules, as it has a homogenous structure. The properties of such graphs were investigated thoroughly by Paul Erdös and Alfred Renyi in the 1950s and 1960s.

 Random graphs do not represent the way natural and artificial systems are organized. Natural systems tend to show greater clustering; that is, vertices are grouped together into clusters or modules (see Sections 5.4.2, "Scale-Free Networks," and 5.4.3, "Small-World Networks").

In a random graph, the probability of any vertex having a given degree approximates a Poisson distribution, with average degree $z = (n - 1)p$, where p is the probability of an edge between two vertices and n is the total number of vertices in the graph. As the value of z increases, a *phase transition* is reached where the graph rapidly becomes connected. The phase transition also applies in the reverse situation, where links are progressively removed from a network until catastrophic fragmentation occurs. This has implications, for example, in the fault tolerance of communications networks.

The average length l of a path between any two vertices is given by

$$l = \frac{\log n}{\log z}$$

This means that the average path length can be relatively small even in very large networks. In communications networks, it is desirable to minimize the length of path on which a message must travel between vertices (i.e., computers), as each edge traversed increases the propagation time for signals and increases the probability of errors. Also, the presence of cycles in such graphs translates to fault tolerance in communication networks; there are alternative paths for messages to take.

5.4.2 Scale-Free Networks

A scale-free network is a network in which the probability of any vertex having a given degree follows a power law. A few nodes have many connections, while most nodes have few. The variable patterns of connectivity form cliques or modules of highly connected nodes, with a smaller number of connections between modules themselves. They are highly tolerant to random attack but not so tolerant to targeted attack.

That is, if a node is removed at random, the graph is largely unaffected, but if a node with high connectivity is removed, the graph may become fragmented. This implies that the Internet, which forms a scale-free network, is vulnerable to attacks on specific servers, such as malicious attacks by hackers. This explains why the Internet is dominated by a few highly connected nodes or large hubs such as Yahoo! or Amazon as well as explaining the dominance of Microsoft Windows on desktops. It also explains the high degree of robustness exhibited by many complex systems: individual nodes can be removed without removing the connected property of the network. Similarly, in a separate context, it explains how a few individuals with an extraordinary ability to make friendships keep society together.

 Unlike the catastrophic fragmentations occurring in random graphs, scale-free graphs remain connected even when a large fraction of edges is removed.

5.4.3 Small-World Networks

The phenomenon of networks is pervasive, and they deeply affect all aspects of human life and relationships. Networks matter because local actions have global consequences, and the relationship between local and global dynamics depends on the network structure. The idea of small worlds is applicable to diverse problems—the community of prospects or customers, organizations, national markets, the global economy, flying routes, postal services, food chains, electrical power grids, disease propagation, ecosystems, language, or the firing of neurons. In 1998, Cornell mathematician Duncan Watts, with his advisor Steve Strogatz, recognized the structural similarity between graph problems describing any collection of dots connected by lines and

- The coordinated lighting of fireflies
- The 1967 theory of sociologist Stanley Milgram that the world's six billion people are all connected by six degrees of separation—that is, the average number of steps needed to get from one selected person to another

They showed that when networks of connected dots have a degree of order to their clustering, the degree of separation is correspondingly high, but adding random links shrinks the degree of separation rapidly.

A small-world network is a network in which the probability of vertices having a given degree follows an exponential distribution. A small-world network is sparse, highly clustered, and has a small diameter. These networks consist of a regular lattice (a tessellation of vertices with uniform connections—e.g., a grid) with a number of links added between pairs of vertices chosen at random. Such models have implications in many areas, particularly where geography constrains the interaction between agents, such as in the epidemiology of disease and the evolution of ecosystems.

5.4.4 Trees

A tree is a connected graph with no cycles. Trees are good models of hierarchical systems—for example, the army with its different levels of rank and a rigid chain of command and communication. The top level of a tree is a single node known as the *root node*. Terminal nodes (those nodes with no branches descending from them) are called *leaves*. A tree is called *balanced* if each node has the same number of branches descending from it. A *subtree* is a subset of nodes that form a tree. Every nonterminal node in a tree forms the root of at least one subtree. A *hierarchy* is a directed graph that forms a tree and in which all nodes fall on paths leading away from (or to) the root of the tree. In a family tree, the descendants of a single individual form a hierarchy.

Information flow in trees can proceed only from one level to another, as there are no peer connections. As a tree has no cycles, it affords no fault tolerance: there is only one path connecting any two nodes; therefore, a tree is vulnerable to attack. The removal of a single node anywhere results in the tree being divided into two trees. On the other hand, trees have the advantage of providing the smallest diameter for a given number of vertices.

  The maximum number of steps between any two nodes in a regular tree with L layers is given by $2(L - 1)$, and L is proportional to the logarithm of the number of nodes.

5.4.5 Network Modules

Because of their universal nature, networks provide a convenient way to define modules mathematically. Within a network, a module is a connected set of nodes that is richly connected internally but has only minimal connections to the rest of the network. In Figure 5.2b, for instance, there are two modules with only a single edge between them. This definition of a network module may seem imprecise, but systems are not necessarily all modular or nonmodular; they can have degrees of modularity. This degree can be measured by the modularity coefficient M.

Various ways of measuring modularity have been proposed, but the most obvious approach is to compare the richness of links within and between modules.

1. Degree of clustering: For any node i in a network of N nodes, the degree of local clustering is given by the ratio between the number of edges E_i that exist between its k_i neighbors and the maximum possible number of links $k_i(k_i - 1)/2$. The clustering coefficient C of the entire network is then given by

$$C = \frac{1}{N} \sum_i \frac{2E_i}{k_i(k_{i-1})}$$

The values of C range from 0 to 1.
2. Pairs of nodes: For any pair of nodes i and j, the local modularity m_{ij} is the ratio between the number of neighbors the nodes share in common and their total number of neighbors. The modularity of the entire network is then the average of this ratio taken over all pairs of nodes.

$$M = \frac{1}{N(N-1)} \sum_i^N \sum_j^N m_{ij}$$

The values of M range from 0 to 1.

5.5 Complex Adaptive System

A complex adaptive system (CAS) is the study of natural systems—how they adapt, interact, and survive over time. Just as biological systems are governed by Darwinian natural selection, which favors those agents that successfully adapt to the (dynamic) constraints and resources offered by their physical environment, so too will any *organic* theory of business network formation be subject to a mechanism that selects those of its members that coevolve and that successfully adapt to

- The environment (as set by globalization)
- The available resources (e.g., various manufacturing and strategy inputs)

CAS theory attempts to categorize the common characteristics of complex systems, wherein individual agents interact and compete for resources within their environment. These agents can aggregate to form more complex multiagents, which often contain highly specialized component agents that might individually have little in common with the function of the overall system. In CASs, small changes are not ignored, and *emergence* rather than *planning* is how things get done.

Some key points of CAS are as follows:

1. They contain *lever points*; these are critical nonlinear features where a small input signal can be magnified to impact the entire system (e.g., a small quantity of pathogen leading to a macro-scale response within the immune system, the principle that underlies vaccines).
2. CAS agents exhibit the capability of foresight; they interact, combine, and replicate by means of an internal (endogenous) mechanism for determining the fitness of the various agents and their interactions. Those agents (or agent aggregates) that are more fit recombine (reproduce) more successfully than those that are less fit, following a sort of natural selection.

The fundamental objective in defining CAS is to describe the properties of the agents and their behavioral abilities; the selection process must follow naturally—a sort of "autopilot" that does not rely on direct external (exogenous) control, though such control can certainly be used to impact the environment in which the agents exist.

5.5.1 Modeling Complex Adaptive Systems

A model must carefully balance two mutually conflicting needs when modeling a complex adaptive system. The model must be complex enough to represent the system, and it must be as simple as possible in order to facilitate a greater understanding of the changeability of the system. Thus, the model must simplify reality in order to be useful, but not so much so that it is useless. Just as a map is a useful simplification and miniaturization of a place, a model must be gainfully simplified by, among other things, defining system boundaries, level of observance, and context.

The various modeling techniques available are as follows:

1. Techniques such as statistical thermodynamics and pattern recognition tools such as neural networks are unsuitable for modeling complex adaptive systems as they are clearly not generative.
2. Techniques such as computable general equilibrium, dynamic systems, and system dynamics use mathematical models based on a top-down paradigm and are unsuitable for modeling complex adaptive systems as they are based on the assumption of a static system structure.
3. Techniques such as discrete event simulation are capable of both generative and dynamic system behavior, are also unsuitable for modeling complex adaptive systems, as the entities are very passive representations and are unable to capture some of the necessary decision making required.
4. Techniques such as agent-based modeling, with their explicitly bottom-up perspective, are capable of both generative and dynamic system behavior. The individual agents, whose algorithmic nature enable many different formalisms, act and react according to internal rules to produce the overall emergent system behavior.

 Models must satisfy the following characteristics:

1. Generative: The central principle of generative science is that phenomena can be described in terms of interconnected networks of (relatively) simple units and that finite, deterministic rules and parameters interact to generate complex behavior.
2. Adaptivity: The model must also be adaptive, with the capacity to evolve over time. There must be selective pressures to respond to and a way to introduce variations for the pressures to act on. Ideally, the selective pressures should also be capable of shifting in response to changes in fitness, making the entire system adaptive, although this is far more difficult to analyze and interpret; it may push the balance of the model toward capturing the complexity of the system at the expense of the insight that might be gained by simplifying the adaptivity.

Agent-based modeling is the most suitable for modeling complex adaptive systems because it is the only one that satisfies Ashby's requirement. The agent-based approach is more general and powerful because it enables the capture of more complex structures and dynamics. The other important advantage is that it provides for the construction of models in the absence of knowledge about the global interdependencies. You may know nothing or very little about how things affect each other at the aggregate level, what the global sequence of operations is, and so on, but if you have some perception of how the individual participants of the process behave, you can construct the agent-based model and then obtain the global behavior.

5.6 Project Management

Modern project management appeared during World War II and was initially dedicated to big military and construction projects. Projects seem to have become increasingly common in all kinds of organizations. Project management is the process of conceiving, designing, preparing, evaluating, scheduling, organizing, monitoring, and controlling the transformation of a system from an initial state to a specific state. Project management is the application of knowledge, skills, tools, and techniques to project activities in order to meet or exceed stakeholders' needs and their expectations of the project.

In today's highly competitive business environment, project management's ability to schedule activities and monitor progress within time, cost, and performance guidelines is becoming increasingly important to obtain competitive priorities. This implies that there are trade-offs that must typically be made when scheduling a project. Typically, projects have three primary objectives: to finish the project quickly, to consume as few resources as possible (especially, to minimize costs), and to produce a high-quality project.

The main dimensions of a project are

1. Time: The project must be completed on time.
2. Resources: The project must be completed within the budgeted cost.
3. Scope: The project must achieve its stated objectives.

A project is a unique set of coordinated activities, with definite starting and finishing points, undertaken by an individual or organization to meet specific objectives within defined schedule, cost, and performance parameters. A project consists of a number of tasks that must be done for the project to be completed. These tasks have durations, typically cost money, and often require nonfinancial limited resources such as people and facilities. They also have precedence relationships that put constraints on what can be done and when.

This concept of a project implies

1. The identification of the system to be transformed.
2. The description of the initial state and the final state that should represent the targets of the project.

3. An organizational framework. Projects need the skills and talents of multiple professions and organizations, which usually have something at stake, because failure would jeopardize the organization or its goal.
4. A set of resources.
5. Methodological support.

5.6.1 Project Modeling

A project can be modeled by a discrete and finite set of entities usually called *jobs* or *activities*; a set of precedence conditions; a discrete and finite set of attributes defined for each activity, describing properties such as time, cost, quality, safety, and so on; and a discrete and finite set of criteria (e.g., total duration, net present value, and so on) that express the values and the preferences of the project manager, so as to compare alternative decisions concerning the management of the project.

The improvement of network models has been pursued along seven different lines:

1. The construction of *generalized networks*: Where some activities just occur with specific probabilities or in terms of the outcomes of previous activities.
2. The construction of *logical networks*: Where the occurrence of each activity is conditioned by logical relationships between precedent activities.
3. The modeling of *overlapping activities*: In terms of the time domain or in terms of the consumed resources expressed by progress lag constraints for activities carried out each time.
4. Morphologic modeling of project networks, which is based on two concepts, the progressive and the regressive levels; and it is important to classify or to simulate networks.
5. The construction of hierarchical networks: Each project can be viewed as a set of interconnected subprojects (macroactivities) and each of these macroactivities can be modeled by another network constructed in terms of more detailed activities. This process of modeling has been studied using multiple hierarchical levels.
6. The aggregation of project networks to be transformed into simpler and more synthetic networks, for which two approaches have been proposed.
   a. The method of modular decomposition, based on the identification of modules that can be synthetized by equivalent macroactivities
   b. The method of network reduction, based on three different types of reduction: series, parallel, and node reduction

5.6.2 Project Evaluation

The purpose of project evaluation is to calculate the benefits and/or costs of projects in such a way as to provide credible and useful information as to whether the project should be undertaken, its design, the effectiveness of its implementation, and the short- and long-term effects on the scope. Evaluation should lead to a decision to continue, rectify, or stop a project, and should look for cost reduction opportunities, along with opportunities to reduce planning budgets, working hours, and so on, at every stage of the project. One of the most important problems in project evaluation concerns the treatment of uncertainty. The problem is that the stream of future benefits and costs is not known with certainty.

Evaluation can be regarded as a joint learning process for all the agents involved in the project, generating useful and relevant information and knowledge to assess the relevance, efficiency, and effectiveness of the project.

The evaluation of projects has been traditionally studied using monetary criteria such as net present value (NPV), payback period, return on investment, and so on. Indicators such as NPV or the risk of delay strongly depend on the schedule, as early (or late) starting times tend to be responsible for lower (or higher) NPV and risk of delay. In addition, this type of index does not consider other important nonmonetary criteria such as quality, safety, and so on. The evaluation process must include the appropriate focus on safety, quality, cost, schedule, and so on, attributes that need not be mutually exclusive. The development of multicriteria decision-making theory can enrich this domain with new contributions as decision aids to support the process of the multicriteria evaluation of a project.

5.6.3 Project Management and Control

Projects are highly unlikely to proceed according to plan. In order to be able to identify and measure the differences between the plan and the actual work performance, progress on the project is required to be controlled and monitored.

The monitoring and control of projects involves the following stages:

1. Measuring the state of the project
2. Comparing actual and planned parameters
3. Reporting the variations between these parameters
4. Taking corrective actions

5.6.4 Project Scheduling

Initially, the study of project scheduling considered just the duration and precedence conditions of the activities, ignoring the resource requirements. Two basic methods were proposed to schedule a project, assuming a deterministic duration: the *critical path method* (CPM) and the *method of potentials*. Since most activity durations have a random nature, PERT was proposed to determine the distribution of the project completion.

The problem of project scheduling under resource constraints was considered and formulated as an optimization problem, where the decision variables are

1. The scheduled starting times of the activities
2. The constraints, including the precedence conditions
3. The maximal (and/or minimal) bounds concerning the available resources

The *objective function* describes the main criteria, such as

1. The minimization of the total duration
2. The maximization of the net present value
3. Other cost–benefit indicators

The process of decision making concerning the scheduling of activities and the allocation of resources to the implementation of activities can be considered *static* or *dynamic*.

- It is static if the decision should be made before starting the project without the acceptance of any latter correction or change.
- It is dynamic if the decision can be changed during the process of implementing the project.

5.6.4.1 Temporal Networks

The theory of networks plays an important role in the planning and scheduling of projects primarily because of the ease with which these projects can be modeled in network form. Networks are easily understood by all levels of personnel in the organizational hierarchy, facilitate the identification of pertinent data, present a mechanism for data collection, and can be used for both communication and analysis purposes.

Networks are composed of events and activities. The following terms are helpful in understanding networks.

- *Event*: Equivalent to a milestone, indicating when an activity starts or finishes.
- *Activity*: The element of work that must be accomplished.
- *Duration*: The total time required to complete the activity.
- *Effort*: The amount of work that is actually performed within the duration. For example, the duration of an activity could be one month, but the effort could be just a two-week period within the duration.
- *Critical path*: This is the longest path through the network and determines the duration of the project. It is also the shortest amount of time necessary to accomplish the project.

The major drawback with Gantt, milestone, or bubble charts is their inability to show the interdependencies between events and activities. These interdependencies must be identified so that a master plan can be developed that provides an up-to-date picture of operations at all times. Interdependencies are shown through the construction of networks. Network analysis can provide valuable information for planning, the integration of plans, time studies, scheduling, and resource management. The primary purpose of network planning is to eliminate the need for crisis management by providing a pictorial representation of the total program.

The following management information can be obtained from such a representation.

1. The interdependencies of activities
2. The project completion time
3. The impact of late starts
4. The impact of early starts
5. Trade-offs between resources and time
6. "What if" exercises
7. The cost of a crash program
8. Slippages in planning/performance
9. An evaluation of performance

Management is continually seeking new and better control techniques to cope with the complexities, masses of data, and tight deadlines that are characteristic of highly competitive industries. Managers also want better methods of presenting technical and cost data to customers.

Scheduling techniques help achieve these goals. The most common techniques are

- Gantt or bar charts
- Milestone charts
- Line of balance
- Networks
- Program evaluation and review technique (PERT)
- Arrow diagram method (ADM), sometimes called the critical path method (CPM)
- Precedence diagram method (PDM)
- Graphical evaluation and review technique (GERT)

The advantages of network scheduling techniques include the following:

- They form the basis for all planning and predicting and help management decide how to use its resources to achieve time and cost goals.
- They provide visibility and enable management to control "one of a kind" programs.
- They help management evaluate alternatives by answering such questions as how time delays will influence project completion, where slack exists between elements, and what elements are crucial to meet the completion date.

- They provide a basis for obtaining facts for decision making.
- They utilize so-called time network analysis as the basic method to determine manpower, material, and capital requirements, as well as provide a means for checking progress.
- They provide the basic structure for reporting information.
- They reveal the interdependencies of activities.
- They facilitate "what if" exercises.
- They identify the longest path or critical paths.
- They aid in scheduling risk analysis.

5.6.4.2 Program Evaluation and Review Technique

PERT was originally developed in 1958 and 1959 to meet the needs of the *age of massive engineering*, where the techniques of Taylor and Gantt were inapplicable. The Special Projects Office of the U.S. Navy, concerned with performance trends in large military development programs, introduced PERT on its Polaris Weapon System in 1958, after the technique had been developed with the aid of the management consulting firm of Booz, Allen, and Hamilton. Since that time, PERT has spread rapidly throughout almost all industries. At about the same time, the DuPont Company initiated the critical path method (CPM), a similar technique that has also spread widely and is particularly concentrated in the construction and process industries.

In the early 1960s, the basic requirements of PERT/time as established by the Navy were as follows:

1. All of the individual tasks to complete a program must be clear enough to be put down in a network that comprises events and activities; that is, follow the work breakdown structure.
2. Events and activities must be sequenced on the network under a highly logical set of ground rules that allow the determination of critical and subcritical paths. Networks may have more than 100 events, but not fewer than 10.
3. Time estimates must be made for each activity on a three-way basis. Optimistic, most likely, and pessimistic elapsed-time figures are estimated by the person(s) most familiar with the activity.
4. Critical path and slack times are computed. The critical path is that sequence of activities and events whose accomplishment will require the greatest time.

 PERT has been criticized on account of the following:

- It is time and labor intensive.
- The decision-making ability is reduced.

■ It lacks functional ownership in estimates.
■ It lacks historical data for time–cost estimates.
■ It assumes unlimited resources.
■ It requires too much detail.

There are distinct advantages to PERT:

1. PERT lays major emphasis on its extensive planning. Network development and critical path analysis reveal interdependencies and problems that are not obvious with other planning methods. PERT therefore determines where the greatest effort should be made to keep a project on schedule.
2. PERT can determine the probability of meeting deadlines by developing alternative plans. If there exists a minimum of uncertainty, one may use the single-time approach, of course, while retaining the advantage of network analysis.
3. PERT can evaluate the effect of changes in the program—for example, a contemplated shift of resources from less critical activities to those identified as probable bottlenecks. PERT can also evaluate the effect of a deviation in the actual time required for an activity from what had been predicted.
4. PERT allows a large amount of sophisticated data to be presented in a well-organized diagram, from which contractors and customers can make joint decisions.

PERT has certain disadvantages. For example, the complexity of PERT adds to implementation problems, and there exist more data requirements for a PERT-organized reporting system than for most others. PERT, therefore, becomes expensive to maintain and is utilized most often in large, complex programs.

5.7 Summary

A complex system is a large network of relatively simple components with no central control, in which emergent complex behavior is exhibited. The complexity of the system's global behavior is typically characterized in terms of the patterns it forms, the information processing that it accomplishes, and the degree to which this pattern formation and information processing are adaptive for the system, that is, increase its success in some evolutionary or competitive context.

Over the past decades it has become clear that the metaphor of *networks*—ensembles of discrete *nodes* connected by *links*—offers a powerful conceptual framework for the description and analysis of many real world systems. The science of networks has grown into a field which is by now firmly established in several disciplines, including mathematics, physics, biology, computer science, economics, and the social sciences. The purpose of characterizing networks according to degree distribution, clustering coefficient, average path length, and the like is both to better understand networks from a scientific point of view and to develop better technologies for designing and managing networks in desired ways. Characterizations of networks are needed to predict the conditions under which they will exhibit resilience to the loss or failure of nodes or links and to determine their vulnerabilities. For example, it is known that in the face of random failures of nodes or links, scale-free networks are far more robust than random networks in the sense that they retain the basic structural and communications characteristics. This is why the Internet exhibits robustness even though individual routers fail all the time. However, scale-free networks are not resilient to failures of their hubs, and are thus quite vulnerable to accidental failures or targeted attacks. Bad weather or other problems at a hub airport, for example, can cause long delays in flights all over the country. While hubs are a reason for short path lengths in scale-free networks, this comes at the price of vulnerability. There is clearly a trade-off between efficiency and robustness.

Chapter 6

Enterprise Networks

To lead in the current business environment, it is essential to be able to embrace change. The modern firm must be highly flexible and able to change its business strategy very quickly. Traditionally it has taken enterprises up to a couple of years to change their strategy, while the human structural organization of the enterprise traditionally changes every 3–6 months. But now enterprises must be able to change faster to meet this required speed of strategic and organizational change. However, the back-end information and communications systems that are needed to facilitate and enable such change were not readily available to the business earlier. Underlying enterprise legacy software has proved to be difficult to integrate, and then changing the infrastructure built on such complex integrations has proved to be even more challenging—traditionally, it has taken between 6 and 10 years to modernize such infrastructure. The advent of enterprise application integration (EAI), middleware, and modern ICT solutions resolved this gap between lagging infrastructure and the required rapid strategic change, as well as to speed up the time for business to take action on this strategy by enabling *networks of enterprises*, which are discussed in this chapter. With the advent of the Internet, this agility and adaptability has been enhanced manifold by recent developments like cloud and big data computing, which are discussed in Chapters 8 and 9 respectively.

6.1 Network of Enterprises

Companies use networks of enterprises to gain a competitive edge. It is important to define the design of a network of enterprises that would allow materials, information, and money to flow in a manner that aligns corporate and business strategies.

Efficient, well-designed supply chains result in higher profits, lowers costs, better operational performance, and higher consumer satisfaction. The design of the network of enterprises requires an organization to make trade-offs based on cost, service levels, and environmental impact to achieve the most optimal operation for that specific organization. Optimization models are used to design the network of enterprises to achieve the lowest cost, mileage, or time in transit.

A well-designed and managed network of enterprises brings many benefits to an organization, such as

1. Products and services delivered to customers in a timely manner, increasing customer goodwill
2. Total supply chain cost reduction
3. Minimized financial and operational risks to the business
4. Environmental impact reduction
5. Tax reduction

The network design decision consists of elements such as

1. How many tiers in the network are necessary?
2. What suppliers should be used and how many of them are there?
3. Where are the facilities located?
4. What channels of distribution are needed?

6.1.1 Theory of Constraints

The *theory of constraints* (TOC) was developed by Eli Goldratt and collaborators. It became broadly known in 1984 when Goldratt's book *Goal* was published. TOC views an enterprise as a system with resources linked together to meet the enterprise's goals. TOC views enterprises as systems with resources linked together to meet an organization's goal. All systems have a constraint that limits the system's capacity to improve and better meet or exceed its goal. Enterprises have limited resources, so it is critical that resources be applied to reduce or eliminate constraints to maximize success. TOC methodology includes improvement tools that use rigorous root-cause analysis to define the solution. The methodology also identifies all the assumptions and conditions needed to ensure the success of a proposed solution. These very conditions and assumptions become the basis of action items for implementation plans. TOC improvement tools are effective both for continuous improvement or breakthrough problem solving.

Over the course of the 1980s, Eli Goldratt introduced a powerful set of concepts. The theory represents a philosophy of operations management, a management system, and a set of tools/principles to improve operations. Initially, TOC promotion focused around the fact that most manufacturing operations have a few bottleneck steps that limit the throughput of the plant under typical product mixes. The goal of planning, then, should be to schedule these bottleneck steps efficiently so as to achieve maximum throughput, to schedule steps before and after the bottlenecks in order to best support the bottlenecks, and to elevate the constraints by adding capacity there, thus shifting the binding constraints to elsewhere in the system. The *drum–buffer–rope scheduling* methodology was invented to support plant operations, so that they might exploit constraints to the maximum possible (i.e., to get maximum throughput through them) and subordinate other manufacturing steps to the constrained ones. As TOC evolved, greater emphasis was placed on the fact that the principles apply not just to manufacturing but to supply chain operations as a whole and even to non–supply chain activities such as project management.

These principles led to a universal five-step methodology for business improvement.

1. Identify the system's constraints.
2. Decide how to exploit the system's constraints.
3. Subordinate everything else to the earlier decision.
4. Elevate the system's constraints.
5. If in the previous steps a constraint has been broken, go back to step 1.

The theory of constraints takes a holistic systems view of all the operations of a plant or supply chain. Applied to a business, TOC's purpose is to increase profit. It focuses system improvement on increasing throughput as the best way to add more value. The improvement or elimination of a current constraint results in more throughput, at which point a new system constraint is identified. This continuous cycle drives performance improvement forever.

TOC includes concepts that are used to schedule operations. The constrained operation is scheduled in a specific product sequence, aligning resource use to meet customer demand. The drum–buffer–rope scheduling system sets the pace for all other operations.

1. Upstream, raw materials are subordinated to the constrained operation to make sure materials are available when needed to support the constrained operations schedule.
2. Downstream operations must flow and are therefore planned and run with sufficient capacity so that all products made by the constrained operation can be processed.
3. Time buffers are used upstream from the constraint so that promised shipment dates are met, protecting promised dates from inevitable process variability. Work is released into production at a rate dictated by the drum and started based on a predetermined total process buffer length.

When sales is the constraint, TOC has an approach for solving these problems that includes using its problem-solving tools combined with TOC accounting, market segmentation, and pricing strategies to identify what needs to change in order to increase sales. This is a unique feature of TOC compared with other problem-solving methodologies.

The metrics used in TOC measure the value-add produced. The key TOC metrics are

- T: The throughput value of sales less the materials cost.
- I: The system's raw materials inventory.
- OE: Operating expenses.
- Conversion ratio: Dividing T by OE gives a productivity measurement—that is, the rate at which operating expenses are converting raw materials into T.
- Inventory turnover: Dividing T by I—the money generated from sales divided by the raw materials inventory cost—measures the inventory turnover.

6.1.1.1 TOC Tools

TOC employs five tools, as follows:
1. What to change

   Current reality tree: The current reality tree is a tool used to identify the root cause of a core problem that has no known solution, in order to eliminate initial undesirable effects. The current reality tree is a type of flowchart that depicts the cause-and-effect relationships that exist for the object of interest. The tree is normally built using a storyboard-type approach, starting with a listing of the effects to be remedied. The contributing factors that perpetuate these effects are associated with them and listed accordingly. This type of analysis is performed again on the perpetuating factors and is continued until what in essence would be the root cause of the problem can be identified. This simplistic explanation can become quite convoluted in practice when the situation under study has multiple effects to remedy and many associated contributing factors.

   One of the expected outputs of creating a current reality tree is to identify the root causes that are perpetuating the effects to be remedied. Once these causes are identified, they provide a focus for subsequent efforts.
2. Objective for change

   Evaporating cloud: The evaporating cloud identifies the requirements that the solution must satisfy. The first step is to state the core problem and define what should replace it. The current core problem exists because it satisfies an organizational need or requirement. This means defined solutions must satisfy needs currently satisfied by whatever caused the core problem and by whatever will replace it.

   Future reality tree: The future reality tree defines the desirable effects of the solution, which will become the improvement project objectives. Future reality trees create a complete picture of the positive and negative consequences of the proposed solution defined in the evaporating cloud process. Each undesirable effect discovered in making the current reality tree is reviewed to define its opposite—that is, desirable—effect. These desirable effects become implementation plan objectives. They are also inputs examined using the prerequisite tree.

3. How to change

Prerequisite tree: The prerequisite tree defines the conditions that need to be in place to achieve the objectives defined by the future reality tree. Prerequisite trees ensure all necessary conditions are identified and objectives are set to ensure the implementation plans meet them. Projects are implemented efficiently by defining the best sequence to meet these conditions, and they are included as input to the transition tree.

Transition tree: The transition tree creates detailed plans to implement the objectives defined in the prerequisite tree. Intermediate objectives and the action plans supporting them are delegated to teams or individuals. Teams use transition trees to break down the actions needed to achieve the assigned objectives. These transition tree objectives and actions are used in implementation reviews to ensure that the overall project objectives are met.

Systems always have constraints to be eliminated, so TOC will always regenerate opportunities for improvement. The heart of the TOC methodology is the focus on the system constraint, which ensures that all resources are applied to maximize the system improvement benefit. The TOC thinking process is based on scientific methods; that is, it identifies the root cause(s) of a problem and develops effective solutions. The thinking process is useful for making both incremental and breakthrough improvements.

6.1.2 Dr. Little's Law

In manufacturing, it is usually written in manufacturing-specific terms as:

$$WIP = TH * CT$$

where:
WIP is work in process
TH is throughput rate
CT is cycle time

Little's Law says the average number of jobs in a system is equal to the average rate jobs go through the system multiplied by the average waiting time in the system. Let WIP denote the average number of jobs and CT denote the average waiting time in the system. The parameter TH not only denotes the arrival rate, but also it is equal to the throughput rate since in a stable system in steady state, over the long-term, the flow in must equal the flow out (assuming there is no loss in the system and nothing is added).

What makes Little's Law so powerful is that it holds regardless of the distribution assumed for the arrival rate or the queue discipline used. You can apply Little's Law to a single server or to the entire system, it is just a matter of defining the boundaries. Little's Law relates the long-term, average values of three important system parameters. The important implication of Little's Law is that if you know any two of the three parameters, then the third parameter is restricted by the equation. This limits your design freedom when specifying system performance.

> Inspired by the Theory of Constraints (TOC), Dr. Little's Law suggests that to achieve target throughput, if internal capabilities and capacities are a constraint, then this constraint can be dissolved by networking with other enterprises with the requisite capabilities and capacities.

6.2 Designing the Network of Enterprises

An organization must establish its mission, objectives, and goals, along with a business strategy. Since the network of enterprises helps an organization attain its mission, objectives, and goals, it is critical to know if the company intends to compete on cost, reliability, or responsiveness, as these elements affect the network design and financial performance. The process of network design involves the consideration of several factors or elements, such as the number and locations of suppliers, manufacturing and assembly plants, distribution centers, and warehouses.

The design of the network of enterprises is an important aspect for any organization; the design impacts costs and customer service levels. Enterprises have a choice of many different network designs; similar enterprises in the same industry often have different network designs. However, enterprises with good network designs have one element in common: they are in alignment with their customers' needs and with the enterprise business strategy, including the following:

1. The types of products and services offered

    The product or service is an important consideration in supply chain design. The product's physical attributes affect the ability of the network to deliver. For washing powder, a stable-demand and high-volume product, it would be appropriate to design an efficient make-to-stock supply chain compared with a make-to-order supply chain that is less efficient but more flexible.

    If the product is in the growth phase, the network is more likely to be designed considering increasing facility and process capacities in the future.

If the product is in the declining phase, capacities will be decreased and fixed assets may need to be unloaded.

2. The location of acceptable materials and suppliers

Location decisions affect cost, service, system, and communication complexity and the level of exposure to supply chain risk. Firms decide where to buy materials, where they want the goods produced, assembled, and stored, and where they will be subsequently sold. If the materials and services purchased are found in limited geographical regions, transportation costs coupled with the customers' location will dictate whether to ship materials to distant assembly plants or move the assembly plants closer to the point where the materials are acquired. An organization might also consider moving its suppliers closer to the assembly plants, much like the automobile industry operates. Along with dispersed locations comes added risk.

Before selecting a location, many factors are considered.
- Proximity to markets
- Proximity to suppliers
- Proximity to materials and material costs
- Labor availability, skill, productivity, union rules, and wages
- Government tax incentives
- Land availability
- Infrastructure, including transportation and utilities
- Risk reduction, including financial, political, and natural disasters
- Trade agreements that reduce import duties and tariffs
- Stable currency

Operating globally offers many advantages. One advantage is obtaining suppliers that can offer better pricing for higher-quality materials. Access to talent and expertise with higher productivity levels is another opportunity provided by global operation. Companies might find that working around the clock—literally, taking advantage of time zones—helps reduce the time to market. Higher productivity levels and reduced time to market generate cash inflows faster, creating value for the organization. On the other hand, there are disadvantages to operating globally or over long distances. Although crossing time zones increases the time available to produce, this also increases the complexity of communicating with suppliers and customers. There are cultural differences and holidays that can interrupt the flow of goods and services. Some countries do not have regulations enforcing high labor or safety standards and are prone to currency exchange volatility.

3. The transportation that connects all of these pieces together

As the number of facilities increases, so do the costs to manage and operate them. To meet existing service levels, inventory costs rise due to additional safety stock requirements. The increase in safety stock is a result of the variation in consumer demand as the network is decentralized. Transportation costs tend to initially decrease as the outbound distance from distribution centers to their delivery points decrease. Lower costs remain as long as the inbound transportation to the facilities can maintain economies of scale. When inbound full truckloads (FTLs) and/or full container loads (FCLs) cannot be maintained any longer, transportation costs begin to increase. Transportation costs begin to grow when too many facilities are added. Outbound costs per unit tend to be higher, since these are generally smaller lot sizes, whereas inbound lot sizes are generally larger. As the number of facilities increases, response time also decreases.

6.3 Ongoing Changes to the Network of Enterprises

Companies often reevaluate supply chain designs for a variety of reasons. Some reasons include the acquisition of another company, cost savings, divesting certain fixed assets or product lines, or changes in consumer buying behavior that prompt a company to enter or leave a market. Moreover, executives are trying to make networks simpler by removing the complexity that may have accumulated in them over time.

While assessing the baseline for envisaged changes, the organization may consider several factors, such as

1. Current and potential new locations of facilities, supply sources, and markets
2. Capacities of the facilities
3. Current and future consumer demand for their products and services
4. Current fixed and variable costs
5. Revenue generated from products and services for the various locations
6. Facility, labor, and material costs by location
7. Transportation costs between locations
8. Inventory costs by location
9. Taxes, tariffs, and duties
10. Response times
11. Risks

Evaluating new network designs may entail the following queries:

- How does the total network cost change if new facilities are added or current facilities are closed?
- How does the cost change if facility locations change?
- How many locations and facilities are needed to meet company goals, objectives, and consumer demand?
- How does the network cost change if facility capacity increases or decreases?
- How do costs change if service levels change?

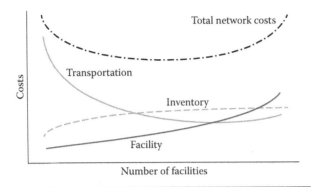

Figure 6.1   Trends of various costs with an increasing number of nodes in a network of enterprises.

Figure 6.1 shows the trends of various costs with an increasing number of nodes in a network of enterprises.

When the design of the network of enterprises changes, so do certain costs. Transportation, inventory, and facility costs characteristically change as the number of facilities change in a distribution network. For instance, as the network is decentralized by increasing the number of distribution and warehouse facilities, total costs decline, then rise again. Inventory and facility costs increase, while transportation costs initially decrease, then increase again.

6.4 Business Processes for the Network of Enterprises

1. The management of relationships with the customer: The first step in enterprise network (EN) management is to identify the customers or group of customers that may be considered essential or important in the company's business mission. It will be vitally important to specify the level of service to be accomplished with these customers by identifying and eliminating the causes generating demand variability. Administration of the relationships with customers involves making performance assessments, which analyze the level of service provided to customers and the profitability of these customers.

2. Customer service management: Thanks to a greater interrelation with the production area and the organization's distribution systems, the customer service department can provide information about its commitments to deliveries, dates, product availability, and so on in real time.

3. Demand management: Inventories are of two types—namely, *essential* and *variable*. An essential inventory includes the products being manufactured and the goods being moved from one place to another through the standard

channels. In a variable inventory, the stocks resulting from the fluctuations in manufacturing processes, supply, and demand are identified. Customer demand is the main source of variability and is made up of irregular patterns. Since customers' orders are unforeseen, demand management is a key element in efficient EN management. During the demand management process, customers' requirements must be balanced with the company's supply capacity in an attempt to determine the exact amount and time to buy by using demand-forecasting techniques. To lower the level of uncertainty, demand management systems use points of sales (POSs) and the relevant customers' databases to improve the efficiency of the physical flow of merchandise throughout the EN.

4. Fulfilling orders: The key to efficient EN management lies in meeting customers' requirements. To achieve this, an efficient process that integrates manufacturing, distribution, and transport plans is required to fulfill orders, and suitable agreements must be reached with the key EN members, especially transport companies, to fulfill the customers' requirements while simultaneously reducing total distribution costs.

5. Manufacturing flow management: In traditional companies, manufacturing flow management follows a common process: producing, storing, and delivering end products to the distribution system in accordance with historical demand forecasts. With this approach, products are manufactured in accordance with a strict production schedule, which usually results in unnecessary and excessive inventories, engendering high costs. In contrast, in the processes-oriented management approach currently employed in EN management, the product is manufactured according to customers' requirements.

   Manufacturing processes can be made flexible to respond to market changes by installing dynamic systems that can be adapted to different product characteristics, as adopted in mass customization. Thus, orders are processed with just-in-time (JIT) systems in minimal amounts and with the manufacturing priorities defined by the delivery date. This approach, emphasizing simple control systems, has brought about changes to the manufacturing process, with shorter cycle times and improved customer service.

6. Supplies or purchases: The main function of the supplies or purchases process is to develop strategic plans with suppliers that support new product development processes as well as the corresponding manufacturing flow management processes. Similarly, suppliers are classified at this stage on the basis of various factors, as per their contribution and importance to the enterprise. As part of this process, long-term strategic alliances are developed with a small group of suppliers for the purpose of obtaining mutual profit, which is protected within *win–win* relationship models.

   The philosophy of this process aims at involving important suppliers in the earliest stages of the design cycle to significantly cut manufacturing cycle and product delivery times. The purchasing area further consolidates and improves its operation by employing information and communication technologies to rapidly transfer the information relating to its requirements to all concerned stakeholders.

7. Product development and commercialization: In EN management, suppliers and their customers work closely to develop newer products faster, with the objective of achieving commercialization faster. When product life cycles shorten, they are launched faster in the market for shorter time periods to remain competitive.

    Thus, the product development and commercialization process involves the following:

    a. Coordinate with the customer service area to identify the end customer's requirements.
    b. Select materials and suppliers along with the supplies department.
    c. Develop technologies to facilitate production and the integration of flows into the EN, thus achieving the best product–market combination.

8. Returns: It is important to have an explicit logistics scheme to provide improved returns management, otherwise known as *reverse logistics*. Efficient returns management helps identify opportunities to improve productivity and to discover new projects. Indeed, it is hoped that, with time, SC elements should do away with all kinds of routines from a previously set up quality decision-making platform so as to enable correct communication and operation to avoid returns altogether.

6.5 Performance of Network of Enterprises

Companies usually focus only on their immediate first-tier suppliers, customers, or third-party logistics providers; consequently, they fail to comprehend the implications of their decisions on the performance of those suppliers residing further upstream or downstream within the chain and, therefore, are ignorant of the performance of the whole system. Such partially valid measurement systems render the enterprise network as a series of disparate elements rather than an inclusive, integrated whole.

As shown in Figure 6.2, the supply chain performance scorecard is comprised of the following four dimensions:

1. *Responsiveness measures* are associated with the flexibility of the pipeline of activities that constitute the enterprise network and include *forecast accuracy*, *enterprise network cycle time*, *pipeline inventory*, and *value-adding contribution* (VAC).

    a. Forecast accuracy

       Forecast accuracy can be established by determining the mean absolute deviation (MAD) between forecasted and actual requirements.

Behavioral measures	Responsiveness measures
Bullwhip index Synchronization index	Demand forecast MAD Inventory level Supply chain cycle time Value-adding contribution
Reliability measures	Cost measures
Stockouts Backorders	Transportation cost Inventory-holding cost

Figure 6.2   Performance measurement system for the networks of enterprises.

The construct for forecast accuracy (FA) is expressed as

$$FA = 100 - \left(\frac{\left(\dfrac{\sum_{i=1}^{p} |a_i - b_i|}{p} \right)}{\mu} \right) * 100$$

where:
    a = final product call-off/consumption (daily demand)
    b = supplier deliveries (daily)
    p = days for the period examined
    μ = mean demand for the period examined

    b. Enterprise network cycle time

Time is the critical component of any assessment of responsiveness. Good responsiveness requires the lead time for materials that travel through the enterprise network pipeline to be kept as short as possible. At each tier, the cycle time (sometimes referred to as *dock-to-dock time*) includes the process time, waiting time, and inventory storage time within each enterprise boundary. Delivery time is included as part of the overall enterprise network cycle time. The overall enterprise network cycle time indicates the total length of the enterprise network pipeline. An enterprise network with short dock-to-dock times can usually respond to demand or market changes quickly because the time for the appropriate modifications to take effect throughout the enterprise network and the restoration of an equilibrium position is shorter.

c. Pipeline inventory

Inventory exists in different forms throughout the enterprise network pipeline—raw materials, works in progress, finished goods, goods in transit, and spare (or service) parts.

An effective inventory management system maintains a low level of inventory while being sufficient to satisfy customer orders or demand. Raw materials, component parts, and finished goods are taken into consideration in the scorecard. The inventory level is calculated from the ratio of the average daily inventory quantity to the average daily usage quantity. Hence, the inventory level is presented in a *days of inventory* format.

d. Value-adding contribution

Value is added to material as it moves through an enterprise network until the final saleable item is produced and ultimately consumed. One of the customer-driven guidelines is to eliminate waste. Waste, or non-value-adding activity, in an enterprise network is an inhibitor to responsiveness. In order to monitor the proportion of value-adding contribution (VAC) for each enterprise network tier, the percentage of value-adding activity is expressed as

$$VAC = \frac{process\ time}{supply\ chain\ cycle\ time} \times 100$$

The overall enterprise network VAC is derived by dividing the sum of the process times (from the involved supply chain tiers) by the overall enterprise network cycle time. A low VAC indicates a high level of non-value-adding activity and vice versa. The higher the VAC, the less non-value-adding activity within the supply chain, hence the higher the expectation of a better degree of responsiveness.

2. *Behavioral measures* are associated with supply chain coordination and include the *bullwhip effect* and *synchronization index*.

a. Bullwhip effect

Bullwhip refers to a cascade of increasing variability of demand further upstream in an enterprise network. A bullwhip metric necessarily establishes the amplification between tiers by comparing the variability of the demand signal from the downstream partner with the variability upstream. *Upstream* refers to demand/orders exhibited at first-, second-, or third-tier enterprises or suppliers, and *downstream* refers to demand/orders at the point of origin (usually an Original Equipment Manufacturer [OEM] or retailer).

The construct for the bullwhip measure is expressed as

$$\omega = \frac{\dfrac{\sigma}{\mu}\text{upstream}}{\dfrac{\sigma}{\mu}\text{downstream}}$$

where:
  σ = the standard deviation of the demand pattern
  μ = the mean of demand pattern

A bullwhip index greater than 1 implies that the variance of the demand registered at the upstream tier is higher than that registered at the point of origin. Situations in which a bullwhip index greater than 1 can be found to include a regular but more infrequent weekly delivery of items from upstream tiers than the consumption of those items at a downstream tier.

A bullwhip index less than 1 implies that the variance of the demand registered at the upstream tier is lower than that registered at the point of origin. Situations in which a bullwhip index less than 1 may occur include more frequent deliveries of items from upstream tiers than the consumption of those items at a downstream tier.

A bullwhip index equal to 1 means a perfectly balanced enterprise network with no demand amplification.

Thus, even if customer demand is constant for a period examined, the size and frequency of enterprises' (i.e., suppliers') deliveries can have a negative impact on the enterprise network index. Weekly deliveries of large batches will often result in a bullwhip index well above 1. Sequenced, synchronized deliveries (one-piece flow) will result in a bullwhip index close to or equal to one.

b. Synchronization index

This measure calculates the mean absolute deviation (MAD) over the examined period, between the appropriate offset OEM demand and the actual demand.

The construct for the synchronization index (SI) of a second-tier supplier is

$$SI = 100 - \left(\left(\frac{\dfrac{\sum_{i=1}^{p}|a_i - b_{i-1}|}{p}}{\mu}\right)\right)*100$$

where:

    a = requested quantities (daily demand)
    b = supplier deliveries (daily)
    p = days for the period examined
    μ = mean demand for the period examined

There is an offset time of 1 day between the OEM and the second-tier supplier, while there is no offset time between the OEM and the first-tier supplier.

The corresponding construct for the synchronization index of a second-tier supplier is

$$SI = 100 - \left(\left(\frac{\left(\frac{\sum\limits_{i=1}^{p}|a_i - b_{i-2}|}{p}\right)}{\mu}\right)\right) * 100$$

There is an offset time of 2 days between the OEM and the third-tier supplier, 1 offset day between the first tier and the second tier, and 1 offset day between the second tier and the third tier. There is no offset time between the OEM and first tier.

3. *Reliability measures* are associated with the satisfaction of customer service as well as the prevention of any of the disruptive effects of activities within the network and include *stockouts* and *backorders*.

Enterprise network reliability is associated with the satisfaction of customer service and is analogous to product reliability in that it conveys the ability to function without disruption and according to an agreement or specification. An unreliable enterprise network is likely to have a negative impact on customer service, partner profitability, and product quality. There are many constructs that can be used to assess supply chain reliability, including metrics for delivery performance, order fulfillment, and the proportion of schedules changed within a supplier's lead time.

One way to attain a reliable enterprise network is to engender trust, share appropriate data and information, and achieve a continuous and smooth material flow throughout the enterprise network pipeline. Reliability assessments via the scorecard focus on monitoring the frequency of stockout incidents and the magnitude of backorders. A late delivery will usually incur additional costs to both the supplier and buyer in the form of compensation costs and production disruption costs.

a. Stockouts

Stockouts refer to the frequency of stockout incidents, and the stockout level indicates the inability of an organization to meet demand at the required time. If one facility in an enterprise network fails to produce according to schedule, it affects the material availability of the next enterprise network facility. This can create a knock-on effect throughout the whole enterprise network and incur additional direct and indirect costs.

The measurement of the stockout level assesses the disruption of material availability by examining the average number of days on which a stockout incident occurred per month. A high stockout level indicates many disruptions have occurred to material provisions and to the desired level of customer service. It may also provide an indication of the reliability of upstream suppliers and the effectiveness of their material management systems.

b. Backorders

Backorders refer to the portion of orders that are not delivered on time, and the backorder level measures the magnitude of material availability disruption. It calculates the average quantities of materials that have been delayed in stockout incidents that were sampled in the stockout level metric.

4. *Cost measures* are associated with transportation and inventory-holding costs and can be used to establish a quantitative cost profile across a chain.

a. Cost of holding inventory

The cost of capital to finance the inventory is the most significant contributor to overall holding costs. Costs can differ significantly from business to business and from inventory item to inventory item, but as a general rule of thumb, 25% of inventory value is regularly attributed to the cost of holding inventory.

The cost of capital (sometimes referred to as the *cost of finance* or the *opportunity cost*), insurance, inventory obsolescence, warehousing and materials handling, deterioration, damage and pilferage, administration, and various other miscellaneous expenses can all contribute to inventory-holding costs and can be interpreted as a percentage of the value of the inventory per holding period. As a cost category, obsolescence can vary considerably, from 10% or more for an inventory item in a high–clock speed electronics enterprise network to as low as 2% for an inventory item in a less ephemeral, slower-moving chemical enterprise network.

b. Transportation costs

Transportation costs are a major component of the cost of logistics. Global markets and the trend to source globally and stretch enterprise networks has made the role of logistics and transportation and their associated costs even more pronounced.

6.6 Characteristics of Network of Enterprises

There are many markets for goods and services that satisfy the characteristics of what we call *network products*. These markets include telephones, e-mail, Internet, computer hardware, computer software, music players, music titles, video players, movies, banking services, airline services, and legal services. The main characteristics of these markets that distinguish them from the markets for grain, dairy products, apples, and treasury bonds are as follows:

- Complementarity, compatibility, and standards
- Network externalities
- Switching costs and lock-in
- Significant economies of scale in production

6.6.1 Complementarity, Compatibility, and Standards

Computers are not useful without having monitors attached or without having software installed. CD players are not useful without CD titles, just as cameras are not useful without film. Stereo receivers are useless without speakers or headphones, and airline companies will not be able to sell tickets without joining a particular reservation system. All these examples demonstrate that, unlike bread, which can be consumed without wine or other types of food, the markets we analyze in this book supply goods that must be consumed together with other products (software and hardware). In the literature of economics, such goods and services are called *complements*. *Complementarity* means that consumers in these markets are shopping for systems (e.g., computers and software, cameras and film, music players and cassettes) rather than individual products. The fact that consumers are buying systems composed of hardware and software or complementary components allows firms to devise all sorts of strategies regarding competition with other firms. A natural question to ask is, for example, whether firms benefit from designing machines that can work with machines produced by rival firms.

On the technical side, the next question to ask would be how complements are produced. In order to produce complementary products, they must be compatible. The CD album must have the same specification as CD players, otherwise it can't be played. A parallel port at the back of each computer must generate the same output voltage as the voltage required for inputting data into a printer attached to this port. Trains must fit on the tracks, and software must be workable with a given operating system (OS). This means that complementary products must operate on the same standard. This creates the problem of coordination as to how firms agree on the standards. The very fact that coordination is needed has the potential to create some antitrust problems; in some cases, firms may need to coordinate their decisions, and while doing that, they may find themselves engaging in price fixing.

Complementarity turns out to be a crucial factor in the markets for information goods. For example, people who subscribe to a fashion magazine are likely to be interested in fashion and clothing catalogs, just as people who read the *New York Times* are likely to be interested in real estate and interior decoration magazines. Advertising agencies have understood these complementarities for quite some time and make use of these complementarities to attract more customers. For example, the publishers of real estate magazines could benefit from purchasing a list of names and addresses of subscribers to the *New York Times* and sending them sample copies to attract their attention. These information complementarities become more and more important with the increase in the use of the Internet for advertising and shopping purposes. For example, those who browse commercial websites offering toys for sale, such as www.etoys.com, are likely to be interested in browsing websites offering children's clothing. Thus, toy sites are likely to sell lists of their site visitors to children's clothing stores.

6.6.2 Network Externalities

What use will anyone have with a telephone if there is no one to talk to? Would people use e-mail knowing that nobody else does? Would people purchase fax machines knowing that nobody else has such a machine? These examples demonstrate that the utility derived from the consumption of these goods is affected by the number of other people using similar or compatible products. Note that this type of externality is not found in the market for tomatoes or the market for salt, as the consumption of these goods does not require compatibility with other consumers. Such externalities are sometimes referred to as *adoption* or *network externalities*.

The presence of these standard-adoption effects can profoundly affect the market behavior of firms. The precise nature of the market outcome (e.g., consumers' adoption of a new standard) depends on how consumers form expectations on the size of the network of users. The reliance on joint consumer expectations generates multiple equilibria, where in one equilibrium, all consumers adopt the new technology, whereas in the other, no one adopts it. Both equilibria are rational from the consumers' viewpoint as they reflect the best response to the decisions made by all other consumers in the market. A good example for this behavior is the fax machine, which was used in the 1950s by flight service stations to transmit weather maps every hour on the hour (the transmission of a single page took about 1 hour at the time). However, fax machines remained a niche product until the mid-1980s. During a 5-year period, the demand and supply of fax machines exploded. Before 1982, almost no one had a fax machine, but after 1987, the majority of businesses had one. The Internet exhibited the same pattern of adoption. The first e-mail message was sent in 1969, but adoption did not take off until the mid-1980s. The Internet did not take off until 1990; however, since 1990, Internet traffic has more than doubled every year. All these examples raise a fundamental question, which is when to expect a new technology to catch on. A related question to ask is, in the presence of adoption externalities, what is the minimal number of users (the critical mass) needed to induce all potential consumers to adopt the technology (Figure 6.3)?

6.6.2.1 Reasons for Obtaining Network Externalities

1. Reduced transaction costs: Compatible standards reduce the transaction costs of trading or interacting across a network. After the dawn of the Internet, for example, compatible standards allowed e-mail transfer across previously incompatible networks that could not share traffic. Likewise, eBay's Web-based standards permitted trading across previously geographically disjointed classified ads markets.
2. Costs of common platform infrastructure: When vertical applications create enough value to justify acquiring the supporting platform, completely unrelated applications benefit. For instance, if applications in Microsoft Office create enough value to justify acquiring Microsoft Windows, then a photo editing package, say, does not need to supply an operating system (OS). Its developers can assume that users will have the OS.
3. Expectations, externalities, and "tippy" outcomes: When users access a network on a recurring basis, their *willingness to pay* (WTP) for participation is broadly based not on the network's current scale but rather on the number of users with whom they expect to be able to interact in the future. With fragmented demand, it can be difficult for prospective users to communicate expectations and coordinate behavior. Facing uncertainty about others' intentions, each prospect may defer adoption, even when network effects are strong. Consequently, networked markets are prone to either stall or tip rapidly toward high adoption rates. Since users' expectations determine which outcome will prevail, platform intermediaries work hard to shape them.

    Network externalities contribute to *excess inertia*. In the absence of a way to internalize externalities—that is, to compensate (or charge) new users for the incremental benefits (or harm) they bring to other users—prospects are less likely to join the network. This happened in the 1980s with the VHS versus Beta competition and is happening again with Blu-Ray versus HD-DVD.
4. Winner-takes-all markets: Network effects and factors that support single-platform dominance frequently lead to *winner-takes-all* markets. At least three factors compound these effects.
    a. Multihoming costs are high. *Homing* costs include all the expenses incurred by network users due to platform affiliation; these are high

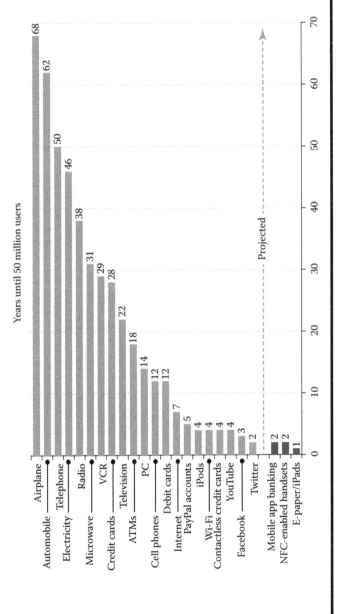

Figure 6.3   Surging contexts of innovations.

enough relative to benefits that they prefer to affiliate with only one plat-form. For example, most PC users typically rely only on the Windows OS because it is expensive to acquire the hardware and software required to use multiple OSs. When multihoming costs are high, users need a good reason to affiliate with multiple platforms.

b. Cross-side network effects are positive and strong, at least for the net-work side with high multihoming costs. When this condition applies, users want access to all potential transaction partners on the network's other side. A subscale platform will be of little interest to them, unless it provides the only way to reach certain partners. The odds of a winner-takes-all outcome also increase when same-side network effects are posi-tive and strong.

c. Neither side's users have strong preferences for inimitable differentiated functionality. If there is little demand for special features, then users will converge on one platform. However, if different user segments have unique needs that are intrinsically difficult or expensive to serve through a single platform, then rival platforms can survive.

6.6.3 Switching Costs and Lock-In

Learning to master a particular OS such as Windows, UNIX, DOS, or macOS takes time (depending on the level of the user). It is an established fact that users are very much annoyed by having to switch between OSs. To some consumers, switching OSs is as hard as learning a new language. On the production side, producers heavily depend on the standards used in the production of other com-ponents of the system. For example, airline companies rely on spare parts and services provided by aircraft manufacturers. Switching costs are significant in ser-vice industries as well. Several estimates provided in this book show that the cost associated with switching between banks (i.e., closing an account in one bank and opening an account and switching the activities to a different bank) could reach 6% of the average account balance. In all of these cases, we say that users are *locked in*. Of course, *lock-in* is not an absolute term. The degree of lock-in is found by calculating the cost of switching to a different service or adopting a new technol-ogy, since these costs determine the degree to which users are locked into a given technology. We call these *switching costs*.

There are several types of switching costs that affect the degree of lock-in.

1. Contracts: Users are sometimes locked into contracts for service, supplying parts, and buying spare parts. Switching costs amount to the damages and compensation that must be paid by the party that breaks the contract.

2. Training and learning: Consumers are trained to use products operating on a specific standard. Switching costs would include learning and training people, as well as the lost productivity resulting from adopting a new system.

3. Data conversion: Each piece of software generates files that are saved using a particular digital format. Once a new software is introduced, a conversion software may be needed in order to be able to use it. Notice that the resulting switching cost increases over time, as the collection of data may grow over time.
4. Search cost: One reason why people do not switch very often is that they would like to avoid the cost of searching and shopping for new products.
5. Loyalty cost: Switching technology may result in losing benefits such as preferred customers' programs—for example, frequent-flyer mileage.

Switching costs affect price competition in two opposing ways. First, if consumers are already locked in to a specific product, firms may raise prices knowing that consumers will not switch unless the price difference exceeds the switching cost to a competing brand. Second, if consumers are not locked in, brand-producing firms will compete intensively by offering discounts and free complimentary products and services in order to attract consumers who later on will be locked into the technology. In the presence of switching costs, once the critical mass is achieved and the sales of the product take off, we say that the seller has accumulated an *installed base* of consumers, which is the number of consumers who are locked into the seller's technology. For example, AT&T's installed base is the number of customers subscribing to its long-distance service, where switching costs include the time and trouble associated with switching to, say, MCI's long-distance service.

6.6.4 Significant Economies of Scale in Production

Software—or more generally, any information—has a highly noticeable production characteristic in which the production of the first copy involves a huge *sunk cost* (a cost that cannot be recovered), whereas the second copy (and the third, the fourth, and so on) costs almost nothing to reproduce. The cost of gathering the information for the *Encyclopædia Britannica* involves more than 100 years of research as well as the lifetime's work of a good number of authors. However, the cost of reproducing it on a set of CDs is less than $5. The cost of developing advanced software involves thousands of hours of programming time; however, the software can now be distributed without cost over the Internet. In economic terms, a very high fixed sunk cost, together with an almost negligible marginal cost, implies that the average cost function declines sharply with the number of copies sold to consumers. This by itself means that a competitive equilibrium does not exist and that markets of this type will often be characterized by dominant leaders that capture most of the market.

6.6.5 Network Effects

Mobile communications, video games, and software are just three examples of businesses where network effects drive market competition and consumer behavior.

One of the most significant distinctive features of these markets is the central role played by the network of users. *Network effects* can be defined as follows: a good exhibits network effects when the utility of a user increases with the number of other users consuming the good. The utility of the user is driven not only by the product itself but by the network that surrounds that product, so that the larger the network, the higher the utility derived from consuming the product.

Network effects have emerged as an area of focus to understand how network effects alter the way in which firms compete. This increasing interest is due to the evidence that network industries seem to challenge much received wisdom in the traditional fields of management and operations. This trend has intensified in recent years with the proliferation of social networks and other new media, which has resulted in an increasingly networking society where individuals can easily interact with each other. In this new environment, a firm's success and survival critically depend on a proper understanding of how these networks operate.

When network effects are present, the firm's installed customer base can be considered a key asset to gain abnormal returns. Network effects have significant implications for the way markets operate and firms compete. For example, when the network of users is large and consumers can derive a high utility from it, customers' willingness to pay increases, with the subsequent potential impact on firm competitive performance. Network effects can also affect the distribution of the market via consumers across the available alternatives across companies. By having a positive effect on customers' utility functions, firms or technologies with a high market share are able to obtain a higher level of profitability. Taken to an extreme, network effects may create winner-takes-all markets, in which one company emerges as dominant and the other firms, which may have superior products or technologies, must abandon the market.

Fundamentally, there are two types of networks:

1. *Direct or pure network effects*: In which each individual in the network contributes equally to creating value for the others. This implies that adding one customer to the market equally increases the utility of all users who are already in the network. Direct network effects emerge as a result of the pricing strategies implemented by cell phone carriers and based on the origin and destination of the calls (the price discrimination between on-net and off-net calls). Direct network effects are present when adoption by different users is complementary, so that each user's adoption payoff, and his incentive to adopt, increases as more number of others users adopt it. This type of network effect is easily understood when we think of examples such as e-mail, fax, or telecommunications, where none of these technologies have any value in isolation. It can only produce utility to consumers when other users adopt the technology.

   More formally, each user's utility function increases with the number of additional users of the technology/product; so, the larger the installed user network, the higher the utility derived from the product. This is because a large installed base allows the firm to offer more benefits to potential customers compared with companies with smaller customer bases. These benefits can take the form of reduced uncertainty, compatibility, the transfer of technical and nontechnical information between members of the network, and the increased availability and quality of complements. The presence of these benefits encourages consumer adoption of the product and increases its utility over and above its stand-alone product performance.

2. *Indirect or market mediated*: In which the utility of each user is not directly influenced by other users consuming the good at the same time but by the growth in the other side of the market. Indirect network effects arise through improved opportunities to trade with the other side of a market. They imply that customer utility from the primary product (i.e., the hardware) increases as more complements become available (i.e., software). In turn, this availability of complementary products depends on the installed user network of the primary product. Prior research has typically referred to the primary product, such as a television set, a mobile handset, or a DVD player, as *hardware*, and to the product that complements the primary product, such as television programs, mobile phone applications, and music or movies, as *software*.

   In the presence of indirect network effects, we can observe the "chicken and egg" paradox. This happens when consumers wait to adopt the primary product until enough complements are available. At the same time, manufacturers of complements delay releasing new complements until enough consumers have adopted the product. This effect can be dangerous for the diffusion of the technology, as it may delay consumer adoption and reduce the interest of manufacturers in designing and releasing new complementary products.

3. *Personal network effects*: In which network effects may be localized. For instance, a mobile phone user gains more when his/her friends join the mobile network than when a stranger does. Personal network effects refer to those instances where mobile service providers offer special tariffs for calls to members of the social network (family, friends, etc.). Personal network effects explicitly take into account the differences that exist in the contribution of each network member to the utility function. They refer to the utility that an individual obtains from the adoption by a given individual. This utility may be positive, neutral, or negative, depending on the person that joins the network. For example, a mobile user may derive high utility when her boyfriend or her brother joins the network, while this utility becomes zero when a stranger does. Thus, network benefits are not homogeneous; consumers find more benefits from interacting with their social subset than with the rest of the installed base.

   Local or personal network effects play a key role in determining mobile users' choice of supplier. In other words, the probability that a user selects a service provider increases with the number of members of his/her social network that are already subscribed to that provider.

6.6.5.1 Network Effects in the Mobile Telecommunications Industry

Mobile telecommunications is a paradigmatic example of an industry where network effects drive market competition.

Direct network effects are present in the mobile communications industry even when the networks are perfectly compatible. In this market, pure network effects mainly arise due to the differences between *on-net* and *off-net* tariffs. Operators charge different prices depending on whether the call made by the user is directed to a member of the same operator (low or on-net tariff) or to a member outside the operator (high or off-net tariff). These strategies aim to encourage existing customers to stay with the provider and to attract new customers, because the larger the user network, the lower the average cost of the calls for their customers. At the same time, these strategies increase consumer switching costs because leaving the company implies losing the benefits derived from making cheaper calls to members of the same network, which reduces competition in the market and confers market power to the firms.

Indirect network effects are associated with the increase in utility derived from the availability of complements to the primary product or service. In mobile communications, as more and more individuals are interested in the technology, software manufacturers will also have higher incentives to design and release new applications, features, or devices that will increase the utility of using the primary product. For example, as more and more individuals become mobile users, handset manufacturers are encouraged to introduce new devices with more complex features and with a wider range of options (e.g., front camera, GPS technology, Bluetooth technology) to increase the utility of the mobile experience.

Personal network effects also come mainly from pricing strategies implemented by mobile operators. In this case, the benefit for the user is not associated with the calls directed to the members of the same operator but with the calls made to a particular group of users that constitutes his/her social subset (family, friends, etc.). The underlying logic is that, although all users in a network are a potential source of network effects, some users matter more than others. Thus, network benefits are not homogeneous, but consumers find more benefits from interacting with their social subset than with the rest of the installed base. Consequently, a customer's choice behavior will be more influenced by his/her social subset than by the rest of the users in the network. For instance, the probability that a customer selects a cell phone company increases with the number of members of his/her social network already subscribed to that firm.

6.6.5.2 Network Effects and Competitive Advantage

The user network is a critical strategic asset for assessing a firm's current and future competitive position. This is because there are strong interdependencies within the market, and customers derive utility not only from the product or service itself but also, even more importantly, from the network of users surrounding these products. One of the greatest challenges that practitioners face in mobile communications is to manage the user network optimally in order to maximize current and future profitability.

Firms can implement strategies that make both existing consumers more willing to stay in the network and new customers more predisposed to join the network. This can be done, for example, by price discriminating against customers who call other networks (off-net calls), as these calls are significantly more expensive than those made to members of the same network. Alternatively, firms can use additional incentives (e.g., promotions, rewards) to encourage customers to join the network. This increase in the size of the network will increase the probability that other users join the network in the future (marginal network effects).

When competition is intense, gaining market share is critical for survival because the presence of network effects increases the probability that individuals will join the firm with the largest user network. This is why we see price wars and huge investments by firms directed at expanding the customer base. Once a firm has built a large market share, it becomes one of its most critical assets. In addition to the direct benefits that the company can obtain from the large number of users of its products, the company benefits from

- Higher acquisition rates
- Higher barriers to entry (It is very difficult for competitors to enter a market with network effects dominated by companies with large market shares.)
- Lower price sensitivity
- Increased market power

Firms pay attention to the social networks, as customers' choices are mainly driven by the behavior of their social group. Thus, in addition to implementing general strategies to promote pure network effects, firms also develop strategies to increase personal network effects in an attempt to build a large network made up of many smaller social networks. To achieve this goal, the firm may offer price discounts to groups of friends and family if they all belong to the same network. The importance of these strategies, which promote the building of social networks inside the company's installed base, arises from empirical evidence showing that, according to the *Pareto principle* (or the *80/20 rule*), 80% of the calls are directed to less than 20% of the people that belong to the social network.

6.7 Summary

This chapter described enterprise networks, that is, the network of real enterprises which are enabled by inter-firm business processes that are in turn enabled by requisite ICT. Inspired by the Theory of Constraints (TOC), Dr. Little's Law suggests that to achieve target throughput, if internal capabilities and capacities are a constraint, then this constraint can be dissolved by networking with other enterprises with the requisite capabilities and capacities. The last part of the chapter dealt with the networks of enterprise performance and characteristics that can be gainfully employed for enhanced performance of the enterprises.

Chapter 7

Agent Systems

A virtual enterprise (VE) is a form of cooperation between independent enterprises that combine their core competencies in order to manufacture a product or provide a service. Its success is critically based on the ability to create temporary cooperation and to realize the value of a short business opportunity that the partners cannot capture on their own. VEs address problems ranging from simple membership to distributed inventory management and the synchronization of supply, production, and distribution schedules; these problems are inherently distributed, with each organization willing to share only limited information and having its own business goals in conjunction with the overall goal. The distributed and goal-oriented nature of VEs provides a strong motivation for the use of agents to model them. Agents introduce a conceptual model for distributed problem solving, declaring autonomy as a core feature of its building blocks. This makes them aware of the environment, supports interactions among them and the environment, and realizes different actions focused on fulfilling the goal assigned to them by the user or designer. It seems that implementation of such complex systems should follow an established methodology and needs adequate tools, in order to create robust, flexible, and reliable software that will be easily extensible for all the interested users.

7.1 Agent Systems

An agent-based system may contain one or more agents. There are cases in which a single-agent solution is appropriate. However, the multiagent case—where the system is designed and implemented as several interacting agents—is arguably more widespread and more interesting from a software engineering standpoint. Multiagent systems (MASs) can be defined as a collection of possibly heterogeneous computational agents, each with their own problem-solving capabilities and which are able to interact in order to reach an overall goal. MASs are ideally suited to representing problems that have multiple problem-solving methods, multiple perspectives, and/or multiple problem-solving entities. Such systems have the traditional advantages of distributed and concurrent problem solving but have the additional advantage of sophisticated patterns of interaction. Examples of common types of interactions include

- Coordination (working together toward a common aim)
- Cooperation (organizing problem-solving activities so that harmful interactions are avoided or beneficial interactions are exploited)
- Collaboration (coming to an agreement that is acceptable to all parties involved)

If a problem domain is particularly complex, large, or unpredictable, the only way it can reasonably be addressed is to develop a number of functionally specific and modular agents that are specialized at solving a particular problem aspect. In MASs, applications are designed and developed in terms of autonomous software agents that can flexibly achieve their objectives by interacting with one another in terms of high-level protocols and languages.

7.1.1 Agent Properties

The primary properties of agents are as follows:

1. Autonomy: The agent can act without direct intervention by humans or other agents and has control over its own actions and internal state.
2. Reactivity/situatedness/sensing and acting: The agent receives some form of sensory input from its environment and performs some action that changes its environment in some way.
3. Proactiveness/goal-directed behavior: The agent does not simply act in response to its environment; it is able to exhibit goal-directed behavior by taking the initiative.
4. Social ability: The agent interacts, and friendliness or pleasant social relations mark this interaction; that is, the agent is affable, companionable, or friendly.

Additional properties are as follows:

1. Coordination: The agent is able to perform some activity in a shared environment with other agents. Activities are often coordinated via plans, workflows, or some other process management mechanism.
2. Cooperation/collaboration: The agent is able to coordinate with other agents to achieve a common purpose; nonantagonistic agents succeed or fail together.

3. Flexibility: The system is responsive (the agents should perceive their environment and respond in a timely fashion to changes that occur in it), proactive, and social.
4. Learning/adaptivity: The agent is capable of
   a. Reacting flexibly to changes in its environment
   b. Taking goal-directed initiative when appropriate
   c. Learning from its own experience, its environment, and interactions with others
5. Mobility: The agent is able to transport itself from one machine to another and across different system architectures and platforms.
6. Temporal continuity: The agent is a continuously running process, not a *one-shot* computation that maps a single input to a single output, then terminates.
7. Reusability: Processes or subsequent instances can require keeping instances of the class agent for an information handover or to check and analyze them as per the results.
8. Resource limitation: An agent can only act as long as it has resources at its disposal. These resources are changed by its acting and possibly also by delegating.
9. Rationality: The assumption that an agent will act in order to achieve its goals and will not act in such a way as to prevent its goals being achieved—at least insofar as its beliefs permit.
10. Inferential capability: An agent can act on abstract task specification using prior knowledge of general goals and preferred methods to achieve flexibility; it goes beyond the information given and may have explicit models of itself, users, situations, and/or other agents.
11. *Knowledge-level* communication ability: The ability to communicate with persons and other agents with language resembling humanlike *speech acts* more than typical symbol-level program-to-program protocols.
12. Prediction ability: An agent is predictive if its model of how the world works is sufficiently accurate to allow it to correctly predict how it can achieve the task.
13. Interpretation ability: An agent is interpretive if it can correctly interpret its sensor readings.
14. Proxy ability: An agent can act on behalf of someone or something—that is, in the interest of, as a representative of, or for the benefit of some entity.
15. Intelligence: The agent's state is formalized by knowledge and it interacts with other agents using symbolic language.
16. Unpredictability: An agent is able to act in ways that are not fully predictable, even if all the initial conditions are known. It is capable of nondeterministic behavior.
17. Personality/character: An agent has a well-defined, believable personality and emotional state.

18. Soundness: An agent is sound if it is predictive, interpretive, and rational.
19. Credibility: An agent has a believable personality and emotional state.
20. Transparency and accountability: An agent must be transparent when required and must provide a log of its activities on demand.
21. Competitiveness: An agent is able to coordinate with other agents except when the success of one agent implies the failure of others.
22. Ruggedness: An agent is able to deal with errors and incomplete data robustly.
23. Trustworthiness: An agent adheres to the laws of robotics and is truthful.
24. Veracity: The assumption that an agent will not knowingly communicate false information.
25. Benevolence: The assumption that agents do not have conflicting goals and that every agent will therefore always try to do what is asked of it.

7.1.2 Agent Taxonomy

1. *Collaborative agents* are able to act rationally and autonomously in open and time-constrained multiagent environments.
   a. Outstanding characteristics: Cooperate with other agents
   b. Key characteristics: Autonomy, social ability, responsiveness, and proactiveness
2. *Interface agents* support and assist the user when interacting with one or more computer applications by learning during the collaboration process with the user and with other software agents.
   a. Outstanding characteristics: Act mainly as personal assistants to human users
   b. Key characteristics: Autonomy, learning (mainly from the user but also from other agents), and cooperation with the user and/or other agents
3. *Mobile agents* are autonomous software programs capable of roaming wide area networks (such as the WWW) and cooperating while performing duties (e.g., flight reservations, managing a telecommunications network) on behalf of its user.
   a. Outstanding characteristics: Can migrate between hosting systems to enhance the efficiency of computation and reduce the network traffic
   b. Key characteristics: Mobility, autonomy, and cooperation (with other agents—e.g., to exchange data or information)
4. *Information/Internet agents* are designed to manage, manipulate, or collate the vast amount of information available from many distributed sources (i.e., information explosion). These agents have varying characteristics: they may be static or mobile; they may be noncooperative or social; and they may or may not learn.

    a. Outstanding characteristics: Play the role of managing, manipulating, or collating information from many distributed sources

    b. Key characteristics: The collation, fusion (disparate formats), and amalgamation (unified metadata) of information

5. *Reactive agents* act/respond to the current state of their environment based on a stimulus response scheme. These agents are relatively simple and interact with other agents in basic ways, but they have the potential to form more robust and fault-tolerant agent-based systems.

    a. Outstanding characteristics: Respond in a stimulus response manner to the present state of the environment in which they are embedded

    b. Key characteristics: Autonomy and reactivity

6. *Hybrid agents* combine two or more agent philosophies into a single agent in order to maximize the strengths and minimize the deficiencies of the most relevant techniques (for a particular purpose).

    a. Outstanding characteristics: A combination of two or more agent categories within a single agent

    b. Key characteristics: A combination of key characteristics of two or more agent categories.

7. *Smart agents*

    a. Outstanding characteristics: Capable of learning from their actions

    b. Key characteristics: Equally characterized by autonomy, cooperation, and learning

7.1.3 Agent Architectures

An agent architecture is essentially a map of the internals of an agent—its data structures, the operations that may be performed on these data structures, and the control flow between these data structures.

Agent architectures are of three types:

1. *Deliberative* or *symbolic* architectures are those designed along the lines proposed by traditional, symbolic artificial intelligence (AI).
2. *Reactive* architectures are those that eschew central symbolic representations of the agent's environment and do not rely on symbolic reasoning.
3. *Hybrid* architectures are those that try to marry the deliberative and reactive approaches.

The corresponding inference architectures for reaching a decision are

1. *Logic-based agents*: In which decision making is realized through logical deduction.

2. *Reactive agents*: In which decision making is implemented in some form of direct mapping from situation to action.

3. *Belief–desire–intention* (BDI) *agents*: In which decision making depends on the manipulation of data structures representing the beliefs, desires, and intentions of the agent.

   The basic idea of the BDI approach is to describe the internal processing state of an agent by means of a set of mental categories, and to define a control architecture by which the agent rationally selects its course of action based on their representation. The mental categories are

   a. Beliefs: These express the agent's expectations about the current state of the world. Beliefs can be environmental beliefs that reflect the state of the environment, social beliefs that relate to the role and the functions of the other agents in the society, relational beliefs that are concerned about the skills, intentions, plans, and so on of the other agents, or personal beliefs that include beliefs of the agent about itself.

   b. Desire: An abstract notion that specifies preferences over future world states or courses of action. An agent is allowed to have inconsistent desires. It does not have to believe that its desires are achievable.

   c. Intention: Since an agent is resource bounded, it must concentrate on a subset of its desires and intend to materialize them.

   d. BDI is often supplemented by the notions of *goals* and *plans*.

   e. Goals are stronger notions than desires. Goals must be believed by the agent to be achievable. The agent thus selects a consistent subset of its goals to pursue. The commitment of an agent to a certain goal describes the transition from goals to intentions.

   f. Plans are very important for the programmatic implementation of intentions. In fact, intentions can be viewed as the partial plans of actions that the agent is committed to execute to achieve its goals. Plan development is a central point in MAS.

4. *Layered architectures*: In which decision making is realized via various software layers, each of which is more or less explicitly reasoning about the environment at different levels of abstraction.

7.1.4 Agent Communications

Agents recurrently interact to share information and to perform tasks to achieve their goals. Communications are critical for agents to identify other agents and how they can coordinate, cooperate, or collaborate.

Communications can be enabled in two ways:

1. Communication protocols
2. Communication languages

7.2 Agents for Virtual Enterprises

The virtual enterprise (VE) creation can be viewed as a cooperative system design problem. A *cooperative system* is a system in which a set of autonomous agents (computational and human) interact with each other through sharing their information, decision-making capabilities, and other resources, and distributing the corresponding workload among themselves, in order to achieve common and complementary goals. The underlying parallelism indicates the suitability of a system of agents to model a VE; the nature of agents, by definition, enables the decentralized control of the enterprise, which is desirable in a dynamic and flexible environment, and the behavior of the complete enterprise emerges as a result of the behaviors of the individual agents.

7.2.1 Agents and Expert Systems

Since the early 1980s, *expert systems* (ES) have become the most important artificial intelligence technology. ES technology provides a software representation of organizational expertise dealing with specific problems, and it will remain a useful mechanism to accomplish knowledge management. However, as an enabler of virtual enterprises that require a more flexible and integrative type of intelligence, traditional ES technology has several shortcomings:

1. ES components typically are not intelligent enough to learn from their experiences while interacting directly with users; thus, the rules encoded initially do not evolve on their own but must be modified directly by developers to reflect changes in the environment. ES are typically brittle, dealing poorly with situations that deviate from the relevant rules.
2. ESs are typically isolated, self-contained software entities; very little emphasis is placed on tool kits that support interaction with other ES or external software components.
3. As ESs evolve, functionality increases are accompanied by an ever-growing knowledge base in which inconsistencies and redundancies are difficult to avoid.
4. Over time, portions of the process that initially required human intervention become well understood and can be totally automated, but there is no mechanism in place to support the transition from human-activated objects to autonomous objects.

These are exactly the types of shortcomings *agent technology* (AT) was developed to address. AT represents a new and exciting means of decomposing, abstracting, and organizing large, complex problems. Agents, as autonomous, cooperating entities, represent a more powerful and flexible alternative for conceptualizing complex problems. As attention is increasingly placed on distributed applications such as mobile and Web-based systems, applications will not necessarily run from a central location. Communications can be costly in such environments. The direct routing of data to the recipient must be fast and efficient to make additional bandwidth available to others. Agent architectures provide a template for a distributed architecture that lends itself to many of these emerging applications. Agents can be used as mediators between heterogeneous data sources, providing the means to interoperate, using ontologies for describing the data contained in their information sources, and communicating with the others via an agent communication language.

The inherent autonomy of agents enables the agent-based system to perform its tasks without direct external intervention. Agents can not only react to specific events but can also be proactive, polling the environment for events to determine the proper action in a given circumstance. Despite the increased level of autonomy in an agent-based system, however, the system itself may not be able to automate all levels of intelligent activity. Human users may be required to perform higher-level intelligent tasks. An intelligent distributed agent architecture that allows flexible interactions between participating agents maps well to applications that require seamless integration with humans.

For problems characterized by dynamic knowledge, it is infeasible to predict and analyze all possible interactions between modules at design time. Flexible interaction among agents at runtime enables an agent-based system to effectively handle dynamic, unpredictable knowledge. Although the knowledge of some problems is dynamic, the change is often local, affecting a subset of requirements. Therefore, some agents can be designated to deal with the dynamic knowledge of a problem, and the functionality of those agents can evolve, reflecting the changes that are encountered.

Agent technology offers mechanisms for knowledge sharing and interoperability between autonomous software and hardware systems characterized by heterogeneous languages and platforms. Agents can be used as mediators between these various systems, facilitating interoperability.

There are some important distinctions between ESs and agent-based systems, which make the latter ideal for integrating individual ESs with other ESs and other systems. Expert systems rely on the user to initiate the reasoning process and to accomplish any action associated with the recommendations provided by the system. The integration of human interaction, then, is assumed and has been greatly facilitated by development tool kits and environments. Expert systems have a fixed set of rules that clearly define their reasoning process. Further, the expert system's knowledge base impacts the modularity and scalability of the system. As new functions are introduced into the system, the central knowledge base grows increasingly large. New rules risk conflicts with old, and changed rules potentially impact more functions than the developer may have planned.

Expert systems are fundamentally built as a cohesive product with a single overarching goal. Despite early emphasis on linking knowledge bases and integrating expertise, those goals are rarely achieved, perhaps because of the issues of combining knowledge bases without the benefit of a standard interface technique. Further, the system components are rarely reused outside the system for which they were built. In fact, it is quite common to throw away one prototype and completely rebuild the next version from scratch. Thus, tools are built with an emphasis on rapid prototyping rather than on facilitating component reuse.

On the other hand, agents are inherently autonomous. That does not mean that the integration of human interaction is necessarily complex; the human is simply another agent in the society of agents. Agents interact with their environment and adapt to new conditions. Thus, an application that characteristically incorporates dynamic changes in its data and rules is more naturally accommodated by agent-based techniques. Agents, on the other hand, are extremely modular, such as self-contained programs that can readily be reused across applications. The social interaction inherent in agents facilitates mobile and distributed systems, with formal standards in place outlining interfaces even between agents assumed to be heterogeneous in design.

7.2.2 Agents and Service-Oriented Architecture Solutions

A virtual enterprise is a temporary alliance where different economic organizations are combining their strengths to provide a specific service traditionally provided by a single enterprise. They come together to share skills and resources in order to better respond to business opportunities, and whose cooperation is supported by computer networks and adequate IT tools and protocols.

7.2.3 Agent-Oriented Software Engineering

The way to manage complexity is by decomposing a complex system or process into smaller modules that can be designed independently—that is, *modularization*. Modularization ensures easy maintenance and updates of complex systems by separating the high-frequency intramodule linkages from the low-frequency intermodule linkages, limiting the scope of interactions between the modules by hiding the intramodule relations inside a module box. Based on the idea of modularity, constructs such as objects, components, software agents, and Web services have been continuously invented and evolved for developing software applications.

Object-oriented programming (OOP) provides a foundation for software engineering that uses objects and their interactions to design applications and computer programs. Component-based development (CBD) provides a coarser-grained construct for larger systems, and separates the interface from the behavior of the construct to support public communication between the components that know about each other before runtime. SOA goes further by using XML-based and network-addressable interface as well as XML-based messages and standard protocols for open communication among all software applications on the Internet. Unlike OOP, CBD, and SOA, agent-oriented computing (AOC) is used to model and implement solutions to semi- or ill-structured problems, which are too complex to be completely characterized and precisely described. An agent is used to perform more autonomous activities in solving complex problems. To achieve this, the knowledge or rules for governing the behavior of an agent are separated from the behavior of the agent.

7.2.3.1 Object-Oriented Programming

Object-oriented programming (OOP) is a software engineering paradigm that uses *objects* and their interactions to design applications and computer programs. A program is seen as a collection of cooperating objects, as opposed to the traditional view in which a program is seen as a list of instructions to the computer. The OOP paradigm addressed issues of reuse and maintenance by encapsulating data and their corresponding operations within an object class. To change a data structure, it is often necessary to change all the functions related to the data structure. OOP was deployed as an attempt to promote greater flexibility and maintainability, since the concepts of objects in the problem domain have a higher chance of being stable than functions and data structures.

7.2.3.2 Component-Based Development

Component-based development (CBD) is another branch of the software engineering discipline, with an emphasis on the decomposition of the engineered systems into functional or logical components with well-defined interfaces used for communication across the components. CBD includes a component model and an interface model. The component model specifies for each component how the component behaves in an arbitrary environment, and the interface model specifies for each component how the component interacts with its environment.

OOP versus CBD: A *component* is a small group of objects working together to provide a system function. It can be viewed as a black box at the level of a large system function. At a fine level of granularity, we use objects to hide behavior and data. At a coarser level of granularity, we use components to do the same. OOP focuses on the encapsulation of both data and the behavior of an object. CBD goes further by supporting public interfaces used for communication across the components.

Object-oriented (OO) technologies provide rich models to describe problem domains; however, it is not enough to adapt to the changing requirements of real-world software systems. OOP assumes that it is possible to identify and solve almost all problems before coding, while CBD, and later SOA and AOC, adopt a more pragmatic approach that believes business system development is an incremental process and changes are an inescapable aspect of software design. Specifically, objects are too fine grained and do not make a clear separation between computational and compositional aspects. Components were then proposed to encapsulate the computational details. Software development can be improved using CBD, since applications can be quickly assembled from a large collection of prefabricated and interoperable software components.

Components inherit much of the characteristics of objects in the OO paradigm. But the component notion goes further by separating the interface from the component model. OO reuse usually means reusing class libraries in a particular OO programming language or environment. For example, to be able to reuse a SmallTalk or Java class in OO programming, you have to be conversant in the SmallTalk or Java languages. A component, by using a public interface, can be reused without even knowing which programming language or platform it uses internally.

7.2.3.3 Service-Oriented Architecture

A service is defined as an act or performance that one party can offer to another that is essentially intangible and does not result in the ownership of anything. Its production may or may not be tied to a physical product.

A *Web service*, as defined by the World Wide Web Consortium (W3C), is a software application identified by a Uniform Resource Identifier (URI) whose interfaces and bindings are capable of being defined, described, and discovered by XML and which supports direct interactions with other software applications using XML-based messages via Internet-based protocols. Web services are self-contained and modular business applications based on open standards. They can share information using standardized communication protocols and ask each other to do something—that is, ask for a service.

Service-oriented architecture (SOA) utilizes Web services as fundamental elements for developing applications. It is an emerging paradigm for architecting and implementing business collaborations within and across organizational boundaries. SOA enables the seamless and flexible integration of Web services or applications over the Internet. It supports universal interoperability and location transparency. SOA reduces the complexity of business applications in large-scale and open environments by providing flexibility through the service-based abstraction of organizational applications.

SOA versus CBD: Compared with a component, a service is relatively coarse grained and should be able to encapsulate more details. SOA is an extension of earlier OOP and CBD concepts. CBD supports close system architecture where the exact source of the required functionality and communication is predetermined. Propriety standards and the implementation-dependent specification of components have hindered CBD from achieving its primary goal of facilitating reuse. The point of SOA is service specification rather than implementation. SOA focuses on the user's view of a computing object or application—that is, the services that are provided and the metadata that define how the services behave. In SOA, a service has a published network-addressable interface. A published interface is exposed to the network and may not be changed so easily because the clients of the published interface are not known.

The difference between a component and a service in the interface is analogous to an intranet-based site only accessible by employees of the company and an Internet site accessible by anyone. A service does not define any structural constraints for the loose coupling of services over the Internet. CBD architectures, on the other hand, represent a case of tight coupling. For example, in CORBA, there is a tight coupling between the client and the server, as both must share the same interface, with a stub on the client side and the corresponding skeleton on the server side. Composing a system from a number of components is relatively controlled compared with dynamic service composition. Moreover, CBD assumes the early binding of components; that is, the caller unit knows exactly which component to contact before runtime. SOA adopts a more flexible approach where the binding is deferred to runtime, enabling a change of the source of provision each time.

The idea of the service model differs from CBD by the fact that SOA supports the logical separation of service need from service fulfillment. Delivering software as a service brings about new business models and opportunities for software development and service provision in demand-driven dynamic environments.

7.2.3.4 Agent-Oriented Computing

Recently, the agent-oriented computing paradigm has gained popularity among researchers attempting to develop complex systems for business process management. Terms such as *autonomous agent* and *agency* are now commonly used in computer science literature. On the other hand, a rich body of literature on the concept of agency and the role of agents already exists in the institutional economics and business fields. We will attempt to reconcile the various terms from the two research traditions.

Table 7.1 shows a comparison between the object-oriented, component-based, and agent-oriented methods.

An *actor* is someone who performs an act—that is, does something. An actor may be a person, an organizational unit, or a computer program. An actor may be

Table 7.1   Comparison between Object-Oriented, Component-Based, and Agent-Oriented Methods

	Object Oriented	*Component Based*	*Agent Oriented*
Origin	Semantic net	Semantic net	Symbolic AI and behavior-based AI
Computational entity	Objects	Components	Agents
State parameters for an entity	Unlimited	Unlimited	Intentional stance like belief, desire of an agent
Activity	Passive	Passive	Proactive with self-control thread, automated
Computational process	Message passing and method response	Message passing and method response	Message passing and method response
Message types	Unlimited, handle messages by method vocation	Unlimited, handle messages by method vocation	Speech act
Language abstraction elements	Objects, classes, modules	Reuse, design patterns, application framework	Agents, class, modules, design patterns, framework, organization, roles, society, goal
Modeling abstraction mechanism	Fine object as an action entity, method invocation used for describing interaction. Static organizational modeling, no semantics	Stronger abstraction mechanism, e.g., component, reuse, design patterns, application frameworks	Agents as coarse and automated computing entity, social ability (organization, roles, etc.), dynamic organizational modeling

(Continued)

Table 7.1 (Continued) Comparison between Object-Oriented, Component-Based, and Agent-Oriented Methods

	Object Oriented	Component Based	Agent Oriented
Analysis and design	Abstraction in fine granularity; object model, dynamic model, function model	Abstraction in coarser granularity; component library, framework library, object bus	Coarser abstraction; role model, interaction model, agent model, service model, acquaintance model
Encapsulation	State and behavior	State and behavior, application framework	State and behavior, behavior activation
Organizational relationship	Static syntactic inheritance	Static syntactic and structural inheritance	An interactive network with inter- and intra-subsystem element interactions, multiple organizational relationships (hierarchy, marketing, etc.)
Interaction	Syntactic interaction, invoking methods or functions, simple message passing	Syntactic interaction, invoking methods or functions, simple message passing	Interaction on knowledge and social levels
System problem-solving	Event/behavior driven; design-time decision; no automated problem-solving; predefined execution	Event driven; design-time decision making	Goal-driven automated, and flexible problem-solving; active decision making at run time, reasoning ability

(Continued)

Table 7.1 (Continued) Comparison between Object-Oriented, Component-Based, and Agent-Oriented Methods

	Object Oriented	*Component Based*	*Agent Oriented*
Complexity in problem-solving	Generic system, with predefined interactive relationships	Not strong enough for modeling complex systems	Building complex distributed systems (data, ability, and control)
System property	Somehow encapsulation, autonomy, passivity, and interaction	Somehow encapsulation, autonomy, passivity, and interaction	Autonomy, reactivity, sociality, proactiveness; loss of control, greater freedom, uncertainty, and indeterminism
Interrelationship		Evolution (specialization) of OO	Evolution (specialization) of OO and CB

completely autonomous; that is, it acts of its own volition. If the actor is authorized to do something on behalf of someone else, the actor is an *agent* of the other party.

An *agent* is an actor (performer) who acts on the behalf of a principal by performing a service. The agent provides the service when it receives a request for service from the principal. The principal–agent relationship is found in most employer–employee relationships. A classic example of the agency relationship occurs when stockholders hire top executives to run the corporation on their behalf. To manage the relationship between a principle and an agent of the principle, agency theory is concerned with various mechanisms used for aligning the interests of the agent with those of the principal, such as piece rates/commissions and profit sharing.

A *broker* is a special type of agent that acts on behalf of two symmetrical parties or principals: the buyer and the seller. A broker mediates between the buyer (the service-requesting party) and the seller (the service-providing party). Acting as an intermediary between two or more parties in negotiating agreements, brokers use appropriate mediating techniques or processes to improve the dialogue between the parties, aiming to help them reach an agreement. Normally, all parties must view the mediator as neutral or impartial.

Autonomy is the power or right of self-government. It refers to the capacity of a rational individual to make an informed, uncoerced decision. Being *autonomous* means that the actor is independent; that is, the actor can decide what to do and how to do it. An autonomous agent, therefore, is a system that is situated in, and part of, an environment; it senses the environment and acts on it, over time, in pursuit of its agenda as derived from its principal. As an agent acts on behalf of the principal, the agent cannot be fully autonomous. The principal may give the agent different levels of choice in performing the task. For example, the principal can tell the agent what to do but leave it to the agent to decide how to do it.

In computer science, the term *agent* is used to describe a piece of software or code that acts on behalf of a human user or another program in a relationship of agency. A *software agent* may denote a software-based entity that enjoys the properties of autonomy (agents operate without the direct intervention of its principal humans), social ability (agents communicate with other agents), reactivity (agents perceive their environment and respond to changes in a timely fashion), and proactivity (agents do not simply act in response to their environment but are able to exhibit goal-directed behavior by taking some initiative). The agent-based computing paradigm is devised to help computers know what to do, solve problems on behalf of human beings, and support cooperative working. The behavior of software agents is empowered by humans and implemented by software.

Agent-oriented computing (AOC) is based on the idea of delegating tasks and the responsibility of solving a complex problem to a group of software agents. It emphasizes the autonomy and mutual cooperation of agents in performing tasks in open and complex environments. A complex system can be viewed as a network of agents acting concurrently, each finding itself in an environment produced by its interactions with the other agents in the system. AOC is used to model and implement intelligent solutions to semi- or ill-structured problems, which are too complex to be completely characterized and precisely described. AOC offers a natural way to view and describe systems as individual problem-solving agents pursuing high-level goals defined by their principals. It represents an emerging computing paradigm that helps understand and model complex real-world problems and systems, by concentrating on high-level abstractions of autonomous entities.

7.2.3.4.1 AOC versus OOP

From a software engineering point of view, object-oriented methodologies provide a solid foundation for agent-oriented modeling. AOC can be viewed as a specialization of OOP. OOP proposes viewing a computational system as made up of modules that are able to communicate with one another. AOC specializes the framework by representing the mental states and rich interactions of the modules (agents). While objects emphasize passive behavior (i.e., they are invoked in response to a message), agents support more autonomous behavior, which can be achieved by specifying a number of rules for interpreting the environmental states and knowledge for governing multiple degrees of freedom of activities. In relation to this, mechanisms of knowledge acquisition, modeling, and maintenance have become important foundations for the building of autonomous agents.

7.2.3.4.2 AOC versus SOA

A software agent is a software-based entity that enjoys the properties of autonomy, social ability, reactivity, and proactivity. A Web service is a software application on the Web based on open standards. Though both of them are computer applications that perform tasks on behalf of principals (human beings or other programs), the focus of software agents is on their autonomous properties for solving complex problems, while Web services are characterized by their open access standards and protocols over the Internet. While a Web service may only know about itself, agents often have awareness of other agents and their capabilities as interactions occur among the agents. Agents are inherently communicative, whereas Web services are passive until invoked. Agents cooperate autonomously and flexibly, and by forming teams and coalitions, they can assemble higher-level and more comprehensive services. However, current standards or languages for Web services do not provide for flexible composing functionalities, such as brokering and negotiation in e-marketplaces. Web services are inherently less autonomous and independent than software agents.

7.3 Developing Agent-Based Systems

7.3.1 Design of Agent-based Systems

The design of agent-based systems is driven by a number *constraints*, including autonomy, the need to interact, information overload, multiple interface, ensuring quality, adaptability, privacy concerns, search costs, and the need to track identity. Not all of these constraints can be equally satisfied by a given design, and trade-offs need to be made.

   a. *Autonomy*: Autonomy is the capability of an agent to follow its goals without interactions or commands from the user or another agent. An autonomous agent does not require the user's approval at every step of executing its task, but is able to act on its own. Agents can be used to implement a complementary interaction style, in which users *delegate* some of their tasks to software agents which then perform them autonomously on their behalf. This indirect manipulation style engages the user in a cooperative process in which human and software agents both initiate communication, monitor events, and perform tasks. In contrast, direct manipulation requires the user to initiate all tasks explicitly and to monitor all events.

With agents performing autonomous actions, users are now facing issues of trust and control over their agents. The issue of *trust* is that by engaging an agent to perform tasks (such as selecting a seller), the user must be able to trust the agent to do so in an informed and unbiased manner. The user would also like to specify the *degree of autonomy* of the agent. For example, the user may not want to delegate decisions to the agent that have legal or financial consequences, although a buyer agent is capable of not only finding the cheapest seller, but also placing a purchase order.

b. *Interactions*: The behavior of an individual agent is thus often not comprehensible outside its social structure—its relationships with other agents. For example, the behavior of a buyer agent in an auction cannot be fully explained outside the context of the auction itself, and of the conventions that govern it (for example, in which order—ascending or descending— bids must be made, and how many rounds of bidding there are in the auction). Agents typically only have *a partial representation* of their environment, and are thus *limited* in their ability in terms of their expertise, access to resources, location, and so forth—to interact with it. Thus, they rely on other agents to achieve goals that are outside their scope or reach. They also need to coordinate their activities with those of other agents to ensure that their goals can be met, avoiding interference with one another.

> As we do not control all the agents, one can also not assume that the agents are cooperative. Some agents may be benevolent and agree on some protocol of interaction, but others will be *self-interested* and follow their own best interests. For example, in an electronic marketplace, buyer and seller agents are pursuing their own best interests (making profit) and need to be constrained by conventions.

c. *Information overload*: Organizations wish to find relevant information and offerings to make good deals and generate profit. However, the large set of sellers, in conjunction with the *multiple interfaces* they use, makes it almost impossible for an individual human to have a comprehensive overview the market. One solution has been to provide *portals* or common entry points to the Web; these portals periodically collect information from a multitude of information sources and condense then into a format that users find easier to process, typically taking the form of a hierarchical index.

d. *Interfaces*: One of the difficulties in finding information (e.g., when comparing the offerings of different sellers) is the large number of different interfaces used to present the information. Not only are store fronts organized differently, sellers do not follow the same conventions when describing their products and terms of sale. For instance, some sellers include the shipping costs in the posted price; others will advertise one price, but add a handling charge to each order. A solution is to agree on common vocabularies, but to be useful, these must also be widely adopted. This has become achievable with the advent of extensible markup language (XML) for associating metacontent with data and the developments like ontology representation languages (OWL) in the Semantic Webs.

e. *Adaptability*: Users differ in their status, level of expertise, needs, and preferences. The issue of adaptability is that of tailoring information to the features of the user, for example, by selecting the products most suitable for the user from a catalog, or adapting the presentation style during the interaction with the user. Any approach to tailoring information involves creating and maintaining a user model. When creating a user model, two cases need to be distinguished: for first time visitors no information is available about them, and the user characteristics must be recognized during the interaction; on subsequent visits, a detailed user model about a visitor is already available and can be used to tailor the information.

f. *Identity*: Buyers and sellers need to be represented by unique identities for the benefit of authentication, nonrepudiation, and tracking. One way of assigning a unique identity to trading partners is to use one of the many unique labels which are readily available on the Internet, for example, an e-mail address, or a Yahoo! account name. A problem with this approach is that it is also very easy to obtain a new identity, thus making authentication, nonrepudiation, or tracking schemes that rely on such identities impractical. Similarly, a user could obtain multiple identities and pretend to represent multiple different parties, where instead there is only one.

g. *Quality*: Shopping online lack the immediate mechanisms for establishing trustworthiness. How can you trust a seller, with whom you have had no previous encounter, whether the order you placed would be fulfilled satisfactorily? For example, any seller in an online auction could claim that the item offered for sale is in superior condition, when the buyer cannot physically verify that claim. One solution is to solicit feedback about the performance of a seller (respectively, buyer) from buyers (respectively, sellers) after order fulfilment which is then made available and shared with the future buyers.

h. *Privacy*: One way of personalizing interactions between buyers and sellers is for the seller to collect information about a buyer from the buyer's behavior (e.g., their clickstream). The buyer may not be aware of the information collected, nor does she always have control over what information is gathered about her. Although effective from the seller's perspective, this is not a desirable situation from the perspective of the buyer. Users are typically not willing to allow just anyone to examine their preferences and usage patterns, in particular without their knowledge or consent. They want to remain in control, and decide on an interaction-by-interaction basis which information is conveyed to the seller. A solution that addresses the force of privacy concerns must put the user in charge of which information is collected and who it is made available to.

i. *Search:* It can be quite challenging for appropriate buyers and sellers to find each other. In a static marketplace, each buyer can store a contact list of sellers for each product, and then quickly locate an appropriate seller when a particular product is needed. However, an electronic marketplace is dynamic, buyers and sellers can join and leave the marketplace, and change their requirements and offerings qualitatively and quantitatively at any point in time. One possible solution to these problems is to use a mediator which can match potential trading partners in the market. With the introduction of mediators, buyers and sellers no longer maintain their own lists of contacts, or need to contact a large number of alternate trading partners to find the optimal one.

7.3.2 Agent-Based E-Business Systems

One of the most promising areas of applications for agent technology is e-business. In this section, we describe a group of architectural patterns for agent-based e-business systems. These patterns relate to front-end e-business activities that involve interaction with the user, and delegation of user tasks to agents. Patterns capture well-proven, common solutions, and guide developers through the process of designing systems.

Patterns are reusable solutions to recurring design problems and provide a vocabulary for communicating these solutions to others. The documentation of a pattern goes beyond documenting a problem and its solution. It also describes the forces or design constraints that give rise to the proposed solution; these are the undocumented and generally misunderstood features of a design. Constraints can be thought of as pushing or pulling the problem toward different solutions. A good pattern balances these constraints. A set of patterns, where one pattern leads to other patterns that refine or are used by it, is known as a pattern language. A pattern language can be likened to a process: it guides designers who wants to use those patterns through their application in an organic manner. As each pattern of the pattern language is applied, some of the constraints affecting the design will be resolved, while new unresolved constraints will arise as a consequence. The process of using a pattern language in a design is complete when all constraints have been resolved.

Figure 7.1 depicts the patterns that are important for any agent-based e-business system.

The starting point for the language is the *Agent Society* pattern, which motivates the use of agents for building the application. At the next level of refinement, the diagram leads the designer to consider the patterns *Agent as Delegate*, *Agent as Mediator*, and *Common Vocabulary*.

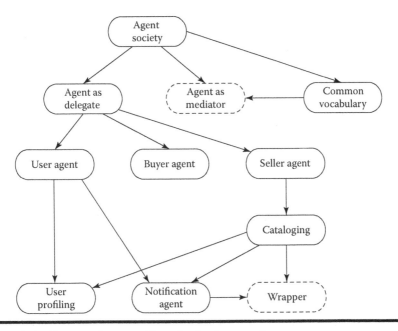

Figure 7.1   Patterns for agent-based e-business systems.

Agent as Delegate and the patterns it links to deal with the design of agents that act on behalf of a single user. The agent as mediator pattern guides the designer through the design of agents that facilitate between a group of agents and their users. *Common Vocabulary* provides guidelines for defining exchange formats between agents. The rest of Figure 7.1 shows refinement of the *Agent as Delegate* pattern. For example, the *User Agent* pattern prescribes to use a single locus of interaction with the user and represent the concurrent transactions a user participates in as buyer and seller agents. User interaction also includes profiling the user (*User Profiling*) and subscribing to information (e.g., the status of an auction) relevant to the user (*Notification Agent*).

1. *Agent Society*: The application is modeled as a society of agents. Agents are autonomous computational entities (autonomy), which interact with their environment (reactivity) and other agents (social ability) in order to achieve their own goals (proactiveness). These computational entities act on behalf of users or groups of users.

   A society of agents can be viewed from two perspectives:

   a. *Micro View*: A society of agents emerges as a result of the interaction of agents; this approach constructs an agent society incrementally from a catalog of interaction patterns. These interaction patterns are described in terms of roles that agents can play and their interactions and may also specify any societal constraints or policies that need to be satisfied. Roles are *abstract* loci of control. Protocols (or patterns of interaction) describe the way the roles interact.

b. *Macro View*: The society of agents imposes constraints and policies on its component agents; this approach identifies top-level goals for the system and decompose them recursively, until we can assign them to individual agents.

Micro- and macro views of the society mutually reinforce each other. For example, emergent behaviors such as specialization of agents leads to the notion of roles that agents play, which allow us to codify expectations about an agent. Roles, in turn, impose restrictions on the possible behaviors of agents. Policies defines constraints imposed by the societies on these roles. As an example of a policy, consider an agent-mediated auction, which specifies conventions specific to its auction type (for example, regarding the order of bids; ascending in an English auction, descending in a Dutch auction) that participating agents must comply with in order for the auction to function correctly.

Many types of applications, including electronic commerce systems, can be modeled using User, Task, Service, and Resource roles, and their sub-types. The User role encapsulates the behaviour of managing a user's task agents, providing a presentation interface to the user and collecting profile information about the user, among other responsibilities. A Task role represents users in a specific task, typically long-lived, rather than one-shot transaction. A Mediator role typically provides a service to a group of users. It mediates the interaction between two or more agents through this service.

The Resource role abstracts information sources. These can be legacy data sources wrapped by "glue" that converts generic requests from other agents to the API of the data source

2. *Agent as Delegate*: This agent acts *on behalf* of the user. They are the system's interface to the user and manage task specific agents such as buyer and seller agents on the user's behalf. User agents can also learn about the needs of the user by building a user profile from a history of interactions. This user profile allows sellers to customize their offerings to specific user tastes, while the user profile controls what part of a profile sellers can access.

3. *Common Vocabulary*: In the example, for buyer and seller agents to understand each other, they need to agree on a common message format that is grounded in a common ontology. The ontology defines product-related concepts that each party must use during interaction, their attributes, and valid value ranges. On receiving a message, the seller agent translates the request to seller-specific format and fetches the contents of the product database.

It is impractical to define general-purpose ontology for agent interaction. These are unlikely to include the intricacies of all possible domains. Instead, the common ontology will be application-specific. Given such an ontology, the communicating agents need to map their internal representations to the shared ontology. Examples are XML-based ontologies for electronic commerce like xCBL, cXML, and RosettaNet.

4. *User Agent*: User agents form the *interface* between the user and the system receive the user's queries and feedback, and present information *tailored* to users. A user agent delegates the user's queries or orders (offers to buy/sell an item) to a trader agent and manages the various buyer and seller agents on behalf of its user. The user agent manages the user's profile and controls who can access it. Sections of the profile can be restricted to a subset of the sellers.

5. *Buyer Agent*: A buyer agent can *tailor* the selection and presentation of products to the needs of its user. It *locates* seller agents that offer the requested product or service and negotiates with them about price and other terms of sale (e.g., shipping).

6. *Seller Agent*: A seller agent *offers* products and services to buyer agents (directly or through a market). It answers queries for information about its owner's products or services, responds to RFPs, and enters into negotiation with buyer agents. A seller agent encapsulates its *execution state* and the seller's selling *strategy* (e.g., a function for setting bids).

7. *User Profiling*: During the interaction with a user, the system builds a user profile by static user modelling, classifying the user into pre-defined user classes (stereotypes), or dynamic user modeling (monitoring the user activity and changing the profile dynamically). In addition to generic information about the user, user profiles contain a collection of interests. Interests contain descriptions of the topics the user is interested in. Interests may also contain weights (e.g., fuzzy logic quantifiers) that define the degree of interest the user has in a topic. The agent may also tailor its interaction style, providing more or less detail depending on the user's receptivity.

It is advisable to limit the amount of explicit input required from the user, for example, in the form of rules. Although manual setting of the user profile results in a very precise profile, this may be feasible only for a few advanced users. On the other hand, while starting with an order, it is advantageous to know as much as possible about the user in order to keep the learning phase short. The user agent can request the user to provide demographic information such as sex, age, and profession, which allow us to group the user into a class. The interests of the user are then initialized to those typical for this class of users.

From the point of view of limiting user input, initializing the user profile by observing the user's behavior over time is most desirable. The user's personal preferences can then be deduced using cluster analysis. This has the added advantage that it is easy to adapt the user profile to changes in their interests. Once the user profiles have been initialized, the user agent can update the profile by soliciting feedback on query results from the user, or to rate a seller on her quality of service after the order has been fulfilled.

8. *Cataloging*: Existing product catalogs can be integrated with the agent-based subsystem through catalog agents. Each catalog agent is a WRAPPER that agentifies an existing catalog, converting a catalog-specific scheme to a common schema schema used by the product extractor. In addition to filtering the contents of the catalog against the buyer's profile, discounts can also be offered to individual customers to entice existing customers to remain loyal to the business, as well as attract new customers.

A user profile contains predictive information about the user's preferences toward product features as defined by the product categories. The view may also be customized regarding generic traits of the user (e.g., his level of expertise, job, or age). A product extractor dynamically creates a customized view on the catalog. It selects the products that best match the customer's preferences by comparing the product features with those contained in the profile.

Tailoring the product catalog to the user resolves the constraint of information overload. A large electronics parts catalog, for example, may contain 50,000 parts, of which only a small subset are relevant to the needs of an individual customer. By extracting a customized view of the catalog we show only those parts matching features specified in the user profile.

9. *Notification Agent:* A notification agent resides close to the information source and monitors the information source for changes of interest by registering with the information source or by continuously polling it. Notification agent can be considered a special type of mobile agent that only move to a single remote location. A notification agent is created with a condition, typically comprising an event (such as the posting of a product for sale) and a boolean expression on the event data (such as the name of a product). Whenever it detects an event of the specified type at the remote location, it evaluates this condition. If the condition is satisfied, the agent notifies the user agent.

7.3.3 Agent-Based Software Engineering

Agent platforms deliver communication mechanisms and basic functions for identification and localization of agents and their services. Agent platform is akin to a middleware, supporting actions and communications among the agents, as well as sometimes delivering functionalities of an integrated development environment supporting design, implementation and running of the agent-based systems.

The platform is usually distributed as a library of classes or modules, consisting of basic, easily extensible implementations of key functions of the system. The agent platforms can be very diverse considering the goal and the way of realization of particular agent features; consequently, these platforms are very different considering their structure, agent model, and the communication methods.

7.3.3.1 Agent-Based Platform JADE

JADE (Java Agent Development) is a Java-based environment facilitating implementation of distributed systems conforming to Foundation for Intelligent Physical Agents (FIPA) standards.

JADE introduces two important organization entities:

1. Platform can be distributed among several nodes, consists of many agent containers, the communication among them is realized using IIOP, agent container is a process that is transparent for agents, provides them with a complete execution environment and makes possible their running in parallel; the communication among the containers is realized using RMI.
2. Containers provide implementation of the basic agents: AMS, DF, and ACC that are activated during the initialization of the platform:
   - *Agent Management System* (AMS) deals with naming, agent localization, and authentication services.
   - *Directory Facilitator* (DF) deals with registration and service localization services.
   - *Message Transport Services* (MTS) deals with Agent Communication Channel (ACC), providing communication method among the agents inside and outside the platform.

Agent Management (AM) provides a work environment for the agents—it fixes the logical reference model for creating, registering, localization, communication, and migration of agents, describing the behavior of the Agent Platform (AP). It describes necessary platform elements and defines basic services as well as ontologies needed for their realization.

The communication among the agents is realized using asynchronous exchange of messages. The agents have their own queues where the messages coming from other agents are placed (after placing the message the recipient is notified by the platform). The platform describes three main schemes of the communication:

- If the recipient is placed in the same container, the message is passed as an event, no unnecessary conversions are realized.
- If the recipient is placed in another container on the same platform, the message is passed using RMI.
- If the recipient is placed on another platform, Agent Communication Channel (ACC) is requested to deliver an appropriate messaging service. Next, a relevant Message Transport Protocol (MTP) is found, that will be used for delivering the message.

7.4 Summary

Software agents are among those software technologies that hold particular promise for an IT infrastructure that enhances rather than inhibits the rapid response of business processes to newly arising requirements. This chapter introduced the concept of agents and related aspects like properties, taxonomy, architecture, and communications. It looked into the characteristics of agents essential for virtual enterprises. The chapter ended with various aspects related to the development of agent-based e-business system.

Chapter 8

Cloud Computing

Many motivating factors have led to the emergence of cloud computing. Businesses require services that include both infrastructure and application workload requests while meeting defined service levels for capacity, resource tiering, and availability. IT delivery often necessitates costs and efficiencies that create a perception of IT as a hindrance, not a strategic partner. Issues include underutilized resources, the overprovisioning or underprovisioning of resources, lengthy deployment times, and a lack of cost visibility. Virtualization is the first step toward addressing some of these challenges by enabling improved utilization through server consolidation, workload mobility through hardware independence, and the efficient management of hardware resources.

The virtualization system is a key foundation for the cloud computing system. We stitch together computer resources so as to appear as one large computer behind which the complexity is hidden. By coordinating, managing, and scheduling resources such as CPUs, networks, storage, and firewalls in a consistent way across internal and external premises, we create a flexible cloud infrastructure platform. This platform includes security, automation and management, interoperability and openness, self-service, pooling, and dynamic resource allocation. In the view of cloud computing we are advocating, applications can run within an external provider, in internal IT premises, or in combination as a hybrid system; what matters is how they are run, not where they are run.

Cloud computing builds on virtualization to create a service-oriented computing model. This is done through the addition of resource abstractions and controls to create dynamic pools of resources that can be consumed through the network. Benefits include economies of scale, elastic resources, self-service provisioning, and cost transparency. The consumption of cloud resources is enforced through resource metering and pricing models that shape user behavior. Consumers benefit through leveraging allocation models such as pay-as-you-go to gain greater cost efficiency, lower barriers to entry, and immediate access to infrastructure resources.

8.1 Cloud Definition

The National Institute of Standards and Technology (NIST) working definition is as follows:

> *Cloud computing is a model for enabling convenient, on-demand network access to a shared pool of configurable computing resources (e.g., networks, servers, storage, applications, and services) that can be rapidly provisioned and released with minimal management effort or service provider interaction. This cloud model promotes availability and is composed of five essential characteristics, three delivery models, and four deployment models.*

The five essential characteristics are

- On-demand self-service
- Broad network access
- Resource pooling
- Rapid elasticity
- Measured service

The three delivery models are

1. Infrastructure as a service (IaaS)
2. Platform as a service (PaaS)
3. Software as a service (SaaS)

The four deployment models are

1. Public cloud
2. Private cloud
3. Hybrid cloud
4. Community cloud

Cloud computing is the IT foundation for cloud services and consists of technologies that enable cloud services. The key attributes of cloud computing are shown in Table 8.1. The key attributes of cloud services are described in Table 8.2.

Table 8.1   Key Attributes of Cloud Computing

Attributes	Description
Offsite, third-party provider	In the cloud execution, it is assumed that third party provides services. There is also a possibility of in-house cloud service delivery.
Accessed via the Internet	Services are accessed via standard-based, universal network access. It can also include security and quality-of-service options.
Minimal or no IT skill required	There is a simplified specification of requirements.
Provisioning	It includes self-service requesting, near real-time deployment, and dynamic and fine-grained scaling.
Pricing	Pricing is based on usage-based capability and it is fine grained.
User interface	User interface includes browsers for a variety of devices and with rich capabilities.
System interface	System interfaces are based on Web Services APIs providing a standard framework for accessing and integrating among cloud services.
Shared resources	Resources are shared among cloud services users; however, via configuration options with the service, there is the ability to customize.

8.2 Cloud Characteristics

Large organizations such as IBM, Dell, Microsoft, Google, Amazon, and Sun have already started to take strong positions with respect to cloud computing provision. They are so invested in this latest paradigm that the success is virtually guaranteed. The essential characteristics of cloud environments include the following:

1. On-demand self-service that enables users to consume computing capabilities (e.g., applications, server time, network storage) as and when required.
2. Rapid elasticity and scalability that allows functionalities and resources to be rapidly, elastically, and automatically scaled out or in, as demand rises

Table 8.2 Key Attributes of Cloud Services

Attributes	Description
Infrastructure systems	It includes servers, storage, and networks that can scale as per user demand.
Application software	It provides web-based user interface, Web Services APIs, and a rich variety of configurations.
Application development and deployment software	It supports the development and integration of cloud application software.
System and application management software	It supports rapid self-service provisioning and configuration and usage monitoring.
IP networks	They connect end users to the cloud and the infrastructure components

or drops. Automatic services are provided according to the current demand requirement. This is done automatically using software automation, enabling the expansion and contraction of service capability, as needed. This dynamic scaling needs to be done while maintaining high levels of reliability and security.

These characteristics have the following features:

a. An economical model of cloud computing that enables consumers to order required services (computing machines and/or storage devices). The requested service could scale rapidly upward or downward on demand.

b. Machine responsibility that does not require any human to control the requested services. The cloud architecture manages on-demand requests (increases or decreases in service requests), availability, allocation, subscription, and the customer's bill.

3. Broad network access. Capabilities are available over the network and accessed through standard mechanisms that promote use by heterogeneous thin or thick client platforms (e.g., cell phones, tablets, laptops, and workstations). Capabilities are available over the network and a continuous Internet connection is required for a broad range of devices such as PCs, laptops, and mobile devices, using standards-based APIs (e.g., ones based on HTTP). Deployments of services in the cloud include everything from using business applications to the latest application on the newest smartphones.

4. Multitenancy and resource pooling that allows heterogeneous computing resources (e.g., hardware, software, processing, servers, network bandwidth) to be combined to serve multiple consumers—such resources being

dynamically assigned. A virtualized software model is used that enables the sharing of physical services, storage, and networking capabilities. Regardless of the deployment model, whether it be a public cloud or private cloud, the cloud infrastructure is shared across a number of users. A cloud vendor provides a pool of resources (e.g., computing machines, storage devices and network) to customers. The cloud architecture manages all available resources via global and local managers for different sites and local sites, respectively. This feature allows big data to be distributed on different servers, which is not possible in traditional models such as supercomputing systems.

5. Measured provision to automatically control and optimize resource allocation and to provide a metering capability to determine the usage for billing purpose, allowing easy monitoring, controlling, and reporting. Resource usage can be monitored, controlled, and reported, providing transparency for both the provider and consumer of the utilized service. Uses metering for managing and optimizing the service and to provide reporting and billing information. In this way, consumers are billed for services according to how much they have actually used during the billing period. In short, cloud computing allows for the sharing and scalable deployment of services, as needed, from almost any location, and for which the customer can be billed based on actual usage.

Thus, in summation, cloud computing allows for the sharing and scalable deployment of services, as needed, from almost any location, and for which the customer can be billed based on actual usage.

8.2.1 Cloud Storage Infrastructure Requirements

Data are growing at an immense rate, and with the combination of technology trends such as virtualization with increased economic pressures, the exploding growth of unstructured data, and regulatory environments that require enterprises to keep data for longer periods of time, it is easy to see the need for a trustworthy and appropriate storage infrastructure. Storage infrastructure is the backbone of every business. Whether a cloud is public or private, the key to success is creating a storage infrastructure in which all resources can be efficiently utilized and shared. Because all data reside on storage systems, data storage becomes even more crucial in a shared infrastructure model.

The most important cloud infrastructure requirements are as follows:

1. Elasticity: Cloud storage must be elastic, so that it can quickly adjust with the underlying infrastructure according to changing customer demands and comply with service-level agreements (SLAs).

2. Automatic: Cloud storage must have the ability to be automated so that policies can be leveraged to make underlying infrastructural changes such as placing user and content management in different storage tiers and geographic locations quickly and without human intervention.

3. Scalability: Cloud storage needs to scale quickly up and down according to the needs of the customer. This is one of the most important requirements and what makes cloud storage so popular.

4. Recovery performance: Cloud storage infrastructure must provide fast and robust data recovery as an essential element of the service.

5. Reliability: As more and more users are depending on the services offered by the cloud, reliability becomes increasingly important. Various users of cloud storage want to make sure that their data are reliably backed up for disaster recovery purposes, and the cloud should be able to continue to run in the presence of hardware and software failures.

6. Operational efficiency: Operational efficiency is key to successful business enterprise, which can be ensured by better management of storage capacities and cost benefit. Both these features should be integral to cloud storage.

7. Latency: Cloud storage models are not suitable for all applications, especially real-time applications. It is important to measure and test network latency before committing to a migration. Virtual machines (VMs) can introduce additional latency through the time-sharing nature of the underlying hardware, and the unanticipated sharing and reallocation of machines can significantly affect runtimes.

8. Data retrieval: Once the data are stored on the cloud, they should be easily accessible from anywhere at anytime if a network connection is available. Ease of access to data in the cloud is critical in enabling the seamless integration of cloud storage into existing enterprise workflows and to minimize the learning curve for cloud storage adoption.

9. Data security: Security is one of the major concerns of cloud users. As different users store more of their own data in a cloud, they want to ensure that their private data are not accessible to other users who are not authorized to use it. If this is the case, then users should use private clouds, because security is assumed to be tightly controlled in this case. But in the case of public clouds, data should either be stored on a partition of a shared storage system, or cloud storage providers must establish multitenancy policies to allow multiple business units or separate companies to securely share the same storage hardware.

Storage is the most important component of IT infrastructure. Unfortunately, it is almost always managed as a scarce resource because it is relatively expensive and the consequences of running out of storage capacity can be severe. Nobody wants to take on the responsibilities of storage managers, thus storage management suffers from slow provisioning practices.

8.3 Cloud Delivery Models

Cloud computing is not a completely new concept for the development and operation of Web applications. It allows for the most cost-effective development of scalable Web portals on highly available and fail-safe infrastructures. In the cloud computing system, we have to address different fundamentals such as virtualization, scalability, interoperability, quality of service, failover mechanisms, and cloud deployment models (private, public, hybrid) within the context of the taxonomy. The taxonomy of the cloud includes the different participants along with the attributes and technologies that are coupled to address their needs and the different types of services—for example, *X as a service* (XaaS) offerings, where *X* is software, hardware, platforms, infrastructure, data, or business (Figures 8.1 and 8.2).

8.3.1 Infrastructure as a Service (IaaS)

The IaaS model is about providing computing and storage resources as a service. According to NIST, IaaS is defined as follows:

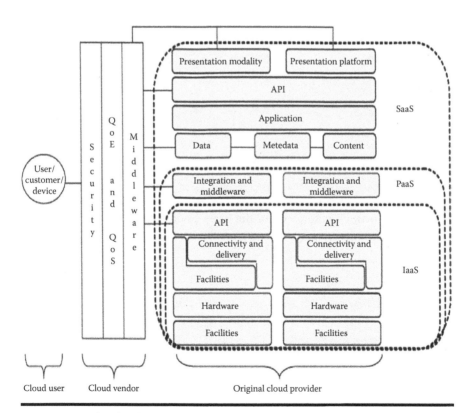

Figure 8.1   Cloud reference model.

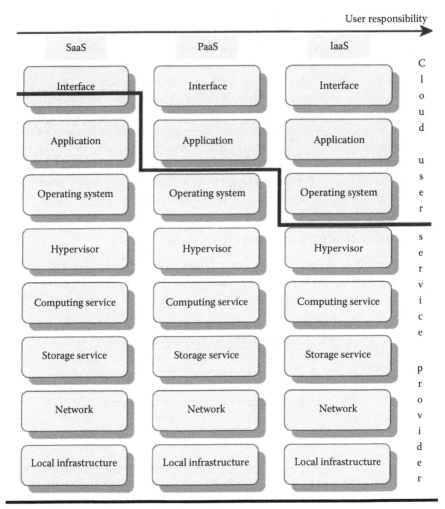

Figure 8.2 Portfolio of services for the three cloud delivery models.

The capability provided to the consumer is to provision processing, storage, networks, and other fundamental computing resources where the consumer is able to deploy and run arbitrary software, which can include operating systems and applications. The consumer does not manage or control the underlying cloud infrastructure but has control over operating systems, storage, deployed applications, and possibly limited control of select networking components (e.g., host firewalls).

The user of IaaS has single ownership of the hardware infrastructure allotted to him/her (it may be a virtual machine) and can use it as if it is his/her own machine on a remote network and he/she has control over the operating system and software on it. IaaS is illustrated in Figure 8.1. The IaaS provider has control over the actual hardware, and the cloud user can request an allocation of virtual resources, which are then allocated by the IaaS provider to the hardware (generally without any manual intervention). The cloud user can manage the virtual resources as desired, including installing any desired operating system, software, and applications. Therefore, IaaS is well suited for users who want complete control over the software stack that they run; for example, the user may be using heterogeneous software platforms from different vendors, and they may not like switching to a platform service where only selected middleware is available. Well-known IaaS platforms include Amazon EC2, Rackspace, and Rightscale. Additionally, traditional vendors such as HP, IBM, and Microsoft offer solutions that can be used to build a private IaaS.

8.3.2 Platform as a Service (PaaS)

The PaaS model is to provide a system stack or platform for application deployment as a service. NIST defines PaaS as follows:

> *The capability provided to the consumer is to deploy into the cloud infrastructure consumer-created or acquired applications created using programming languages and tools supported by the provider. The consumer does not manage or control the underlying cloud infrastructure including network, servers, operating systems, or storage, but has control over the deployed applications and possibly application hosting environment configurations.*

Figure 8.2 shows a PaaS model diagrammatically. The hardware, as well as any mapping of hardware to virtual resources such as virtual servers, is controlled by the PaaS provider. Additionally, the PaaS provider supports selected middleware, such as a database, Web application server, and so on, as shown in the figure. The cloud user can configure and build on top of this middleware—for example, to define a new database table in a database. The PaaS provider maps this new table onto their cloud infrastructure. Subsequently, the cloud user can manage the database as needed and develop applications on top of this database. PaaS platforms are well suited to those cloud users who find that the middleware they are using matches the middleware provided by one of the PaaS vendors. This enables them to focus on the application. Windows Azure, Google App Engine, and Hadoop are some well-known PaaS platforms. As in the case of IaaS, traditional vendors such as HP, IBM, and Microsoft offer solutions that can be used to build a private PaaS.

8.3.3 Software as a Service (SaaS)

SaaS is about providing the complete application as a service. SaaS has been defined by NIST as follows:

> *The capability provided to the consumer is to use the provider's applications running on a cloud infrastructure. The applications are accessible from various client devices through a thin client interface such as a web browser (e.g., web-based email). The consumer does not manage or control the underlying cloud infrastructure including network, servers, operating systems, storage, or even individual application capabilities, with the possible exception of limited user-specific application configuration settings.*

Any application that can be accessed using a Web browser can be considered an SaaS. These points are illustrated in Figure 8.2. The SaaS provider controls all the layers apart from the application. Users who log in to the SaaS service can both use and configure the application for their use. For example, users can use Salesforce.com to store their customer data. They can also configure the application—for example, requesting additional space for storage or adding additional fields to the customer data that are already being used. When configuration settings are changed, the SaaS infrastructure performs any management tasks needed (such as allocating additional storage) to support the changed configuration. SaaS platforms are targeted toward users who want to use the application without any software installation (in fact, the motto of Salesforce.com, a prominent SaaS vendor, is "No software"). However, for advanced usage, some small amount of programming or scripting may be necessary to customize the application for usage by the business (e.g., adding additional fields to customer data). In fact, SaaS platforms such as Salesforce.com allow many of these customizations to be performed without programming, instead specifying business rules that are simple enough for nonprogrammers to implement. Prominent SaaS applications include Salesforce.com for CRM, Google Docs for document sharing, and Web e-mail systems such as Gmail, Hotmail, and Yahoo! Mail. IT vendors such as HP and IBM also sell systems that can be configured to set up SaaS in a private cloud; SAP, for example, can be used as an SaaS offering inside an enterprise.

Table 8.3 presents a comparison of the three cloud delivery models.

8.4 Cloud Deployment Models

8.4.1 Private Clouds

A private cloud has an exclusive purpose for a particular organization. The cloud resources may be located on or off the premises and may be owned and managed by the consuming organization or a third party. This might be an organization

Table 8.3   Comparison of Cloud Delivery Models

Service Type	IaaS	PaaS	SaaS
Service category	VM rental; online storage	Online operating environment, online database, online message queue	Application and software rental
Service customization	Server template	Logic resource template	Application template
Service provisioning	Automation	Automation	Automation
Service accessing and using	Remote console, Web 2.0	Online development and debugging, integration of offline development tools and cloud	Web 2.0
Service monitoring	Physical resource monitoring	Logic resource monitoring	Application monitoring
Service-level management	Dynamic orchestration of physical resources	Dynamic orchestration of logic resources	Dynamic orchestration of application
Service resource optimization	Network virtualization, server visualization, storage visualization	Large-scale distributed file system. Database, middleware, etc.	Multitenancy
Service measurement	physical resource Metering	Logic resource usage metering	Business resource usage metering
Service integration and combination	Load balance	SOA	SOA, mashup
Service security	Storage encryption and isolation, VM isolation, VLAN; SSL/SSH	Data isolation, operating environment isolation, SSL	Data isolation, operating environment isolation, SSL; Web authentication and authorization

who has decided to harness the potential infrastructure cost savings of a virtualized architecture on top of its existing hardware. The organization feels unable to remotely host their data, so they are looking to the cloud to improve their resource utilization and automate the management of such resources. Alternatively, an organization may wish to extend its current IT capability by using an exclusive, private cloud that is remotely accessible and provisioned by a third party. Such an organization may feel uncomfortable with their data being held alongside a potential competitor's data in the multitenancy model.

8.4.2 Public Clouds

A public cloud, as its name implies, is available to the general public and is managed by an organization. The organization may be a business (such as Google) or an academic or governmental department. The cloud computing provider owns and manages the cloud infrastructure. The existence of many different consumers within one cloud architecture is referred to as a *multitenancy* model.

8.4.3 Hybrid Clouds

Hybrid clouds are formed when more than one type of cloud infrastructure is utilized for a particular situation. For instance, an organization may utilize a public cloud for some aspect of its business, yet also have a private cloud on the premises for sensitive data. As organizations begin to exploit cloud service models, it is increasingly likely that a hybrid model will be adopted, as the specific characteristics of each of the different service models are harnessed. The key enablers here are the open standards by which data and applications are implemented, since if portability does not exist, then vendor lock-in to a particular cloud computing provider becomes likely. The lack of data and application portability has been a major hindrance to the widespread uptake of grid computing, and this is one aspect of cloud computing that can facilitate much more flexible, abstract architectures.

8.4.4 Community Clouds

Community clouds are a model of cloud computing where the resources exist for a number of parties who have a shared interest or cause. This model is very similar to the single-purpose grids that collaborating research and academic organizations have created to conduct large-scale scientific experiments (*e-science*). The cloud is owned and managed by one or more of the collaborators in the community, and it may exist either on or off the premises.

8.5 Cloud Benefits

Cloud computing is an attractive paradigm that promises numerous benefits inherent to the characteristics, as mentioned previously. These include

- The optimization of a company's capital investment by reducing the cost of purchasing hardware and software, resulting in a much lower total cost of ownership and, ultimately, a whole new way of looking at the economics of scale and operational IT
- The simplicity and agility of operations and use, requiring minimal time and effort to provision additional resources
- Enabling an enterprise to tap into a talent pool, as and when needed, for a fraction of the cost of hiring staff or retaining the existing staff and, thus, enabling the key personnel in the organizations to focus more on producing value and innovation for the business
- Enabling small organizations to access the IT services and resources that would otherwise be out of their reach, thus placing large organizations and small businesses on a level playing field
- Providing novel and complex computing architectures and innovation potential
- Providing mechanisms for disaster recovery and business continuity through a variety of fully outsourced information and communications technology (ICT) services and resources

Cloud computing can be massively scalable, and there are built-in benefits to efficiency, availability, and high utilization that, in turn, result in reduced capital expenditure and operational costs. It permits seamless sharing and collaboration through virtualization. In general, cloud computing promises cost savings, agility, innovation, flexibility, and simplicity. The offerings from vendors, in terms of services of the application, platform, and infrastructure nature, are continuing to mature, and the cost savings are becoming particularly attractive in the current competitive economic climate. Another broader aim of cloud technology is to make supercomputing available to enterprises in particular and the public in general.

The major benefits of the cloud paradigm can be distilled into its inherent flexibility and resiliency, the potential for reducing costs, the availability of very large amounts of centralized data storage, the means to rapidly deploy computing resources, and its scalability.

1. Flexibility and resiliency: A major benefit of cloud computing is its flexibility, though cloud providers cannot provide infinite configurations for provisioning flexibility and will seek to offer structured alternatives. They might offer a choice among a number of computing and storage resource configurations at different capabilities and costs, and the cloud customer will have to adjust his or her requirements to fit one of those models.

The flexibility offered by cloud computing can be in terms of

- The automated provisioning of new services and technologies
- Acquiring increased resources on an as-needed basis
- The ability to focus on innovation instead of maintenance details
- Device independence
- Freedom from having to install software patches
- Freedom from concerns about updating servers

Resiliency is achieved through the availability of multiple redundant resources and locations. As autonomic computing becomes more mature, self-management and self-healing mechanisms can ensure the increased reliability and robustness of cloud resources. Also, disaster recovery and business continuity planning are inherent in using the provider's cloud computing platforms.

2. Reduced costs: Cloud computing offers reductions in system administration, provisioning expenses, energy costs, software licensing fees, and hardware costs. The cloud paradigm, in general, is a basis for cost savings because capabilities and resources can be paid for incrementally without the need for large investments in computing infrastructure. This model is especially true for adding the storage costs of large database applications. Therefore, capital costs are reduced and replaced by manageable, scalable operating expenses.

There may be some instances, particularly for long-term, stable computing configurations, where cloud computation might not have a cost advantage over using one's internal resources or directly leasing equipment. For example, if the volume of data storage and computational resources required are essentially constant and there is no need for rapid provisioning and flexibility, an organization's local computational capabilities might be more cost effective than using a cloud.

Resources are used more efficiently in cloud computing, resulting in substantial support and energy cost savings. The need for highly trained and expensive IT personnel is also reduced; client organizational support and maintenance costs are reduced dramatically because these expenses are transferred to the cloud provider, including 24/7 support that in turn is spread onto a much larger base of multiple tenants or clients.

Another reason for migrating to the cloud is the drastic reduction in the cost of power and energy consumption.

3. Centralized data storage: Many data centers are an ensemble of legacy applications, operating systems, hardware, and software and are a support and maintenance nightmare. This situation requires more specialized maintenance personnel, increased costs because of a lack of standardization, and a higher risk of crashes. The cloud not only offers larger amounts of data storage resources than are normally available in local, corporate computing systems, it also enables decreases or increases in the resources used as per the requirements, with the corresponding adjustments in operating cost. This centralization of storage infrastructure results in cost efficiencies in utilities, real estate, and trained personnel. Also, data protection mechanisms are much easier to implement and monitor in a centralized system than in large numbers of computing platforms that might be widely distributed geographically and in different parts of an organization.

4. Reduced time to deployment: In a competitive environment where the rapid evaluation, development, and deployment of new approaches, processes, solutions, or offerings is critical, the cloud offers the means to use powerful computational or large storage resources at short notice, without requiring sizable initial investments of finances, effort, or time (for hardware, software, and personnel). Thus, this rapid provisioning of the latest technologically upgraded and enhanced resources can be accomplished at relatively low cost (with a minimal cost of replacing discontinued resources) and offers the client access to advanced technologies that are constantly being acquired by the cloud provider. The improved delivery of services obtained by rapid cloud provisioning improves time to market and, hence, market growth.

5. Scalability: Cloud computing provides the means, within limits, for a client to rapidly provision computational resources to meet increases or decreases in demand. Cloud scalability provides for optimal resources so that computing resources are provisioned as per the requirements, seamlessly ensuring maximum cost benefit to the clients. Since the cloud provider operates on a multitenancy utility model, the client organization has to pay only for the resources it is using at any particular time.

8.6 Cloud Technologies

Virtualization is widely used to deliver customizable computing environments on demand. Virtualization technology is one of the fundamental components of cloud computing, allowing the creation of a secure, customizable, and isolated execution environment for running applications without affecting other users' applications. The basis of this technology is the ability of a computer program—or a combination of software and hardware—to emulate an executing environment separate from the one that hosts such programs. For instance, we can run Windows on top of a virtual machine that is itself running on Linux. Virtualization provides a great opportunity to build elastically scalable systems that can provision additional capability with minimum costs.

8.6.1 Virtualization

Resource virtualization is at the heart of most cloud architectures. The concept of virtualization allows an abstract, logical view on the physical resources and includes servers, data stores, networks, and software. The basic idea is to pool physical resources and manage them as a whole. Individual requests can then be served as required from these resource pools. For instance, it is possible to dynamically generate a certain platform for a specific application at the very moment when it is needed; instead of a real machine, a virtual machine is instituted.

Resource management grows increasingly complex as the scale of a system as well as the number of users and the diversity of applications using the system increase. Resource management for a community of users with a wide range of applications running under different operating systems is a very difficult problem. Resource management becomes even more complex when resources are oversubscribed and users are uncooperative. In addition to external factors, resource management is affected by internal factors, such as the heterogeneity of the hardware and software systems, the ability to approximate the global state of the system and to redistribute the load, and the failure rates of different components. The traditional solution for these in a data center is to install standard operating systems on individual systems and rely on conventional operating system techniques to ensure resource sharing, application protection, and performance isolation. System administration, accounting, security, and resource management are very challenging for the service providers in this setup; application development and performance optimization are equally challenging for the users.

The alternative is resource virtualization, a technique analyzed in this chapter. Virtualization is a basic tenet of cloud computing—which simplifies some of the resource management tasks. For instance, the state of a virtual machine (VM) running under a virtual machine monitor (VMM) can be saved and migrated to another server to balance the load. At the same time, virtualization allows users to operate in environments with which they are familiar rather than forcing them to work in idiosyncratic environments. Resource sharing in a VM environment requires not only ample hardware support and, in particular, powerful processors but also architectural support for multilevel control. Indeed, resources such as CPU cycles, memory, secondary storage, and I/O and communication bandwidth are shared among several VMs; for each VM, resources must be shared among multiple instances of an application. There are two distinct approaches for virtualization:

- *Full virtualization* is feasible when the hardware abstraction provided by the VMM is an exact replica of the physical hardware. In this case, any operating system running on the hardware will run without modifications under the VMM.
- *Paravirtualization* requires some modifications of the guest operating systems because the hardware abstraction provided by the VMM does not support all the functions the hardware does.

One of the primary reasons that companies implement virtualization is to improve the performance and efficiency of the processing of a diverse mix of workloads. Rather than assigning a dedicated set of physical resources to each set of tasks, a pooled set of virtual resources can be quickly allocated as needed across all workloads. Reliance on the pool of virtual resources allows companies to improve latency. This increase in service delivery speed and efficiency is a function of the distributed nature of virtualized environments and helps to improve the overall time-to-realize value. Using a distributed set of physical resources, such as servers, in a more flexible and efficient way delivers significant benefits in terms of cost savings and improvements in productivity.

1. The virtualization of physical resources (such as servers, storage, and networks) enables substantial improvement in the utilization of these resources.
2. Virtualization enables improved control over the usage and performance of the IT resources.
3. Virtualization provides a level of automation and standardization to optimize your computing environment.
4. Virtualization provides a foundation for cloud computing.

Virtualization increases the efficiency of the cloud, which makes many complex systems easier to optimize. As a result, organizations are able to achieve the necessary performance and optimization to be able to access data that were previously either unavailable or very hard to collect. Big data platforms are increasingly used as sources of enormous amounts of data about customer preferences, sentiment, and behaviors (see Chapter 8, Section 8.1.1, "What Is Big Data?"). Companies can integrate this information with internal sales and product data to gain insight into customer preferences to make more targeted and personalized offers.

8.6.1.1 Characteristics of Virtualized Environments

In a virtualized environment, there are three major components: *guest*, *host*, and *virtualization layer*. The guest represents the system component that interacts with the virtualization layer rather than with the host, as would normally happen. The host represents the original environment where the guest is supposed to be managed. The virtualization layer is responsible for recreating the same or a different environment where the guest will operate.

Virtualization has three characteristics that support the scalability and operating efficiency required for big data environments:

1. *Partitioning*: In virtualization, many applications and operating systems are supported in a single physical system by partitioning (separating) the available resources.
2. *Isolation*: Each virtual machine is isolated from its host physical system and other virtualized machines. Because of this isolation, if one virtual instance crashes, the other virtual machines and the host system are not affected. In addition, data are not shared between one virtual instance and another.
3. *Encapsulation*: A virtual machine can be represented (and even stored) as a single file, so you can identify it easily based on the services it provides. For example, the file containing the encapsulated process could be a complete business service. This encapsulated virtual machine could be presented to an application as a complete entity. Thus, encapsulation could protect each application so that it does not interfere with another application.

Virtualization abstracts the underlying resources and simplifies their use, isolates users from one another, and supports replication, which, in turn, increases the elasticity of the system. Virtualization is a critical aspect of cloud computing, equally important to the providers and consumers of cloud services, and plays an important role in

■ System security, because it allows the isolation of services running on the same hardware
■ Portable performance and reliability, because it allows applications to migrate from one platform to another
■ The development and management of services offered by a provider
■ Performance isolation

8.6.1.1.1 Virtualization Advantages

Virtualization—the process of using computer resources to imitate other resources—is valued for its capability to increase IT resource utilization, efficiency, and scalability. One obvious application of virtualization is server virtualization, which helps organizations to increase the utilization of physical servers and potentially save on infrastructure costs; companies are increasingly finding that virtualization is not limited only to servers but is valid and applicable across the entire IT infrastructure, including networks, storage, and software. For instance, one of the most important requirements for success with big data is having the right level of performance to support the analysis of large volumes and varied types of data. If a company only virtualizes the servers, they may experience bottlenecks from other infrastructure elements such as storage and networks; furthermore, they are less likely to achieve the latency and efficiency that they need and are more likely to expose the company to higher costs and increased security risks. As a result, a company's entire IT environment needs to be optimized at every layer from the network to the databases, storage, and servers—virtualization adds efficiency at every layer of the IT infrastructure.

For a provider of IT services, the use of virtualization techniques has a number of advantages:

1. Resource usage: Physical servers rarely work to capacity because their operators usually allow for sufficient computing resources to cover peak usage. If virtual machines are used, any load requirement can be satisfied from the resource pool. If the demand increases, it is possible to delay or even avoid the purchase of new capacities.
2. Management: It is possible to automate resource pool management. Virtual machines can be created and configured automatically as required.
3. Consolidation: Different application classes can be consolidated to run on a smaller number of physical components. Besides server or storage consolidation, it is also possible to include entire system landscapes, data and databases, networks, and desktops. Consolidation leads to increased efficiency and thus to cost reduction.
4. Energy consumption: Supplying large data centers with electric power has become increasingly difficult, and seen over its lifetime, the cost of energy required to operate a server is higher than its purchase price. Consolidation reduces the number of physical components. This, in turn, reduces the expenses of energy supply.
5. Less space required: Each and every square yard of data center space is scarce and expensive. With consolidation, the same performance can be obtained with a smaller footprint, and the costly expansion of an existing data center might possibly be avoided.
6. Emergency planning: It is possible to move virtual machines from one resource pool to another. This ensures better availability of the services and makes it easier to comply with service-level agreements. Hardware maintenance windows are inherently no longer required.

8.6.1.1.2 Virtualization Benefits

Since the providers of cloud services tend to build very large resource centers, virtualization leads not only to a size advantage but also to a more favorable cost situation. This results in the following benefits for the customer:

1. Dynamic behavior: Any request can be satisfied just in time and without any delays. In case of bottlenecks, a virtual machine can draw on additional resources (such as storage space and I/O capabilities).
2. Availability: Services are highly available and can be used day and night without stopping. In the event of technology upgrades, it is possible to hot-migrate applications because virtual machines can easily be moved to an up-to-date system.
3. Access: The virtualization layer isolates each virtual machine from the others and from the physical infrastructure. This way, virtual systems feature multitenant capabilities and, using the *roles* concept, it is possible to safely delegate management functionality to the customer. Customers can purchase IT capabilities from a self-service portal (*customer emancipation*).

> The most direct benefit from virtualization is to ensure that MapReduce engines work better. Virtualization will result in better scale and performance for MapReduce. Each one of the map and reduce tasks needs to be executed independently. If the MapReduce engine is parallelized and configured to run in a virtual environment, you can reduce management overheads and allow for expansions and contractions in the task workloads. MapReduce itself is inherently parallel and distributed. By encapsulating the MapReduce engine in a virtual container, you can run what you need whenever you need it. With virtualization, you can increase your utilization of the assets you have already paid for by turning them into generic pools of resources.

8.6.1.1.3 Virtualization Challenges

There are side effects of virtualization—notably, the performance penalty and the hardware costs. All privileged operations of a VM must be trapped and validated by the VMM, which ultimately controls system behavior; the increased overhead has a negative impact on performance. The cost of the hardware for a VM is higher than the cost for a system running a traditional operating system because the physical hardware is shared among a set of guest operating systems and it is typically configured with faster and/or multicore processors, more memory, larger disks, and additional network interfaces compared with a system running a traditional operating system.

A drawback of virtualization is the fact that the operation of the abstraction layer itself requires resources. Modern virtualization techniques, however, are so sophisticated that this overhead is not too significant; due to the particularly effective interaction of current multicore systems with virtualization technology, this performance loss plays only a minor role in today's systems. In view of possible savings and the quality benefits perceived by the customers, the use of virtualization pays off in nearly all cases.

8.6.2 Service-Oriented Architecture

Service-oriented architecture (SOA) introduces a flexible architectural style that provides an integration framework through which software architects can build applications using a collection of reusable functional units (services) with well-defined interfaces, which it combines in a logical flow. Applications are integrated at the interface (i.e., contract) level, not at the implementation level. This allows greater flexibility since applications are built to work with any implementation of a contract, rather than take advantage of a feature or idiosyncrasy of a particular system or implementation. For example, different service providers (of the same interface) can be dynamically chosen based on policies such as price, performance, or other quality of system (QoS) guarantees, current transaction volume, and so on.

Another important characteristic of an SOA is that it allows many-to-many integration; that is, a variety of consumers across an enterprise can use and reuse applications in a variety of ways. This ability can dramatically reduce the cost/complexity of integrating incompatible applications and increase the ability of developers to quickly create, reconfigure, and repurpose applications as business needs arise. Benefits include reduced IT administration costs, easier business process integration across organizational departments and with trading partners, and increased business adaptability.

SOA is a logical way of designing a software system to provide services to either end-user applications or to other services distributed in a network, via published and discoverable interfaces. To achieve this, SOA reorganizes a portfolio of previously siloed software applications and support infrastructure in an organization into an interconnected collection of services, each of which is discoverable and accessible through standard interfaces and messaging protocols. Once all the elements of an SOA are in place, existing and future applications can access the SOA-based services as necessary. This architectural approach is particularly applicable when multiple applications running on varied technologies and platforms need to communicate with each other.

The essential goal of an SOA is to enable general-purpose interoperability among existing technologies and extensibility to future purposes and architectures. SOA lowers interoperability hurdles by converting monolithic and static systems into modular and flexible components, which it represents as services that can be requested through an industry-standard protocol. Much of SOA's power and flexibility derives from its ability to leverage standards-based functional services, calling them when needed on an individual basis or aggregating them to create composite applications or multistage business processes. The building-block services might employ preexisting components that are reused and can also be updated or replaced without affecting the functionality or integrity of other independent services. In this latter regard, the services model offers numerous advantages over large monolithic applications, in which modifications to some portions of the code can have unintended and unpredictable effects on the rest of the code to which it is tightly bundled. Simply put, an SOA is an architectural style, inspired by the service-oriented approach to computing, for enabling extensible interoperability.

SOA as a design philosophy is independent of any specific technology—for example, Web services or J2EE. Although the concept of SOA is often discussed in conjunction with Web services, these two are not synonymous. In fact, SOA can be implemented without the use of Web services—for example, using Java, C#, or J2EE. However, Web services should be seen as a primary example of a message delivery model that makes it much easier to deploy an SOA. Web service standards are key to enabling interoperability as well as other key issues, including quality of system (QoS), system semantics, security, management, and reliable messaging.

8.6.2.1 Advantages of SOA

Enterprises may use SOA for the following:

- Implementing end-to-end collaborative business processes: The term *end-to-end business process* signifies that a succession of automated business processes and information systems in different enterprises (which are typically involved in intercompany business transactions) are successfully integrated. The aim is to provide seamless interoperation and interactive links between all the relevant members in an extended enterprise—ranging from product designers, suppliers, trading partners, and logistics providers to end customers. At this stage, an organization moves into the highest strategic level of SOA implementation. The deployment of services becomes ubiquitous, and federated services collaborate across enterprise boundaries to create complex products and services. Individual services in this extended enterprise may originate from many providers, irrespective of company-specific systems or applications.
- Implementing enterprise service orchestrations: This basic SOA entry point focuses on a typical implementation within a department or between a small number of departments and enterprise assets and comprises two steps. The first step is transforming enterprise assets and applications into an SOA implementation. This can start by service enabling existing individual applications or creating new applications using Web services technology. This can begin by specifying a Web service interface into an individual application or application element (including legacy systems). The next step after this basic Web service implementation is implementing service orchestrations out of the service-enabled assets or newly created service applications.

- Service enabling the entire enterprise: The next stage in the SOA entry point hierarchy is when an enterprise seeks to provide a set of common services based on SOA components that can be used across the entire organization. Enterprise-wide service integration is achieved on the basis of commonly accepted standards. This results in achieving service consistency across departmental boundaries and is a precursor to integrating an organization with its partners and suppliers. Consistency is an important factor for this configuration as it provides both a uniform view to the enterprise and its customers as well as ensuring compliance with statutory or business policy requirements.

One problem when implementing an SOA at the enterprise level or implementing a cross-enterprise collaborative SOA is how to manage the SOA model, how to categorize the elements in this model, and how to organize them in such a way that the different stakeholders reviewing the model can understand it. Toward this end, it is often convenient to think of the SOA as comprising a number of distinct layers of abstraction that emphasize service interfaces, service realizations, and compositions of services into higher-level business processes. Each of these describes a logical separation of concerns by defining a set of common enterprise elements; each layer uses the functionality of the layer below it, adding new functionality, to accomplish its objective. The logical flow employed in the layered SOA development model may focus on a top-down development approach, which emphasizes how business processes are decomposed into a collection of business services and how these services are implemented in terms of preexisting enterprise assets.

8.6.2.2 Layers in SOA

SOA is comprised of the following six distinct layers:

1. Domains: A business domain is a functional domain comprising a set of current and future business processes that share common capabilities and functionality and can collaborate with each other to accomplish a higher-level business objective, such as loans, insurance, banking, finance, manufacturing, marketing, and human resources.
2. Business processes: This layer is formed by subdividing a business domain, such as distribution, into a small number of core business processes, such as purchasing, order management, and inventory, which are made entirely standard for use throughout the enterprise; having a large number of fine-grained processes leads to tremendous overheads and inefficiency, and hence,

having a small collection of coarser-grained processes that are usable in multiple scenarios is a better option.

3. Business services: For any process, the the right business service is to subdivide it into increasingly smaller subprocesses until the process cannot be divided any further. The resulting subprocesses then become candidate indivisible (i.e., singular) business services for implementation. Business services automate generic business tasks that provide value to an enterprise and are part of standard business processes. The more processes that an enterprise decomposes in this way, the more commonality across these subprocesses can be achieved. In this way, an enterprise has the chance of building an appropriate set of reusable business services.

This layer relies on the orchestration interface of a collection of business-aligned services to realize reconfigurable end-to-end business processes. Individual services or collections of services that exhibit various levels of granularity are combined and orchestrated to produce new composite services that not only introduce new levels of reuse but also allow the reconfiguration of business processes.

The interfaces get exported as service descriptions in this layer using a service description language such as Web Services Description Language (WSDL). The service description can be implemented by a number of service providers, each offering various choices of qualities of service based on technical requirements in the areas of availability, performance, scalability, and security.

During the exercise of defining business services, it is also important to take existing utility logic, ingrained in code, and expose it as a collection of services, which themselves become candidate services that specify not the overall business process but rather the mechanism for implementing the process. This exercise should thus yield two categories of services: business functionality services that are reusable across multiple processes and a collection of fine-grained utility (or commodity) services, which provide value to and are shared by business services across the organization. Examples of utility services include services implementing calculations, algorithms, and directory management services.

4. Infrastructure services: Infrastructure services are subdivided into technical utility services, access services, management and monitoring services, and interaction services; these are not specific to a single line of business but are reusable across multiple lines of business. They also include mechanisms that seamlessly interlink services that span enterprises. This can, for example, include the policies, constraints, and specific industry messages and interchange standards (such as the need to conform to specific industry

message and interchange standards such as EDIFACT, SWIFT, xCBL, ebXML BPSS, or RosettaNet) that an enterprise—say, within a particular vertical marketplace—must conform to in order to work with other similar processes. Access services are dedicated to transforming data and integrating legacy applications and functions into the SOA environment. This includes the wrapping and service enablement of legacy functions.

5. Service realizations: This layer is the component realization layer that uses components for implementing services out of preexisting applications and systems found in the operational systems layer. Components comprise autonomous units of software that may provide a useful service or a set of functionality to a client (business service) and have meaning in isolation from other components with which they interoperate.

6. Operational systems: This layer is used by components to implement business services and processes. This layer contains existing enterprise systems or applications, including customer relationship management (CRM) and ERP systems and applications, legacy applications, database systems and applications, and other packaged applications. These systems are usually known as *enterprise information systems*.

8.7 Business Processes with SOA

Every enterprise has unique characteristics that are embedded in its business processes. Most enterprises perform a similar set of repeatable routine activities that may include the development of manufacturing products and services, bringing these products and services to market, and satisfying the customers who purchase them. Automated business processes can perform such activities. We may view an automated business process as a precisely choreographed sequence of activities systematically directed toward performing a certain business task and bringing it to completion. Examples of typical processes in manufacturing firms include among other things new product development (which cuts across research and development, marketing, and manufacturing), customer order fulfillment (which combines sales, manufacturing, warehousing, transportation, and billing), and financial asset management. The potential to design, structure, and measure processes and determine their contribution to customer value makes them an important starting point for business improvement and innovation initiatives.

The largest possible process in an organization is the value chain. The value chain is decomposed into a set of core business processes and support processes necessary to produce a product or product line. These core business processes are subdivided into activities. An activity is an element that performs a specific function within a process. Activities can be as simple as sending or receiving a message or as complex as coordinating the execution of other processes and activities. A business process may encompass complex activities, some of which run on back-end systems, such as credit checks, automated billing, purchase orders, stock updates, and shipping, or even such frivolous activities as sending a document and filling out a form. A business process activity may invoke another business process in the same or a different business system domain. Activities will inevitably vary greatly from one company to another and from one business analysis effort to another.

At runtime, a business process definition may have multiple instantiations, each operating independently of the other, and each instantiation may have multiple activities that are concurrently active. A process instance is a defined thread of activity that is being enacted (managed) by a workflow engine. In general, instances of a process, its current state, and the history of its actions will be visible at runtime and expressed in terms of the business process definition so that

- Users can determine the status of business activities and business
- Specialists can monitor the activity and identify potential improvements to the business process definition

8.7.1 Process

A *process* is an ordering of activities with a beginning and an end; it has inputs (in terms of resources, materials, and information) and a specified output (the results it produces). We may thus define a process as any sequence of steps that is initiated by an event; transforms information, materials, or commitments; and produces an output. A business process is typically associated with operational objectives and business relationships—for example, an insurance claims process or an engineering development process. A process may be wholly contained within a single organizational unit or may span different enterprises, such as in a customer–supplier relationship. Typical examples of processes that cross organizational boundaries are purchasing and sales processes jointly set up by buying and selling organizations, supported by EDI and value-added networks. The Internet is now a trigger for the design of new business processes and the redesign of existing ones.

A business process is a set of logically related tasks performed to achieve a well-defined business outcome. A (business) process view implies a horizontal view of a business organization and looks at processes as sets of interdependent activities designed and structured to produce a specific output for a customer or a market. A business process defines the results to be achieved, the context of the activities, the relationships between the activities, and the interactions with other processes and resources. A business process may receive events that alter the state of the process and the sequence of activities. A business process may produce events as input to other applications or processes. It may also invoke applications to perform computational functions, and it may post assignments to human work lists to request actions by human actors. Business processes can be measured, and different performance measures apply, such as cost, quality, time, and customer satisfaction.

A business process exhibits the following behaviors:

- It may contain defined conditions triggering its initiation in each new instance (e.g., the arrival of a claim) and defined outputs at its completion.
- It may involve formal or relatively informal interactions between participants.
- It has a duration that may vary widely.
- It may contain a series of automated activities and/or manual activities. Activities may be large and complex, involving the flow of materials, information, and business commitments.
- It exhibits a very dynamic nature, so it can respond to demands from customers and to changing market conditions.
- It is widely distributed and customized across boundaries within and between enterprises, often spanning multiple applications with very different technology platforms.
- It is usually long running; a single instance of a process such as an order to cash may run for months or even years.

Every business process implies processing—a series of activities (processing steps) leading to some form of transformation of data or products for which the process exists. Transformations may be executed manually or in an automated way. A transformation will encompass multiple processing steps. Finally, every process delivers a product, such as a mortgage or an authorized invoice. The extent to which the end product of a process can be specified in advance and can be standardized impacts the way that processes and their workflows can be structured and automated.

Processes have decision points. Decisions have to be made with regard to the routing and allocation of processing capacity. In a highly predictable and standardized environment, the trajectory in the process of a customer order will be established in advance in a standard way. Only if the process is complex and if the conditions of the process are not predictable will routing decisions have to be made on the spot. In general, the customer orders will be split into a category that is highly proceduralized (and thus automated) and a category that is complex and uncertain. Here, human experts will be needed, and manual processing is a key element of the process.

8.7.2 Workflow

A workflow system automates a business process, in whole or in part, during which documents, information, or tasks are passed from one participant to another for action, according to a set of procedural rules. Workflows are based on document life cycles and form-based information processing, so they generally support well-defined, static, clerical processes. They provide transparency, since business processes are clearly articulated in the software, and they are agile because they produce definitions that are fast to deploy and change.

A *workflow* can be defined as a sequence of processing steps (i.e., the execution of business operations, tasks, and transactions), during which information and physical objects are passed from one processing step to another. Workflow is a concept that links together technologies and tools able to automatically route events and tasks with programs or users.

Process-oriented workflows are used to automate processes whose structure is well defined and stable over time, often coordinate subprocesses executed by machines, and only require minor user involvement (often only in specific cases). An order management process or a loan request is an example of a well-defined process. Certain process-oriented workflows may have transactional properties. The process-oriented workflow is made up of tasks that follow routes, with checkpoints represented by business rules—for example, a pause for a credit approval. Such business process rules govern the overall processing of activities, including the routing of requests, the assignment or distribution of requests to designated roles, the passing of workflow data from activity to activity, and the dependencies and relationships between business process activities.

A workflow involves activities, decision points, rules, routes, and roles. These are briefly described later. Just like a process, a workflow normally comprises a number of logical steps, each of which is known as an *activity*. An activity is a set of actions that are guided by the workflow. An activity may involve manual interaction with a user or workflow participant or may be executed using diverse resources such as application programs or databases. A work item or data set is created and is processed and changed in stages at a number of processing or decision points to meet specific business goals. Most workflow engines can handle very complex series of processes.

A workflow can depict various aspects of a business process, including automated and manual activities, decision points and business rules, parallel and sequential work routes, and how to manage exceptions to the normal business process. A workflow can have logical decision points that determine which branch of the flow a work item may take in the event of alternative paths. Every alternate path within the flow is identified and controlled through a bounded set of logical decision points. An instantiation of a workflow to support a work item includes all possible paths from beginning to end.

Within a workflow, business rules at each decision point determine how workflow-related data are to be processed, routed, tracked, and controlled. Business rules are core business policies that capture the nature of an enterprise's business model and define the conditions that must be met in order to move to the next stage of the workflow. Business rules are represented as compact statements about an aspect of the business that can be expressed within an application, and as such, they determine the route to be followed. For instance, for a health-care application, business rules may include policies on how new claim validation, referral requirements, or special procedure approvals are implemented. Business rules can represent among other things typical business situations such as escalation (e.g.,

"Send this document to a supervisor for approval") and managing exceptions (e.g., "This loan is more than $50,000; send it to the MD").

8.7.3 Business Process Management (BPM)

BPM is a commitment to expressing, understanding, representing, and managing a business (or the portion of business to which it is applied) in terms of a collection of business processes that are responsive to a business environment of internal or external events. The term *business process management* includes process analysis, process definition and redefinition, resource allocation, scheduling, the measurement of process quality and efficiency, and process optimization. Process optimization includes the collection and analysis of both real-time measures (monitoring) and strategic measures (performance management) and their correlation as the basis for process improvement and innovation. A BPM solution is a graphical productivity tool for modeling, integrating, monitoring, and optimizing process flows of all sizes, crossing any application, company boundary, or human interaction. BPM codifies value-driven processes and institutionalizes their execution within the enterprise. This implies that BPM tools can help analyze, define, and enforce process standardization. BPM provides a modeling tool to visually construct, analyze, and execute cross-functional business processes.

BPM is more than process automation or traditional workflow. BPM within the context of (Enterprise Application Architecture EAI) and e-business integration provides the flexibility necessary to automate cross-functional processes. It adds conceptual innovations and technology from EAI and e-business integration and reimplements it within an e-business infrastructure based on Web and XML standards. Conventional applications provide traditional workflow features that work well only within their local environment. However, integrated process management is then required for processes spanning enterprises. Automating cross-functional activities, such as checking or confirming inventory between an enterprise and its distribution partners, enables corporations to manage processes by exception based on real-time events driven from the integrated environment. Process execution then becomes automated, requiring human intervention only in situations where exceptions occur—for example, when inventory level has fallen below a critical threshold or manual tasks and approvals are required.

The distinction between BPM and workflow is mainly based on the management aspect of BPM systems; BPM tools place considerable emphasis on management and business functions. Although BPM technology covers the same space as workflow, its focus is on the business user and provides more sophisticated management and analysis capabilities. With a BPM tool, the business user is able to manage all the processes of a certain type (e.g., claim processes) and should be able to study them from historical or current data and produce costs or other business measurements. In addition, the business user should also be able to analyze and compare the data or business measurements based on the different types of claims. This type of functionality is typically not provided by modern workflow systems.

8.7.4 Business Processes via Web Services

Business process management and workflow systems today support the definition, execution, and monitoring of long-running processes that coordinate the activities of multiple business applications. However, because these systems are activity oriented and not communication (message) oriented, they do not separate internal implementation from external protocol description. When processes span business boundaries, loose coupling based on precise external protocols is required because the parties involved do not share application and workflow implementation technologies and will not allow external control over the use of their back-end applications. Such business interaction protocols are by necessity message-centric; they specify the flow of messages representing business actions among trading partners without requiring any specific implementation mechanism. With such applications, the loosely coupled, distributed nature of the Web enables exhaustive and full orchestration, choreography, and monitoring of the enterprise applications that expose the Web services participating in the message exchanges.

Web services provide a standard and interoperable means of integrating loosely coupled Web-based components that expose well-defined interfaces, while abstracting the implementation- and platform-specific details. Core Web service standards such as SOAP, WSDL, and UDDI provide a solid foundation to accomplish this. However, these specifications primarily enable the development of simple Web service applications that can conduct simple interactions. However, the ultimate goal of Web services is to facilitate and automate business process collaborations both inside and outside enterprise boundaries. Useful business applications of Web services in EAI and business-to-business environments require the ability to compose complex and distributed Web service integrations and the ability to describe the relationships between the constituent low-level services. In this way, collaborative business processes can be realized as Web service integrations.

A business process specifies the potential execution order of operations originating from a logically interrelated collection of Web services, each of which performs a well-defined activity within the process. A business process also specifies the shared data passed between these services, the external partners' roles with respect to the process, joint exception-handling conditions for the collection of Web services, and other factors that may influence how Web services or organizations participate in a process. This would enable long-running transactions between Web services in order to increase the consistency and reliability of business processes that are composed of these Web services.

The orchestration and choreography of Web services are enabled under three specification standards—namely, the Business Process Execution Language for Web Services (BPEL4WS or BPEL for short), WS-Coordination (WS-C), and

WS-Transaction (WS-T). These three specifications work together to form the bedrock for reliably choreographing Web service–based applications, providing BPM, transactional integrity, and generic coordination facilities. BPEL is a workflow-like definition language that describes sophisticated business processes that can orchestrate Web services. WS-C and WS-T complement BPEL to provide mechanisms for defining specific standard protocols for use by transaction processing systems, workflow systems, or other applications that wish to coordinate multiple Web services.

8.7.4.1 Service Composition

The platform-neutral nature of services creates the opportunity for building composite services by combining existing elementary or complex services (i.e., component services) from different enterprises and in turn offering them as high-level services or processes. Composite services (and, thus, processes) integrate multiple services—and put together new business functions—by combining new and existing application assets in a logical flow.

The definition of composite services requires coordinating the flow of control and data between the constituent services. Business logic can be seen as the ingredient that sequences, coordinates, and manages interactions among Web services. By programming a complex cross-enterprise workflow task or business transaction, it is possible to logically chain discrete Web service activities into cross-enterprise business processes. This is enabled through orchestration and choreography (Web service technologies support coordination and offer an asynchronous and message-oriented way to communicate and interact with application logic).

1. *Orchestration* describes how Web services can interact with each other at the message level, including the business logic and execution order of the interactions from the perspective and under the control of a single end point. For instance, this is the case when the business process flow is seen from the vantage point of a single supplier. Orchestration refers to an executable business process that may result in a long-lived, transactional, multistep process model. With orchestration, business process interactions are always controlled from the (private) perspective of one of the business parties involved in the process.

2. *Choreography* is typically associated with the public (globally visible) message exchanges, rules of interaction, and agreements that occur between multiple business process end points, rather than a specific business process that is executed by a single party. Choreography tracks the sequence of messages that may involve multiple parties and multiple sources, including customers, suppliers, and partners, where each party involved in the process

describes the part it plays in the interaction and no party owns the conversation. Choreography is more collaborative in nature than orchestration. It is described from the perspectives of all parties (i.e., a common view) and, in essence, defines the shared state of the interactions between business entities. This common view can be used to determine specific deployment implementations for each individual entity. Choreography offers a means by which the rules of participation for collaboration can be clearly defined and agreed to, jointly. Each entity may then implement its portion of the choreography as determined by their common view.

8.8 Summary

This chapter introduced the concept of cloud computing. It described its definition, presents the cloud delivery and deployment models, and highlights its benefits for enterprises. In the last part of the chapter, we discussed the primary challenges faced while provisioning a cloud service—namely, scalability, multitenancy, and availability. The later part of the chapter described virtualization technology, which is one of the fundamental components of cloud computing, Virtualization allows the creation of a secure, customizable, and isolated execution environment for running applications without affecting other users' applications. One of the primary reasons companies implement virtualization is to improve the performance and efficiency of processing a diverse mix of workloads. Rather than assigning a dedicated set of physical resources to each set of tasks, a pooled set of virtual resources can be quickly allocated as needed across all workloads. Virtualization provides a great opportunity to build elastically scalable systems that can provision additional capabilities at minimum cost. The chapter introduced service-oriented architecture (SOA) to explain the realization of processes in terms of Web services.

Chapter 9

Big Data Computing and Graph Databases

The rapid growth of the Internet and the World Wide Web has led to vast amounts of information becoming available online. In addition, business and government organizations create large amounts of both structured and unstructured information, which needs to be processed, analyzed, and linked. It is estimated the amount of information stored in digital form in 2007 stood at 281 exabytes, with the overall compound growth rate at 57% and information in organizations growing at even a faster rate. It is also estimated that 95% of all current information exists in unstructured forms, which have greater data-processing requirements than structured information. The storing, managing, accessing, and processing of this vast amount of data represents a fundamental need, and it will be an immense challenge to satisfy needs to search, analyze, mine, and visualize these data as information.

The Web is believed to have well over a trillion Web pages, of which at least 50 billion have been catalogued and indexed by search engines such as Google, making them searchable by all of us. This massive Web content spans well over 100 million domains (i.e., locations where we point our browsers, such as http://www.wikipedia.org). These are themselves growing at a rate of more than 20,000 net domain additions daily. Facebook and Twitter each have over 900 million users, who between them generate over 300 million posts a day (roughly 250 million tweets and over 60 million Facebook updates). Add to this over 10,000 credit card payments made per second, well over 30 billion point-of-sale transactions per year (via dial-up devices), and finally, over 6 billion mobile phones, of which almost 1 billion are smartphones, many of which are GPS-enabled and can access the

Internet for e-commerce, tweets, and updates on Facebook. And last but not least, there are the images and videos on YouTube and other sites, which by themselves outstrip all these put together in terms of the sheer volume of data they represent.

9.1 Big Data

This deluge of data, along with the emerging techniques and technologies used to handle it, is commonly referred to today as *big data*. Such big data is both valuable and challenging because of its sheer volume; the amount of data created in the years 2010 through 2015 far exceeded all the data generated in human history. The Web, where all these data are being produced and where they reside, consists of millions of servers, with data storage soon to be measured in zetabytes.

Cloud computing provides an opportunity for organizations with limited internal resources to implement large-scale big data computing applications in a cost-effective manner. The fundamental challenges of big data computing are managing and processing exponentially growing data volumes, significantly reducing the associated data analysis cycles to support practical, timely applications, and developing new algorithms that can scale to search and process massive amounts of data. The answer to these challenges is a scalable, integrated computer systems hardware and software architecture designed for the parallel processing of big data computing applications. This chapter explores the challenges of big data computing.

9.1.1 What Is Big Data?

Big data can be defined as volumes of data available in varying degrees of complexity, generated at different velocities and varying degrees of ambiguity, that cannot be processed using traditional technologies, processing methods, algorithms, or any off-the-shelf commercial solutions (Figure 9.1).

Big data includes weather, geospatial, and GIS data; consumer-driven data from social media; enterprise-generated data from legal, sales, marketing, procurement, finance, and human resources departments; and device-generated data from sensor networks, nuclear plants, X-ray and scanning devices, and airplane engines.

9.1.1.1 Data Volume

The most interesting data for any organization to tap into today is social media data. The amount of data generated by consumers every minute provides extremely important insights into choices, opinions, influences, connections, brand loyalty, brand management, and much more. Social media sites provide not only consumer perspectives but also competitive positioning, trends, and access to communities formed by common interests. Organizations today leverage social media to personalize the marketing of products and services to each customer.

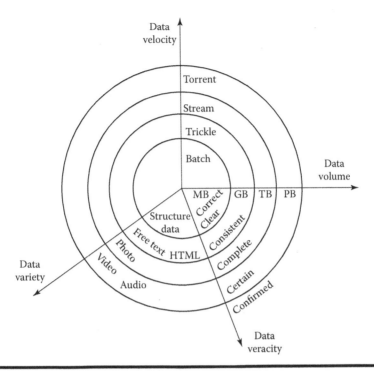

Figure 9.1 4V characteristics of big data.

Many additional applications are being developed and are slowly becoming a reality. These applications include using remote sensing to detect underground sources of energy, environmental monitoring, traffic monitoring and regulation by automatic sensors mounted on vehicles and roads, the remote monitoring of patients using special scanners and equipment, and the tighter control and replenishment of inventories using radio frequency identification (RFID) and other technologies. All these developments will have associated with them a large volume of data. Social networks such as Twitter and Facebook have hundreds of millions of subscribers worldwide who generate new data with every message they send or post they make.

Every enterprise has massive amounts of e-mails that are generated by its employees, customers, and executives on a daily basis. These e-mails are all considered an asset of the corporation and need to be managed as such. After Enron and the collapse of many audits in enterprises, the U.S. government mandated that all enterprises should have a clear life cycle management of e-mails, and that e-mails should be available and auditable on a case-by-case basis. There are several examples that come to mind, such as insider trading, intellectual property, competitive analysis, and much more, that justify the governance and management of e-mails.

Table 9.1 Scale of Data

Size of Data	Scale of Data
1000 megabytes	1 gigabyte (GB)
1000 gigabytes	1 terabyte (TB)
1000 terabytes	1 petabyte (PB)
1000 petabytes	1 exabyte (EB)
1000 exabytes	1 zettabyte (ZB)
1000 zetabytes	1 yottabyte (YB)

If companies can analyze petabytes of data (equivalent to 20 million four-drawer file cabinets filled with text files or 13.3 years of HD video content) with acceptable performance to discern patterns and anomalies, businesses can begin to make sense of data in new ways. Table 9.1 indicates the escalating scale of data.

The list of features for handling data volumes include the following:

■ Nontraditional and unorthodox data-processing techniques need to be innovated for processing this data type.
■ Metadata are essential for processing these data successfully.
■ Metrics and KPIs are key to providing visualization.
■ Raw data do not need to be stored online for access.
■ Processed outputs need to be integrated into enterprise-level analytical ecosystems to provide better insights and visibility into the trends and outcomes of business exercises, including CRM, the optimization of inventory, clickstream analysis and more.
■ An enterprise data warehouse (EDW) is needed for analytics and reporting

9.1.1.2 Data Velocity

The business models adopted by Amazon, Facebook, Yahoo, and Google, which became the de facto business models for most Web-based companies, operate on the fact that by tracking customer clicks and navigations on a website, you can deliver personalized browsing and shopping experiences. In this process of clickstreams, there are millions of clicks gathered from users every second, amounting to large volumes of data. These data can be processed, segmented, and modeled to study population behaviors based on the time of day, geography, advertisement effectiveness, click behavior, and guided navigation response. The result sets of these models can be stored to create a better experience for the next set of clicks exhibiting similar behaviors. The velocity of data produced by user clicks on any website today is a prime example for big data velocity.

Real-time data and streaming data are accumulated by the likes of Twitter and Facebook at a very high velocity. Velocity is helpful in detecting trends among people that are tweeting a million times every 3 minutes. The processing of streaming data for analysis also involves velocity. Similarly, high velocity is attributed to data associated with the typical speed of transactions on stock exchanges; this speed reaches billions of transactions per day on certain days. If these transactions must be processed to detect potential fraud or billions of cell phone records must be processed to detect malicious activity, we are dealing with the velocity dimension.

The most popular way to share pictures, music, and data today is via mobile devices. The sheer volume of data that is transmitted by mobile networks provides insights to the providers on the performance of their network, the amount of data processed at each tower, times of day, the associated geographies, user demographics, locations, latencies, and much more. The velocity of data movement is unpredictable and sometimes can cause a network to crash. Data movement and its study have enabled mobile service providers to improve their quality of service (QoS), and associating these data with social media inputs has enabled insights into competitive intelligence.

The list of features necessary for handling data velocity include the following:

■ The system must be elastic, for handling data velocity along with volume.
■ The system must scale up and scale down as needed without increasing costs.
■ The system must be able to process data across the infrastructure in the least processing time.
■ The system throughput should remain stable, independent of data velocity.
■ The system should be able to process data on a distributed platform (Figure 9.2)

9.1.1.3 Data Variety

Data comes in multiple formats, ranging from e-mails to tweets to social media and sensor data. There is no control over the input data format or the structure of the data. The processing complexity associated with a variety of formats is the availability of appropriate metadata for identifying what is contained in the actual data. This is critical when we process images, audio, video, and large chunks of text. The absence of metadata or partial metadata means processing delays from the ingestion of data to producing the final metrics, and, more importantly, in integrating the results with the data warehouse.

Sources of data in traditional applications were mainly transactions involving the financial, insurance, travel, health-care, and retail industries and governmental and judicial processing. The types of sources have expanded dramatically and include Internet data (e.g., clickstream and social media), research data (e.g., surveys and industry reports), location data (e.g., mobile device data and geospatial data), images (e.g., surveillance, satellites, and medical scanning), e-mails, supply chain data (e.g., electronic data interchange [EDI], vendor catalogs), signal

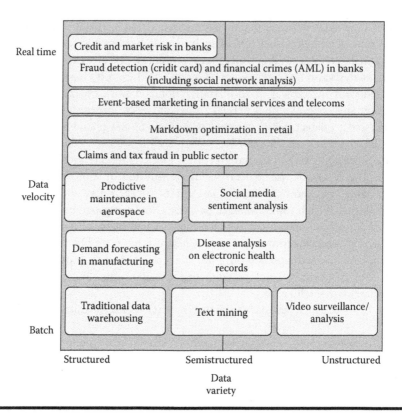

Figure 9.2   Use cases for big data computing.

data (e.g., sensors and RFID devices), and videos (YouTube gathers hundreds of minutes of video every minute). Big data includes structured, semistructured, and unstructured data in different proportions based on context (Tables 9.2 and 9.3).

The list of features for handling data variety include the following:

■ Scalability
■ Distributed processing capabilities
■ Image-processing capabilities
■ Graph-processing capabilities
■ Video- and audio-processing capabilities

9.1.1.4 Data Veracity

The veracity dimension of big data is a more recent addition than the advent of the Internet. Veracity has two built-in features: the credibility of the source and the suitability of the data for its target audience. It is closely related to trust; listing veracity as one of the dimensions of big data amounts to saying that data coming into so-called big data applications have a variety of trustworthiness, and

Table 9.2 Big Data Values across Industries

	Volume of Data	Velocity of Data	Variety of Data	Underutilized Data (Dark Data)	Big Data Value Potential
Banking and securities	High	High	Low	Medium	High
Communications and media services	High	High	High	Medium	High
Education	Very low	Very low	Very low	High	Medium
Government	High	Medium	High	High	High
Health-care providers	Medium	High	Medium	Medium	High
Insurance	Medium	Medium	Medium	Medium	Medium
Manufacturing	High	High	High	High	High
Chemicals and natural resources	High	High	High	High	Medium
Retail	High	High	High	Low	High
Transportation	Medium	Medium	Medium	High	Medium
Utilities	Medium	Medium	Medium	Medium	Medium

therefore, before we accept the data for analytical or other applications, it must go through some degree of quality testing and credibility analysis. Many sources generate data that is uncertain, incomplete, and inaccurate, therefore making its veracity questionable.

9.1.2 Common Characteristics of Big Data Computing Systems

There are several important common characteristics of big data computing systems that distinguish them from other forms of computing.

1. Colocation of the data and programs or algorithms to perform the computation: To achieve high performance in big data computing, it is important to minimize the movement of data. This principle—*move the code to the data*—which was designed into the data-parallel processing architecture

Table 9.3   Industry Use Cases for Big Data

Manufacturing	Retail
Product research	Customer relationship management
Engineering analysis	Store location and layout
Predictive maintenance	Fraud detection and prevention
Process and quality metrics	Supply-chain optimization
Distribution optimization	Dynamic pricing
Media and telecommunications	**Financial services**
Network optimization	Algorithmic trading
Customer scoring	Risk analysis
Churn prevention	Fraud detection
Fraud prevention	Portfolio analysis
Energy	**Advertising and public relations**
Smart grid	Demand signaling
Exploration	Targeted advertising
Operational modeling	Sentiment analysis
Power-line sensors	Customer acquisition
Health care and life sciences	**Government**
Pharmacogenomics	Market governance
Bioinformatics	Weapon systems and counter terrorism
Pharmaceutical research	Econometrics
Clinical outcomes research	Health informatics

implemented by Seisint in 2003, is extremely effective, since program size is usually small in comparison with the large data sets processed by big data systems, and results in much less network traffic, since data can be read locally instead of across the network. In direct contrast with other types of computing and supercomputing that utilize data stored in a separate repository or servers and transfer the data to the processing system for computation, big data computing uses distributed data and distributed file systems in which data are located across a cluster of processing nodes, and instead of moving the data, the program or algorithm is transferred to the nodes with the data that need to be processed. This characteristic allows processing algorithms to execute on the nodes where the data reside, reducing system overhead and increasing performance.

2. Programming model utilized: Big data computing systems utilize a machine-independent approach in which applications are expressed in terms of high-level operations on data, and the runtime system transparently controls the scheduling, execution, load balancing, communications, and movement of programs and data across the distributed computing cluster. The programming abstraction and language tools allow the processing to be expressed in terms of data flows and transformations, incorporating new dataflow programming languages and shared libraries of common data manipulation algorithms such as sorting. Conventional supercomputing and distributed computing systems typically utilize machine-dependent programming models, which can require low-level programmer control of processing and node communications using conventional imperative programming languages and specialized software packages, which adds complexity to the parallel programming task and reduces programmer productivity. A machine-dependent programming model also requires significant tuning and is more susceptible to single points of failure.

3. Focus on reliability and availability: Large-scale systems with hundreds or thousands of processing nodes are inherently more susceptible to hardware failures, communications errors, and software bugs. Big data computing systems are designed to be fault resilient. This includes redundant copies of all data files on disk, the storage of intermediate processing results on disk, the automatic detection of node or processing failures, and the selective recomputation of results. A processing cluster configured for big data computing is typically able to continue operation with a reduced number of nodes following a node failure, with the automatic and transparent recovery of incomplete processing.

A final important characteristic of big data computing systems is the inherent scalability of the underlying hardware and software architecture. Big data computing systems can typically be scaled in a linear fashion to accommodate virtually any amount of data or to meet time-critical performance requirements by simply adding additional processing nodes to a system configuration in order to achieve billions of records per second (BORPS) processing rates. The number of nodes and processing tasks assigned for a specific application can be variable or fixed depending on the hardware, software, communications, and distributed file system architecture. This scalability solves computing problems once considered to be intractable due to the amount of data or processing time required and affords opportunities for new breakthroughs in data analysis and information processing.

One of the key characteristics of the cloud is elastic scalability: users can add or subtract resources in almost real time based on changing requirements. The cloud plays an important role within the big data world. Dramatic changes happen when these infrastructure components are combined with the advances in data management. Horizontally expandable and optimized infrastructure supports the practical implementation of big data. Cloudware technologies such as virtualization increase the efficiency of the cloud, which makes many complex systems easier to optimize. As a result, organizations have the performance and optimization to be able to access data that was previously either unavailable or very hard to collect. Big data platforms are increasingly used as sources of enormous amounts of data about customer preferences, sentiment, and behaviors. Companies can integrate this information with internal sales and product data to gain insight into customer preferences to make more targeted and personalized offers.

9.1.3 Big Data Appliances

Big data analytics applications combine the means for developing and implementing algorithms that must access, consume, and manage data. In essence, the framework relies on a technology ecosystem of components that must be combined in a variety of ways to address each application's requirements, which can range from general information technology (IT) performance scalability to detailed performance improvement objectives associated with specific algorithmic demands. For example, some algorithms expect massive amounts of data to be immediately and quickly available, necessitating large amounts of core memory. Other applications may need numerous iterative exchanges of data between different computing nodes, which would require high-speed networks.

The big data technology ecosystem stack may include

1. Scalable storage systems that are used for capturing, manipulating, and analyzing massive data sets.
2. A computing platform, sometimes configured specifically for large-scale analytics, often composed of multiple (typically multicore) processing nodes connected via a high-speed network to memory and disk storage subsystems. These are often referred to as *appliances*.
3. A data management environment, whose configurations may range from a traditional database management system scaled to massive parallelism to databases configured with alternative distributions and layouts, as well as newer graph-based or other NoSQL data management schemes.
4. An application development framework to simplify the process of developing, executing, testing, and debugging new application code. This framework

should include programming models, development tools, program execution and scheduling, and system configuration and management capabilities.

5. Methods of scalable analytics (including statistical and data-mining models) that can be configured by analysts and other business consumers to help improve the ability to design and build analytical and predictive models.

6. Management processes and tools that are necessary to ensure alignment with the enterprise analytics infrastructure and collaboration among the developers, analysts, and other business users.

9.2 Tools and Techniques of Big Data

9.2.1 Processing Approach

Current big data computing platforms use a *divide-and-conquer* parallel processing approach combining multiple processors and disks in large computing clusters connected via high-speed communications switches and networks, which allows the data to be partitioned among the available computing resources and processed independently to achieve performance and scalability based on the amount of data (Table 9.1). We define a *cluster* as a type of parallel and distributed system that consists of a collection of interconnected stand-alone computers working together as a single integrated computing resource.

This approach to parallel processing is often referred to as the *shared-nothing* approach, since each node, consisting of a processor, local memory, and disk resources, shares nothing with other nodes in the cluster. In parallel computing this approach is considered suitable for data-processing problems that are *embarrassingly parallel*—that is, where it is relatively easy to separate the problem into a number of parallel tasks and there is no dependency or communication required between the tasks other than their overall management. These types of data-processing problems are inherently adaptable to various forms of distributed computing including clusters and data grids and cloud computing.

Analytical environments are deployed in different architectural models. Even on parallel platforms, many databases are built with a *shared-everything* approach in which the persistent storage and memory components are all shared by the different processing units.

Parallel architectures are classified by which shared resources each processor can directly access. One typically distinguishes *shared-memory*, *shared-disk*, and *shared-nothing* architectures (as depicted in Figure 9.3).

1. In a shared-memory system, all processors have direct access to all memory via a shared bus. Typical examples are common symmetric multiprocessor systems, where each processor core can access the complete memory via the shared memory bus. To preserve the abstraction, processor caches, buffering a subset of the data closer to the processor for fast access, have to be kept

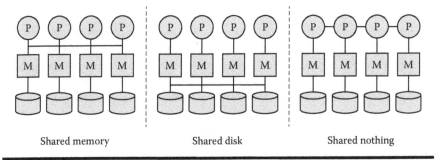

Shared memory   Shared disk   Shared nothing

Figure 9.3 Parallel architectures.

consistent with specialized protocols. Because disks are typically accessed via the memory, all processes also have access to all disks.

2. In a shared-disk architecture, all processes have their own private memory, but all disks are shared. A cluster of computers connected to an SAN is a representative for this architecture.

3. In a shared-nothing architecture, each processor has its own private memory and private disk. The data are distributed across all disks, and each processor is responsible only for the data on its own connected memory and disks. To operate on data that spans the different memories or disks, the processors have to explicitly send data to other processors. If a processor fails, data held by its memory and disks are unavailable. Therefore, the shared-nothing architecture requires special considerations to prevent data loss.

When scaling out the system, the two main bottlenecks are typically the bandwidth of the shared medium and the overhead of maintaining a consistent view of the shared data in the presence of cache hierarchies. For that reason, shared-nothing architecture is considered the most scalable because it has no shared medium and no shared data. While it is often argued that shared-disk architectures have certain advantages for transaction processing, shared-nothing is the undisputed architecture of choice for analytical queries.

A shared-disk approach may have isolated processors, each with its own memory, but the persistent storage on disk is still shared across the system. These types of architectures are layered on top of symmetric multiprocessing (SMP) machines. While there may be applications that are suited to this approach, there are bottlenecks that exist because of the sharing, because all I/O and memory requests are transferred (and satisfied) over the same bus. As more processors are added, the synchronization and communication needs increase exponentially; therefore, the bus is less able to handle the increased need for bandwidth. This means that, unless the need for bandwidth is satisfied, there will be limits to the degree of scalability.

In contrast, in the shared-nothing approach, each processor has its own dedicated disk storage. This approach, which maps nicely to (massively parallel processing MPP) architecture, is not only more suitable to the discrete allocation and distribution of data but also enables more effective parallelization, and consequently, does not introduce the same kind of bus bottlenecks from which the SMP/shared-memory and shared-disk approaches suffer. Most big data appliances use a collection of computing resources, typically a combination of processing nodes and storage nodes.

9.2.2 Big Data System Architecture

A variety of system architectures have been implemented for big data and large-scale data analysis applications, including parallel and distributed relational database management systems, which have been available to run on shared-nothing clusters of processing nodes for more than two decades. These include database systems from Teradata, Netezza, Vertica, Exadata/Oracle, and others, which provide high-performance parallel database platforms. Although these systems have the ability to run parallel applications and queries expressed in the SQL language, they are typically not general-purpose processing platforms and usually run as a back end to a separate front-end application processing system.

Although this approach offers benefits when the data utilized is primarily structured in nature and fits easily into the constraints of a relational database, and often excels for transaction-processing applications, most data growth is with data in unstructured forms, and new processing paradigms with more flexible data models are needed. Internet companies such as Google, Yahoo, Microsoft, Facebook, and others required a new processing approach to effectively deal with the enormous amount of Web data for applications such as search engines and social networking. In addition, many government and business organizations were overwhelmed with data that could not be effectively processed, linked, and analyzed with traditional computing approaches.

Several solutions have emerged, including the MapReduce architecture pioneered by Google and now available in the open-source implementation Hadoop, as used by Yahoo, Facebook, and others.

9.2.2.1 Basically Available, Soft State, Eventual Consistency (BASE)

BASE follows an optimistic approach that accepts stale data and approximate answers while favoring availability. Some ways to achieve this are by supporting partial failures without total system failures, decoupling updates on different tables (i.e., relaxing consistency), and item-potent operations that can be applied multiple times with the same result. In this sense, BASE describes more a spectrum of architectural styles than a single model. The eventual state of consistency can be provided as a result of a read repair, where any outdated data are refreshed with the latest versions as a result of the system detecting stale data during a read operation. Another approach is that of weak consistency. In this case, the read operation will return the first value found, not checking for staleness. Any stale nodes discovered are simply marked for updating at some stage in the future. This is a performance-focused approach but has the associated risk that data retrieved may not be the most current. In the following sections we will discuss several techniques for implementing services following the BASE principle.

Conventional storage techniques may not be adequate for big data and, hence, cloud applications. To scale storage systems to the cloud, the basic technique is to partition and replicate the data over multiple independent storage systems. The word *independent* is emphasized, since it is well known that databases can be partitioned into mutually dependent subdatabases that are automatically synchronized for reasons of performance and availability. Partitioning and replication increases the overall throughput of the system, since the total throughput of the combined system is the aggregate of the individual storage systems. To scale both the throughput and the maximum size of the data that can be stored beyond the limits of traditional database deployments, it is possible to partition the data and store each partition in its own database. For scaling the throughput only, it is possible to use replication. Partitioning and replication also increase the capacity of a storage system by reducing the amount of data that needs to be stored in each partition. However, this creates synchronization and consistency problems, and the discussion of this aspect is out of scope for this book.

The other technology for scaling storage is known by the name Not Only SQL (NoSQL). NoSQL was developed as a reaction to the perception that conventional databases, which are focused on the need to ensure data integrity for enterprise applications, were too rigid to scale to cloud levels. As an example, conventional databases enforce a schema on the data being stored, and changing the schema is not easy. However, changing the schema may be a necessity in a rapidly changing environment like the cloud. NoSQL storage systems provide more flexibility and simplicity compared with relational databases. The disadvantage, however, is greater application complexity. NoSQL systems, for example, do not enforce a rigid schema. The trade-off is that applications have to be written to deal with data records of varying formats (schema). BASE is the NoSQL operating premise, in the same way that traditional transactionally focused databases use ACID: one moves from a world of certainty in terms of data consistency to a world where all we are promised is that all copies of the data will, at some point, be the same.

The partitioning and replication techniques used for scaling are as follows:

1. The first method is to store different tables in different databases (as in multidatabase systems).
2. The second approach is to partition the data within a single table onto different databases. There are two natural ways to partition the data from within a table: store different rows in different databases and store different columns in different databases (this is more common for NoSQL databases).

9.2.2.2 Functional Decomposition

As stated previously, one technique for partitioning the data to be stored is to store different tables in different databases, leading to the storage of the data in a multi-database system (MDBS).

9.2.2.3 Master–Slave Replication

To increase the throughput of transactions from the database, it is possible to have multiple copies of the database. A common replication method is master–slave replication. The master and slave databases are replicas of each other. All writes go to the master and the master keeps the slaves in sync. However, reads can be distributed to any database. Since this configuration distributes the reads among multiple databases, it is a good technology for read-intensive workloads. For write-intensive workloads, it is possible to have multiple masters, but ensuring consistency when multiple processes update different replicas simultaneously is a complex problem. Additionally, the time to write increases, due to the necessity of writing to all masters, and the synchronization overhead between the masters rapidly becomes limiting overhead.

9.2.3 Row Partitioning or Sharding

In cloud technology, *sharding* is used to refer to the technique of partitioning a table among multiple independent databases by row. However, the partitioning of data by row in relational databases is not new and is referred to as *horizontal partitioning* in parallel database technology. The distinction between sharding and horizontal partitioning is that horizontal partitioning is done transparently to the application by the database, whereas sharding is explicit partitioning done by the application. However, the two techniques have begun to converge, since traditional database vendors have started offering support for more sophisticated partitioning strategies. Since sharding is similar to horizontal partitioning, we shall first discuss the different horizontal partitioning techniques. It can be seen that a good sharding technique depends on both the organization of the data and the types of queries expected.

9.2.4 Row versus Column-Oriented Data Layouts

Most traditional database systems employ a row-oriented layout, in which all the values associated with a specific row are laid out consecutively in memory. That layout may work well for transaction-processing applications that focus on updating specific records associated with a limited number of transactions (or transaction steps) at a time. These are manifested as algorithmic scans performed using multiway joins; accessing whole rows at a time when only the values of a smaller set of columns are needed may flood the network with extraneous data that are not immediately needed and will ultimately increase the execution time.

Big data analytics applications scan, aggregate, and summarize over massive data sets. Analytical applications and queries will only need to access the data elements needed to satisfy join conditions. With row-oriented layouts, the entire record must be read in order to access the required attributes, with significantly more data read than is needed to satisfy the request. Also, the row-oriented layout is often misaligned with the characteristics of the different types of memory systems (core, cache, disk, etc.), leading to increased access latencies. Subsequently, row-oriented data layouts will not enable the types of joins or aggregations typical of analytic queries to execute with the anticipated level of performance.

Hence, a number of appliances for big data use a database management system that uses an alternate, columnar layout for data that can help to reduce the negative performance impacts of data latency that plague databases with a row-oriented data layout. The values for each column can be stored separately, and because of this, for any query, the system is able to selectively access the specific column values requested to evaluate the join conditions. Instead of requiring separate indexes to tune queries, the data values themselves within each column form the index. This speeds up data access while reducing the overall database footprint and dramatically improving query performance. The simplicity of the columnar approach provides many benefits, especially for those seeking a high-performance environment to meet the growing needs of extremely large analytic data sets.

9.2.5 NoSQL Data Management

Not Only SQL (NoSQL), suggests environments that combine traditional SQL (or SQL-like query languages) with alternative means of querying and access. NoSQL data systems hold out the promise of greater flexibility in database management while reducing the dependence on more formal database administration. NoSQL databases have more relaxed modeling constraints, which may benefit both the application developer and the end-user analysts when their interactive analyses are not throttled by the need to cast each query in terms of a relational table-based environment.

Different NoSQL frameworks are optimized for different types of analyses. For example, some are implemented as key–value stores, which nicely align to certain big data programming models, while another emerging model is the graph database, in which a graph abstraction is implemented to embed both semantics and connectivity within its structure. In fact, the general concepts for NoSQL include schema-less modeling in which the semantics of the data are embedded within a flexible connectivity and storage model; this provides for the automatic distribution of data and elasticity with respect to the use of computing, storage, and network bandwidth in ways that don't force specific bindings of data to be persistently stored in particular physical locations. NoSQL databases also provide for integrated data caching that helps reduce data access latency and speed performance.

NoSQL data management environments are engineered for two key criteria:

- Fast accessibility, whether that means inserting data into the model or pulling it out via some query or access method
- Scalability for volume, so as to support the accumulation and management of massive amounts of data

NoSQL databases have been classified into four subcategories:

1. Column family stores: An extension of the key–value architecture with columns and column families; the overall goal was to process distributed data over a pool of infrastructure—for example, HBase and Cassandra.
2. Key–value pairs: This model is implemented using a hash table where there is a unique key and a pointer to a particular item of data creating a key–value pair—for example, Voldemort.
3. Document databases: This class of databases is modeled after Lotus Notes and is similar to key–value stores. The data are stored as a document and represented in the JSON or XML formats. The biggest design feature is the flexibility to list multiple levels of key–value pairs—for example, Riak and CouchDB.
4. Graph databases: Based on graph theory, this class of database supports scalability across a cluster of machines. The complexity of representation for extremely complex sets of documents is evolvin—for example, Neo4j.

 The model will not inherently provide any kind of traditional database capabilities (e.g., the atomicity of transactions, or consistency when multiple transactions are executed simultaneously); those capabilities must be provided by the application itself.

9.3 Graph Databases

A graph database uses structures called *nodes* (or *vertices*) and *relationships* (or *edges* or *links* or *arcs*). A node is an object that has an identifier and a set of attributes; a relationship is a link between two nodes that contains attributes about that relation. For instance, a node could be a city, and a relationship between cities could be used to store information about the distance and travel time between cities. Much like nodes, relationships have properties; the weight of the relationship represents some value about the relationship. A common problem encountered when working with graphs is to find the least weighted path between two vertices. The weight can represent the cost of using the edge, the time required to traverse the edge, or some other metric that you are trying to minimize.

> ✎ Graph theory is not related to the study of charts and other visualizations sometimes referred to as graphs; it is the branch of mathematics from which graph databases get their name. Graph theory is the study of objects, represented by vertices, and the relations between them, represented by edges.

Both nodes and relationships can have complex structures. There are two types of relationship: directed and undirected. Directed edges have a direction. A path through a graph is a set of vertices along the edges between those vertices; paths are important because they capture information about how vertices in a graph are related. If edges are directed, the path is a directed path. If the graph is undirected, the paths in it are undirected paths.

Graph databases are designed to model the adjacency between objects; every node in the database contains pointers to adjacent objects in the database. This allows for fast operations that require following paths through a graph. Graph databases allow for more efficient querying when paths through graphs are involved.

Many application areas are efficiently modeled as graphs; in those cases, a graph database may streamline application development and minimize the amount of code you would have to write.

Graph databases are the most specialized of the four types of NoSQL databases.

9.3.1 OrientDB

OrientDB is an open-source graph-document NoSQL data model. It largely extends the graph data model but conglomerates the features of both document and graph data models to a certain extent. At the data level for the schema-less content, it is document based in nature, whereas to traverse the relationship, it is graph oriented and, therefore, fully supports schema-less, schema-full, or schema-mixed data. The database is completely distributed in nature and can be spanned across several servers. It supports state-of-the-art multimaster replication distributed systems. It is a full ACID-compliant data model and also offers role-based security profiles to users. This database engine is lightweight, written in Java, and is hence portable in nature and platform independent, so it can run on Windows, Linux, and so on. One of the salient features of OrientDB is its fast indexing system for lookups and insertion that is based on the MVRB-Tree algorithm, which originated from Red-Black Tree and B+ Tree.

OrientDB relies on SQL for basic operations and uses graph operator extensions to avoid SQL joins in order to deal with relationships in data; graph traversal language is used as the query-processing language and can loosely be termed *OrientDB's SQL*. OrientDB has out-of-the-box support for the Web, including HTTP, RESTful, and JSON, without any external intermediaries.

9.3.2 Neo4j

Neo4j is considered the world's leading graph data model and is a potential member of the NoSQL family. It is an open-source, robust, disk-based graph data model that fully supports ACID transactions and is implemented in Java. The graph nature of Neo4j imparts it with agility and speediness and in comparison to relational databases; for the similar set of operations, it is rated significantly faster and outperforms the former with greater than 1000 times performance for several potentially important realtime scenarios.

Similar to an ordinary property graph (with simple key–value pairs), the Neo4j graph data model consists of nodes and edges, where every node represents an entity and an edge between two nodes corresponds to the relationship between those attached entities. As location has become an important aspect of data today, most applications have to deal with highly associative data, forming a network (or graph); social networking sites are an obvious example of such applications. Unlike relational database models, which require upfront schemas that restrict the absorption of the agile and ad hoc data, Neo4j is a schema-less data model that works with a bottom-up approach, enabling the easy expansion of the database to accommodate ad hoc and dynamic data.

Neo4j has its own declarative and expressive query language called Cypher, which has pattern-matching capabilities among the nodes and relationships during data mining and data updating. Cypher is extremely useful when it comes to creating, updating, or removing nodes, properties, and relationships in the graph. Simplicity is one of the salient features of Cypher, evolving as humane query language and is designed for not only developers but also for naïve users who can write ad hoc queries.

9.3.2.1 Neo4j Features

9.3.2.1.1 Consistency

Since graph databases operate on connected nodes, most graph database solutions usually do not support the distribution of nodes on different servers. Within a single server, data are always consistent, especially in Neo4j, which is fully ACID compliant. When running Neo4j in a cluster, a write to the master is eventually synchronized to the slaves, while slaves are always available for read. Writes to slaves are allowed and are immediately synchronized to the master; other slaves will not be synchronized immediately, though; they will have to wait for the data to propagate from the master.

9.3.2.1.2 Transactions

Though Neo4j is ACID compliant, the way of managing transactions differs from the standard way of RDBMS.

9.3.2.1.3 Availability

Neo4j achieves high availability by providing for replicated slaves. These slaves can also handle writes: when they are written to, they synchronize the write to the current master, and the write is committed first at the master and then at the slave. Other slaves will eventually receive the update.

9.3.2.1.4 Query

Neo4j allows you to query the graph for the properties of the nodes, traverse the graph, or navigate the node relationships using language bindings. The properties of a node can be indexed using the indexing service. Similarly, the properties of relationships or edges can be indexed, so a node or edge can be found by the value. Indexes should be queried to find the starting node to begin a traversal. Neo4j uses Lucene as its indexing service.

Graph databases are very powerful when you want to traverse the graphs at any depth and specify a starting node for the traversal. This is especially useful when you are trying to find nodes that are related to the starting node at more than one level down. As the depth of the graph increases, it makes more sense to traverse the relationships by using a *traverser*, where you can specify that you are looking for INCOMING, OUTGOING, or BOTH types of relationships. You can also make the traverser go top down or sideways on the graph by using the order values BREADTH_FIRST or DEPTH_FIRST.

9.3.2.1.5 Scaling

With graph databases, sharding is difficult, as graph databases are not aggregate oriented but relationship oriented. Since any given node can be related to any other node, storing related nodes on the same server is better for graph traversal. Since traversing a graph when the nodes are on different machines is not good for performance, graph database scaling can be achieved by using some common techniques:

- We can add enough RAM to the server so that the working set of nodes and relationships is held entirely in memory. This technique is only helpful if the data set that we are working with will fit in a realistic amount of RAM.

■ We can improve the read scaling of the database by adding more slaves with read-only access to the data, with all the writes going to the master. This pattern of writing once and reading from many servers is useful when the data set is large enough to not fit in a single machine's RAM but small enough to be replicated across multiple machines. Slaves can also contribute to availability and read scaling, as they can be configured to never become a master, remaining always read only.

■ When the data set size makes replication impractical, we can shard the data from the application side using domain-specific knowledge.

9.3.2.2 Neo4j Data Model

The data model in Neo4j organizes data using the concepts of nodes and relationships. Both nodes and relationships can have properties that store the data items associated with nodes and relationships. Nodes can have labels—zero, one, or several; nodes that have the same label are grouped into a collection that identifies a subset of the nodes in the database graph for querying purposes. Relationships are directed; each relationship has a start node and an end node, as well as a relationship type, which serves a similar role to a node label by identifying similar relationships that have the same relationship type. Properties can be specified via a map pattern, which is made of one or more *name: value* pairs enclosed in curly brackets—for example, {Lname: "Bacchan," Fname: "Amitabh," Minit: "B"}.

There are various ways in which nodes and relationships can be created—for example, by calling appropriate Neo4j operations from various Neo4j APIs. We will just show the high-level syntax for creating nodes and relationships; to do so, we will use the Neo4j CREATE command, which is part of the high-level declarative query language Cypher. Neo4j has many options and variations for creating nodes and relationships using various scripting interfaces, but a full discussion is outside the scope of our presentation.

1. Indexing and node identifiers: When a node is created, the Neo4j system creates an internal, unique system-defined identifier for each node. To retrieve individual nodes using other properties of the nodes efficiently, the user can create indexes for a collection of nodes that have a particular label. Typically, one or more of the properties of the nodes in that collection can be indexed. For example, Empid can be used to index nodes with the EMPLOYEE label, Dno to index the nodes with the DEPARTMENT label, and Pno to index the nodes with the PROJECT label.

2. Optional schema: A schema is optional in Neo4j. Graphs can be created and used without a schema, but in Neo4j version 2.0, a few schema-related functions were added. The main features related to schema creation involve creating indexes and constraints based on the labels and properties. For example, it is possible to create the equivalent of a key constraint on the property of a

label, so all nodes in the collection of nodes associated with the label must have unique values for that property.

9.4 Summary

This chapter introduced big data systems that are associated with big volume, variety, velocity, and veracity. It described the characteristic features of such systems, including big data architecture and NoSQL data management. It introduced the characteristics and examples of NoSQL databases, namely, column, key-value, document, and graph databases. The chapter provided a snapshot overview of graph databases OrientDB and Neo4j.

NETWORK
BUSINESSES

This section deals with network businesses. Chapter 10 introduces the characteristics of virtual organization and explores brands as a virtual organization, that is, a network enterprise. Chapter 11 deals with the management of network enterprises. Collaborative network enterprises are covered in Chapter 12.

Chapter 10

Network Enterprises

Network businesses have emerged as an organizational paradigm for collaboration and coordination across loosely connected individual organizations. Customers in geographically dispersed, emerging, and established global markets nowadays demand higher quality products in a greater variety, at lower cost, and in a shorter time. As a result, enterprises have moved from centralized, vertically integrated, few-sites manufacturing facilities to geographically dispersed networks of capabilities, competencies, and resources, namely, network businesses. Enterprises are now constructing more fluid network businesses in which each member focuses on its differentiation and relies increasingly on its partners, suppliers, and customers to provide the rest.

Network businesses or enterprises are a realization of the vision of IT/IS-enabled virtual network enterprises that reform and reconfigure automatically to address the opportunities available in the market. They have especially become viable and governable after the advent of cloud computing and big data computing. Big data computing systems and environments combine the power of elastic infrastructure (via cloud computing) and information management with the ability to analyze and discern recurring patterns in the colossal pools of operational and transactions data (via big data computing) to leverage and transform them into success patterns for an enterprise's business. These extremes of requirements for storage and processing arose primarily from developments of the past decade in the areas of e-business networks, social networks, wireless networks, and so on.

Network enterprises are an avatar of virtual organizations. *Virtual organization* is the name for the network form of an organization based on information technology (IT). It can be created very rapidly to meet specific, sometimes transitory, sets of circumstances. It can just as easily be dismantled and reformed as circumstances and profit opportunities change. A classic example of a virtual organization is the traditional brand; a *brand* is a virtual embodiment of the marketing strategy encompassing the collective of product(s), position, price, and promotion. This chapter starts with a description of the characteristics, benefits, and management of a virtual organization. After identifying network enterprises as virtual organizations, the later part of the chapter discusses characteristic dimensions of brands.

10.1 Virtual Organization

The virtual organization differs from the strategic alliance in that it primarily places its emphasis not on how two or more firms can work together to their mutual advantage but on how one firm can be created with flexible boundaries and ownership, aided by the facilities provided by electronic data exchange and communication.

Successful alliances are not composed of partners involved in skill substitution; that is, one partner produces and leaves the selling to the other. They are concerned with learning from each other and thus strengthening the areas in which they are weak. This does not apply to the virtual organization. In this intraorganizational form, companies each provide different functions and are linked electronically. Organizational learning is not a basic objective of the exercise; rather, it is the creation of a flexible organization of companies, each carrying out one or more functions in order to deliver a competitive product to the customer.

The organization thus has virtual (logical) qualities and physical existence in its traditional form. The virtual and physical aspects of a firm coexist and interact with each other. Power, cultural communication, knowledge perception, and self are seen as virtual characteristics, while resources, management, personnel, organization structure, information systems, and production are seen as epitomes of the physical organization. The virtual characteristics are less clearly bounded and are more dominant in some types of businesses than in others. The organization itself is shaped by the interaction of its virtual and physical parts. Information technology unbalances the firm toward virtuality, which can limit or increase effectiveness, according to how its introduction is handled.

Virtuality is dependent upon six prime characteristics:

1. A repertoire of variably connectable modules built around an electronic information network.
2. Flexible workforces able to be expanded or contracted to meet changing needs. The *shamrock* pattern may well be an appropriate one here, with a small central core and several groups of self-employed workers selling their time as required.
3. Outsourcing but to cooperating firms with strong and regular relationships, as in the Japanese *keiretsu*.
4. A web of strategic partnerships.

5. A clear understanding among all participating units of the current central objectives of the virtual organization. In the absence of such an understanding, there is a high risk that the corporation will lack the will and purpose to compete successfully with more integrated corporations.

6. An enabling environment in which employees are expected to work out for themselves the best way of operating and then get things done. This is in contrast to the traditional system of working according to orders conveyed with the aid of operations manuals, organigrams, and job descriptions.

The concept of virtuality is applicable from the corporation to the value chain that depicts graphically the activities carried out by the corporation. The physical value chain (PVC) has the typical primary activities of inbound logistics, operations, outbound logistics, marketing and sales, and after-sales service. These activities are supported by activities such as technology development, human resource functions, the firm's infrastructure, and procurement. The PVC incurs costs, sometimes very high, as activities move from one link in the chain to another, and the most efficiently configured PVC takes advantage of what economies of scale and scope exist in the technologies and processes of the firm. In the age of the microchip, the virtual value chain (VVC) exists alongside the PVC and needs to be managed separately from the PVC but in concert with it. It does not require the realization of scale-and-scope economies to achieve cost efficiency. Often, advantages can be gained by moving an activity from the PVC to the VVC; thus, Ford conducted product design by gathering an engineering team in a specific location and charging it with the job of designing a car. This can now be done by a virtual team in different parts of the world operating through CAD/CAM, e-mail, and teleconferencing.

The three great strategic challenges faced by a corporation in the turbulent, global economy of the current and immediate future are

1. Demand risk means the risk that capacity will have been created to produce and sell in a market that then fluctuates widely, either booming or rapidly melting away. In such circumstances, a virtual organization, or at least one with a relatively limited fixed central core and a large and flexible periphery, is in a better position to survive and adjust to changed market conditions than a wholly integrated corporation.

2. Efficiency risk alludes to the ever-changing nature of costs as technologies change. Here, the virtual organization would seem to have an advantage over the vertically integrated hierarchy, as virtual companies, coupled on the basis of specialization, are likely to be well equipped to achieve optimal scale

economies, and consequently, to contribute low-cost parts to aid the production of an aggregatively low-cost product.

3. Innovation risk refers to the risk of falling behind rivals in the race for the new generation of products. There are mixed arguments for the virtual organization here. Child advances the view that a specialized core, buying in parts outside that specialization, helps innovation by concentrating the specialists on developing new products and technologies related to their area of core competence.

Certain phrases are commonly used to identify the virtual organization.

- A lack of physical structure
- Reliance on information and communications technology (ICT)
- Fluidity and mobility
- The transcending of conventional boundaries
- Networks
- Flexibility

Definitions of the virtual organization tend to emphasize one or more of these characteristics and therefore vary considerably. Some stress the role of information and technology, regarding the virtual organization as one that organizes these things rather than people. Others stress the networking aspects, applying the idea of virtuality to webs of partnerships between individuals or firms that come together to achieve a task or make a product. Virtual integration is the idea of interweaving distinct businesses so that the partners are treated as if they are inside the company. A further variant is the idea of flexible workforces that are brought together to perform a given need and then disband. In all these respects, virtual organization is seen as an attempt to avoid the rigid hierarchies and boundaries that often characterize conventional organizations.

Virtual organizations may be realized in a largely incremental way. Thus, a firm may start out by performing some activities itself and subcontracting others. As it grows and establishes trust and commitment relationships with its subcontractors, it may establish single-source relationships not unlike those of the Japanese *keiretsu*, where a high degree of operational interdependence is developed between firms at different stages of the value chain of activities, but with little if any common ownership.

Like any other organization, a virtual organization requires management. The continuing significance of management in a virtual organization stems from the fact that such an organization requires both operational and strategic direction. At the operation level, it is necessary to put together a set of competent value chain performers that are able to deliver the required output on time and to specification. This is the central nervous system of the virtual organization, providing communications and processes to ensure the necessary standards of quality and delivery are met. While having such a system is an obviously necessary condition, it is not sufficient. A virtual organization also requires strategic direction; it requires a brain as well as a central nervous system. The brain is a center that provides strategic direction and makes difficult choices according to a consistent vision, including whom to add and whom to discard from the collective network.

10.1.1 Advantages

1. Lack of physical structure: Virtual organizations have a lower physical presence than their conventional counterparts. They have fewer tangible assets such as office buildings and warehouses, and those they do have are often geographically dispersed. Some have suggested that in the future, firms may be structured in virtual reality formats with computer links taking the place of physical infrastructure and firms existing only in cyberspace.

2. Reliance on communications technology: Modern ICT plays a vital role in enabling virtual organizations, and many see it as being at the heart of the virtual organization. Whereas conventional organizations use physical structures to provide their framework, virtual organizations use networks of communication supported by the Internet and other systems. However, technology is an enabler of virtual organization rather than the organization itself.

3. Mobile work: The use of communications networks rather than buildings and tangible assets means that it is now less important where work is physically located. As a result, departments and teams no longer have to work in close contact with each other. Project teams can be—and, in sectors such as publishing, routinely are—assembled from persons in different countries or on different continents to work together without ever coming into physical contact.

4. Hybrid forms: Because virtual organizations often involve collaboration between individuals or firms, they have been referred to as *hybrids*—networks, consortia, or webs working together within a loose framework to achieve a mutual goal. Such hybrids can be short term, such as consortia with a limited life bringing players together to undertake risky research and development projects, or they can be longer term, such as virtual supply chains.

5. Boundaryless and inclusive: This characteristic is associated with the way that virtual organizations are not confined to legal entities. They can encompass suppliers and distributors working in tight relationships with producers, and bring customers into the production process through the concept of relationship marketing. Online financial services are a highly developed example of this latter phenomenon.

6. Flexible and responsive: Virtual organizations are, in principle, very responsive and flexible. They should be amenable to rapid assembly from a variety

of disparate elements used to achieve a certain business goal and then dismantled. Much in practice, however, will depend on the people involved: whether they can negotiate mutually satisfactory arrangements quickly, and whether managers and employees are willing to work flexibly.

There are, of course, limitations and disadvantages too with the virtual organization, such as difficulties in achieving scale-or-scope economies, difficulty in transferring tacit knowledge, problems with proprietary information leakage, and difficulty in financing critical mass–level R&D, maintaining commitment, and so forth.

10.1.2 Forms of Virtual Organization

It is important to recognize that there can be different degrees and different forms of virtuality in organizations. The exact mix of virtual and tangible aspects in an organization depends on the nature of its product or service and the way it adds value in relation to the needs of customers and suppliers. It is useful here to distinguish between the mix of virtual and tangible organizational assets and the extent to which these are managed in a virtual or tangible manner.

The traditional way to manage tangible assets is nonvirtual. This uses the conventional form of organization in which most people and assets are physically concentrated in factories and offices and are managed through hierarchies. It is, in fact, difficult for technical reasons to envisage anything other than the nonvirtual configuration and management of integrated process production, unless such processes can be completely automated. Tangible assets can be managed in a partly virtual manner when the value chain can be separated into stages. Global virtual supply chains, as are common in the automobile and computer industries, come into this category.

Some organizations may organize certain activities on a virtual basis while organizing others in a conventional manner. For example, the operations inside supermarkets are physical and tangible. By contrast, their links with many suppliers are often made virtual through the use of automated reordering systems. In addition, specialist programmers working from their homes maintain the software for these and other systems. Very few companies, however, are suited to complete virtuality throughout all their activities. They may have to maintain a physical connection with their customers and they may also still be producing tangible goods.

The most comprehensively virtual organization is found when both its assets and management system are highly virtual. Many financial service firms fall into this category. They are trading a largely virtual commodity—financial instruments and currencies—across dispersed networks of offices around the world, managing the transactions through various communication technologies. Other cases illustrate the management of virtual assets in a nonvirtual way. These are often found in knowledge industries, where intellectual property is created or processed through project teams, teaching program teams, or publishing houses. There is always the potential for the management and coordination of such virtual assets to be managed in a more virtual manner. There is, for instance, growing interest in the use of virtual global teams for research and development (R&D).

10.1.3 Potential Benefits of Virtual Organization

Companies also need to respond more rapidly to changes in order to preserve their competitive advantage; the flexibility offered by virtual organization assists the capacity for rapid response. Virtual organization also addresses the needs that most companies face as a consequence of the pressure to offer increased value along with lower costs. Virtual organization promises to reduce costs in several ways, not least by offering a viable way of managing outsourcing to lower-cost sources of supply.

> Virtual organization can also benefit small companies by combining their advantages with those of large companies. Independent but closely linked companies can cooperate within a virtual organization to achieve their common business goals in an efficient way. Their relatively small size helps them to be highly innovative and to react swiftly to changing market demands. On the other hand, their combination into a virtual organization allows them to act as a single large company and to benefit from their aggregated market power.

While the operation of virtual organization is greatly facilitated by the development of ICT, the benefits resulting from the operations of virtual organization include
1. The reduction of costs by eliminating mediated transactions

In conventional modes of organization, the imperfections inherent in transacting in a mediated way—through, for example, the intervention of staff placing orders for supplies or requesting a technical specialist to visit a site in person to provide assistance—generate costs associated with waiting times because the physical and organizational distance between transacting parties creates delays. Oftentimes, components and parts have to wait in the form of inventory; people have to wait until personal assistance becomes available. A related benefit of a virtual organization lies in the way it can reduce costs by eliminating mediated transactions. By transacting in a virtual mode, it is possible to reduce if not eliminate waiting costs such as these, as well as the costs of managerial intervention. Supplies can now be ordered automatically through electronic order placing, guided by a stock check and reorder system. Technical advice can often be given speedily on the basis of an electronic representation of the problem parameters, either through applying an expert system or through electronic communication with technical staff working at their distant location, which may be their home.

2. Efficient coordination across the boundaries of time and space

This aspect of virtuality clearly can provide considerable benefits for the organization of related activities across physical distances, such as with a global supply chain. The savings in time, cost, travel fatigue, and so forth can be considerable. They offer the benefits of both reduced cost and faster response speed. Organizing in a virtual mode therefore offers a constructive response to the coordination and control requirements that follow from the trend toward the networking of business on a global scale.

The use of ICT-based systems opens the door to efficient coordination across boundaries of time and space. E-mail systems overcome the need to synchronize communication across time zones and to ensure that the other party is immediately available, as is necessary for telephone conversations. Moreover, they readily overcome the limitations of geographical space by permitting the simultaneous distribution of information across a network of recipients in dispersed locations. Other systems, such as video conferencing, effectively eliminate spatial distance by creating the virtuality of a single space between people who are at a considerable distance. It is possible to hold meetings between people located thousands of miles from each other, and also to deliver services such as education simultaneously and interactively to different groups located far away from one another. Online financial services reduce the unit costs borne by banks as well as being readily available at times outside the normal working day that suit many customers.

3. A more flexible combination of activities

Virtual organization permits a more flexible combination of activities that form a value chain. By providing an alternative means of managing linked activities by placing them under a unified hierarchical structure, virtual organization allows for their coordinated disaggregation, often spread between different firms. With virtual modes of management, it becomes easier to separate the stages of production and other activities in the value chain, while retaining a basis for coordinating them effectively. The speedy communication of information through common protocols within a virtual system permits the disaggregated activities to be recombined in a variety of ways to meet the needs of the specific situation.

This approach promises considerable economic benefits:

a. The firm can select the most suitable partners with which to join to form a complete value chain. The partners should also benefit from the ability to focus on their core competencies.

b. Partnerships within a network are bound together by contracts that can be subject to periodic review and renewal, and which include provisions for contingencies. Such arrangements should permit greater flexibility in adjusting to changing market demand compared with a mode of organization in which all activities are integrated within a single company.

c. It permits a firm to specialize on those activities for which it enjoys a relative advantage based on its core competencies and/or specific location. The firm can then focus its efforts on enhancing this core advantage so as to maintain the basis for its competitive position.

d. When a company focuses its staff down to a small central core and constructs a virtual organization to take care of other value chain activities, it can use flexible employment arrangements to permit the workforce to be expanded or contracted as needs change. Virtuality can offer an extra degree of loose coupling, which provides more flexibility in adjusting employment compared with a conventional organization. The extra loose coupling comes through the spatial dispersion of work units and flexible employment arrangements such as home-based contract work.

e. The use of communications networks rather than a physical concentration of people and equipment opens up much greater choice in the location of work. People and their activities can now be located in the lowest-cost places, which is one of the prime reasons why outsourcing has become so attractive to firms. Even staff working in the core organization do not need to be located in central offices; many can work at home or in their local community. This can dramatically reduce costs; for example, the overhead per capita cost of home working can be under one-third that of working in a city center office.

f. The simplification of management: The use of virtuality should permit the simplification of management and a corresponding reduction in administrative overheads. It is natural to devolve initiative within a virtual organization, and this saves on management time and effort partly by automating much information processing on the basis of shared protocols, and partly by facilitating direct communications between anyone in the network. A number of the potential benefits offered by virtual organization are closely associated with a reduction in the need for managerial intervention.

 Virtual organizations also have inherent challenges, limitations, and disadvantages, such as

- Difficulties in achieving scale-or-scope economies
- Difficulty in transferring tacit knowledge
- Problems with proprietary information leakage
- Difficulty in financing critical mass–level R&D
- Difficulties in maintaining commitments

The risk of vulnerability when working within a virtual network is illustrated by a well-known example where an innovation partnership operating in a virtual fashion actually worked against the long-term interests of the lead company. When IBM, although far from being a virtual organization itself, decided to develop and make its PC in a virtual manner, it coupled its hardware with Microsoft software and an Intel microprocessor. This gave Microsoft and Intel the impetus to grow from small beginnings to become larger than IBM itself. The company missed the opportunity to make the microprocessor and develop the software in-house, which it certainly had the resources to do. Instead, it effectively gave away some of its core competencies. It made a mistake in entering into a virtual partnership and not doing in-house the things that it was both good at and which had strategic importance.

10.1.4 Managing the Virtual Organization

The task of managing a virtual organization has close affinities with the general management of conventional organizations. General managers are not expected to get closely involved with operational control and coordination; in a virtual organization, IT-based systems are expected to provide a considerable amount of the operational coordination that is required.

General management involves the following seven tasks (POSDCORB):

1. Planning
2. Organizing
3. Staffing
4. Directing
5. Coordinating
6. Reporting
7. Budgeting

An important issue that arises with virtual networks is what to centralize into the lead firm and what to leave to the partners. The *critical processes* that have to be managed in virtual organizations are the management of people, relationships, work, knowledge, and technology. They argue that the effective management of these processes in a virtual organization can be a source of major business benefits such as shorter time to market, a superior response to competitors' moves, more effective management of integrated supply chains, and the better use of staff with flexible work schedules. The key difference between managing the processes in a conventional organization and a virtual organization lies in the very low incidence of face-to-face contacts in the latter.

The nature of a virtual organization means that its management process has to be characterized above all by

- The guidance and motivation of the organization through a vision that is articulated through strategy and communicated effectively to its members
- A strong focus on information processing and knowledge management
- An emphasis on the coordination of others
- The constant reinforcement of skills and a willingness to cooperate among staff

The last requirement stems from the fact that, while a virtual organization depends on advanced technology to facilitate its processes, its distinctive competitive edge depends primarily on its network of people and how this functions. One aspect of this is to give priority to the development of their relevant skills, appreciating that these skills must include the ability to work together within a virtual format. It is therefore vital to manage the staff of a virtual organization in a manner that promotes their willingness to trust each other, and consequently to communicate openly in ways that enhance the potential competitive advantages of a virtual organization with respect to learning and flexible adaptation.

All firms comprise a mixture of virtual and physical components that are deployed using both tangible and intangible assets. The right combination between the two can be addressed by reference to the combination of organizational, economic, and technological factors.

10.1.4.1 Organizational Factors

One of the problems that frequently arise when organizations adopt virtual modes is a loss of control and motivation. Control may not be too much of a problem if the quantity and quality of what people produce can readily be measured or assessed. Even so, people working at a distance from their organization can feel cut off and develop a demotivating sense of being neglected by management. Therefore, if virtual arrangements are to replace physical and social proximity between managers and employees, this will probably have to be compensated for by mechanisms that ensure the relationship remains sufficiently tight.

In a virtual organization, the management of the work involves

1. Control: In virtual organizations, the approach to control has to shift from attention to how work is done toward the outcomes of that work. Initiative is generally highly devolved in virtual organizations; to work effectively in geographically dispersed locations, workers must have the autonomy to make important decisions on how to perform their work—for example, how to respond immediately to specific client requests. This means that managers

have to develop new approaches toward evaluating and monitoring the performances of remote workers.

2. Coordination: The coordination of activities within a virtual organization becomes more complex because goals and priorities have to be communicated to people in a variety of different locations. Local needs and circumstances have also to be communicated back to managers. In a conventional work environment, managers can often achieve this coordination speedily and effectively through face-to-face interactions, either informally or through scheduled meetings. In a virtual organization, electronic protocols have to be substituted and rules implemented to make this effective—for instance, an instruction that all staff must check their e-mail boxes at least once a day. When the units of a virtual organization are distributed globally, special support is needed to assist their working together.

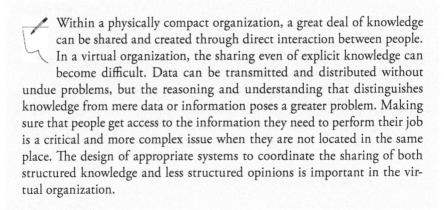

Within a physically compact organization, a great deal of knowledge can be shared and created through direct interaction between people. In a virtual organization, the sharing even of explicit knowledge can become difficult. Data can be transmitted and distributed without undue problems, but the reasoning and understanding that distinguishes knowledge from mere data or information poses a greater problem. Making sure that people get access to the information they need to perform their job is a critical and more complex issue when they are not located in the same place. The design of appropriate systems to coordinate the sharing of both structured knowledge and less structured opinions is important in the virtual organization.

10.1.4.2 Economical Factors

10.1.4.2.1 Relationship with Customers

If the product is standardized and an established brand, there will not normally be any need for customers to have personal contact with the producer, and the relationship can take a virtual form. In other cases, the transference of customer provision to a virtual mode is technically possible but may hinder the provision of other linked services that customers prefer to receive through a more personal mode of delivery. For example, banks were concerned about losing touch with their customers once they introduced automated teller machines (ATMs).

10.1.4.2.2 Relationship with Suppliers

Virtual supplier relationships also depend on the nature of the goods or services being supplied. Normally, the organization of supplies, and indeed a whole supply chain, can be accomplished on a virtual basis. In manufacturing, components and parts require physical shipment and may be sourced very locally so as to facilitate just-in-time delivery. This shipment clearly cannot be done on a virtual basis, although the accompanying information processing—of components or parts specifications and their delivery schedule—can be.

Services that consist of information provision, such as booking airline flights, are increasingly being provided through the Internet. Other support services such as consultancy and media promotion have to be tailored to the needs of a particular firm as they require personal interaction between the supplier and members of the organization and cannot be conducted on a virtual basis. When the supply of goods or services can be provided and transacted on a virtual basis, considerable savings of cost and time are normally available through the elimination of "middlemen" such as wholesalers and travel agents.

10.1.4.3 Technological Factors

There are a number of areas of work that can operate and be managed quite well on a virtual basis. Sales teams are often physically dispersed and work through virtual links. They can be brought together periodically through sales conferences in order to share experiences and discuss possible improvements on a face-to-face basis.

If a firm undertakes advanced research and/or design work, the need to promote creativity and share tacit knowledge through group work may limit the extent to which this can successfully be carried out on a virtual basis. This is despite the keen interest now being shown in virtual teams. Managers may have to assess the trade-off between

1. Optimizing the processes conducive to creativity
2. Optimizing the availability and cost of creative resources, especially when these are spread across different regions and time zones

The first component of the trade-off speaks in favor of working in a nonvirtual mode with teams of people who are in close physical proximity, whereas the second component speaks in favor of bringing together the most appropriate, but dispersed, people through a virtual system.

10.1.5 Technology Management

Information technology clearly plays a vital role in virtual organizations. The need to service a number of interaction and transaction modalities means that an IT strategy for supporting the processes within a virtual organization has to take into account the entire range of interactions in an integrated manner. Managers also need to give attention in their IT policy to supporting the totality of virtual work, including personal interactions as well as purely business matters.

The technology is required to support virtual working in a number of modalities:

1. Structured, as in the use of systems for managing and reporting structured tasks such as sending purchase orders as EDI messages in a supply chain
2. Semistructured, as in the use of workflow management systems—for example, sending invoices for payment that may entail several levels of review in both the purchasing and selling units within a virtual network
3. Unstructured, as in the use of groupware and e-mail to cope with distances and/or nonsynchronized work schedules

 In light of the characteristics of virtual organizations discussed above, it should be clear that network enterprises are virtual organizations.

10.2 Network Enterprise as a Virtual Organization

Network enterprises can be defined as virtual partnerships formed by separate firms to enable them to operate as integral elements of a greater organization while retaining their own authority in major budgeting and pricing matters. Consequently, the term network enterprise is synonymous with modular organizations, virtual organization, organic network, value-adding partnership, and interorganizational configuration.

Network enterprises, which are a long-term arrangement among distinct, but related, for profit organizations, can be perceived as intermediary organizational forms between markets and hierarchies. Compared to a market, a network has more structure, produces more interaction among the network enterprises, provides *thicker* information channels, demands more loyalty, exhibits more trust, and puts less emphasis on prices. Compared to hierarchies, a network enterprise is comparatively *unorganized* by reason of the loose coupling of the network enterprises, and the open boundaries of the network itself.

Network enterprises can be defined as the relationship between an identified set of distinct firms (the network structure) and their interaction (the network process).

Network enterprise exhibit many common characteristics and features, like:

1. Network enterprises consist of nodes and relations; their nodes are the independent firms that participate, and the relationships between these participants are based on specific exchanges of decisions, information, and goods or materials (that is, not just simple transactional links).
2. Network enterprises are an organizational form to manage interdependence between companies; they differ from mergers fusing firms into single companies, as well as from coordination through only market signals (such as

pricing). Network enterprises are based on purposeful collaboration and specific communication patterns.

3. Network enterprises may vary with respect to their goals, boundaries, structures, processes, and other attributes

A network enterprise needs to be differentiated from the traditional focal firm acting as an orchestrator or systems integrator: the traditional focal firm seldom plays simultaneous differing roles in different network of enterprises. In contrast, the focal firm within a network enterprise may participate simultaneously in differing roles to differing degrees in more than one but disparate network enterprises.

10.3 Brands as Network Enterprises

Brands are clearly virtual organizations and the best examples of network enterprises formed by a set of enterprises dependent upon the personality of the envisaged brand.

A brand network enterprise can be managed and assessed based on a 9S framework that is inspired by the pioneering McKinsey 7S model, namely, shared values, strategy, structure, stuff, style, staff, skills, systems, and sequence. The various aspects related to managing an network enterprise have been explained in Section 11.1, "Network Enterprise Management."

The remaining part of this chapter presents an overview of the 9S framework.

10.3.1 Shared Values

These are appropriate cultures and beliefs that support the needs and environment of the business. These are ideas about what is right and desirable. For example:

- Quality and customer satisfaction (John Lewis)
- Entrepreneurialism (Virgin)
- Customer service (IBM)
- Innovative culture (HP/3M)
- Willingness to change

10.3.2 Strategy

This is the clear and communicated direction and goal for the enterprise, supported by a coherent set of actions aimed at gaining a sustainable advantage over competition. The orientation of each other factor must be evaluated and changes introduced to ensure compatibility with the strategy.

10.3.3 Structure

This is the management and overall organizational structure to match the future needs. For example:

- Responsibilities and accountabilities defined
- Clear, relevant, and simple
- Provides for career development and motivation of staff
- Flexible and responsive to change
- Organizational hierarchy

10.3.4 Stuff

- Product
- Service
- Experience

10.3.5 Style

This also reflects aspects of culture. It is linked to the management paradigm—*the way we do things here*. For example:

- Autocratic versus democratic
- Concentration on consensus building to ensure commitment to change
- Enthusiasm
- Focus on external achievement and continuous progress
- Integrity
- Open culture

10.3.6 Staff

These are appropriate resources to meet the demands of the existing business and future strategy. For example:

- Ability to recruit, develop, and retain staff of sufficient quality
- Staff retention
- High fliers versus team players
- Quality of resources
- Old versus young
- Levels of competence
- Creative versus analytical

10.3.7 Skills

These are the capabilities possessed by the enterprise as a whole, as distinct from those of individuals. Some companies perform extraordinary feats with ordinary people. For example:

■ Strategic thinking ability
■ Responsiveness to change
■ Ability to analyze based on fact not opinion
■ Ability to turn ideas into action
■ Product development capability
■ Entrepreneurial focus
■ Marketing competence
■ Production control

10.3.8 Systems

These are the techniques, working procedures, computer systems, communication systems, and so on. They may be formal or informal *customary practices*. These are processes through which things get done on a day-to-day basis. For example:

■ Management information systems
■ Customer information systems
■ Authority levels
■ Manpower planning

10.3.9 Sequence

■ Economic order quantity (EOQ)
■ Safety stock/cycle stock/reorder point
■ Production planning
■ Material requirements planning
■ Master production scheduling (MPS)
■ Master planning
■ Final assembly scheduling
■ Lot sizing
■ Shop floor scheduling
■ Finite capacity scheduling (FCS)
■ Roughcut Capacity Planning
■ Capacity requirements planning
■ Supply management
■ Demand planning
■ Demand-based management

- Distribution requirements planning
- Inventory deployment
- Adaptive supply chain networks
- Advanced planning system (APS)
- Order profitability
- Order sourcing
- Hierarchical planning
- Strategic planning
- Tactical planning
- Sales and operations planning
- Workforce planning
- Supply planning
- Collaborative planning (and collaborative planning, forecasting, and replenishment [CPFR])
- Operational planning/scheduling
- Shop floor control
- Warehouse management
- Pick wave optimization
- Available to promise/capable to promise
- Toyota Production System (TPS)
- JIT
- Kanban
- Zero inventories
- Drum–buffer–rope scheduling (theory of constraints)
- Pull versus push inventory management
- Transportation management
- Load building
- Carrier assignment
- Routing
- Vendor-managed inventory/continuous replenishment

10.4 Summary

This chapter started by identifying the features that are common to the newer organizational form of virtual organization. It then described different forms of virtual organization and the conditions under which such organizations emerge, listing the benefits to be achieved from virtual organizations and their limitations. It went on to describe how to manage the virtual organization, emphasizing the economic, technological, and organizational factors that need to be considered, and highlighting the need for well-developed teamwork in virtual organizations. The important role of IT in the management of a virtual organization was also stressed.

Chapter 11

Management of Network Enterprises

Companies have always known that leveraging the strengths of business partners can compensate for their own operational deficiencies, thereby enabling them to expand their marketplace footprint without expanding their costs. Still, there are limits to how robust these alliances can be, due to their resistance to share market and product data, limitations in communication mechanisms, and an inability to network the many independent channel nodes that constitute their business channels. In addition, companies are often reluctant to form closer dependences for fear of losing leverage when it comes to working and negotiating with channel players. Supply chain management (SCM) is important because companies have come to recognize that their capacity to continuously reinvent competitive advantage depends less on internal capabilities and more on their ability to look outward to their networks of business partners in search of the resources to assemble the right blend of competencies that will resonate with their own organizations and their core product and process strategies.

In today's business environment, no enterprise can expect to build competitive advantage without integrating their strategies with those of the supply chain systems in which they are entwined. In the past, what occurred outside the four walls of the business was of secondary importance in comparison with the effective management of internal engineering, marketing, sales, manufacturing, distribution, and finance activities. Today, a company' s ability to look outward to its channel alliances to gain access to sources of unique competencies, physical resources, and marketplace value is considered a critical requirement; creating *chains* of business partners has become one of today's most powerful competitive strategies. No company can survive and prosper isolated from its channels of suppliers and customers. The ultimate core competency an enterprise may possess is in its ability to continuously assemble and implement market-winning capabilities arising from collaborative alliances with its supply chain partners.

11.1 Network Enterprises Management

Network enterprises management aims to establish structures and mechanisms that are needed to sustain ongoing coordination efforts among members of the network enterprise. Management within a network environment faces a series of complexities: coordinating different actors with different knowledge and backgrounds, creating an environment where collaborative action can evolve and take place, and dynamically aligning different strategic, organizational, and technological perspectives and systems.

11.1.1 Firm Perspective

Enterprise networks can be dealt with from the perspective of a single firm. Single firms are the players in networks; they initiate and manage networks or they simply participate in networks. Firms establish networks, act in networks, and are influenced by the participation in networks. The relationship between the network members and the network is reciprocal: the network shapes and confines the actions, policies, and identity of its members as it is shaped by them. The results and quality of network operations are often attributed to both the individual firm and to the network as a whole.

Management at the single-firm level can be discussed in the three domains:

1. *Strategy*: Generally, a firm has to position itself strategically in the market in a way that ensures an advantageous competitive position. It must gain access to a superior resource base in order to be able to set-up a unique service portfolio. Setting up or joining a network enterprise becomes a strategic option to extend the reach of a company's activities and still retain a high level of autonomy.

   Network initiatives can be motivated by either market-based or resource-based perspectives:
   - From a market-based perspective, reasons for network participation might be to enter or develop new markets, to overcome barriers to market entry by collaborating with incumbent players, to collaboratively offer services/products, to reduce competition within the market, or to extend control over the market environment.
   - From a resource-based perspective, reasons for participation might be to focus on the collaborative development or the sharing of different types of resources like knowledge, technology, human resources,

infrastructure, etc. Well-known examples are research and development (R&D) and innovation partnerships, collaborative procurement initiatives, and information partnerships.

Networks enterprises often are complex arrangements with many different players and it is crucial for firms to search for an appropriate position or role within the network. Each company strives for a superior or at least equal position to assure its participation in the distribution of the positive effects of the network, either in terms of revenue streams, collaborative knowledge or other. Moreover, a good and powerful position allows the company to influence the network strategy to assure the achievement of its own goals, which may differ from the other participants' goals. Especially in networks where companies cooperate with their competitors ("co-opetition"), strategic positioning remains very important. The network enterprise has to position itself in the market and in the network at the same time.

To be part of the overall network, the enterprise has to link its resources and activities into the overall value creation of the network enterprise. Integration in this sense means to carefully design process interfaces and to contribute to the network resource pool. On the one hand the own resources (e.g. production processes, knowledge, services) have to be adjusted and documented, so that it becomes transparent for the other network partners, what resources are available, and furthermore how the firm resources may be used by the other partners. On the other hand, the company has to ensure the integration of network benefits and of external resources offered by other partners into the internal operations. Here, organizational learning is very important in that the firm learns from the network partners in terms of innovation, product design, process competence, and other strategic capabilities.

Firms are members not just in one but in a portfolio of crisscrossing and overlapping networks. While a portfolio of relationships offers access to a broader range of resources and a reduced dependency on a single network, it makes the managing and balancing of the various network relations even more demanding

2. *Organization*: The firm has to design appropriate organizational structures that ensure efficiency, flexibility, and sustainability Network enterprises often promise efficiency improvements and access to new (external) organizational capabilities (learning, benchmarking).

Network enterprises are often initiated with the intent to improve the coordination of activities along the value chain between different partners in the market. In doing so, inter-firm business processes have to be aligned and integrated. Driven by efficiency concerns these networks aim at decreasing cost and improving process cycle times within the supply chain. Here, network enterprise participation is less strategic but motivated by operational and efficiency concerns. Such efficiency-oriented cooperation concentrates on synergies, transactional benefits, or increasing economies of scale. Examples are procurement partnerships or supply chain collaborations, which concentrate on gaining advantages within the market by jointly decreasing their costs Additionally, they might aim at offering new services to the end customer (e.g. the Efficient Consumer Response [ECR] initiatives in the grocery industry).

Firms have to integrate network processes and to align internal processes to external requirements of the network enterprise. More specifically, firms have to develop their own networkability, the ability to cooperate and to participate in networks. Networkability covers not only the process issues, but also the networkability of products and services, employees, the organizational structure, and a cooperative culture. Firms in this sense have to be able to learn how to collaborate and to create inter-firm interfaces for their processes and products.

The firm has to staff its network teams and decide who will work in various network-related roles or on the network level itself. A crucial role is played by the so called boundary spanners, who link firm- and network-level operations. The boundary spanner role embodies the promises of the extended enterprise as well as the tensions between firm and network. Boundary spanners are often torn in their loyalty between their own firm and the network. A related role is that of a relationship promoter.

3. *Technology*: The technology (or information management) perspective highlights the increasing relevance of ICT infrastructures and information systems (IOIS) for conducting business. Firms set up new network enterprises business models, flexibly integrating services from different partners. Furthermore, firms collaborate to get access to or develop new technologies through collaboration in networks. On the other side, participation in networks also has implications on the technology level.

The increasing role of ICT within companies is reflected in the set-up of ICT-focused network arrangements. Firms are keen to expand their technological resource base and to pool or share information, information systems, or infrastructures with other firms. Outsourcing of IT services is one particular way to achieve this goal. While outsourcing is often chosen by firms who do not see technology as their own core competence, it requires not only relationship management capabilities in order to achieve a productive working relationship with the service provider, but also information management capabilities in order to be able to evaluate the business value of ICT and, in particular, the strategic potential of ICT innovations.

Network enterprise information resources, systems, and infrastructure management need to be mirrored on the firm level. Network-relevant information assets need to be identified and policies for sharing, pooling, developing, or protecting need to be devised. The above-mentioned concept of networkability does also refer to the interoperability of information systems (IS) and infrastructures as another factor to ensure the ability to cooperate. Firms have to develop the ability to connect IS that contribute to collaborative processes in the network enterprise (e.g., to exchange order data, product development sketches, or to couple manufacturing and inventory (ERP) systems). This aspect is similar to the networkability of products; to make IS "networkable" one needs to describe the software interfaces, exchange formats, and increase systems interoperability by using common standards.

11.1.2 Network Perspective

Network enterprises can be dealt with from the perspective of the lifecycle of the network itself.

 To avoid being tedious, we may refer to network enterprises as networks, but the reader should not lose the sight of the fact that every time we refer to network we are truly referring to network enterprises.

1. *Network enterprises life cycle:* This is used to structure network enterprises management according to the typical phases a network enterprise might go through from initiation to transformation or its final dissolution. It highlights the challenges of an ongoing transformation and the balancing between facets of management as well as the inherent contradictions of network arrangements.
   a. *Initiation:* The initiation stage inaugurates the formation of network enterprises, which can occur in two ways:
      i. *Top-down process:* The decision-making authorities of each partner decide to establish interfirm collaboration. In this case, the efforts of the participating firms are concentrated in the partner selection. The relevant aspects are:
         ▪ Avoidance of opportunistic behavior: participation in network enterprises always entails the danger of opportunistic behavior. Partners that intend to enter the alliance exploit the common resources and offer nothing in return must be traced at this initial stage and excluded from the arrangement.

■ Selection of partners: Partners need to share common values and beliefs in order to achieve the necessary fit inside a network enterprise. Network enterprise participation is a risky investment, and for this reason managers must have some cues on the attitude of their prospective partners. These cues can be usually found on the values of each company and on its overall behavior over time.

ii. *Bottom-up process:* The network enterprise evolves out of the initiatives undertaken by individuals within organizations. In these cases, the network has to ensure institutional support that will provide a steady flow of financial and human resources to the network and backup its operations in times of abrupt changes of market conditions.

The relevant aspects are:

■ Design of the initiative: while designing their initiative, the individual incubators must make sure that they have identified and incorporated in the network enterprise activities all the relevant stakeholders and especially the ones deriving from the institutional environment.

■ Value-adding proposition: in cases where network initiation is a bottom-up initiative, organizations tend to accept network enterprise plans if they are innovative in terms of partners, operating scheme or product. Therefore, the value-adding proposition must concern a networking activity that will bring together major players within an industry. In the case where individuals bring together organizations that already collaborate, then the new network enterprise must hold operations in a different but still profitable way. Finally, the product must be innovative in its market, although solely an innovative product is considered a high-risk strategy and therefore the emerging network gains very difficult institutional support.

b. *Configuration*: In this stage, the network partners are selected and the major challenge that must be addressed by the members in order to officially launch the operation of the network is the definition of the scope of the network enterprise.

Once the major building blocks of the network enterprise are in place, the partners are ready to launch its operation. However, there is an intermediary step that concerns mainly the introduction of technological solutions in an interfirm environment. More specifically, this stage concerns the implementation of collaborative solutions that will facilitate interaction.

The relevant aspects are:

• Definition of tasks: collaboration between companies entails great complexity that stems out of the different routines inherent in the practice of every organization. In a network enterprise the major challenge for managers is to achieve equilibrium among these routines and thus balance the actions that must be performed in the network level with the everyday routines at the firm level. This can only be achieved through the definition of specific tasks to be performed by each partner in order to provide a common ground for collaboration and contain conflict at these initial stages.

- Structuring of an efficient interface: another issue that needs careful design at the initial stages of the life cycle is the type of communication among partners. Managers need also to establish frequent face-to-face meetings among these persons in order to facilitate the establishment of a common context of reference for all the involved parties and moreover reduce the equivocality generated by the use of electronic media for communication.
- Establishment of governance mechanisms: there are two major governance mechanisms to be deployed in a network enterprise, contractual collaboration, or trust-based collaboration. Whatever type of collaboration they will choose, managers must first assess the pros and the cons and decide the one that best suits the scope and strategic goals of the network enterprise.
- Valuation of contributions: in every network enterprise the contribution of partners may involve products, technologies, know-how, information, or management practices. Whatever their nature these contributions are some of the most sensitive issues of network enterprise management since they are tightly related to the perceptions of each partner regarding what it offers to the common effort and what it subsequently expects to receive.

c. *Implementation*: This stage concerns existing network enterprises that are reshaped by the adoption of new collaborative technologies like collaboration platforms. The technological solution implemented in a preexisting interfirm arrangement influences the status quo among partners. In order to stress the importance of explicit management of this transition, this process is presented as a separate stage.

These issues can occur in newly founded networks, as well, when the technological solutions adopted at the network enterprise level are different from the ones that each partner uses at the firm level. Furthermore, the implementation stage deals also with the efforts of one important node to impose its technological platforms on to the rest of the partners.

The relevant aspects are:

- Management of information exchange: preexisting networks have their own way of exchanging information among the nodes, which is fixed by everyday practice. The introduction of new collaboration platforms usually rearranges the existing information flows and subsequently affects the power of the various nodes. But in new networks, as well, the mentality of information exchange (e.g., who reports to whom, in which format etc.) at the network level, if different from the one at the firm level, can also generate problems. This is why it must be explicitly managed in order to facilitate the transition to the new situation.

- Introducing the new working arrangements: with the introduction of a new technology, the existing working practices of the network participants are bound to change drastically. To this end, managers need to help workers and staff to incorporate the new system in their practices. This type of assistance is crucial since a potential rejection of the system by its users will destabilize the network.

d. *Stabilization*: After the formation stage follows the stabilization stage; partners have a more realistic picture of each other's capabilities, and conflict can easily emerge and spread.

The relevant aspects are:

- Reinforcement of social ties: a very efficient mechanism that can bind the network enterprise together and help it endure the shocks of reality is the social network underneath the organizational one. The existence of social ties among network enterprise partners reinforces the sentiment of trust within the network and constitutes a fertile ground for trust to flourish.

- Creation of a common identity: the existence of a common identity that unites all partners under the vision of a common effort can fortify this stage of the network enterprise arrangement, since it gives people something to look up to, especially at this stage where there are not any external challenges that can act as a bonding mechanism.

- Facilitate procedural alignment: although the effort to establish common procedures has been explicit from the initial stages of the network enterprise life cycle, at the stabilization phase partners are in the position to have a more realistic outlook of the partnership and allocate more realistic tasks that will eventually lead to common processes.

e. *Transformation*: In a fast-changing environment, network enterprise arrangements cannot be unaffected by the external pressures, and sooner or later they will be forced to change. In this stage network partners face changing environmental conditions and realize the need to adjust in order to survive.

The relevant aspects are:

- Exploitation of interpartner learning: collaboration for a long period of time that usually precedes transformation permits a thorough evaluation of each partner's capabilities, strategic intent, and general vision. By working together network enterprise partners co-evolve and therefore they can learn from each other. Managers at this stage need to exploit this learning and use it for the benefit of the alliance.
- Assessment of partners: this managerial task is complementary to the first one of this stage. Managers must use the knowledge they possess and the experience they have after a significant time of collaboration in order to evaluate the contribution of each partner and remove some nodes if necessary.
- Adjustment of scope: to cope with a changing environment, managers need to adjust the scope of the network to reflect current needs. However, this process entails the repetition of the negotiation among partners that took place at the initial stages of the network enterprise formation.
- Facilitate the entry of new partners: very cohesive networks contain the risk to lose contact with the outside environment and therefore miss business opportunities. To this end, managers must always be alert and open to new opportunities and prospective partners in order to infuse the network enterprise with new innovative ideas that will prevent decline.

If transition to another more up-to-date model is successful, then the interfirm arrangement enters to a negotiation phase among old and new partners that resemble the initial stages of network life cycle. However, if the attempt to change fails, then the network decline and finally dissolution follow.

f. *Dissolution*: This is the final stage of the network life cycle. It is usually the outcome of unsuccessful attempts to change. However, there are networks with a more precarious character, like construction projects that dissolve after the completion of the common tasks.

The relevant aspects are:

- Allocation of common resources: when the dissolved interfirm arrangements had been strategic collaboration with specific investments for the creation of common resources, an allocation of the common property is in order. This is a very critical point of the dissolution stage, and network enterprise managers must be very careful in its management.
- Detection of new opportunities for collaboration: it is not unlikely for new opportunities to flourish after the dissolution of old collaborations. Network enterprise managers must be alert to detect these opportunities and even pursue new interfirm collaboration with

partners that may potentially prove invaluable during the time of common pursuits. The decline of collaboration must be confronted gracefully in order to avoid rivalries and fierce competition among old partners.

2. Building blocks of network enterprise management

   a. Network strategy: The network enterprise strategy is defined as the interplay between the internal resources and structures of the network, and the external market situation and the network environment. The strategy domain comprises the network mission, network resources, market positioning, and the network business model. Generally, there are two approaches to the formulation of corporate strategy:

   • the market-based view, which takes an outside-in look on strategy starting from the market environment
   • the resource-based view, which views strategy inside-out focusing on the resource portfolio

   Both approaches can be applied to network enterprises. To formulate a more detailed network strategy, the network business model is specified.

   The initiation of a network normally starts from an idea for a joint product, service, or any other project. The formulation of the network purpose and more specifically its goals lead to the creation of a network mission. A mission statement is the most top-level document to describe the network. While the network mission might change throughout the life cycle of the network, it is important as a reference point for the network enterprise members and is the starting point to form a network enterprise identity.

   The proliferation of networks is supposed to impact entire industries by shifting competition from a firm level to a group or network enterprise level. In this scenario, entire network enterprises compete with each other, making it necessary for networks to position themselves and build out a competitive advantage. The market-based view (MBV) on strategy assumes that economic success is determined by both the structure of the market in which a network enterprise operates and by its behavior in relation to the five market forces: rivalry among competitors, power of customers, power of suppliers, new entrants, and substitutes.

   Competitive advantage derives from unique (core) resources and the ability (capabilities) to develop products that provide a unique selling proposition as an outcome of these resources. The resource-based view (RBV) on strategy concentrates on the development, maintenance, and exploitation of (core) resources. While RBV initially focused on the single firm as the locus of control over resources and their development, it has subsequently been expanded to the network enterprises level, where resources are developed jointly in order compete with larger companies or other networks

A network enterprise business model can be characterized using three elements:

i. value proposition,
ii. revenue streams
iii. architecture

The configuration of network business models has to focus on the value creation network, its structure, and the roles of the players involved in network value creation. More specifically, in the network context the balancing of value propositions and revenue streams between partners is a crucial task in order to achieve an incentive compatible solution for the participating players. The network business model thus specifies the group of actors, their roles in terms of value creation activities ("who does what"), the interplay between the actors ("how does it work together"), and the value flow between the partners.

b. *Network enterprises organization*: Network enterprises comprise a structural dimension with linkages among actors, and a behavioral dimension with interactions that take place between the people within the structure of the network. Additionally, network policies and governance mechanisms are necessary to govern the network operations within the network structures

Designing sustainable and viable network structures is a crucial management task to enable the intended network enterprise operations. Toward this end, network tasks have to be identified and assigned to appropriate roles fulfilled by the participating firms. The linkages (dyads) between the partners have to be spelled out and network-wide (interfirm) processes have to be specified and agreed upon.

Institutional arrangements and governance structures are needed to deal with the complexity of the network relations and to ensure the implementation of strategies. Normally, a separate umbrella organization is established to deal with the issues of network enterprise management. However, these structural arrangements have to reflect the network strategy and the constraints resulting from the fact that the network participants are autonomous organizations. They have to combine flexible institutional arrangements, limited power, and the medium-term commitment of the participants. As the participating organizations relinquish some of their managerial sovereignty and some control over their own organizational boundaries, they are particularly concerned about the development of network boundaries and very sensitive about emerging governance structures.

c. *Network enterprises information management*: Network enterprise management deals with the coordination of the activities and resource sharing between the network participants. Normally network management addresses organizational and strategic concerns. Nevertheless, the role of

ICT as enabler of interorganizational relationships creates a link between information management and network management.

The goal of network information management (NIM) is to manage information infrastructures, systems, and resources to ensure that information can be deployed throughout the network efficiently and effectively. NIM comprises the information and ICT issues and extends the notion of information management to interfirm networks. From a systemic point of view, the focus of NIM is to improve the management of information flows in the network; from a strategic and relational point of view, the focus is on enabling information partnerships between the participating firms.

11.1.3 Environmental Perspective

Enterprise networks can be dealt with from the perspectives of the industry and the market. The environment or context of the firm and the network provides explanations for the initiation of networks (collaborative advantages, level of fragmentation) and the existence of specific types or configurations (dominant patterns, business logic, standards), as well as the micro conditions that might lead a firm to initiate a new network. At the same time, the formation of networks affects and shapes markets, industries, and geographical regions.

1. Market drivers for network enterprise formation

   There are general macro-level market conditions that favor the formation of organizational networks and can account for the increase in cooperation among firms in the last decades.

   a. *Technological changes*: New ways of communication and information processing technology, specially based on the Internet, allow new forms of organizing and value creation: The significantly lower costs of obtaining, processing, and transmitting information allow new efficient information links between firms. The drivers for network formation are new opportunities of an increasingly efficient way of interfirm coordination based on IT, as well as the reaction to the above-mentioned competition challenges in terms of collaborative investment strategies or joint R&D projects in terms of risk reduction and acceleration of time-to-market.

   b. *Changing customer needs and fragmented markets*: The trend toward individualization and customization of products and services has led to increasingly fragmented markets and the emergence of microsegments. This fragmentation forces companies to likewise increase their amount of product variants, to increase the specificity of their products to better meet customer needs, and to develop new mass customization strategies.

This leads to business approaches which are meant to be better applied in a collaborative manner.

The propensity of firms to form interorganizational networks is triggered not only by general market forces but also by the specific types of organizing that are prevalent in a specific industry or a market segment.

c. *Globalization*: The phenomenon of globalization is driven by technological changes like the emergence of the Internet, deregulation and opening of national markets, global reporting in mass media, and changes in people's minds; it causes the erosion of market structures, confronting companies with the entrance of new competitors and an increasing competition within the market, leading to shifting of market boundaries. The turbulent business environment is forcing organizations to reevaluate their processes and structures, indicating an increasing need for networking and cooperative arrangements.

On the other hand, globalization opens the opportunity to get access to new markets. To face competition challenges, overcome barriers of distance, and become global players, network collaboration promises to be a sound solution for enterprises. Strategic alliances in the airline industry are only one example of this phenomenon.

2. Typical industry patterns that favour formation of network enterprises

The propensity of firms to form interorganizational networks is triggered not only by general market forces, but also by the specific types of organizing that are prevalent in a specific industry or a market segment.

a. *Outsourcing*: In many industries, companies are increasingly seeing the need to focus on their core competencies and to collaborate with other firms for the fulfillment of the rest of the activities necessary for the delivery of their product. Up until the 1990s, companies tried to accomplish all processes necessary for their operation by themselves. However, this tactic resulted in the creation of large bureaucratic companies that were perceived to be unable to flexibly react to shifts in customer demand. For this reason, companies started to reevaluate their processes, focus on value-adding activities, and outsource peripheral activities to companies with superior expertise in these areas. This practice gradually led to network enterprises for the delivery of a host of specific products.

This trend is quite evident in the construction industry, where the complexity of the task demands close collaboration among a variety of companies that cannot undertake the project by themselves. Close collaboration during the construction period forges stable relationships and leads to network enterprises.

b. *Co-opetition*: The outsourcing of firm-specific activities and the close cooperation with other firms for the accomplishment of common goals paved the road for more audacious collaborations: cooperation among competitors, that is, co-opetition. It is often linked to the metaphor of a business ecosystem, which emphasises the coexistence of competition and collaboration as a prerequisite for a dynamic and innovative industry. An example is the biotechnology industry. The need for constant innovation in combination with the small size of many of the biotechnology companies led to collaboration among competitors for the sake of risk sharing and achieving virtual size.

c. *Standardization*: In various industrial sectors, initiatives that aim to establish standard procedures for collaboration between industry actors become the precursor of industry-wide networking activity. These initiatives do not explicitly intend to form interorganizational networks, but rather focus on the standardization of common activities that are performed on a frequent basis. Since standardization usually imposes a rearrangement of firm-specific processes toward common processes among value chain partners, the transition from single units to a network enterprise is easier.

In the retail industry, for example, the ECR movement aimed to bring about the close collaboration between retailers and suppliers for the alignment of the entire value chain. This initiative led to the creation of supply chain hubs around the major retailers worldwide. In this particular industry the notion of networking was the natural outcome of an initiative that made major players aware of the benefits of collaborative processes and thus facilitated the formation of network enterprises.

Before proceeding to discuss supply chain management (SCM), it is important to highlight the fact that even though SCM is quite familiar territory, the context has changed altogether; the reference here is to SCM for the *network enterprise* as a whole rather than a selected part of it—as is done customarily. The disappointing impact of supply chain management efforts and solutions in the 1990s may have been related to the fact that most of these solutions were implemented primarily for the focal company along with a few of its important partners (i.e., for the main part of the *network of enterprises* anchored on the focal company) rather than the network enterprise (i.e., the whole of the *virtual enterprise* anchored on the focal company).

As a corollary, this implies that the most impactful, value-adding but challenging, and profitable business in that space would be that of fourth-party logistics (4PLs) rather than 3PLs. The real business opportunity in the SCM space is in 4PLs.

11.2 Concept of Supply Chain Management (SCM)

The supply chain focus of today's enterprise has arisen in response to several critical business requirements that have arisen over the past two decades. To begin with, companies have begun to look to their supplier and customer channels as sources of cost reduction and process improvement. Computerized techniques and management methods such as enterprise resource planning (ERP), business process management (BPM), Six-Sigma, and *lean* process management have been extended to the management of the supply chain in an effort to optimize and activate highly agile, scalable manufacturing and distribution functions across a network of supply and delivery partners. The goal is to relentlessly eradicate all forms of waste where supply chain entities touch, while enabling the creation of a linked, customer-centric, *virtual* supply channel capable of superlative quality and service.

In the twenty-first century, companies have all but abandoned strategies based on the vertical integration of resources. On one side, businesses have continued to divest themselves of functions that were either not profitable or for which they had weak competencies. On the other side, companies have found that by closely collaborating with their supply chain partners, new avenues for competitive advantage can be uncovered. Achieving these advantages can only occur when entire supply chains work seamlessly to leverage complementary competencies. Collaboration can take the form of outsourcing noncore operations to channel specialists or leveraging complimentary partner capabilities to facilitate the creation of new products or speed delivery to the marketplace.

As the world becomes increasingly "flat" and the philosophies of lean and continuous improvement seek to reduce costs and optimize channel connections, the element of risk has grown proportionally. Companies have become acutely aware that they need agile yet robust connections with their supply chain partners to withstand any disruption, whether a terrorist attack, a catastrophe at a key port, a financial recession, or a devastating natural event like Hurricane Katrina. Enterprises such as Dell Computers, Microsoft, Siemens, and Amazon.com have been able to tap into the tremendous enabling power of SCM to tear down internal functional boundaries, leverage channel-wide human and technological capacities, and engineer *virtual enterprises* capable of responding to new marketplace opportunities. With the application of integrative information technologies to SCM, these and other visionary companies are now generating agile, scalable enterprises capable of delivering to their customers revolutionary levels of convenience, delivery reliability, speed to market, and product/service customization.

SCM provides companies with the ability to be both flexible (i.e., able to manipulate productive assets, outsource, deploy dynamic pricing and promotions, etc.) and responsive (i.e., able to meet changes in customer needs for alternate delivery quantities, transport modes, returns, etc.). SCM enables whole channel ecosystems to proactively reconfigure themselves in response to market events, such as the introduction of a disruptive product or service, regulatory and environmental policies, financial uncertainty, and massive market restructuring, without compromising on operational efficiencies and customer service. Today's marketplace requirement that companies be agile as well as efficient has spawned the engineering of virtual enterprises and interoperable processes that are impossible without supply chain collaboration. The conventional business paradigms assume that each company is an island and that collaboration with other organizations, even direct customers and suppliers, is undesirable. In contrast, market-leading enterprises depend on the creation of pan-channel integrated processes that require the generation of organizational structures capable of merging similar capabilities, designing teams for the joint development of new products, productive processes, and information technologies, and structuring radically new forms of vertical integration.

Globalization has opened up new markets and new forms of competition virtually inaccessible just a decade ago. Globalization is transforming businesses and, therefore, supply chains—strategically, tactically, and operationally. As they expand worldwide in the search of new markets, profit from location economies and efficiencies, establish a presence in emerging markets, and leverage global communications and media, companies have had to develop channel structures that provide them with the ability to sell and source beyond their own national boundaries. Integrating these supply channels has been facilitated by leveraging the power of today's communications technologies, the ubiquitous presence of the Internet, and breakthroughs in international logistics.

The merger of the SCM management concept and the enabling power of integrated information technologies is providing the basis for a profound transformation of the marketplace and the way business will be conducted in the twenty-first century. The application of breakthrough information technologies has enabled companies to look at their supply chains as a revolutionary source of competitive advantage. Before the advent of integrative technologies, businesses used their supply chain partners to realize tactical advantages, such as linking logistics functions or leveraging a special competency. With the advent of integrative technologies, these tactical advantages have been dramatically enhanced with the addition of strategic capabilities that enable whole supply chains to create radically new regions of marketplace value virtually impossible in the past. As companies implement increasingly integrative technologies that connect all channel information, transactions, and decisions, whole channel systems will be able to continuously generate new sources of competitive advantage through electronic collaboration, enabling joint product innovation, online buying markets, networked planning and operations management, and customer fulfillment.

11.2.1 SCM Challenges

The major business challenges for companies developing supply chain strategies include developing capabilities to manage the following:

1. Value: The value challenge is for suppliers to anticipate and identify what customers value in order to supply a bundle of goods and services that equate with value in order to exchange money for products.
2. Volume: The volume challenge is for suppliers to supply in volumes of their choice, at a time determined by the supplier, preferably in a standardized form. This was a characteristic of the mass production era.
3. Volatility: The volatility challenge is for suppliers to meet the demands of customers when required by ensuring that capacity can be increased when demand is high and lowered when demand is low, without incurring excessive or unnecessary cost.
4. Velocity: The velocity challenge is for suppliers to enhance or degrade the speed of response.
5. Variety: The variety challenge is for suppliers to customize products and services per the customer requirements.
6. Variability: The variability challenge is for suppliers to exercise management control in ensuring that goods and services satisfy the quality and deliver criteria as per the customer's requirements.
7. Visibility: The visibility challenge is a supplier's core capability for managing the total supply chain from source to consumer. Visibility or transparency ensures that parties within the total supply chain know what the current pipeline looks like.

The integration of systems, policies, and procedures across organizational boundaries between enterprises working together within a supply chain to satisfy the customer has been the catalyst for visibility, while technology has provided the means for achieving the same. Information and communication technology (ICT) has allowed enterprises to frequently view status reports on sourcing, procurement, production, logistics, and customer demand, ensuring that there are no blockages, unnecessary inventories, or unplanned cost build-ups.

8. Virtuality: The virtuality challenge is for suppliers to replace inventory with information through the creation of digital supply chains supported by ICT. Companies need to focus their attention on customers by creating capabilities that deliver market-driven supply chain strategies.

    Companies need to look at the ways in which they interact with customers at every level and view each of the preceding challenges from a customer perspective to devise corresponding supply chain strategies:

■ Sustainability: Offering customers consistent value—for example, based on preferences, not simply in their preferences for time, place, cost, flexibility, dependability, and quality. Companies must identify order qualifiers and order winners and compete while managing complexity.

■ Service: The ability to deliver different quantities of goods by managing capacity not simply operationally but strategically (it is no longer sufficient to rely on economies of scale). Developing capabilities to manage capacity flexibly in order to deliver products and services to customers when they are required in the quantities demanded—for example, from mass production to mass customization (from n to 1).

■ Speedy response: Developing responsive capabilities to deliver goods and services when they are required—for example, efficient consumer response, quick response.

■ Suited to customer requirements: Developing flexibility capabilities—for example, agile, lean supply chains, innovations, and new product developments.

■ Standards: Developing supply chain strategies to ensure customer quality standards are met effectively and cooperate within supply chains to compete across them.

■ Systems focused on customer satisfaction: Redesigning business processes and developing enabling strategies for all relevant parties, including customers, to view supply chain information relevant to them (e.g., collaborative, cooperative strategies rather than competitive ones).

■ Structures and relationships: For example, developing digital supply chain strategies to replace unnecessary inventory movements by moving and exchanging information instead of goods.

There is a substantial difference between the concept of supply chain management (SCM) and supply chain management systems (SCM systems). SCM is a concept of much broader scope than SCM systems, which implement a subset of the tenets of SCM. After introducing the concept of SCM, the chapter focuses on leveraging the SCM-oriented capabilities of enterprises.

11.2.2 Supply Chain Management (SCM)

SCM can be defined as the management of intra- and interorganizational processes and activities, with the objective of fulfilling customer requirements by delivering goods and services from the point of origin to the point of consumption at the overall lowest cost at the right time and at the highest level of quality.

In order to realize a supply chain, apart from the focal company, numerous different companies are involved, from the point of origin of raw materials to the point of consumption by end users; they include raw material/component suppliers, manufacturers, wholesalers/distributors, retailers, and customers. Different customers may need different products and different services, and a different set of companies may be involved for delivering to different customers. Even for the same portfolio of products, different customers may require a different set of value-added services. The last key element in the definition of SCM is the simultaneous focus on cost minimization, time reduction, and quality optimization.

11.2.2.1 SCM Characteristics

Supply chains can be structured in different forms to improve business performance in areas such as operational efficiency, agility, lean management, customer satisfaction, inventory levels, and response time to market. Once a supply chain is completed and integrated, the supply chain partners need to evaluate how they are performing in terms of the supply chain's major functions: the decision, information, and physical flows.

11.2.2.1.1 Decision flow

When goods move or services are provided, business partners expect monetary compensation from their customers. Decisions, and hence funds, need to flow in order to support the movement of goods and services from their origins to their final delivery to the end user and vice versa.

The flow of decisions and consequent funds is essential to sustain the operation of a supply chain because

- A total of 80% of revenue dollars is spent on supply chain activities.
- Services account for 18% of the total revenue.
- An internal physical supply chain typically contains more than 70% of organizational assets.
- An average of 55% of total revenue in a company is spent on purchased materials.
- Maintenance, repair, and operations (MRO) activities account for 7% of the total revenue in a company.

11.2.2.1.2 Information flow

When goods move from one location to another, information requires updating and dissemination to supply chain partners. The absence of information synchronicity can result in overstocking, backorders, poor decision-making processes, distrust between supply chain partners, and slow responses to market changes. The real significance of information emerges when information substitutes for traditional physical and funds flow as far as possible until such time when physical goods or funds actually have to be moved.

11.2.2.1.3 Physical Flow

Physical flow is the actual movement of goods or the delivery of services across the supply chain. All supply chain partners attempt to optimize the physical flow to ensure that customers receive goods on time and at a reasonable price; information and funds flows play supporting roles to ensure the core supply chain functions smoothly and efficiently from one business partner to another. At the same time, business partners must closely collaborate with each other and streamline the physical flow to reduce waste. Success at moving physical flow can lower costs and increase revenues. Retailers promote goods to customers in an effective manner so that revenues increase and the quality of customer service improves. If customers are satisfied with the goods purchased, retailers will continue to order from manufacturers. Seamlessly moving physical goods from upstream to downstream in the supply chain is indispensable to its sustainability.

Figure 11.1 shows the components of an agile supply chain.

> The JIT ideals suggest an aspect of the Japanese production techniques that is truly revolutionary: the extent to which the Japanese have regarded the production environment as a control. Rather than simply reacting to such things as machine setup times, vendor deliveries, quality problems, and production schedules, they have worked proactively to

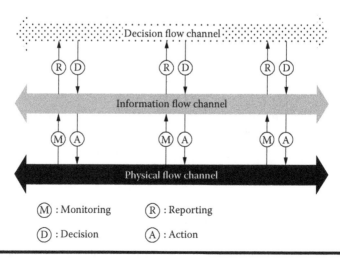

Figure 11.1 Components of an agile supply chain.

shape the environment. By doing this, they have consciously made their manufacturing systems easier to manage. This is in sync with the constructal law that applies to all flow systems: for a finite-size (flow) system to persist in time (to live), its configuration must evolve such that it provides easier access to the imposed currents that flow through it (Bejan and Zane 2012). The constructal theory of global optimization under local constraints explains in a simple manner the shapes that arise in nature. The theory allows one to design and analyze systems under constraints in a quest for optimality. This law was proposed by Adrian Bejan in 1976. He coined the term "constructal" from the Latin verb "construere" (to construct).From a theoretical point of view, constructal is to construct—in order to designate the naturally optimized forms. Examples include rivers, trees and branches, lungs, and the engineered forms that come from an evolutionary process that maximizes flow access in time. The constructal theory posits that in nature the generation of design (configuration, pattern, geometry, etc.) is a phenomenon of physics that unites all animate and inanimate systems. The two worlds of inanimate and animate matter are connected by a theory that flow systems—from animal locomotion to the formation of river deltas—evolve in time to balance and minimize imperfections; flows evolve to reduce friction or other forms of resistance, so that they flow more easily with time. Constructal theory also explains the reason and a scientific basis for the prevalence of S-curve (also known as the sigmoid function) in nature and man-made systems like biological populations, chemical reactions, contaminants, language, information, and economic activity; the ubiquitous S-curve can be viewed as a natural design of flow systems. A new technology, for example, begins with slow acceptance, followed by explosive growth, only to level off before hitting the wall. When plotted on a graph, this pattern of growth takes the shape of an S. For the example of a new technology, per constructal theory, after a slow initial acceptance, the rise can be imagined moving fast through established, though narrow, channels into the market place. This is the steep upslope of the S.

11.2.2.2 SCM Functional Components

1. *Demand management* is the SCM process that balances the customers' requirements with the capabilities of the supply chain. With the right process in place, management can proactively match supply with demand and execute the plan with minimal disruptions. In particular, if managers are proactively managing the demand management process, they need to manage the company's activities that influence customer demand patterns, such as end-of-quarter promotions or financial terms of sale, which cause customers to

react in totally unexpected ways. Thus, the demand process not only includes forecasting but also strategies for synchronizing supply and demand, increasing flexibility, and reducing variability. A good demand management system uses point-of-sale and key customer data to reduce uncertainty and provide efficient flows throughout the supply chain. In advanced applications, customer demand and production rates are synchronized to manage inventories globally.

The output from demand management is important for several reasons. It can help the company with decisions regarding inventory levels, production planning, transportation requirements, and so on. It also provides the information required to organize labor, equipment, raw materials, and semi-manufactured goods. It may also be useful in predicting future cost levels for assessing the challenges of future procurements.

2. *Order fulfillment* is the SCM process that includes all the activities necessary to define customer requirements, design a logistics network, and enable an enterprise to meet customer orders while minimizing the total cost of delivery. More than the functional logistics requirements, order fulfillment needs to be executed cross-functionally and also with the coordination of key suppliers and customers. For example, in complex global enterprises, the finance function provides the requisite information regarding tax rates, tariffs, and exchange rates that determines the selection of the appropriate network configuration, thus affecting overall profitability. The objective is to develop a seamless process from the suppliers through the focal enterprise and on to its various customer segments.

3. *Customer relationship management* is the SCM process that includes all activities related to identifying customers, building and continuously enhancing customer relationships, increasing the awareness of the company's products and services that address the needs of the customer, and enabling the company's sales, marketing, services, and support to the final satisfaction of the customer.

4. *Product development and commercialization* is the SCM process that includes all activities for developing and bringing products to market jointly with customers and suppliers. The product development and commercialization process team coordinates with the CRM process teams to identify customers' articulated and unarticulated needs; develop production technology with the manufacturing flow management process team, keeping in mind the manufacturability aspects of the product; and selects materials and their suppliers in conjunction with the supplier relationship management (SRM) process teams to manufacture and provide the best overall supply chain process for a particular market/product combination.

5. *Manufacturing flow management* is the SCM process that includes all activities necessary to move products through their plants and facilities and to

obtain, implement, and manage manufacturing flexibility in the supply chain via the network of suppliers' and subsuppliers' manufacturing facilities. Manufacturing flexibility reflects the ability to make a wide variety of products in a timely manner at the lowest possible cost. To achieve the desired level of manufacturing flexibility, planning and execution must extend beyond the four walls of the manufacturer to other concerned members of the supply chain.

6. *Sourcing management* is the SCM process that includes activities for matching the manufacturing plan to the corresponding requirements of raw materials and components. Sourcing decisions are especially important when product costs become a significant portion of the price. This involves sales forecasts being broken down into the actual items necessary for manufacturing the products. Some components might be manufactured internally, and only the corresponding raw materials need to be procured for producing them. For others, semimanufactured or even finished goods can be procured from other company-operated locations or from external suppliers.

7. *Supplier relationship management* (SRM) is the SCM process that includes all activities related to interactions with its suppliers. It is the counterpart to customer relationship management in that, just as a company needs to develop relationships with its customers, it also needs to foster relationships with its suppliers. It forges close relationships with a small subset of its key suppliers and manages arm's-length relationships with others. The objective of SRM is to build and maintain relationships with its key suppliers to enhance its value, creating capability and advantage. SRM processes are focused on data that provide information regarding suppliers of raw materials, components, semimanufactured goods and services, and so on.

8. *Returns management* is the SCM process by which activities associated with *returns, reverse logistics, gatekeeping,* and *avoidance* are managed within the enterprise and across key members of the supply chain. The correct implementation of this process enables management not only to manage the reverse product flow efficiently but also to identify opportunities to reduce unwanted returns and to control reusable assets, such as containers. The concept of returns avoidance is a key aspect of this process and differentiates it from reverse logistics. The largest types of returns are consumer returns since they are the result of the perception that a flexible returns policy increases total revenue; marketing returns consist of product returns from downstream inventory positions; products are returned by reason of slow sales turnover, quality problems, or changes in the product mix; asset returns comprise the recapture and repositioning of assets, as in the case of reusable containers; product recall involves recalling a product due to quality or safety issues; and environmental returns are typically triggered by

government regulations. Avoidance has to do with activities that minimize the number of return requests; this dictates that the quality standards must be met before the products leave the company. Gatekeeping refers to the process of minimizing the number of items that are allowed to flow from the reverse channels. This must be achieved without any adverse effect on customer service.

11.2.2.3 Supply Chain Management Maturity (SCMM) Framework

The SCMM methodology defines five stages through which a supply chain progresses—namely, initial, defined, linked, integrated, and extended.

1. Initial
   - Unstructured processes
   - Unpredictable performance
   - High costs
   - Low customer satisfaction
   - Low functional cooperation
2. Defined
   - Basic definitions of processes
   - Traditional definitions
   - High costs
   - Improved customer satisfaction
3. Linked
   - Cooperation
   - Cost decreases
   - High customer satisfaction
4. Integrated
   - Cooperation improved
   - SCM procedures
   - SCM performance measures
   - SCM management systems
   - Marked cost reduction
5. Extended
   - Total cooperation
   - Common processes
   - Common goals

Figure 11.2 shows the various stages of the supply chain maturity framework.

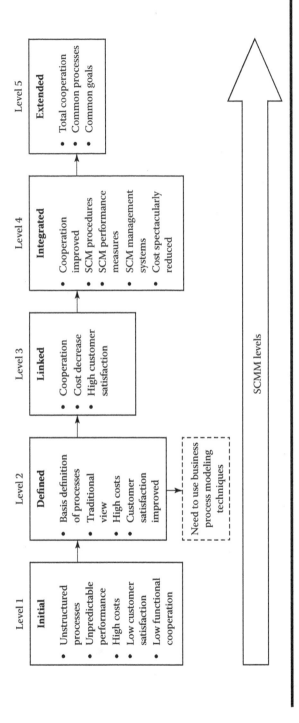

Figure 11.2 SCMM framework.

11.3 Supply Chain Management Framework

Figure 11.3 shows the supply chain operating model, consisting of three principal flows—namely, materials, information, and cash. In Figure 11.4, the squares represent different companies and the lines of connection represent the flows between different companies. The company under consideration is termed the *focal* company, shown in the middle of the figure. Activities and processes related to the conversion of goods from the suppliers (and supplier's suppliers and so forth) up to the focal company are called *upstream*. And activities and processes from the same focal company to its customers (and customer's customers and so forth) are

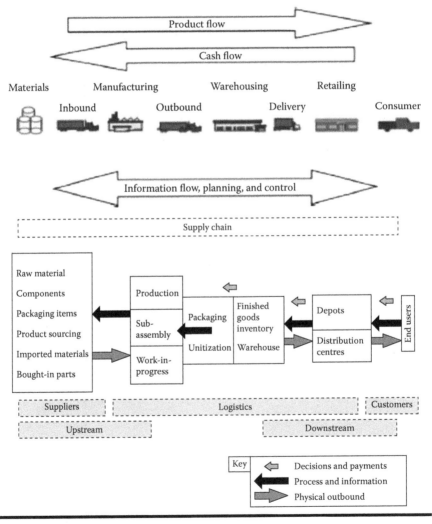

Figure 11.3   Classic supply chain operating model.

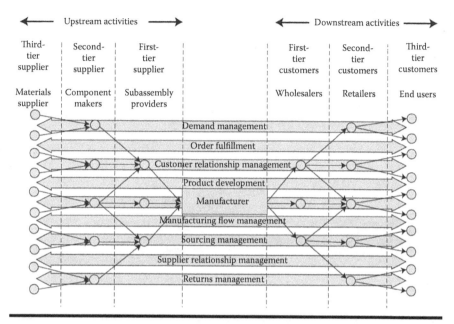

Figure 11.4   Network structure in a supply chain.

called *downstream*. A network structure appears in the figure, containing different layers of suppliers as well as customers. Up to and from the focal company, there are first-tier customers and first-tier suppliers. Upstream, the supplier's supplier is the second-tier supplier and the same tier structure occurs downstream.

Figure 11.5 shows supply chain structures for different industries.

Four SCM patterns can be highlighted.

1. Internal pattern: This corresponds to the activities and process flows of material, information, and cash within the company under focus. Elements in the internal supply chain may be the function and process related to demand management, order handling, planning, sourcing and purchasing, inventory management, warehousing, manufacturing, transportation, and quality inspection.

2. Bilateral pattern: This corresponds to the activities and process flows of material, information, and cash between two companies or two companies within the same group. The bilateral pattern spans the whole spectrum of business relationships from transaction-based arm's-length relations to close business relationships based on trust and shared information. This pattern can be applied in projects such as vendor-managed inventory (VMI), which seek to create optimization between the focal company and one of its suppliers.

3. Chain pattern: This corresponds to a linear chain of companies engaging in goods and services. The chain is only as vulnerable as the weakest link.

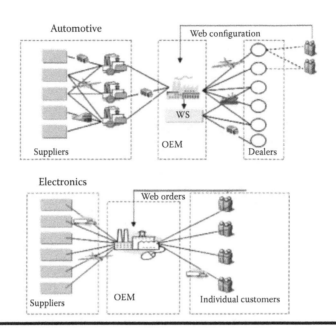

Figure 11.5 Supply chain structure examples.

4. Network pattern: This corresponds to the richest interaction in global and complex business networks, with the exchange of material and information occurring both horizontally and vertically. Moving beyond the traditional linear chain, the network pattern highlights optimization between the focal company and several of its competing suppliers.

11.3.1 Supply Chain Performance Framework

The growing importance of the management of supply chains has motivated researchers and practitioners to develop and implement measures that can be used to establish supply chain performance. The measurement of supply chain performance requires the creation of an interorganizational assessment system. Such systems can feasibly be used to identify high-performance entities and best practices.

11.3.1.1 Volume

Customers now prefer customized products that are aligned with their specifications and preferences.

The key concepts associated with volume are as follows:

1. Product functionality and features are co-created with customers.
2. Products are engineered on platforms incorporating all the prerequisite systems and support.

3. Production processes use postponement to configure the final product as close as possible to the point of delivery.

11.3.1.2 Volatility

Enterprises need the ability to promptly scale up or scale down operations, or engage or disengage outsourced capacities, depending on the surge or slack in customer demand. This will avoid lost sales or prevent lost operational capacities, matching the volatility in customer demands.

The key concepts associated with volatility are

1. The lead time essential for scaling up or down internal capacities, or engaging or disengaging external outsourced capacities
2. The resources essential for scaling up or down internal capacities, or engaging or disengaging external outsourced capacities

11.3.1.3 Velocity

The result of increasing operational velocity will translate into an increase in asset velocity inventory and cash flow. Far too often, enterprises try to increase asset velocity by reducing inventory without the appropriate changes in policies and processes to reduce time and/or increase frequency. This customarily results in poorer customer service. Without the underlying changes (in reducing time and increasing frequency), inventory reduction will only result in lost sales and poorer customer service.

Inventory turns or the number of days of inventory are the two most popular ways to measure inventory velocity. Inventory turns is a measure of the number of times the inventory turns over during a year. It is calculated as the annual *cost of goods sold* (COGS)/average inventory during the year. The number of days of inventory is the average inventory/average daily COGS. Correspondingly, the *cash flow velocity* is the sum of the *accounts receivable* days minus the *accounts payable* days.

While reducing time, one distinguishes between four characteristic times:

■ Need time: The time between when a customer requests a product or service and when they need to receive the product or have the service fulfilled
■ Lead time: The time it takes for you to fulfill a customer request
■ Cycle time: The time taken for each of the process elements
■ Wait time: The time between process elements spent waiting for people, resources, assets, materials, cash, and so forth to start a process element

The gap between the need time and lead time is what creates the need for inventory.

Unlike the time element of velocity, the frequency aspect of velocity has largely been neglected. The frequency of sourcing, manufacturing, replenishment, and customer service has a critical role in improving velocity. Improving frequency directly improves the velocity of operations and reduces cycle stock requirements dramatically. Since forecasts have to be made over a shorter duration, the safety stock requirements also decline. Just as manufacturing frequency needs to be traded off with setup time and costs, replenishment frequency will have to be traded off with truckload considerations. If truckload considerations get in the way of increasing frequency, multistop routes that together make a truckload can be another strategy to increase the replenishment frequency.

Thus, the key concepts associated with velocity are as follows:

1. Asset velocity is the result of improving operational velocity.
2. The gap between need time and lead time determines the amount of inventory needed.
3. Frequency is a largely untapped way of increasing velocity.

11.3.1.4 Variety

Customers demand more and more differentiated offerings. If there is a way you can deal with variety without the associated costs of complexity, you will have the best of both worlds—the variety that customers love and the simplicity that employees and shareholders love. The 80/20 rule is one of the best ways to measure variety; this rule states that 20% of causes contribute to 80% of the results. The 20% of businesses, customers, employees, processes, facilities, and products that contribute to 80% of the revenues, economic surplus, and cash flow represent good variety.

Thus, the key concepts associated with variety are as follows:

1. Variety or complexity tends to slow down systems.
2. Distinguish between good and bad variety in the context of businesses.
3. The costs of differentiation and increased variety are more than compensated for by increased revenues.
4. The complexities and costs associated with increased variety outweigh the increased revenues.

11.3.1.5 Variability

Processes will always have variability—in the inputs they receive (e.g., supplier lead time variability, yield, etc.), the outputs they produce (e.g., customer demand variability, product quality, etc.), and the products and services they deliver (e.g., fill rate, plan compliance, etc.).

The key concepts associated with variability are as follows:

1. All processes have variability: There is variability in the inputs they receive, the outputs they produce, and in the resources, costs, and time they consume to produce those outputs.
2. Controlling variability: Minimize variability wherever possible; if it is not possible, minimize its impact by buffering against variability where it matters most.
3. Differentiate between common causes that do not need intervention and special causes that can be improved.

11.3.1.6 Visibility

Visibility problems exist not only between enterprises but are also equally prevalent within enterprises. Enterprises create teams to ensure specialized competencies are created and nurtured. Over time, each of the teams starts to work within its silo, and the walls that are created distort visibility across the enterprise. Each team begins to create its own set of numbers (forecasts, inventory buffers, etc.), which results in a lot of local optimization but at the cost of global optimization. This distorts *demand* and creates *bullwhip* effects within the enterprise.

The *beer game* illustrates the distortions caused by poor visibility. The three participants in the game—the retailer, the wholesaler, and the marketer or manufacturer—share few data among themselves other than the orders placed. Each participant also tries to maximize his or her "patch." As a result, when there is a small change in demand at the retailer's end, it causes a bullwhip effect that results in bigger changes in demand for the wholesaler, and even bigger changes in demand for the marketer/manufacturer. First there is growing demand that cannot be met. Orders build throughout the system, inventories become depleted, and backlogs grow. Then the beer arrives en masse, while incoming orders suddenly decline, and everyone ends up with large inventories they cannot unload.

The key concepts associated with visibility are as follows:

1. Improve visibility within the organization by designing policies, processes, performance measures, and systems that break down the visibility barriers between marketing, sales, planning, manufacturing, distribution, and transportation.
2. Gain visibility to customers' sales at the stores, the events and promotions they are planning and their impact on forecasts, and the inventories they have at the stores and DCs.
3. Provide visibility to suppliers.

11.3.1.7 Virtuality

Enterprises need the ability to instantiate the business e-processes essential for any part of the operation, be they internal and real, or, outsourced and virtual.

The key concepts associated with virtuality are

1. Interoperable business e-processes
2. Characteristic metrics and measures for monitoring the virtual processes that can be looped back to the virtual process for fine-tuning the performance of the concerned operations

11.3.2 Supply Chain Performance Measurement

The growing importance of the management of supply chains has motivated researchers and practitioners to develop and implement measures that can be used to establish supply chain performance. The measurement of supply chain performance requires the creation of an interorganizational assessment system. Such systems can feasibly be used to identify opportunities for improved supply chain efficiency and competitiveness, to help understand how companies operating in supply chains affect each other's performance, to support the supply chain in satisfying consumer requirements, and to assess the result of an implemented initiative.

Any business should be able to identify a multitude of measures to provide some perspective on supply chain performance. These can be categorized as follows:

1. Strategic
    a. Total cash flow time
    b. Rate of return on investment
    c. Flexibility to meet particular customer needs
    d. Delivery lead time
    e. Total cycle time
    f. Level and degree of buyer–supplier partnership
    g. Customer query time
2. Tactical
    a. Extent of cooperation to improve quality
    b. Total transportation cost
    c. Truthfulness of demand predictability/forecasting methods
3. Operational
    a. Manufacturing cost
    b. Capacity utilization
    c. Information carrying cost
    d. Inventory-carrying cost

11.4 Summary

After introducing the concept of SCM, the chapter described the characteristics and components of SCM. It reinterpreted the traditional supply chain (SC) in terms of the flow of decisions, information, and materials, which eventually leads to the trifurcation of the traditional SC networks into mutually separable decision networks (like Fourth-Party Logistics [4PL]), information networks (like wireless sensor networks [WSN]), and logistics networks (like Third-Party Logistics [3PL]) (see Chapter 13, "Supplier Networks"). The chapter then presented a supply chain performance framework covering dimensions including volume, volatility, velocity, variety, variability, visibility, and virtuality. In the end it described the issues of measurement of the supply chain performance.

Chapter 12

Collaborative Network Enterprises

The concept of collaboration means that participants contribute something for the betterment of the whole. In doing so, the relationship changes from traditional business rules to those based on mutual trust; these are enhanced by performance and contribution. One example is the sharing of new product development information with a vendor. The first commitment a vendor must provide is one of absolute confidentiality: information will not be shared beyond those required to contribute. The supplier agrees to product development confidentiality while the host agrees to not share product innovation or production ideas provided by the supplier. The results are better ideas, lower cost (perhaps shared), and committed production benefiting both supplier and host. It's a win-win arrangement that is likely to provide a better product and improved business success for both parties. For many years, this relationship has been evident in certain industries and some companies, including automotive and electronics manufacturers, and contrasts sharply with the tough adversarial beat-down-the-price and beat-up-the-vendor relationship that exists in many supply chains.

This chapter focuses on the structure, behavior, and evolving dynamics of networks of autonomous entities that collaborate to better achieve common and compatible goals. Instead of focusing on the internal specificities and tight interconnections among the internal components of an enterprise, *the focus* in collaborative networks is directed to the external interactions among autonomous (and heterogeneous) entities (e.g., interoperability mechanisms and tools), the roles of those entities (e.g., coordinator, member, cluster-manager, broker), the main components that define the proper interaction among entities (e.g., common ontologies, contracts, distributed business processes, distributed multi-tasking, collaborative language), the value systems that regulate the evolution of the collaborative association (e.g., collaborative performance records), and the emerging collective behavior (e.g., trust, teamwork), among others.

12.1 Process Networks

Process networks unlock the real economic value of business collaboration. Business collaboration generates meaningful economic value only when it focuses on enhancing the performance of specific business processes that extend across multiple enterprises. Process networks become the mechanism that achieves this performance improvement. As the following examples illustrate, process networks are expanding groups of companies organized by an orchestrator across multiple levels of activity in a business process to improve performance; the long-term economic power of process networks resides in accelerated performance improvement. The core business processes addressed by process networks include customer relationship management, supply chain management, and product innovation and commercialization.

Nike's key business challenge involved coping with a highly volatile fashion business—the athletic shoe product line. Fashions rapidly and unexpectedly emerged and just as rapidly and unexpectedly vanished. Product volumes for specific models could skyrocket and then plummet. Market demand was uncertain, but there was also considerable uncertainty regarding tariff levels and other trading regulations in countries around the world. These tended to change frequently and unpredictably, significantly affecting the cost of a shoe delivered to a retailer. At a much earlier stage in its development, Nike confronted the extreme uncertainty that a growing number of businesses are experiencing. As a result, it needed to create a highly flexible network of production partners around the world that could help it cope with this uncertainty.

Few people realize that Nike does not manufacture any of the shoes that carry its logo. Instead, the company has developed a highly differentiated network of *production partners* (Nike uses this term, rather than *suppliers*, to highlight the importance of business partnership) to meet its needs. First-tier production partners assemble the finished shoes and sell them directly to Nike. Nike segments this first tier into three broad categories:

1. *Developed partners* are focused on producing the leading edge, and most expensive, models of Nike shoes. These tend to be relatively low-volume lines. Nike works closely with these partners in terms of collaborative product development (often pushing shoe technologies to their performance limits) and coinvesting technologies.
2. *Volume producers* are focused more on high-volume shoe lines and often develop a specialization in certain styles of shoes. These partners tend to be more vertically integrated, and they cope with the volatility in volume by working for other customers in addition to Nike.

3. *Developing partners* are focused on the more margin-sensitive shoe lines, for which the ability to take advantage of low labor costs is most critical. As a result, these partners tend to be focused in less-developed economies such as China, Thailand, and Indonesia. They usually produce exclusively for Nike, and in return, Nike works with them to upgrade their capabilities in a *tutelage* program, so that they can evolve into higher-level categories of production partners.

Process networks succeed because they create loosely coupled business processes that are much more flexible and can be tailored to the needs of specific products, customers, or both. Loosely coupled business processes are modular; the modules represent either work groups within a company or, in the case of process networks, entire companies. Standardized interfaces for each module enable the modules to be dynamically swapped to tailor the business process. Loosely coupled business processes today are found largely within emerging process networks; loosely coupled business processes will become much more prevalent within as well as across enterprises. Process networks are different because the role of the orchestrator extends beyond two levels of activity in the business process. For instance, in the case of a supply network, orchestrators are making choices not just regarding their direct suppliers but also regarding the suppliers to their suppliers and even farther back into the supply chain.

Since orchestrators are much less involved in managing the day-to-day activities of service providers, the information architecture of a loosely coupled business process is quite different from a more conventional business process. In a conventional process, managers focused on directing microactivities across the business process require full information transparency. All information about all activities must be accessible at all times for the managers to perform their role. This is why conventional business process reengineering often requires massive changes in the architectures of corporate databases. Fragmented and imperfect information becomes a significant source of process inefficiencies. In a more loosely coupled business process, the needs for information are much more selective across the process network. Rather than full information transparency, in which all information about all activities must be accessible to process managers at all times, a process network requires selective information visibility. Selective visibility means that only certain information is provided to selected participants at the appropriate times.

Service providers need two types of operating information from the orchestrator:

■ They need selective operating information to perform the task at hand.
■ Beyond task-related operating information, service providers also need tailored capability-building programs to keep up with the evolution of broader product platforms.

Conventional business processes create economic value through experience effects. As a business gains more experience with a process, it uses that experience to find ways to deliver more value at lower cost. These experience effects can also be achieved across a limited number of enterprises working together to support a specific business process. However, managers quickly encounter diminishing returns as the number of enterprises working together increases. Given traditional approaches to managing hardwired business processes, the escalating costs of complexity involved in coordinating multiple enterprises at a detailed activity level soon overwhelm any potential experience effects. Process networks with loosely coupled business processes also benefit from experience effects, but the real economic power comes from the opportunity available to each service provider to increasingly specialize in the activities for which it has world-class capabilities.

Rather than encountering diminishing returns at the overall process level as the number of participants increases, process networks encounter increasing returns; the value delivered by the process network increases as the number of participants increases. With an increasing number of participants, each service provider has a greater opportunity to specialize and improve its own performance accordingly. The orchestrator also has more flexibility in tailoring the business process to the specific needs of the individual product, customer, or both.

Process networks are also very different from business-to-business marketplaces, which focus on facilitating transactions, helping to connect buyers and sellers, and providing transaction-processing support. Most of the economic value of a business is concentrated in the processes that surround a transaction, rather than in the transaction itself. Process networks focus on improving the performance of business processes across many levels of an industry value chain. In this way, they can provide far more value than business-to-business marketplaces can provide.

12.2 Collaboration

Collaboration between enterprises can be defined as a form of organizing in which people from autonomous organizations go into durable agreements and, consequently, mutually harmonize elements of the work between themselves.

There are different ways of specifying the precise form of the collaborative efforts. Collaborative models can be arrayed around two dimensions:

1. The *sharing to exchange* dimension
    Exchanging versus *sharing* mainly deals with the extent to which the partnership demands that the partners dare to relativize their uniqueness in exchange for synergy. On the one hand, there are partnerships in which the participating organizations enter into very close relationships and mutually align their work methods and even their strategies to one another; they share organizational aspects. However, you don't just go ahead and do that; you only do it with a partner that brings some very unique competencies to the table. It is worth investing in the "togetherness," in the mutual alignment

of the work methods, and in letting go of other opportunities to make this opportunity work. The partners are prepared to enter into an exclusive relationship, and they consolidate their mutual dependency in agreements that will prevent their investment from draining away through the togetherness or failing to yield worthwhile returns. This is the case, for example, when you want to outsource a job or where you see a specific business opportunity that you wish to explore in a partnership with a specific party. In this kind of situation, it is preferable to do business with a specific partner; however, if that does not work out, then you can always find an alternative party.

You also have partnerships on the other side of the spectrum, in which the partners enter into much looser relationships. The mutual dependency is limited, which means that it is always possible to change partners. The partnerships are focused on the exchange of products, services, experiences, knowledge, and data, without there being any need for the partners to make radical organizational changes or to relinquish their uniqueness: this is not about assimilation but coexistence. The partners do not need to agree on everything (i.e., reach a consensus), as long as they agree at the level at which they exchange their products, services, and so on. These types of partnerships often flourish in environments where the relationship is expanded over several different parties. This includes partnerships in retail chains (with producers, distribution centers, transporters, wholesale chains, etc.), regional chains in the care sector (with general practitioners, hospitals, nursing homes, rehabilitation centers, and homecare), or the public order and safety chain (consisting of the police, the public prosecutor, the penitentiary services, the reclassification system, etc.). These types of relationships regularly feature in environments in which the partners form a group focused on a specific theme or on creating shared preconditions. It includes themes such as *underground building, public services, regional development*, or *software for production companies*. The venture is undertaken by several partners, the parties can decide whether they wish to collaborate or not, and the group can also attract other parties or dispose of existing ones.

2. The *improving to renewal* dimension

Some forms of cooperation are aimed at improvement; this includes doing everything we have been doing before, but only better and smarter. One organization transfers one of its jobs to another organization (e.g., part of the production process, the execution of the operational processes, etc.), which results in a cooperative relationship. In that sense, the partnership is primarily an extension of one of the partners' ambitions. You have a recognizable initiator/principal on the one hand and a contractor on the other. The result or performance that one partner receives from the other is the key focus of the relationship. The collaboration is characterized by the optimal control of the performance; the collaboration benefits from stability.

The other side of the story is collaboration aimed at renewal; this is a question of gaining access to new opportunities through smart combinations.

The partner organizations can vary greatly in size, but they share a sense of equality in terms of the collaboration. It is not obvious, in advance, what the partnership will ultimately yield; it is only possible to define this in terms of objectives, intentions, and ambitions. The guidelines are not determined by the quality of the results but by the quality of the process. These types of partnerships are future oriented and flourish in environments with an abundance of entrepreneurial behavior, creativity, and innovative strength in the relationship.

12.2.1 Transactional Collaboration

The section outlines the organizational principles of transactional cooperation.

1. Making agreements on result description: The focus is on the result, which is also the connecting point in the partnership. It is the basis for the exchange of cooperation (the transaction). The joint determination of the result therefore demands detailed care and attention. To enhance the level of commitment, you need to jointly formulate the result description.
2. Assurance of connectability: Partnerships work best if the contact point between the partner organizations is well organized. The use of information and communication technology offers a wide range of options to improve the efficiency of the contact point in chains in which this basic model is frequently used.
3. Steering on transaction costs and chain efficiency: The partners obviously assess one another and the partnership based on all sorts of relationship characteristics; however, below the line, the legitimacy of the partnership is based on the height of the transaction costs and the level of chain efficiency. It's not so much about the price the one party charges the other as it is about the cost of the product or service for both organizations, including the costs related to the maintenance of the partnership.
4. Using a results-oriented management style: Transactional partnerships do well under results-oriented managers who, with due consideration to the relational conditions, continuously monitor the process to ensure that the legitimacy of the partnership is consistently proven in the quality and cost of the result.

12.2.2 Functional Collaboration

This section offers an outline of the organizational principles of functional collaboration.

1. Making agreements on service levels: Organizations in a functional partnership are closely intertwined and mutually harmonize their organizational systems. The central themes in that regard are performance agreements

known as *service-level agreements* (SLAs). It is preferable for the partners to determine the service levels jointly and not for one of the partners to dictate them to the other.

2. Assurances of principalship and contractorship: Functional partnerships are often interpreted as purchasing relationships that are not supposed to demand a great deal of care and attention. The contrary is in fact true: it is precisely this intimate form of partnership, which often also has a longer duration, that demands serious attention to the contact points between the organizations and the quality of the relationship. Therefore, this also entails a serious approach to the question of principalship and contractorship in both organizations.

3. Steering on process integration and service quality: The supplying partner is asked to crawl under the skin of the receiving partner and to adopt a whole lot of customs, business-operational principles, and cultural values from the receiving organization. The extent to which the organizations succeed in doing that is evident from the extent of the process integration and the realized service quality.

4. Using a service-oriented management style: The functional partnership is not a domain for remote management, because it demands a high level of intensive involvement on both sides. One of the more common misunderstandings is that the required service-oriented management style should mainly be displayed on the contractor side. That attitude is, however, also a basic condition, on the principal side, for a successful functional partnership.

12.2.3 Explorative Collaboration

The organizational principles of explorative collaboration are as follows:

1. Making agreements on the rules of the game: The purpose of an explorative collaboration is for the participating partners to explore together. There is no clearly delineated result but, at most, there is a catalytic theme. The partners do, however, need some baseline set of conditions for collaboration, which is formulated in the rules of the game. For example, they make agreements on the confidentiality and reciprocity of the information exchange. It is quite often the case that there is no natural compulsion to determine the rules of the game, but experience has shown that these ground rules do contribute to the clear arrangements and appointments and to the quality of the partnership.

2. Assurance of the professional added value: Explorative partnerships often have a somewhat looser structure. This means that an explorative partnership also attracts parties that are not able to add any additional professional value or do not plan to do so. This poses a threat to the quality of the partnership, and as a result, it is important to constantly monitor the professional and balanced contributions of the partners.

3. Steering on accessibility and optimal interaction: The downside of the "looseness" of the explorative collaboration, as mentioned previously, is that bonding and connectedness are sometimes a bit tricky to organize: professional interaction is hard to bring about. It is therefore important to minimize the barriers to collaboration for the desired partners and to make sure to create effective opportunities for interaction. This is one of the top priorities for the moderator of the explorative partnership.

4. Using a facilitating management style: An explorative partnership demands a management style that puts accessibility and interaction center stage in terms of attitude and behavior. The positional exercise of power has a counterproductive effect and is more about influence than about power. It should not, however, be confused with modesty and a predominantly cautious action repertoire. Decisiveness is in fact what is needed in this type of environment, with the understanding that it must be exercised with due diplomacy. One of the most important instruments available to the facilitating manager, in an explorative collaboration, is the set of agreed rules of the game.

12.2.4 Entrepreneurial Collaboration

1. Making agreements on procedures: Procedures play the same role in the entrepreneurial partnership that the rules of the game play in the explorative partnership. The procedures are however much more clearly formulated and have a substantially bigger impact. Transgressing the procedures of, for example, confidentiality will not only potentially compromise the relationship, but is potentially a threat to the continuity of the cooperating organizations. Procedures rely on confidentiality, admission, withdrawal, appreciation/valuation, and the division of the development, copyrights and property rights, and so on. The organizational principle in the entrepreneurial partnership is to take these procedural aspects of the partnership seriously and to organize them well.

2. Ensuring exclusivity: The foundation of the mutual understanding between the cooperative partners is the shared vision and the agreements that the partners make in terms of what they can and will do inside and outside the partnership. This demands a clear determination of the scope of the partnership, observance of the related agreements, regular refreshment of the agreements, and transparency concerning apparently competitive initiatives.

3. Steering goals and synergy: Although the parties involved in an entrepreneurial partnership don't simply start cooperating out of the blue, they also do not operate based on any precise descriptions of the expected results. The partners do commit to certain goals, and the jointly established synergy does offer a view of the feasibility of the goals. It is therefore important to approach the goal-steering process in a professional way and to routinely put the level of mutual synergy on the agenda. Programmatic work procedures can yield benefits in this type of situation.

4. Using a goal-oriented management style to create room to maneuver: This basic partnership model demands a goal-oriented management style—with a view to legitimizing the partnership, but not in such a way as to undermine the explorative aspect of the partnership. It is a question of balance between exploration and exploitation, between design and development, and between diverging and converging. It is quite obvious that this is a special task for people with special qualities. Whatever applies to the transactional and functional basic models also applies to the explorative and entrepreneurial basic models; an explorative partnership could be the run-up to a more intensive form of collaboration in the form of an entrepreneurial partnership. As a matter of fact, most partnership forms are actually interim forms and thereby derive qualities from two or more basic models.

12.3 Collaboration Strategies

Collaborative networks engender collaborative advantage for the members of the collaborative networks.

12.3.1 Product Life Cycle Management

The practice of sharing and collaborating on product design using supply chain partners has emerged as a significant management tool, especially in industries using outside contract manufacturing facilities and those with multiple design engineering input locations. Included in this category is real-time information sharing on product tracking and product genealogy throughout the life of the product. These data could include the following: complete product design history from initial concept to product disposal, quality assurance data, and use and repair information throughout the useful life of the product to disposal or recycle.

Product life cycle management describes software information systems used to manage the information and events associated with a product, from concept through design through manufacturing through distribution; it also includes user feedback processes. The capabilities of an effective system enable interaction among departments within a company or an extended enterprise of supply chain partners. Collaboration is based on the idea of interactive co-development and management. Participants in co-development may be within a company, sharing information among product development, manufacturing, marketing, and purchasing as also the extended enterprise. In many businesses, the participants include suppliers and their suppliers, and it is not unusual to include customers and their customers at some points in the process. Some companies have hundreds of people involved on product project teams that can last for years.

Modern applications of product life cycle management are built around a closed-loop process that begins with customer requirements information management and concludes with collection and management of customer feedback information to start the process over again. These systems have evolved from early computer-aided design (CAD) and computer-aided engineering (CAE) to product data management systems that support and connect global network nodes with proactive system tools built around creating, storing, and managing product and process information across the extended enterprise. The use of the Internet provides a global reach that can include real-time interactive sessions with participants anywhere.

The benefits of using a collaborative product development system are as follows:

- Collaborative design allows participants of an interactive design session to discuss design concepts and direction. Several concepts may be developed and discussed in a single interactive session using an online system. Design teams may interact via a Web browser and review several variations of a design done interactively using input from both the customer and in-house design teams. The ability to collaborate with colleagues in different locations around the world results in the best ideas being exchanged simultaneously, reducing re-engineering efforts and the best product offerings at the lowest costs throughout the program.
- Faster product development cycle times (fewer design turns) and greater efficiency also result from automated workflow, 24/7 capability, and effective sharing and visibility of common information. Many suppliers believe that the potential exists for significant reductions in product development time using collaborative tools and processes.
- Workflow functionality can ensure that necessary follow-up actions take place, thereby avoiding potential delays and allowing engineers to meet key milestones.
- Real-time review and approval of data and program-related information allow customers, suppliers, and internal users to improve efficiency and quality through earlier design involvement and participation. Teams will be able to mark up and annotate designs and provide manufacturing feasibility in a real-time capacity.
- Using workflow to manage access and approval of designs in a central repository would reduce cycle time in the development process and facilitate informed decision making.
- A collaborative development system will allow process/procedure tracking and an audit trail useful in ISO 9000 certification.
- New employee effectiveness can be enhanced as a result of the predefined workflow process and documentation availability through a central repository and virtual workspace.
- Standardized processes for completing development tasks can be communicated more effectively within organizations.

12.3.2 Synchronized Inventories and Production

The objective of these collaborations is to synchronize inventories across supply chain partners. This entails removing the inventory buffers that most companies put in place to preserve their ability to provide products to customers when unanticipated adverse events impact the production plan. Another major factor is basing production plans on a demand forecast that is shared between supply chain partners as much as is practical and useful. Within this view is the growing requirement of mass customization to meet individual customer desires. Inventory management is a crucial element in accomplishing individualized unit production without a major adverse cost impact, and the key to inventory management is to produce to actual demand, not anticipated or forecast demand.

One of the major factors effecting inventory overbuild is the bullwhip effect, which describes the demand amplification primarily due to misinformation as requirements move up the supply chain. Demand distortion is generally used to describe an overreaction to actual demand, but it could equally describe an under-response. The underreaction would have adverse effects in that customer service could suffer and sales likely would be lost. Over-responding or amplifying the demand information results in peaks and valleys in manufacturing, causing problems of cost and inventory build-up.

Bullwhip effect is caused because of:

1. Demand forecast updating: Every company prepares forecasts to guide their organization on subjects such as production quantities, inventory levels, material requirements, and financial requirements. Because people are using available information when making or adjusting forecasts, they tend to react to obvious demand information. When a customer places an order with a supplier, the individual receiving the order is likely to see that as an indication of future demand. Forecasts are based on historical and the latest current information, with individuals likely to overreact to positive trends by increasing their orders to upstream suppliers to ensure their ability to deliver. In a supply chain of any size, the cascading effect of the distorted demand can be very significant.
2. Order batching: Ordering cycles can distort demand by accumulating quantities into infrequently placed orders. An example is a company that sells 1 of an item each day but places orders every 2 months because of internal reasons. The supplier sees something quite different from the actual demand of one per day.
3. Price fluctuation: Special pricing, such as promotions or seasonality, can cause customers to overbuy to meet future needs, resulting in inventory that exceeds current demand.
4. Rationing and shortage gaming: A shortage, real or imagined, can be seen as a threat to future supply causing buyers to overbuy today to ensure inventory availability tomorrow.

Another kind of distortion occurs within companies as plants, departments, and individuals accumulate inventory that was produced to counteract adverse events within production processes. Usually referred to as buffer inventories, they can exist anywhere in the supply chain production process. Some production systems have automatic built-in buffers in areas such as lot sizing or scheduling algorithms.

Both of these effects are the result of rational decision making by members of the supply chain. By understanding the underlying issues, companies can reduce the effects through more effective information systems and more collaborative relationships with supply chain partners. Collaboration is used to address the fundamental causes of what are obviously dysfunctional system processes by first giving visibility to the processes and events on a holistic basis. It is not enough to view just a department or a plant, but each decision point of the entire value chain must be included in the examination of existing methods. The solution will include most of the following steps:

- Synchronization of demand and supply: This requires the participants to see the actual demand requirements, with the value chain host providing leadership on demand identification for all value chain participants and processes. Decision points must be highly visible with absolutely correct real-time information and a single schedule.
- On-line information transfer: Communications channels must provide timely and accurate transmittal of compliance, as well as condition change information, such as quantity revisions or exceptions to planned events. Modern information technology, including Internet access, e-mail, and automatic integrated system updates, are required.
- Time buffers: Time buffers should be the tool used to respond to unanticipated events, not inventory buffers.

12.3.3 Distribution Order Fulfillment

The most successful implementation of collaboration to date appears to be Collaborative Planning, Forecasting, and Replenishment (CPFR®), a model developed by the Voluntary Interindustry Commerce Standards (VICS) Association. VICS is made up of a number of large-scale, consumer goods manufacturers and retailing corporations that set out to improve manufacturing scheduling and responsiveness to demand fluctuations. It deals with methods regarding inventory management between the manufacturer and the retail store, and methods for determining demand in the value chain.

The traditional answer to addressing customer service problems has been to increase inventories. If inventory is in the pipeline, including the stores, then consumers will never have to deal with products being out of stock. Unfortunately, inventory is expensive in terms of capital consumption and expense. Participants have also found that inventory management initiatives frequently involve direct inventory reductions and shifting of inventory burden. Inventory has a way of hiding inefficiencies in processes and generates some of its own. The supply process variability is an area of significant inefficiencies. Inventory also drives storage costs, increases the handling of products and inventory inhibits flexibility. Within the store, inventory affects shelf productivity and impacts assortment opportunities.

The most significant driver in nearly all inventory decisions is management of uncertain demand. The more unpredictable the demand, the more inventory is required to manage the risk of lost sales. In addition, the farther away from the consumer an inventory buffer is in the value chain process, the more demand variability that inventory buffer will have to address. This is referred to as the Forrester effect. The Forrester effect is created by the lack of coordination of downstream demand information with supply processes back through the value chain. Each demand and supply pairing is managed independently; the cost of inventory generated by this lack of coordination ultimately is buried in the product cost to the consumer.

Another potential source of inventory distortion is the uncertainty of supply processes. Supply variability drives inventory at both the beginning and the end of value chain nodes:

- At the input stage of a supply chain node the reason for variability is a supplier failing to deliver what is ordered.
- At the output stage of a supply node, inventory depends on the flexibility of the node process, expressed as process cycle time, to react to demands on it. It is fairly common for output inventories to be equal to the node process cycle times (in contrast, finished goods inventories for manufacturers are frequently equal to production lead times.) It is also common for process cycle times to have hidden time buffers to compensate for process inconsistencies. These time buffers are ultimately equal to output inventory buffers.

Collaboration allows value chain participants to coordinate the planning for supply processes to reduce the multiple sources of supply variability and subsequent inventory.

There are three forecasting and replenishment processes being used by the retail value chain:

- Aggregate forecasting and replenishment are the traditional methods of interaction between business trading partners. The manufacturer and retailer views of this process along with some of their deficiencies will be reviewed. The manufacturing approach generally follows these steps:
  - Assemble data: The core data used for forecasting include historical shipments, syndicated data, and sales forecasts. Typically, the data are aggregated to the product family or brand level by week or month, and by market regions.

- Forecast sales: The available data input and plans from marketing that focus on influencing demand are used to generate an aggregated consumer demand forecast. The best practice is to use this forecast to drive integrated planning across the corporation. Frequently this does not happen, as the desire for meeting short-term targets often preempts the best forecasting algorithms.
- Forecast orders: The aggregated consumer forecast drives a coordinated effort to create a supply plan that supports the designated level of sales. The demand and supply are matched by planning the customer-order flow and finished-goods inventory flow into distribution centers. Planning systems with conventional distribution requirements are sometimes used to facilitate a customer pull-through process.
- Order generation: As the execution phase begins, a retailer places a purchase order. One primary driver of the ordering process is replenishment activity; the key to this is warehousing withdrawals by stores. Other input involves the basic ordering parameters that factor inventory targets and transportation costs into ordering quantities. The third primary driver is promotional activity.
- Order fulfillment: Once retail orders are received, manufacturers look to the available inventory and determine whether the order will be filled completely. If an allocation needs to take place, the manufacturer notifies the retailer. This contact marks the first collaboration within the process.
- Frequently the first notification of a shortage occurs when the retail receiver opens the back of the truck. In either case, given the short order cycles, the retailer and the manufacturer have little recourse for remedying the shortage. If the retailer has been carrying enough inventory, the consumer may not be disappointed. If not, sales are lost. Either outcome is costly.

The retailer goes through a series of steps similar to that of the manufacturer.

■ Vendor-managed inventory (VMI): The VMI approach was developed to avoid some of the process problems identified above. A key technology component that has made VMI possible is the ability of supply chain applications to manage inventories at retailer locations. Demand and supply now come together at the retail receiving location. This is frequently the distribution center, yet store-level VMI is also common. VMI practices and technology provide a broader view of the inventory holding locations and pipeline activities; this gives the manufacturers better information for planning inventory deployment across the pipeline. It also allows the manufacturer to be more customer-specific in their planning and to plan at a much lower level.
■ Jointly managed inventory (JMI): The JMI approach focuses on collaboratively planning and executing the business at a much lower level of detail.

This allows an increased focus on the consumer and on exploiting opportunities frequently hidden in the aggregated data. Jointly managed inventory uses teams of people working only with key accounts. Frequently, team members are located geographically close to each other, which allows frequent face-to-face meetings. This fosters open communication between functional counterparts, which in turn furthers process customization. The improved understanding of each other's operations and the increased interaction that results helps foster trust between the trading partners.

Table 12.1 gives a comparison of the three forecasting and replenishment processes used in retail value chain.

CPFR principles have been developed from the best practices of both VMI and JMI. The trading partner framework and operating processes focus on consumers and are oriented toward the value chain process:

1. Trading partners manage the development of a single shared forecast of consumer demand that drives planning across the value chain. Embedded in the concept of a single shared forecast is the orientation of forecasting toward a level of detail that supports the identification of consumer opportunities. While information sharing and demand planning at some level of aggregation are practical, the ability to work together to discover and exploit these opportunities requires an interactive flow of information within a framework of collaboration.

   The value of having a single demand plan is to better coordinate value chain process activities. This coordination would yield significant, but not dramatic benefits. Dramatic benefits come from using the demand plan to affect the constraints inhibiting supply process performance, for example:
   a. Manufacturing flexibility: Manufacturing capacity is not used because retailers' normally short order cycle times are inconsistent with longer manufacturing cycle times. By extending the retailers' order cycle and thus making it consistent with the manufacturing cycle, production could move to a "make-to-order" process for some products. This removes the need to hold a significant number of finished goods inventories in the value chain and improves customer service.
   b. Dynamic interenterprise scheduling to optimize asset utilization across manufacturing.
2. Trading partners jointly commit to the shared forecast through risk sharing in the removal of supply process constraints, transportation, and distribution centres.

The underlying principles of the process are what generate the dramatic potential benefits of collaboration. Building a trading partner framework, creating a

Table 12.1 Comparison of Forecasting and Replenishment Processes Used in Retail Value Chain

	Aggregate Forecasting	Vendor Managed Inventory	Jointly Managed Inventory
Joint Business Planning	Limited joint business plan development	Limited joint-business plan development	Heavy emphasis on joint-business planning and coordinated execution planning
Assemble Data	Syndicated data and historical sales	POS, warehouse withdrawal data, syndicated data	POS data by product, store, and week; syndicated data
Sales Forecasting	Sales forecast done at a high level of detail: category, week or month, market or region	Sales forecast generated by: product, customer DC, by week. Store-level VMI is by product, store, week	Sales forecast generated at the store level by product by week. Identifies micro-marketing and micro-merchandising opportunities
Order Forecasting	Primarily focused on manufacturing support to its own distribution centers. Frequently not done by retailers	Focused on retailer DC driven by inventory and transportation cost targets; store-level VMI focused on store inventory; still focused on supply coming from supplier DC	Time-phased replenishment of stores, retail DCs, and supplier DCs
Order Generation	Generated by retailer expecting 100% fulfillment from supplier	Generated by supplier based on the pull from store replenishment or consumer demand for store-level VMI	Could be generated by either party based on store-level sales that are lime-phased to supply capabilities
Order Fulfillment	Supplier provides what is available at its DC	Supplier fills orders from its DCs, giving priority to VMI customers	Supplier fills orders from its DCs or manufacturing, depending on the extent of integrated planning

single forecast of consumer demand, and synchronizing manufacturer- and retailer-order cycles all focus on creating an inter-enterprise, value chain environment that reduces waste and cost. Collaboration supports marketing, promotion, management, manufacturing, transportation, and planning activities. The information shared as part of this process enhances the accuracy of the forecast and order fulfillment. The extension of the collaboration into the value chain environment is the fundamental change that creates new opportunities.

For most companies, the return on investment generated by CPFR will be substantial. Financial improvement comes through revenue growth due to improved customer service, balance sheet improvement from reduced inventories, and expense reduction from improved supply-process efficiency and productivity improvement. A basic assumption behind CPFR is that technology investments for improving internal integration can be leveraged if companies extend the technologies to their trading partners.

> A fundamental part of the ideas behind both synchronized inventories and CPFR collaboration is an intense focus on manufacturing products to an actual demand as opposed to a forecast demand. Although any production environment other than a build-to-order method will have some degree of an estimate, the idea is to eliminate as much of the guesswork as possible and to use time buffers, not inventory buffers, to address any discrepancy. This is best accomplished through a scheduling system that integrates each node of the supply chain into a single schedule and provides actual demand information to each participant. This approach requires complete visibility and accuracy of production events and processes, and is a part of the trust equation that is so important to successful collaboration.

12.4 Innovation Networks

This subsection discusses the functioning of collaborative networks with the aid of an innovation framework that deals with the following overall workflow:

1. Influences from the environment provide stimuli on people inside the organization.
2. Realization occurs and a knowledge exploration, modeling, and ideation cycle starts.
3. This cycle, which is a high-level business process, includes several mid-level business processes.
4. During this cycle, many knowledge objects are retrieved and used, and some are newly created.

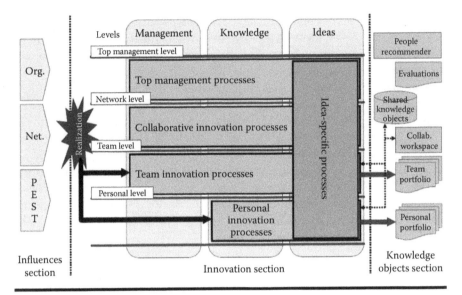

Figure 12.1 Innovation framework business processes.

12.4.1 Influences Phase

The *influences* phase captures all sources of stimuli that might have some impact on the innovation process. Depending on their origin, three types of influences have been identified:

1. Influences from inside the company or organization: The primary source of influences lies within the company or organization, originating mainly from the corporate strategy, policies, rules, and operational tactics, as well as from the corporate culture and value system. The procedures, structures (explicit or implicit), hierarchies (formal or informal), and social networks have a great impact on the innovation process, as they might control access to valuable knowledge resources and also provide the context needed for innovation to take place and propagate to the decision makers.

2. Influences from the external company or organization network: The secondary source of influences lies within the company's network of partners, suppliers, and customers. Partners and suppliers can help in improving and rationalizing the organization's business processes and structures in order to increase efficiency. Customers are the users of companies' products and/ or services, and therefore, they can provide valuable feedback about product and service functioning, characteristics, and suitability for purpose, as well as providing insights on their own actual needs that must be met by new products and services.

3. Influences from the broader environment: The supplementary source of influences lies in the broader context of the political, economical, social and technological (PEST) environment within which the company or organization exists and operates. Technology in the last few decades has proven to be a quite versatile environment and simultaneously a driving factor for innovation.

12.4.2 Innovation Phase

The *innovation* phase is the core part of the innovation process. In the real world, innovation can occur as a result of several interacting and interrelating business processes; not all of them aim to generate new ideas, but they might lead to innovative results as a by-product. However, in the innovation process, the focus is on processes that explicitly seek new idea generation (e.g., knowledge modeling) as well as idea management.

1. Areas of interest

    The *areas of interest* identify three domains (areas) that are involved in innovation processes and innovation management:

    a. The *management* area of interest includes the activities of the strategic innovation process, which relates to the decision making and management of people, teams, projects, and resources. These activities do not generate new knowledge or ideas but provide the necessary operational environment for innovation to take place.

    b. The *knowledge* area of interest includes the activities of the innovation process that relate to knowledge exploration, exploitation, leveraging, creation, modeling, and knowledge management. The *knowledge cycle* falls into this area of interest. The activities of this area are usually providing the necessary influence, context, and background needed for ideation to occur. For this reason we can consider the ideas area as an extension of the knowledge area.

    c. The *ideas* area of interest includes all activities of the innovation process, which relate to the generation of new ideas (ideation), the development and evolution of already proposed ones, and the management of proposed ideas. The *ideation cycle* falls into this area of interest. This area focuses specifically on ideas, not on knowledge in general.

2. Levels

    The *levels* concept helps in distinguishing and grouping the interacting structures and the related business processes, depending on the level of complexity and/or authority.

    a. Top management: The processes, methods, tools, or any other concepts used by the top management of the company and their assistants, both for managing the whole innovation process as well as making informed decisions on innovations and ideas.

b. Network or open team: The processes, methods, tools, or any other concepts used by networks formed from interacting and collaborating teams.

c. Team or group: The processes, methods, tools, or any other related concepts used by (planned) teams. Such teams do not necessarily have a formal internal structure.

d. Individual: The processes, methods, tools, or any other related concepts used by a single individual.

3. Business processes

Business processes refer to those processes that take place within a company or organization and are explicitly aimed at idea generation and management. Generally, a business process is a set of linked activities that create value by transforming an input into a more valuable output; both input and output can be artifacts and/or information, and the transformation can be performed by human actors, machines, or both. Such business processes exist at every level of the organization and span several areas of interest. Interactions occur among business processes both within the same area and level, as well as across different areas and levels.

A business process can be decomposed into several subprocesses that have their own attributes but also contribute to achieving the goal of the superprocess. The analysis of business processes typically includes the mapping of processes and subprocesses down to the activity level. Activities are the parts of the business process that are devoid of decision making and, for lack of insight, are not worth decomposing any further.

Innovation frameworks consist of two classes of business processes:

a. Horizontal processes, including personal innovation–related processes, team innovation–related processes, collaborative innovation–related processes, and top management innovation–related processes. Horizontal processes span all areas of interest and reside at any one of the levels. An innovation-related business process includes activities residing in many areas of interest—that is, knowledge-related, innovation-related, and management-related activities. Also, business processes at different levels have different attributes, as the goals, tools, and practices used at each level are different.

b. Vertical processes are associated with ideation-specific processes. Vertical processes reside in the ideas area of interest and can span all levels of the innovation framework. These processes are of special interest because they focus on pure innovation activities such as

- Ideation
- Idea development
- Idea management
- Prediction

4. Business process interactions

As indicated earlier, interactions occur among business processes and their activities; these interactions can be of many different types, such as
- Workflow
- Activity ordering
- Decision points
- Influences or other implicit impacts

Management activities tightly interact with knowledge activities to enable them to produce and disseminate new knowledge. This basic interaction leads to the generation and evolution of new ideas, thus starting and influencing the innovation activities (Figure 12.2).

5. Knowledge cycle

The *knowledge cycle* involves activities related to the knowledge life cycle and knowledge management.
- The initial definition of process goals and strategy
- Knowledge exploration or seeking
- Knowledge retrieval or extraction
- Knowledge use, exploitation, and leveraging
- New knowledge capture, modeling, and storing
- Knowledge sharing or dissemination
- The reframing and redefinition of exploration purpose or point of view
- Other knowledge management activities

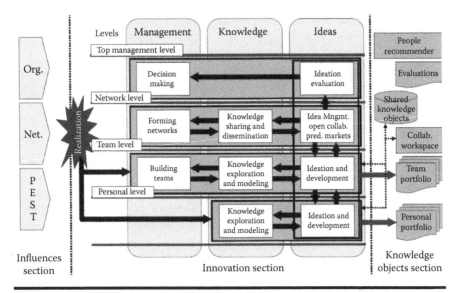

Figure 12.2 Innovation framework business process interactions.

6. Ideation cycle

The *ideation cycle* involves activities related to the idea life cycle and idea management.

- The initial definition of process goals and strategy.
- Existing idea searching, reuse, and leveraging. Existing ideas will then be used as the starting point for further innovation.
- Idea generation or ideation. The leveraging of existing knowledge assets.
- Idea elaboration or development. The leveraging of existing knowledge assets.
- Idea capturing, modeling, and storing.
- Idea sharing or dissemination.
- The reframing and redefinition of ideation purpose.
- Other idea management activities.

12.4.3 Knowledge Objects Phase

The *knowledge objects* phase includes all entities and media containing or conveying knowledge. Knowledge objects can be a *database* or *knowledge base*, a folder of documents, a single document, a software package, and so on. A knowledge object can be of various types:

- Those residing in knowledge stores
- Idea models
- Idea portfolios
- Those residing in collaboration workspaces
- Evaluation reports

The knowledge and information contained in knowledge objects can be represented in various different formats (e.g., database records, plain text, rich text, XML, voice recordings, pictures, drawings etc.).

12.5 Summary

This chapter focused on the structure, behavior, and evolving dynamics of networks of autonomous entities that collaborate to better achieve common and compatible goals. Instead of focusing on the internal specificities and tight interconnections among the internal components of an enterprise, *the focus* in collaborative networks is directed to the external interactions among autonomous (and heterogeneous) entities. After describing various types of collaborations, the chapter introduced the innovation framework business processes. In the last part, the chapter discussed collaborative strategies in the areas of product life cycle management, inventory management, and order fulfillment.

NETWORK BUSINESSES EXAMPLES

This section deals with examples of network enterprises. Chapters 13 and 14 present the supplier and manufacturing network enterprises respectively. Chapter 15 and 16 describe e-business and platform network enterprises respectively. Chapter 17 is on popular social network enterprise applications like Facebook and Twitter. Chapter 18 introduces the sensor network enterprises.

 To avoid being tedious, we may refer to network enterprises as networks, but the reader should not lose the sight of the fact that every time we refer to network we are truly referring to network enterprises.

Chapter 13

Supplier Networks

Enterprises that wish to engage in e-business find that they must be involved in managing the network of all upstream companies (supplier side) that provide input directly or indirectly, as well as the network of all downstream companies (customer side) that are responsible for delivery and aftermarket service of a particular product to a customer. Essentially, a supply chain is a network of interlinked suppliers and customers, where each customer is, in turn, a supplier to the next downstream organization, until a complete product reaches the end customer. We may define a supply network enterprise as the network that encompasses all the organizations and activities associated with the flow and transformation of decisions, information, and goods from the raw material stage, through to the end user.

In this definition, decisions, information, and materials flow both up and down the supply chain, while the supply network manages the ICT infrastructure, enterprise information systems, sourcing and procurement, production scheduling, order processing, inventory management, warehousing, customer service, and overarching policies and strategies that oversee enterprise operations. Supply networks are typically comprised of geographically dispersed facilities and capabilities, including sources of raw materials, product design, and engineering organizations, manufacturing plants, distribution centers, retail outlets, and customers, as well as the transportation and communication links between them. The supply network includes all of the capabilities and functions required to design, fabricate, distribute, sell, support, use, recycle, and dispose of a product, as well as the associated decisions and information that flows up and down the network enterprise.

13.1 Suppliers

Suppliers can be categorized into the following types:

1. Facilities and equipment builders or vendors: These are companies involved in the construction of supply chain network (SCN) facilities or in the production–distribution of manufacturing and warehousing equipment. They provide the lasting resources used by the company to perform insourced activities.
2. Contract manufacturers: These are the subcontractors selected by the firm to perform outsourced manufacturing activities.
3. Logistics service providers: These are warehousing and/or transportation companies providing storage space for outsourced storage activities and transportation means for the movement of products between activity locations.
4. Material vendors: These are external raw material, component, or product sources. In a manufacturing context, they provide the material associated with the leaves of bill of material (BOM) trees. In a distribution context, they provide the products sold to customers. In an activity graph, they provide the material identified on the arcs adjacent to the generic supply activity.
5. MRO vendors: MROs are *maintenance*, *repair*, and *operating* supplies. They are required to perform activities, but they do not become part of the end product or are not central to the firm's output. MRO items include consumables such as cleaning, testing, or office supplies; minor industrial equipment such as measurement instruments and safety equipment; spare parts, lubricants, and repair tools required to maintain facilities and equipment; computers; furniture; and so on. MRO items are usually not shown explicitly on activity graphs.

The nature of the relationship developed with suppliers is significantly influenced by three contextual factors:

1. The value creation impact of the product or service: The value creation impact is related in particular to technology. A commodity has much less value than a high-tech component based on proprietary technology.
2. The complexity of the supply process: Supply complexity depends on how easily a product or service can be obtained. A commodity largely available on the market is easy to procure. However, if only a few vendors qualify to supply the product, if capacity is limited, if just-in-time (JIT) deliveries are required, or if quality is critical, then it is much more difficult to find good suppliers.
3. The risks involved.: Risks are related mainly to the possible disruption of the supply line and to price fluctuations. If an item is procured close by in the same country, risks are lower than if it is purchased overseas in a country with highly fluctuating exchange rates and strong inflation.

The nature of the relationships developed with suppliers depends on whether the need for its products or services is repetitive or not. Most buying and outsourcing relationships involve repetitive needs. They may also involve a single product or a family of products. This is important because significant economies of scope may be generated when several items are procured from the same vendor. In this context, some kind of contract must be negotiated with suppliers. These can range from mid-term commodity-specific contracts to long-term partnerships. For example, contracts with material vendors could take the following forms:

1. Fixed price: The vendor sets a unit price based on expected volumes and the buyer has the flexibility to order any quantity at any time during the contract period. This type of contract is widely used in practice.
2. Fixed commitment: A periodic (say, monthly) fixed delivery quantity is specified by the contract. Discounts are offered based on the level of the fixed quantity commitment.
3. Minimum quantity commitment: Periodic minimum quantities are imposed by the contract and the buyer has the flexibility to order any quantity above this minimum in each period of the contract (say, each month of a yearly contract). Discounts are offered based on the level of the minimum commitment.
4. Order band commitment: Periodic minimum and maximum quantities are imposed by the vendor and the buyer has the flexibility to order any quantity in the interval specified. Discounts are offered based on the level of the minimum commitment and the range of the interval.

The procurement of plant, equipment, and MRO supplies is often nonrepetitive. In the former case, it takes the form of investment projects. Alternative proposals are usually evaluated using a life cycle cost approach; that is, the evaluation is based on the total cost of ownership over the life of the asset. In addition to the financing of the construction acquisition costs, the expenditures considered include operations, maintenance, overhaul, and replacement or disposal costs. When relevant, the environmental and social impact of the options considered must also be evaluated. It may also be possible to lease equipment instead of buying it. The acquisition of nonrepetitive MRO supplies often takes the form of spot buys. This involves finding a low-value item or service quickly to fulfill a short-term need. The item may be purchased from a local store, for example, but nowadays, e-procurement is often used. When the item is more expensive, a request for proposal (RFP) may be issued either by phone or via the Internet to be able to evaluate a few options.

13.1.1 Debacle at Cisco

In 2000, Cisco Systems was the world's foremost e-business and the most valuable company on the planet, more valuable even than Microsoft, with a market capitalization of $579 billion.

In April 2001, Cisco announced its first quarterly decline in revenues since it was founded in 1985, along with over 8000 redundancies, a restructuring of the business, and a rationalization of its portfolio of routers, switches, and other equipment that powers the Internet and large corporate networks.

Cisco's own results for the quarter ending January 27, 2001 had already confirmed that something was going badly wrong. It showed that the level of inventory (finished and semifinished goods) on its books had more than doubled from $1.2 to $2.5 billion over the preceding 6 months.

Cisco's operational capabilities came from its online supply chain management system—the most advanced in the world. From the mid-1990s, Cisco's *network strategy* used the Internet to create interactive relationships, linking employees, partners, suppliers, and customers together. The links enabled Cisco itself to concentrate on product design, while other tasks were outsourced to suppliers and contract manufacturers.

The company had always made customer service and on-time order fulfillment key performance indicators internally and throughout its extended enterprise. The Internet-based network allowed customers to order and configure online, and contract manufacturers to begin building systems within 15 minutes of receipt of the order. Third-party logistics suppliers were also linked in to the system, enabling Cisco to provide customers with information on the status of their orders at any time. The network strategy facilitated direct fulfillment, which led to a reduction in inventories and labor and shipping costs, saving Cisco $12 million per year. Cycle times were further shortened by the online prototype testing of customers' new systems, allowing lead times to be reduced from weeks to days and Cisco to monitor demand and revenues on an hour-by-hour basis. This *virtual close* facility not only helped Cisco to run its own business but also became a useful marketing tool to promote its systems to customers.

In June 2000, a booming market led to component shortages, delaying deliveries of customer orders by 3–4 weeks. It was by then becoming apparent that there were also communication and forecasting problems between Cisco and lower tiers of subcontractors in the network. The problem was quickly addressed by the introduction of Cisco Connection Online, linking in all subcontractors. The Integrated Commerce Solution (ICS) was introduced, connecting in any remaining larger customers (mainly telecoms equipment distributors or operators) who had previously been unable to link up. Thus, all parties were connected in real time to the network.

To overcome the problem of component shortages, Cisco entered into long-term contractual agreements with key suppliers of scarce components. The forecasts for these orders were based on the projections of sales staff. These were in turn based on indications of demand from suppliers and partners (systems integration consultants) and customer orders. What Cisco's real-time systems failed to recognize was that waning confidence in delivery lead times was prompting buyers to overorder. Customers were placing multiple orders with several suppliers, accepting only the first to deliver. Cisco was itself actioning orders that would never be confirmed, and its suppliers—who were also receiving multiple orders from other manufacturers—would interpret and duly report this as a surge in demand. Cisco's inventory cycle rose from 53.9 to over 88 days.

The problem was eventually recognized toward the end of 2000, when Cisco began the hurried implementation of its e-hub solution, which would automatically cancel any unconfirmed order within two hours. But the task of implementing the e-hub proved more costly, complex, and time consuming than expected. When the bubble burst, Cisco was left holding the inventory.

13.2 Decision Networks

Responding to demand surges and supply disruptions requires the efficient redistribution and reallocation of resources based on real-time decision making through information sharing and collaboration. Hurricane Katrina provided evidence of the importance of efficient decision making, collaboration, and information sharing in response to demand surges and supply disruptions. Wal-Mart was able to move supplies to areas hit by Hurricane Katrina because it had an emergency operations center that was staffed around the clock by decision makers who had access to all of the company's systems. District managers could call in to request supplies, and the decision makers, with the help of the logistics department, would decide on how to relocate supplies to the affected area. They also relied on historical point-of-purchase data from other hurricanes to forecast consumer demand before and after the hurricane, and used these data to stockpile emergency supplies in distribution centers around the affected areas. Wal-Mart, therefore, mostly relied on reallocating and redirecting existing capacity to meet the demand surge. In contrast, the U.S. government relied on redundant capacity maintained in the Strategic Petroleum Reserve to mitigate the supply disruptions caused by Hurricane Katrina in the Gulf of Mexico.

13.2.1 Decision Graphs

Decision models help the decision maker to choose the best decisions during uncertainty—that is, those decisions that maximize the expected utility of an agent, given its current knowledge (i.e., evidence) and its objectives under a decision-theoretic framework.

Decision theory provides a normative framework for decision making during uncertainty. It is based on the concept of *rationality*—that is, that an agent should try to maximize its utility or minimize its costs. This assumes that there is some way to assign utilities (usually a number that can correspond to monetary value or any other scale) to the result of each alternative action, such that the best decision is the one that has the highest utility. In general, an agent is not sure about the results of each of its possible decisions, so it needs to take this into account when it estimates the value of each alternative. In decision theory, we consider the *expected utility*, which takes an average of all the possible results of a decision, weighted by their probability. Thus, in a nutshell, a rational agent must select the decision that maximizes its expected utility.

13.2.1.1 Fundamentals of Utility Theory

In utility theory, the different scenarios are called *lotteries*. In a lottery, each possible *outcome* or *state*, A, has a certain probability, p, and an associated preference to the agent, which is quantified by a real number, U. For instance, a lottery L with two possible outcomes, A with probability p, and B with probability $1 - p$, will be denoted as

$$L = [p, A; \ 1 - p, B]$$

If an agent prefers A rather than B, it is written as $A > B$, and if it is indifferent between both outcomes, it is denoted as $A \sim B$. In general, a lottery can have any number of outcomes; an outcome can be an atomic state or another lottery.

Utility theory can be defined in an analogous way to probability theory by establishing a set of reasonable constraints on the preferences for a rational agent; these are the axioms of utility theory.

> *Order*: Given two states, an agent prefers one or the other or is indifferent between them.
>
> *Transitivity*: If an agent prefers outcome A to B and prefers B to C, then it must prefer A to C.
>
> *Continuity*: If $A > B > C$, then there is some probability, p, such that the agent is indifferent between getting B with probability one, or the lottery $L = [p, A; \ 1 - p, C]$.
>
> *Substitutability*: If an agent is indifferent between two lotteries A and B, then the agent is indifferent between two more complex lotteries that are the same, except that B is substituted for A in one of them.
>
> *Monotonicity*: There are two lotteries that have the same outcomes, A and B. If the agent prefers A, then it must prefer the lottery in which A has higher probability.
>
> *Decomposability*: Compound lotteries can be decomposed into simple ones using the rules of probability.
>
> Where:
>
> *Alternatives*: The choices that the agent has and are under his control. Each decision has at least two alternatives (e.g., to do or not do some action).

Events: These are produced by the environment or by other agents; they are outside of the agent's control. Each random event has at least two possible results; although we do not know in advance which result will occur, we can assign a probability to each one.

Outcomes: The results of the combination of the agent's decisions and the random events. Each possible outcome has a different preference (*utility*) for the agent.

Preferences: These are established according to the agent's goals and objectives and are assigned by the agent to each possible outcome. They establish a value for the agent for each possible result of its decisions.

The definition of a utility function, then, follows from the axioms of utility.

The *utility principle* states that if an agent's preferences follow the axioms of utility, then there is a real-valued utility function, U, such that

1. $U(A) > U(B)$ if and only if the agent prefers A over B.
2. $U(A) = U(B)$ if and only if the agent is indifferent between A and B.

The *maximum expected utility principle* states that the utility of a lottery is the sum of the utilities of each outcome multiplied by its probability.

$$U[P_1, S_1; P_2, S_2; P_3, S_3; \ldots] = \sum_j P_j U_j$$

Based on this concept of a utility function, we can now define the expected utility (EU) of a certain decision D taken by an agent, considering that there are N possible results of this decision, each with probability P:

$$EU(D) = \sum_{j=1} P\left(\text{result}_j(D)\right) U\left(\text{result}_j(D)\right)$$

The principle of *maximum expected utility* states that a rational agent should choose an action that maximizes its expected utility.

13.2.1.2 Decision Trees

Decision trees are a tool for modeling and solving sequential decision problems, as decisions have to be represented in sequence, as in the previous example. However, the size of the tree (i.e., the number of branches) grows exponentially with the number of decision and event nodes, so this representation is practical only for small problems. An alternative modeling tool is the *influence diagram* (see Section 13.2.1.3), which provides a compact representation of a decision problem.

A decision tree is a graphical representation of a decision problem, which has three types of elements or nodes that represent the three basic components of a decision problem.

1. A *decision* node is depicted as a rectangle that has several branches; each branch represents each of the possible alternatives present at this decision point. At the end of each branch there could be another decision point, an event, or a result.
2. An *event* node is depicted as a circle, and also has several branches, each representing one of the possible outcomes of this uncertain event. These outcomes correspond to all the possible results of this event; that is, they should be mutually exclusive and exhaustive. A probability value is assigned to each branch, such that the sum of the probabilities for all the branches is equal to one. At the end of each branch there could be another event node, a decision node, or a result.
3. The *results* are annotated with the utility they express for the agent and are usually at the end of each branch of the tree (i.e., the leaves).

13.2.1.3 Influence Diagrams

Influence diagrams (IDs) are viewed as extensions of Bayesian networks (BNs), incorporating decision and utility nodes. In the following sections, we present a brief introduction to IDs, including their representation and basic inference techniques.

13.2.1.3.1 Modeling

An influence diagram is a directed acyclic graph, G, that contains nodes representing *random*, *decision*, and *utility* variables.

1. Random nodes (X) represent random variables as in BNs, with an associated CPT. These are represented as ovals.
2. Decision nodes (D) represent decisions to be made. The arcs pointing toward a decision node are informational; that is, the random or decision node at the origin of the arc must be known before the decision is made. Decision nodes are represented as rectangles.
3. Utility nodes (U) represent the costs or utilities associated with the model. Associated with each utility node there is a function that maps each permutation of its parents to a utility value. Utility nodes are represented as diamonds. Utility nodes can be divided into ordinary utility nodes, whose parents are random and/or decision nodes, and supervalue utility nodes, whose parents are ordinary utility nodes. Usually, the supervalue utility node is the (weighted) sum of the ordinary utility nodes.

There are three types of arcs in an ID:

1. Probabilistic: Indicate probabilistic dependencies, pointing toward random nodes.
2. Informational: Indicate information availability, pointing toward decision nodes. That is, $X \to D$ indicates that value of X is known before the decision D is taken.
3. Functional: Indicate functional dependency, pointing toward utility nodes.

In an ID there must be a directed path in the underlying directed graph that includes all the decision nodes, indicating the order in which the decisions are made. This order induces a partition on the random variables in the ID, such that if there are n decision variables, the random variables are partitioned into subsets. Each subset, R_1, contains D_i, all the random variables that are known before the decision and unknown for previous decisions. Some of the algorithms for evaluating influence diagrams take advantage of these properties to make the evaluation more efficient.

IDs are used to aid a decision maker in finding the decisions that maximize its expected utility. That is, the goal in decision analysis is to find an optimal policy, $\pi = \{d_1, d_2, \ldots, d_n\}$, which selects the best decisions for each decision node to maximize the expected utility, $E_\pi(U)$. If there are several utility nodes, in general we consider that we have additive utility, so we will maximize the sum of these individual utilities.

$$E_\pi(U) = \sum_{u_i \in U} E_\pi(u_i)$$

13.2.1.3.2 Evaluation

Evaluating an influence diagram (ID) involves finding the sequence of best decisions or the optimal policy. First, we will see how we can solve a simple ID with only one decision; then we will cover general techniques for solving IDs.

We define a simple ID as one that has a single decision node and a single utility node. For this case, we can simply apply BN inference techniques to obtain the optimal policy with following algorithm:

1. For all $d_i \in D$:
   a. Set $D = d_i$.
   b. Instantiate all known random variables.
   c. Propagate the probabilities, as in a BN.
   d. Obtain the expected value of utility node, U.
2. Select the decision, d_k, that maximizes U.

For more complex decision problems in which there are several decision nodes, the preceding algorithm becomes impractical. In general, there are three main types of approaches for solving IDs:

1. Transform the ID to a decision tree and apply standard solution techniques for decision trees.
2. Solve the ID directly by variable elimination, applying a series of transformations to the graph.
3. Transform the ID to a Bayesian network (BN) and use BN inference techniques.

13.2.2 Hierarchical Decision Model

The hierarchical decision model is more traditional; it is based on following assumptions:

1. Uniformity: There is a certain uniformity within an organization or between organizations.
2. Hierarchy: A second assumption is, of course, that there is a pyramidal power structure with superiors and subordinates. The assumption is that this is not only the formal structure but that it also exists in reality. This assumption is fallacious, primarily because of mutual dependencies, which belies the truth about hierarchy.
3. Open: Agents are open to interventions of a superior agent.
4. Stable: This hierarchical structure is reasonably stable.

 The following discussion refers to the network decision model and network enterprises interchangeably. This should not create any confusion, since the correct meaning should be clear by context.

Table 13.1 presents a comparison between hierarchical and network decision models.

Table 13.1 Comparison between Hierarchical and Network Decision Models

Hierarchy	Network
Uniformity	Variety
Unilateral dependencies	Mutual dependencies
Openness/receptiveness to hierarchical signals	Closedness to hierarchical signals
Stability	Dynamic

13.2.3 Network Decision Model

The network decision model is more traditional; it is based on following assumptions:

1. Variety: The network model is characterized by great variety: many different agents, products, interests, and so on. For instance, in multinational enterprises, which may comprise tens of operating companies, dozens of business or product groups, and a number of country organizations, influencing such a variety of agents calls for so much knowledge and expertise that no single agent can meet all the requirements. Consequently, actors who intervene never know exactly what impact such an intervention will have. If one and the same intervention is used in a world of variety, all kinds of unforeseen effects may occur. An intervention that is effective for agent A, will not work for agent A′, will work even less for agent A″, and will not work at all for agent B.

   Variety limits the reach of the intervention. The risk is that only in a limited number of companies will there be a close fit between the interventions and the company's characteristics. In other companies, all kinds of irregularities might manifest themselves, and this will produce unforeseen effects in the intervention.

2. Interdependence: The agents that together form a network are dependent on each other. This means that, in some cases, agents simply do not accept directives from another agent. Even an agent that regards itself as temporarily superior to the other agents is dependent on others at that particular time, because another agent will be superior next time or with regard to an another subject.

   Interdependencies can be of several types:
   - Single-value–multivalue: Actors have a single-value dependence on each other if the dependence can be expressed in one value. In networks, the dependencies tend to be multivalue ones. Actors are dependent on each other for information, for example, but also for money, land, goodwill, and so on.
   - Bilateral–multilateral: Two actors may be interdependent. The situation is complex where large numbers of actors are interdependent. A is dependent on B, B on C, and C on A. Simple bilateral agreements are then no longer possible; third and fourth parties are needed.
   - Synchronous–asynchronous: A relatively simple situation is one in which actors know that they are all dependent on each other at the same time. A form of barter is then possible by making equal exchanges. In complex situations, the dependencies will be asynchronous: the actors need each other at different times, which may be far removed from each other.

- Sequential–simultaneous: Dependencies in networks may be coupled to each other sequentially: an act by A is possible only if B has performed an act earlier. Set against them are simultaneous dependencies. An act by A depends on B, who should act at the same time.
- Static–dynamic: Many dependencies will change. New subjects, political changes, new and broken coalitions, and the introduction of new technologies may lead to new interdependencies. These are then dynamic rather than static interdependencies. The more dynamic interdependencies are, the less transparent a network is.

3. Closedness: The closedness of an enterprise results from its core values: values that are deeply rooted in the enterprise and that determine most of the enterprise's actions. Closedness tends to be an important precondition for actors to function properly. The business unit within a multinational enterprise, which has its own product range and is responsible for good operating results. A business unit needs room for entrepreneurial behavior. It has its own suppliers and its own customers. Much of the behavior of the business unit will depend on these parties, which implies that a business unit can be relatively closed to interventions from the top of the organization because they may conflict with the interventions from the market.

    This makes closedness one of the main strengths of an organization, one that an intervening actor may utilize. It might be difficult to gain the support of a closed actor, but once this support has been gained, an intervening actor has a strong ally.

4. Dynamic: The positions of the agents in a network change constantly. An agent that used to play an insignificant role in a network may suddenly occupy an important position and be vitally important to the others. The result may be that ignoring this agent is no longer possible and that serious negotiations with this agent are needed. New agents may enter the decision-making process and others will leave. Agents may change their opinions or may learn during the process that they have no prospect of gain, which will change their attitude toward the other actors.

The dynamic nature of networks means that agents' strategies should always be adaptive. If positions in networks change continuously, agents will have to monitor the other agents in the network continuously and will have to be prepared to change their strategies.

13.3 Information Networks

Depending on the capabilities (technology and manpower) of network members, the benefit of information sharing will also range from basic inventory reduction to higher profit earning. Manufacturers can reduce variance in demand forecasts if historical order data are readily available and being used efficiently. Sharing of demand information with upstream members helps in reducing manufacturers' supply chain cost in Collaborative Planning, Forecasting, and Replenishment (CPFR). Knowledge on demand information also helps to reduce the inventory costs of both supplier and customer. Meanwhile, sharing demand information along with the current inventory status facilitates reductions in inventory costs. Updates on point-of-sale (POS) data can improve forecasts of promotions and new products.

The information exchange among network members varies widely across different supply chains. For instance, retailers in the supply chain are more interested in promotional sales and, hence, need to know about recent price reductions and upcoming promotions. On the other hand, manufacturers are interested in having POS data and inventory levels at retail outlets for production planning, material resource planning, and logistics planning, and also for avoiding excess inventory.

Six attributes of information exchanges are as follows:

1. Source of information: The source of information indicates the parties involved in an information exchange. In particular, the source can help to identify who observes or owns the data. In simple terms, the source indicates the whereabouts of the information available.
2. Cost of information: The cost of information denotes the cost incurred by the supply chain members to obtain information.
3. Availability of information: This indicates the status of the availability of the information on a specific time scale, such as always, intermediate, short term, sometimes, and after or before an event. The time scale is dependent on the duration of special events/sales promotions in a particular company.
4. Reliability/accuracy of information: The descriptive nature of the observer and market can alter the reliability of the information. Hence, it is obligatory for managers to know how accurate the information is before using it in the company's decision making.
5. Actionability of information: The extent to which the available information can be used in forecasting, production, and replenishment is represented through actionability. Here, the actionability represents the capability of using the available information in the network.
6. Significance of information in the network processes, such as collaborative planning, forecasting, production, and replenishment, decides the need for information exchange among the network members.

The *bullwhip effect* is an illuminating example of the great importance of information flow to supply networks. The term was coined by executives of Proctor and Gamble, who observed that, even though the consumer demand of nappies was fairly stable, the retailers' orders were highly variable and production orders even more so. Small variations in the retail sales of products become larger variations of distributors' orders on the factory and enormous swings in manufacturers' orders on suppliers. This increase in the variation of demand is similar to the increasing amplitude of cycles in a bullwhip when it is moved at one end. The effect is widely observed in food supply chains.

Four causes of the bullwhip effect have been identified.

■ Links updating their forecasts independently
■ Order batching
■ Price fluctuations
■ Inflated orders during periods of rationing

The simplest solution to this effect is to share the retail sales information with each link back up the supply chain. When partners farther up the chain can see the steady demand by end consumers, the tendency to generate safety stock against feared future increases diminishes significantly.

Building on the *double bell* model of a supplier network, the information framework is proposed to analyze whether sufficient information is available across the whole supply chain. This information framework contains five basic supply network stages (suppliers, manufacturing, distribution, retailing, and customer orders and forecasting) and four decision phases (strategic analysis, planning, execution, and intercompany). The information framework is a tool to investigate whether the information systems available are sufficient to support logistics decisions. It is used by indicating where each of the available sets of information sits in the matrix. The resulting data pattern indicates areas that lack information and data sets that can be coordinated (Figure 13.1).

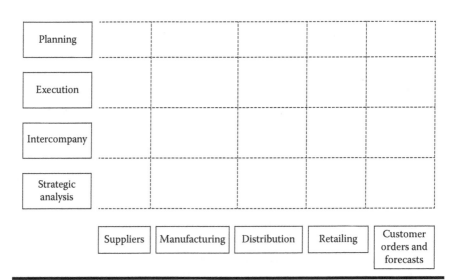

Figure 13.1   Supply network information framework.

The five stages should be populated with the following information:

1. Supplier information: The products available for purchase and their stock availability, lead times, and prices, as well as purchase order status and supplier performance analysis
2. Manufacturing information: The products available for manufacture, in what batch sizes and lead times, at what cost, and what location
3. Distribution information: What is to be transported, to what distribution center, by what mode, and at what price
4. Retail information: Similar to distribution, but more local and detailed
5. Demand information: Who is buying what products, at what price, where, and in what quantity; forecasts of future orders and long-term trends

Table 13.2 lists types of data exchanged in supplier networks.

13.3.1 e-Sensors for Supporting Supplier Networks

The next evolution of the *intelligent agent* concept is the development of integrated hardware/software systems that may be specifically designed to sense (perceive) and respond (act) within certain predefined operational constrains and factors, and respond in a real-time fashion to changes occurring throughout the supply network. These integrated hardware–software systems are termed *e-sensors*. Enterprises will need to create new business applications to put e-sensors at the center of a process if they want to be competitive in this new supply chain environment.

Current supplier network information technology (IT) allows managers to track and gather intelligence about their customers' purchasing habits. In addition to point-of-sale Universal Product Code (UPC) barcode devices, the current IT infrastructure may include retail radio frequency identification (RFID) devices and electronic tagging to identify and track product flow. In addition, there is a need to obtain (sense) real-time data for managing (anticipating, responding) throughout the supplier network. Typically, companies need to synchronize orders by type, quantity, location, and the timing of the delivery in order to reduce waste in the production and delivery process. The data collection and availability provided by the e-sensing infrastructure/architecture allows for a collaborative environment, improves forecast accuracy, and increases cross-enterprise integration among partners in the supplier network.

13.4 Logistic Networks

Logistics network and distribution center (DC) location strategies are aimed at establishing the most appropriate blend of storage and transport at a given customer service level. The interrelationship of the different distribution elements and

Table 13.2　Types of Data Exchanged in Supplier Networks

Information Sharing (Data Type)	Purpose
Inventory	Minimizing inventory cost
Historical data	Decision on technology investment
Demand inventory	Minimizing total inventory cost
POS and inventory	Minimizing inventory cost
Demand and inventory	Minimizing inventory cost through whole SC
Demand information	Minimizing total inventory cost
Order history	Decision on technology investment
Demand information (asymmetric)	Improver supplier benefit
Inventory, sales, order status, sales forecast, production/ delivery schedule	Total supply chain cost saving
POS and market data	Improve responsiveness to demand fluctuations
Demand, recovery yield, capacity utilization	Capacity utilization showed more value than any other information in a capacitated closed-loop supply chain
Demand information	Study changes in inventory level and service level
SKU-store level data	Forecast promotions
Sales data and promotion plans	Improve planning, forecasting, and replenishment

their associated costs thus provide the basis for decision making. To plan an efficient logistics structure, it is necessary to be aware of the interaction between the different distribution costs—specifically, as to how they vary with respect to the different site alternatives (number, size, type, and location) and what the overall logistics costs will be.

There are a number of different types of DC:

■ Finished goods DCs/warehouses, which hold the stock from factories.
■ Distribution centers, which might be central, regional (RDC), national (NDC), or local DCs. All of these will hold stock to a greater or lesser extent.

- Trans-shipment sites or stockless, transit, or cross-docking DCs, which, by and large, do not hold stock but act as intermediate points in the distribution operation for the transfer of goods and picked orders to customers.
- Seasonal stockholding sites.
- Overflow sites.

There are a number of reasons why DCs and warehouses are required.

1. To hold the inventory that is produced from long production runs. Long production runs reduce production costs by minimizing the time spent for machine setup and changeover, enabling *lean* manufacturing.
2. To hold inventory and decouple demand requirements from production capabilities. This helps to smooth the flow of products in the supply chain and assists in operational efficiency, enabling an *agile* response to customer demands. Note that many supply chains have strategic inventory located at several different points, whereas this buffer only needs to be held at what is known as the *decoupling point*, the point at which discrete product orders are received.
3. To hold inventory to cater for large seasonal demands more economically.
4. To hold inventory to help provide good customer service.
5. To enable cost trade-offs with the transport system by allowing full vehicle loads to be used.
6. To facilitate order assembly.

For the best possible customer service, a DC would have to be provided right next to the customer, and it would have to hold adequate stocks of all the goods the customer might require. At the other extreme, the cheapest solution would be to have just one DC (or central warehouse) and to send out a large truck to each customer whenever his or her orders were sufficient to fill the vehicle, so that an economically full load could be delivered. This would be a cheap alternative for the supplier, but as deliveries might then only be made to a customer once or maybe twice a year, the supplier might soon lose the customer's business.

There is obviously a suitable compromise somewhere between these extremes. This will usually consist of the provision of a number of DCs on a regional or area basis, and the use of large primary (line haul) vehicles to service these, with smaller vehicles delivering the orders to customers. For certain operations, of course, even these simple relationships will vary because of the need for very high levels of customer service or the very high value of products.

By its very nature, logistics operates in a dynamic and ever-changing environment, which makes the planning of a logistics structure a difficult process. The component parts of a distribution system necessarily interact with one another to form the system as a whole. Within this system, it is possible to trade off one element with another, and so gain an overall improvement in the cost-effectiveness of the total system. An appreciation of the makeup and relationship of these key costs is thus a vital link to successful distribution planning and operations.

One way of overcoming this problem is to adopt a *total* view of the system, to try to understand and measure the system as a whole as well as in relation to its constituent parts. Total logistics cost analysis allows this approach to be developed on a practical basis. Figure 13.2 shows the effects of a different number of DCs and the related costs on the total distribution cost; it also shows how any changes to one of the major elements within such a structure will affect the system as a whole.

The figure shows that for just a single DC, there is a large local delivery cost to add to the much smaller costs of primary transport, inventory, storage, and systems. It can be seen from the graph that the least expensive overall logistics cost occurs at around 6–8 DCs. Similarly, it is often possible to create total cost savings by making savings in one element, which creates additional costs in another but produces an overall cost benefit.

The cost and service trade-offs within any logistics structure will, of course, vary from one company to another, depending on the role the company plays within the supply chain as a whole. In the main, however, the following major costs and their associated trade-offs may need to be considered and assessed.

1. Production costs: These will vary according to the type of production process or system used and the type of product manufactured. Make-to-stock or make-to-order will also be relevant. Factories may be focused on one or two specific types of product or may make a large range of different products.

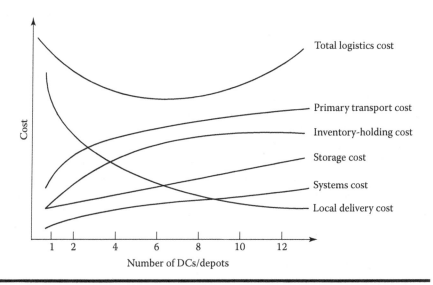

Figure 13.2 Relationship between total and functional logistics costs as the number of depots in a network changes.

Different distribution structures may be required to support different types of product. The effect on primary transport costs will be very relevant.

2. Packaging costs: These are mainly concerned with the trade-off between the type of packaging and the handling and transport costs. The type of load unitization will also be important.

3. Information systems costs: These cover a wide area from order receipt to management information systems. The type of DC network will affect many of these costs.

4. Lost sales costs: These might occur because of inadequate customer service and are very relevant in the context of the proximity of the DC to the customer, together with the reliability and speed of service.

5. Inventory costs: These include the cost of capital tied up in inventory, the cost of obsolescence, and so on. They have a fundamental relationship with the DC network in terms of the number of stockholding points and the hierarchy of stockholding according to DC type.

6. Transport costs: The number and location of sites within the distribution structure and the associated throughputs significantly affect transport costs. Both primary transport and final delivery costs are affected by DC numbers and location.

7. Warehousing costs: These costs vary according to the type of storage and handling systems used, together with the volume and throughput at the site. The size and type of site will thus be important, as will the location.

13.5 Summary

This chapter reinterpreted the traditional supply chain (SC) in terms of the flow of decisions, information, and materials, leading to the trifurcation of SC networks into mutually separable decision networks (like Fourth-Party Logistics [4PLs]), information networks (like wireless sensor networks [WSN]), and logistics networks (like Third-Party Logistics [3PLs]). In relation to decision networks, the chapter discussed two types of modeling techniques for problems with one or many decisions: decision trees and influence diagrams. As in the case of probabilistic models, these techniques take advantage of the dependency structure of the problem to have a more compact representation and a more efficient evaluation.

Chapter 14

Manufacturing Network Enterprises

Taking advantage of the competitive offering of products (and services) to customers in geographically dispersed, emerging, and established global markets nowadays demands higher quality products of a greater variety and at a lower cost with shorter response times. As a result, firms have been forced to reorganize their activities and realign their global strategies in order to provide the speed and flexibility necessary to respond to windows of market opportunity. Consequently, organizations have moved from centralized, vertically integrated, single-site manufacturing facilities to geographically dispersed networks of resources. Additionally, in order to acquire technological know-how and assets quickly, or to acquire a local presence in new and distant markets, strategic partners are increasingly part of the network structure.

14.1 Manufacturing Network Enterprises

Traditionally, small- and medium-sized enterprises (SMEs) either select market segments that require no head-on competition with the giant companies' technological strength, or live with the big companies by working as the diligent members in their supply chain. Manufacturing networks provide a prototype for how SMEs can form a dynamic and adaptive network to create competitive advantages on both collaborative and individual scales. The proposed system is based on the creation of a network of plants that are electronically linked, so that the participating members focus on their specialized tasks yet also share their manufacturing and production resources to create a loosely structured and flexible enterprise—a *manufacturing network enterprise* (MNE).

This vision of the future MNE is based on two principles:

1. The portfolio of manufacturing facilities that may not all be directly owned but which add up to a complete capability
2. The presence of a global brokerage, which has direct and intimate customer relationships and can conceive total business solutions that are tailored to customer needs

MNEs attempt to draw the flexibility of the large-scale global network and the self-organization of the multimember community into a highly customized self-adapting network structure that molds itself to the resources and constraints of the local business environment. Such networks are highly flexible in responding to current market needs. This strategy allows SMEs to leverage their combined capabilities in a dynamic way that strengthens each individual unit through a dynamic competitive process that selects the best possible end product and most efficient production path for the customer.

MNEs are characterized by attributes such as

1. Adaptive organization
2. The provision of knowledge-driven enterprise solutions
3. Collaborative production
4. Niche marketing—many changing models
5. Arbitrary production volume
6. Production to order
7. Individualizable products and services
8. Enduring, interactive customer relationships

These attributes are enabled by

- The enterprise-wide integration of processes/systems
- The intercompany integration of processes/systems
- Neutral databases for information storage and retrieval
- Information exchange standards
- Digital product description standards
- Reusable design tools
- Reusable production/business processes
- Flexible, modular, reconfigurable production technologies
- Cross-functional, entrepreneurial teams
- Physically distributed teams, intra- and intercompany
- Robust groupware
- Interoperable simulation and modeling processes/tools
- Real-time production management/scheduling
- Agility-based quality metrics

- ■ Real-time information access
- ■ Enterprise-wide performance assessment models/metrics

Competition is different for MNEs than for more traditional supply chain structures. The goal of MNEs is self-organization and dynamism in the form of continual adaptation to changing circumstances; the notion of adaptation here is far more drastic than the usual notions of flexibility, agility, and rapid response. When a customer order specification is advertised to the SMEs on the network, particular production units combine to create a competitive production capacity for a portion (or all) of the job order. Management no longer remains production oriented but becomes mission oriented; and since, to be effective, the participative companies need free rein to remain flexible and responsive, hierarchy within the network dissipates and dissolves.

One of the main characteristics of MNEs is their ability to manufacture a high variety products (i.e., mass customization) in a production environment where the emphasis is on both flexibility and speed; as the number of product options increases, and the number of supply chain choices expands, achieving mass customization becomes a daunting task due to the challenges of matching product supply with consumer demand. Thus, a central *pseudo-controller* known as a *hub* is necessary to introduce SMEs to each other on a large enough scale to foster meaningful communication, warranting the cost of maintaining the hub. The hub takes on the role of a global brokerage with regard to interconnecting clients and SMEs; the role of a hub as a pseudo-central controller is to provide a common technological forum to introduce various SMEs and facilitate information exchange, but its role in explicitly coordinating production is rather limited. It actually does very little controlling, which is done cooperatively by the SMEs themselves, and serves more as a coordinating conduit.

It is not necessary for the entire production chain outside of the cluster to be understood. The individual clusters have no need for this information; they must only know how to coordinate to deliver on their stated production capacity. Only the ultimate order-placing customer who chooses among the available clusters for production needs to have this knowledge.

14.1.1 MNEs as Complex Adaptive Systems (CASs)

Discussion on the structure of self-organizing clusters of SMEs capable of forming a cohesive manufacturing strategy would benefit by drawing an analogy with how complex natural networks adapt to their environment using the available and accessible resources. Just as biological systems are governed by Darwinian natural selection, which favors those agents that successfully adapt to the (dynamic) constraints and resources offered by their physical environment, so too will any "organic" theory of business network formation be subject to a mechanism that selects those of its members that coevolve and that successfully adapt to the environment dictated by globalization and the available resources (e.g., various manufacturing and strategy inputs). As per the corresponding *complex adaptive systems* (CAS) theory, agents exhibit the capability of foresight: they interact, combine, and replicate by means of an internal (i.e., endogenous) mechanism for determining the fitness of the various agents and their interactions. Those agents (or agent aggregates) that are more fit recombine (i.e., reproduce) more successfully than those that are less fit. Strategy in the network is directly related to the strategies that agents (i.e., the constituting SMEs) use to compete for scarce resources.

Traditionally, an SME may make itself more efficient in response to a current production strategy, but when another strategy is required it may find itself hard-pressed to adapt its methodologies to the new constraints. An MNE allows SMEs to select, preserve, and strengthen those business processes that are considered positive, while each new cluster formation (i.e., each new generation) gives the opportunity to weed out those deemed inefficient or counterproductive with respective to those particular constraints. In an MNE, each SME is free to change its internal strategy and goals as it adapts to and grows with the changing business environment. It is the adaptability and success of the individual that is paramount, not that of the network cluster per se.

Thus, *survival of the fittest* must apply to individual SMEs and not to the clusters to which they may belong. Clusters become more effective over every successive generation (i.e., each new cluster) of the business model precisely because the strong SMEs survive and are made stronger, while their weak counterparts are weeded out and perish. An MNE is not responsible for turning a member SME into a winner; while the business model can provide all the opportunities to take advantage of the current environment, the onus of success forever remains only with the individual firm.

There is no central command per se; the job requirements are distributed to all nodes via the hubs using a common technology language and interface. The nodes determine on their own whether they have enough resources and connections to manufacture a particular component of the design specification, to meet a certain design requirement, or to facilitate a certain design transaction. Then, this information is passed back to the hub again using the common technology interface, where the customer can then assess the available options and select among viable clusters. Given that any business unit will have deficiencies in a certain area, collaboration can be used as a method to draw resources into that capabilities gap. Not only does this address weaknesses in the production process, it also accounts for a form of knowledge diffusion that enhances the performance of an SME as a unique enterprise, thereby bolstering its ability to operate within a manufacturing network environment. Thus, collaboration in such a network formation prepares small producers to better exploit opportunities in the market while sustaining their growth by drawing in the various resources so critical to new capability formation.

Ultimately, it will be those SMEs that are most fit in their dealings with the hubs that can draw enough resources and thus make sufficient new connections so that they will thrive as well. As each new incoming project offers the chance to reaffirm those processes that were proven highly effective, while discarding those that are deemed ill-suited, the fittest SMEs are able to sustain themselves through this process of continual renewal and adaptation to the most pressing market requirements.

For obtaining true modularity in the business model, two characteristics are essential.

■ Decentralized control
■ Dynamic internal adaptation

Irrespective of how the MNEs form and dismantle with future customer orders, decentralized hub control (also termed *scale-free networking*), combined with a selfish fitness improvement standard, ensures that each SME partaking in the network will be as fit as possible. Those that cannot adapt to changes and maintain an ever-evolving standard of fitness will be weeded out. This implies that those SMEs that participate in the MNE structure will be more responsive to market demands (vis-à-vis those that do not), as they will be in a position to form clusters that meet the precise needs at that instance. Thus, an MNE is an organization that promotes both the efficiency of production and speed in responding to customer needs.

> The benefit of MNEs to SMEs is primarily in expanding their economic outreach in more and bigger contracts, enhancing opportunities for knowledge diffusion and new capabilities formation through close and varied partner relationships, and providing stability by spreading business partnerships over a wide range of producer locations and competencies.

Clusters can continuously form/reshape themselves and readvertise their abilities to the hub; they are highly customizable to the constraints of the business environment and, hence, contribute immensely to overall enterprise agility. In fact, certain dominant or niche clusters can be continuously posted to the hub even if no specific job request demands their existence; but this is how new or strong capabilities could be advertised. Thus, SMEs are not dependent on large corporations for control and leadership of their production processes, but rather only for order placement. The big companies are needed as order placers, such that SMEs can build up confidence in a MNE environment by working together on a large project. This is also how the effective network relations are formed and made persistent. After certain dominant or niche clusters have formed over several generations of MNE, they may find themselves able to challenge larger producers with their combined, effective, and highly streamlined production capacity. It is this capacity that can now be advertised to potential customers via the hubs.

14.1.2 Elements of MNEs

This subsection describes the elements of a manufacturing network enterprise that are over and above the usual properties that are essential for any member of a manufacturing network.

14.1.2.1 Acknowledging Identity and Recognizing Boundaries

Each constituent manufacturing enterprise has to carry its digital presence, uniquely identified in the digital world, which includes an ID and network interface address or other application-specific high-level naming. The existing boundaries of the MNE network must be accepted. This also affects the hierarchies of the (traditional) manufacturing systems in enterprise resource planning (ERP), manufacturing execution systems (MES), and shop floor terms, with clear responsibilities for factory equipment, such as machines, or factory sections. Network access and participation is also dependent on a network consensus; high-level maturity measures and rules have been provided for in the GERAM methodology. The maturity on the shop floor level and its technological readiness is measured by the intensity of participation in the network—temporary, frequent, or even as a core network constituent.

14.1.2.2 Modularity

Enterprises are considered modular if they can be decomposed into subunits that may be interchanged and matched in various configurations. The respective components are able to interact, to connect, and to exchange resources using standardized interfaces. Modularization entails the ability of processes, information systems, and products to be packaged as reusable modules that can be (re)combined with other modules, collectively making up new value-adding compositions.

Modularity relates to the degree of dependency of the elements of the module and is realized by allowing loose coupling between them, implying that modules should have as few interdependencies as possible. In contrast to monolithic systems, modular units are loosely coupled. In networked systems, modularly designed objects behave like autonomous network constituents that can be networked in a relatively straightforward way; it is decisive in which way the units or activities are interconnected. Modularity also implies that, aside from local feedback and local decision making, capabilities are offered for prioritizing task allocation and capabilities, which are available for the execution of partial process chains. Standardization allows modular networked objects to be synthesized in a standard manner, decreasing the need for mutual agreements on interoperability.

Modularity is closely associated with the feature of compositionality, which means that higher-level systems' properties can be derived from the local properties of individual components. Compositionality is critically dependent on the strong interdependencies of software and the embedding of higher-level properties.

14.1.2.3 Heterogeneity

MNEs are intrinsically heterogeneous: enterprises or their constituents connect and configure; the respective networks comprise different types of computing units. In MNEs, heterogeneity may therefore be assumed to be omnipresent; it occurs on all levels and for a number of reasons.

On the informational side, heterogeneity may additionally come with different hardware platforms, operating systems, or programming languages. On the conceptual level, heterogeneities originate from different understandings and modeling principles for the same real-world phenomena.

Heterogeneity relates to the property of enterprises being composed of diverse elements and thereby using dissimilar constituents. On the road to MNE, heterogeneous manufacturing units and their constituents configure networks and also collaborate closely. Thus, due to the variety of involved units and devices, enabling interactions between sets of heterogeneous information and communications technology (ICT) devices of different brands and marks is an essential prerequisite in any MNE scenario.

14.1.2.4 Scalability

Scalability relates to extending or reducing resources such that no major changes in structure or application of technology are necessary. The primary focus for this capability is capacity— that is, the facility to increase or decrease the necessary resources to efficiently accommodate broadly varying capacity loads. For example, cloud manufacturing gives cloud clients new options to quickly search, request, and fully utilize respective procedures—for example, for engaging idle or redundant machines and hard tools in outside organizations, in order to scale up the manufacturing capacity or scale down capacity loads, respectively.

Scalability can be seen as an important feature for realizing self-organization in MNE, as it enables process parameters to be adapted rapidly in highly dynamic environments. Moreover, in MNE, such adaptation processes are gaining importance in plug-and-work applications. Another field of scalability discussions is the scalability of controls, software, and computing power, especially when cloud computing is addressed.

14.1.2.5 Context Awareness

Context awareness is generally defined as the ability to provide services with full characterization of the current operation and execution environment, and any information that can be used to detail the situation of entities (i.e., people, places, or objects) is considered relevant for interactions. Context awareness implies both the enterprise as well its interactions.

Context has two major dimensions:

1. Logical contexts such as goals, tasks, objectives fulfillments, key performance indicators (KPIs), improvement effects, operations, or processes. This entails capturing and verifying a unit's decision space as well as the valid KPI position. The use of operational and performance measures for determining current states, once the gaps and deviations are ascertained with respect to the stated objectives, improvements, and adaptations, may be initiated to exploit the enterprise's potential. Performance will be improved through actions and adequate strategy activation, positively influencing the KPIs defined to measure an objective.

2. Physical contexts, such as information captured by hardware sensors—that is, location, movement, and alignment parameters—or information captured from the market or regulators. Depending on the captured and monitored data, events, or stimuli, a manufacturing object may have to become active to compensate for the observed differential.

14.1.2.6 Autonomy

An enterprise's autonomy is related to its ability to perform its actions and pursue its objectives without the intervention of other entities. Autonomy includes the ability to interact or to self-organize in response to external stimuli, establishing a positive self-feedback loop with the environment. ICT has rapidly contributed to the higher intelligence of a number of manufacturing units, so self-control, self-organization, and eventually full autonomy of factory objects is attainable for most units. The resulting distributed data volumes and the globally dispersed structures can easily be governed by company networks or by third-party services on the cloud.

Autonomous enterprises may do their communication independently and may decide how to handle interactions with other units and the outside world. The results may be interpreted as the unit's own decision-making process or that of the autonomous hub enterprises with their own rules and procedures within a collaborative process or manufacturing network. The member enterprises keep their own objectives aligned with those of the other units in the network, or ascertain alignment for modified structures for collaboration by adapting or renegotiating links and confirming or revising objective bundles.

14.1.2.7 Interoperability

The property that allows diverse network enterprise units or subunits to collaborate (i.e., interoperate) is referred to as *interoperability*. Interoperability refers to the ability to safely and reliably run a setup in line with general and unit-specific requirements. IEEE defines interoperability as the ability of two or more units or components to exchange information and to use the information that has been exchanged.

Interoperability can be understood as the capability of ICT systems, as well as all supporting processes, to exchange data and share information and knowledge.

Service-oriented architecture (SOA) is, therefore, an important vehicle for smart communication in distributed manufacturing and a significant step toward new concepts for addressing and hiring services via networks according to the pay-per-usage services offered by cloud providers.

14.1.2.8 Networkability

In MNEs, the networkability of constituent enterprises primarily has to promote the configuration of interenterprise collaborative processes on all layers. This includes advanced decision abilities, providing all the procedures involved in governing and executing the necessary activities for (re)designing and setting up new or restructured processes.

The networkability of units may be enhanced by sensing and actuating technologies that capture the global and local contexts of products, objects and other units, and communication infrastructures, even IT models. In manufacturing, process and network decisions are especially concerned with generating efficient processes. Toward this objective, MNEs may even carry factory models, equipment geometries, and process and task descriptions, as well as interaction and decision models.

14.2 Cloud Based Manufacturing Network Enterprises

14.2.1 Evolution of Manufacturing

Over the last two centuries, the manufacturing industry has evolved through several paradigms from *craft production* to *cloud manufacturing* (CMfg); the manufacturing paradigms succeeded one another, always seeking smaller volumes and costs, while increasing the product variety.

Craft production, as the first paradigm, responded to a specific customer order based on a model allowing high product variety and flexibility, where highly skilled craftsmen treated each product as unique. However, such a model was time and money consuming. The history of production systems truly began with the introduction of standardized parts for arms, also known as the *American system*.

Mass production enabled the making of products at lower cost through large-scale manufacturing. On the downside, the possible variety of products was very limited, since the model was based on resources performing the same task again and again, leading to significant improvements in speed and the reduction of assembly costs.

Lean manufacturing emerged after World War II as a necessity due to the limited resources in Japan. The lean manufacturing paradigm is a multidimensional approach that encompasses a wide variety of management practices, including just-in-time, quality systems, work teams, cellular manufacturing, and so on, in an integrated system that eliminates *waste* at all levels. It is worth noting that the lean management philosophy is still an important part of all modern production systems.

The fourth paradigm, *mass customization*, came about in the late 1980s, when the customer demand for product variety increased. The underlying model combines business practices from *mass production* and *craft production*, moving toward a customer-centric model. This model requires the mastery of a number of technologies and theories to make manufacturing systems intelligent, faster, more flexible, and interoperable. Within this context, a significant body of research has emerged, particularly with the Intelligent Manufacturing Systems (IMS) community, which is an industry-led, global, collaborative research and development program with worldwide membership, established to develop the next generation of manufacturing and processing technologies. The IMS philosophy adopts heterarchical and collaborative control as its information system architecture. The behavior of the entire manufacturing system therefore becomes collaborative, determined by many interacting subsystems that may have their own independent interests, values, and modes of operation.

The fifth and latest paradigm, CMfg, moves this vision a step further, since it provides service-oriented, networked product development models in which service consumers are able to configure, select, and use customized product realization resources and services, ranging from computer-aided engineering software to reconfigurable manufacturing systems. Several applications relying on cloud infrastructure have been reported in recent years—for example, those used for hosting and exposing services related to manufacturing, such as machine availability monitoring, collaborative and adaptive process planning, online tool path programming based on real-time machine monitoring, collaborative design, and so on.

14.2.2 Cloud Manufacturing (CMfg)

14.2.2.1 Concept of CMfg

CMfg is a new service-oriented smart manufacturing paradigm and approach based on networks (e.g., the Internet, the Internet of Things [IoT], communication networks, broadcasting networks, and mobile networks). It fuses the current informatized manufacturing technology and new information technology (such as e-commerce, service-oriented computing, intelligent science, cloud computing, high-performance computing, big data, modeling and simulation, IoT, etc.) to transform manufacturing resources and capabilities into manufacturing services and to build a manufacturing service pool, which can be managed and operated in an intelligent and unified way to enable users to acquire safe, reliable, high-quality, cheap manufacturing services anytime and anywhere on demand for the whole life cycle of manufacturing.

14.2.2.2 System Architecture

The architecture of the CMfg system can be captured by a five-layer conceptual model that defines the overall structure, including users, Web portals, applications, services, and resources. The representation of the system architecture is a mapping mechanism that links product designs to associated manufacturing processes. The centralized portal enables cloud-based human–computer interaction, facilitates effective data collection, and provides the seamless integration of resources and services into the CMfg system. A product configuration process transforms data collected from the centralized portal layer into conceptual designs and high-level manufacturing specifications and constraints. Service encapsulation transforms conceptual designs into embodiment and detail designs and consolidates services based on the conceptual designs from the application layer. Resources are allocated according to the detailed designs from the service layer. The specific functions of each layer are illustrated as follows:

1. User layer: The key users of the CMfg system include product designers and manufacturing engineers.
2. Centralized portal layer: The key function of the centralized portal layer is to provide cloud providers and consumers with a centralized interface that facilitates communications between them. Specifically, the centralized portal provides forums, wikis, and chat rooms. The portal also provides social networking tools and document sharing tools such as Google Docs.
3. Application layer: The key function of the application layer is to transform information acquired via the centralized portal to requirements, structures, functions, behaviors, design constraints, and manufacturing specifications.
4. Service layer: The key function of the service layer is to provide various engineering services (e.g., CAD/CAM/CAE/CAPP). The service layer delivers detailed designs and manufacturing processes based on information from the application layer.
5. Resource layer: The resource layer encompasses design- and manufacturing-related resources such as fixtures/jigs, 3D printers, CNC machine tools, manufacturing cells, assembly lines, facility, servers, network equipment, and so on.

14.2.2.3 Characteristics of CMfg

1. Digitalization of manufacturing resources and capabilities: This refers to converting attributes—both the static and dynamic behavior of the manufacturing resources—and capabilities into digits, data, and models, in order to carry out a unified analysis, planning, and restructuring process. The integration of digitalization technology and manufacturing resources and capabilities can be used to control, monitor, and manage systems such as

hardware manufacturing resources (i.e., CNC machine tools, robots, etc.) and soft manufacturing resources (i.e., computer-aided design software, management software, etc.).

2. Servalization of manufacturing resources and capabilities: A CMfg system gathers mass virtual manufacturing resources and capabilities, and forms them as on-demand services via service package and computing technologies. The characteristics of CMfg services are on-demand dynamic architecture, interoperability, collaboration, heterogeneous network integration, fast response times, full life cycle smart manufacturing, and so on.

3. Virtualization of manufacturing resources and capabilities: This means providing logical and abstract representation and management of the manufacturing resources and capabilities, which is not limited to the specific physical instances of virtualization technology. For example, a physical manufacturing resource or capability can form multiple isolated, packaged *virtual devices*; multiple physical manufacturing resources and capabilities can aggregate to form a larger-grained *virtual devices* organization, and, when necessary, virtual manufacturing resources and capabilities can achieve live migration and dynamic scheduling. Virtualization technology enables the simplification of representation, access to the manufacturing resources and capabilities, and further optimal management of them uniformly. It is the key technology to realizing service-oriented and collaborative manufacturing resources and capabilities.

4. Collaboration of manufacturing resources and capabilities: Collaboration is a typical feature of advanced manufacturing modes. Through information technology such as virtualization, service-oriented and distributed, or high performance computing, and CMfg, forms the flexible, interconnected, interoperable *manufacturing resources* and *capabilities as a service* module is formed. On a technical level, cloud service modules can achieve the system-wide, full–life cycle, comprehensive interconnection, interoperation, and collaboration to satisfy the users' demands. CMfg also provides comprehensive support to the dynamic, collaborative management of agile virtual enterprise organizations, to achieve the on-demand dynamic construction of virtual enterprise organizations by multiusers, and to achieve seamless integration in the collaboration of virtual enterprise business.

5. Intellectualization of manufacturing resources and capabilities: Another typical technique of CMfg is to achieve system-wide, full–life cycle, comprehensive intelligence. Knowledge and intelligent science is the core to the intelligent operation of the CMfg service system. The manufacturing cloud brings together all kinds of knowledge and builds a multidisciplinary knowledge base. Knowledge and intelligent science penetrate all aspects and levels of manufacturing, to support the two dimensions of the life cycle: the full life cycle of the manufacturing and the full life cycle of the manufacturing resource and capability service.

6. Connection of things of manufacturing resources and capabilities: Integrating the newest information technologies, such as the IoT and cyber-physical systems (CPS), CMfg achieves the comprehensive and thorough accessing and perception of the system-wide, full–life cycle manufacturing resources and capabilities, especially hard manufacturing resources (such as machine tools, machining centers, simulation equipment, test equipment, the logistics of goods) and manufacturing capabilities (such as human, knowledge, organization, performance, and reputation).

14.2.2.4 CMfg Technologies

1. *e-Business* provides the enabling technology for the full–life cycle activities of CMfg and the integration of logistics, information flow, and capital flow; it also takes all production activities and business flows online and makes them much easier for manufacturing enterprises.
2. *Service-oriented technology* provides a series of enabling technologies (such as SOA, Web services, the Semantic Web, and so on) for intelligently constructing and executing a virtual manufacturing and service environment. It makes it possible for manufacturing resources and capabilities to access cloud services.
3. *Intelligent science* provides the enabling technology to make manufacturing resources or capabilities intelligent, and helps to improve the intelligent operation and use of the CMfg service platform, with much more manufacturing-related knowledge generation and management.
4. *Cloud computing* provides a series of enabling technologies and new manufacturing patterns for resources or capabilities in CMfg, as well as the enabling technologies for intelligent information processing and decision making in manufacturing activities. It is the core technology to handle all manufacturing data.
5. *High-performance computing* provides the enabling technologies for solving large-scale and complex manufacturing problems and carrying out large-scale cooperative manufacturing and work.
6. *Big data* provides the enabling technology for accurate, high-efficiency, intelligent, full–life cycle activities in CMfg, with the entire realization of manufacturing informatization, which brings out massive data.
7. *Modeling and simulation* provides the enabling technology for the effective development and running of manufacturing systems.
8. *Automation* provides the enabling technology for the inspection, control, and evaluation of manufacturing systems.
9. The *Internet of Things (IoT)* provides a series of enabling technologies for interconnection between things in the manufacturing domain and the realization of wisdom manufacturing—that is, intelligent perception and effective connection among different things (including person-to-person, machine-to-machine, and person-to-machine). It is for the sourcing and transmission of various manufacturing data.

14.3 Outsourcing

This section describes the various outsourcing operations and services that are offered by third-party logistics (3PL) service providers. There is a vast choice of different operations and services that can be outsourced. A good way to understand the opportunities available is to consider a typical logistics structure as shown in Figure 3.1. This represents the theoretical physical flow, storage, and manufacture of a product all the way through from the supplier of a raw material to the delivery of finished goods to the final customer. Any of these functions could be outsourced to a third-party contractor. Many companies do not actually fulfill all of the many physical logistics functions that are represented in the diagram, but some fast-moving consumer goods (FMCG) manufacturers fit this model.

The decisions to outsource should cover three main broad alternatives:

- physical logistics/delivery operations
- logistics processes
- decision flows

In distribution and logistics, probably every different function can be outsourced. The ultimate option is to outsource the whole operation, keeping in-house only those non-logistics functions that are deemed to be the core business of the company. For example, some high-tech companies, such as 3M, are more concerned with the research and development that goes into the planning and production of new products rather than the sales and logistical operations that support the bringing of these products to market. However, many users do not wish to outsource everything, but they are keen to concentrate their resources on certain aspects of their business and to outsource others. One useful way to understand the breadth of opportunities that are available for outsourcing is to view this as a continuum of services, ranging from total internal logistics management to total external logistics management.

Main drivers for using outsourcing are:

- Organizational
  - One of the prime reasons quoted for outsourcing is the opportunity for users to focus on their *core business or core competence*, be this manufacturing or retailing.
  - Outsourcing can provide the user company with access to wider knowledge.
  - The use of a third party can often mean the loss of direct influence at the *point of delivery* because the driver is delivering a number of different companies' products.
  - There may be a problem with the *confidentiality of information* when using a third-party distribution service.

- Financial
  - Outsourcing has several financial and cost advantages because of the elimination of asset ownership; there are capital cost advantages of using third-party distribution because the client company does not have to invest in facilities and resources such as distribution centres and vehicles, as it would for its own operation.
  - *Improved cash flow* can occur when the service provider pays for existing assets that are owned by the client company but are transferred to the service provider at the start of the contract. The client can then use this cash input to help in other parts of the business.
  - A particular advantage for shared operations is the opportunity to benefit from cost savings through *economies of scale.*
- Service
  - Service levels should improve following a move from in-house to *outsourced operations.*
  - The use of a third-party distribution operation should offer greater flexibility to the user company.
  - Third-party companies are able to offer a number of value-added services.
- Physical
  - *Complexity* of logistics and supply chain structure may best be planned and managed by a third-party company that has a broad international experience of the many different logistics elements.
  - The need to relocate logistics facilities can also be an important reason or opportunity for outsourcing.
  - The move to a third-party operator provides a major opportunity to solve any industrial relations problems that might otherwise be difficult or costly to eradicate.

Once it has been determined that outsourcing is a viable solution, the next step is to clarify whether a dedicated or a shared solution is the most advantageous. A dedicated operation may provide superior opportunities for service but at a high cost; a multi-user operation will provide opportunities for low-cost logistics but could mean a compromise for service requirements.

1. Dedicated operations: From a service perspective, the dedicated operation provides major advantages. All of the organization and resources within the operation are focused on the single client. Dedicated operations also allow staff to become more specialized in terms of product familiarization and operational requirements. This can, for example, help to maximize the accuracy and speed of picking performance, because order pickers are more often than not dealing with the same products and the same product locations. Service is also often enhanced in dedicated operations through the specialization of buildings, depot storage and handling equipment, packaging

requirements, unit loads, and delivery vehicles. Once again, the existence of a single client means that all of these different distribution elements can be designed specifically for that client in terms of what is most suitable for the demand characteristics of the product and the customer service that is required.

2. Shared operations: From a cost perspective, major savings can result from the economies of scale that are achieved with joint operations when the key resources are shared among a number of clients. Most small- and medium-sized companies that have single dedicated operations are unable to maximize the use of a variety of resources such as storage space, warehouse equipment, specialist warehouse labour, delivery vehicles, and delivery drivers. Such operational scale economies are gained through the use of a multi-user option, as well as the scale economies arising from spreading the cost of overheads across a much wider range of activities. The consolidation of loads enables higher delivery frequency to be achieved and also leads to better load utilization in vehicles. There is also often the opportunity to find and link clients with different business seasonality, thus creating an opportunity to maximize the utilization of assets throughout the year. In a shared operation there may be conflicting demands from different clients that might compromise the service that is provided. An example concerning delivery transport might be that one company requires early morning delivery of its products, but another has restricted delivery windows at lunchtimes that need to be met.

It may not be possible to meet both of these requirements within a shared delivery operation because of the implications for cost and vehicle utilization. For shared operations, it is often not possible to deal appropriately with all special requirements because the most standard equipment, organization, procedures, and processes are used by the operating companies. Some, but certainly not all, exceptions can be made—but where they are feasible, they will be at a cost that must be met solely by the client that requires them. Thus some service demands may be adversely affected because not all individual customer requirements can be met.

Staff in a shared operation do not get much opportunity to gain specialist customer knowledge because of the number of different products and clients they deal with.

The standard types of operations covered are:

- Warehousing and storage
    - Distribution depot operation
    - Excess storage
    - Cross-docking
    - Transhipment
    - Break bulk

- ■ Stock and inventory
  - Inventory management
  - Specific stock responsibility
- ■ Transport
  - Primary transport (trunking, line-haul)
  - Secondary transport
  - Collections
  - Fleet management
  - Contract hire
- ■ Packaging and unitization
  - Packaging
  - Labeling and product preparation
  - Unit loads
- ■ Other standard operations
  - Product inspection
  - Reverse logistics
  - Merchandising
  - Telesales and call centres

The ultimate option is to outsource the whole operation, keeping in-house only those non-logistics functions that are deemed to be the core business of the company. For example, some high-tech companies, such as 3M, are more

14.3.1 Foxconn

Foxconn Technology Group, better known by its trading name Foxconn, is a multinational electronics contract manufacturer headquartered in Tucheng, New Taipei, Taiwan. Foxconn is the manufacturer of some of America's most popular consumer electronic devices for companies like Apple and Microsoft, and has widespread manufacturing facilities worldwide, but most of all in China. Foxconn is the world's largest and fastest-growing company in the field of manufacturing services providers for the so-called 3Cs: computers, communication, and consumer electronics.

Foxconn's competitive advantages lie in the aforementioned eCMMS business model and its unique "Foxconnian culture." Foxconn's eCMMS, which stands for e-enabled components, modules, moves, and services, is the vertically integrated business model formed by integrating mechanical, electrical, and optical capabilities. This process means quicker speed to market, higher quality, better engineering services, greater flexibility, and cost savings. Moreover, it allows the company to generate solutions ranging from molding, tooling, mechanical parts, components, modules, and system assembly to design, manufacturing, maintenance, and logistics. On the strength of the eCMMS model, Foxconn's Shenzhen Campus in southern China is both the world's largest 3C manufacturing base and shortest supply chain.

Foxconn provides four different manufacturing services:

1. Contract electronic manufacturing (CEM)
2. Electronic manufacturing services (EMS)
3. Original design manufacturing (ODM)
4. Components, modules, moves, and services (CMMS)

Foxconn provides services for the biggest companies in the field of electronics and information technology. Its clients include American, European, and Japanese companies which outsource the manufacturing of hardware or other components in order to lower production costs and withstand competitive pressures. One of Foxconn's most important contract partners is Apple, as Foxconn draws an estimated 40%–50% of its revenue from assembling their products and other work. It further manufactures components for Amazon, Dell, Blackberry, Intel, HP, Microsoft, and many others.

14.4 Summary

As was pointed out right in the beginning of this chapter, firms have been forced to reorganize their activities and realign their global strategies in order to provide the speed and flexibility necessary to respond to windows of market opportunity. Consequently, organizations have moved from centralized, vertically integrated, single-site manufacturing facilities to geographically dispersed networks of resources. This chapter introduced manufacturing network enterprises (MNE) along with their characteristic elements. The latter part of the chapter focused on cloud-based MNE to highlight various aspects of cloud manufacturing (CMfg) like characteristics, architecture, and technologies. In order to acquire technological know-how and assets quickly, or to acquire a local presence in new and distant markets, strategic partners are increasingly becoming part of the network structure. The chapter ended with an overview of several aspects of outsourcing.

Chapter 15

E-Business Networks

The vision of e-business is that enterprises will have access to a much broader range of trading partners to interact and collaborate with, and not only to buy and sell more efficiently. Also, it is expected that e-business will contribute to the agility of all business organizations, and with that, to reaching higher levels of customization. In this manner, enterprises can maximize supply chain efficiency and improve service to customers and their profit margin. To accomplish this objective, enterprises must make certain that their mission-critical business information systems such as inventory, accounting, manufacturing, and customer support not only can interact with each other but can also become Web-enabled and exposed so that business systems of their partners and customers can interact with them. Additionally, in order to optimize their operational efficiency, enterprises need to develop newer distributed applications that extract data and launch business processes across many or all of these systems.

If e-business processes are integrated end-to-end across the company and with partners, suppliers, and customers, they can respond with flexibility and speed to customer demands and market opportunities. E-business supports business processes along the entire value chain: electronic purchasing and supply chain management, processing orders electronically, customer service and cooperation with partners. One of the objective of e-business is to provide seamless connectivity and integration between business processes and application external to an enterprise and the enterprise's back office applications, such as billing, order processing, accounting, inventory, receivables, and service focused on total supply chain management and partnership including product development, fulfillment, and distribution.

15.1 Business Webs

15.1.1 Mela B-Web

A *business web* (B-Web) of the *mela* type is an electronic marketplace where buyers and sellers meet in order to openly negotiate over the goods offered and their prices. What is important in the mela is the process of dynamic price discovery. In an mela, there are no fixed prices; the prices are negotiated. An mela promotes the exchange of digital and material goods and services, as providers and buyers haggle among themselves over the price. Consumers or buyers inform themselves and discuss the elements of the products, including rights to use and individual prices.

 The term *mela* originates from antiquity and was used to designate the people's assemblies held at that time. Later, the term was also used for a public meeting place where business was conducted, including trade.

Well-functioning marketplaces acting as agoras show advantages for both providers and consumers. The buyers profit since there are a high number of providers offering various products and services. Conversely, the presence of many consumers with different ideas about the value of a certain product will push up the value of the product offered, to the benefit of the provider.

Mela B-Webs have the following advantages:

■ No storage costs: The providers store their own products.
■ Minimal marketing costs: The providers describe and illustrate their products on the platform themselves.
■ Reduced distribution costs: Buyers and providers regulate dispatch and payment among themselves.
■ Low product liability: Products are auctioned; the buyer carries the risk.
■ Low financial risk: The providers authorize the operator of the exchange platform to collect an auction fee.

In an mela, the customers or customer groups often develop into a community. The participants of auctions agree to an organized process involving negotiation, pricing, and the distribution of goods.

15.1.1.1 eBay

Until the 1990s, the auction business was largely fragmented; thousands of small city-based auction houses offered a wide range of merchandise to local buyers. And a few famous global ones, such as Sotheby's and Christie's, offered carefully chosen selections of high-priced antiques and collectibles to limited numbers of dealers and wealthy collectors. However, the auction market was not very efficient, for there was often a shortage of sellers and buyers, and so it was difficult to determine the fair price of a product. Dealers were often able to influence auction prices and so obtain bargains at the expense of sellers. Typically, dealers were able to buy at low prices and then charge buyers high prices in the brick and mortar (B&M) antique stores that are found in every town and city around the world, so they reaped high profits.

The auction business was changed forever in 1995 when Pierre Omidyar developed innovative software that allowed buyers around the world to bid online against each other to determine the fair price for a seller's product. Omidyar founded his online auction site in San Jose on September 4, 1995, under the name AuctionWeb. A computer programmer, Omidyar had previously worked for Microsoft, but he left that company when he realized the potential opportunity to develop new software that provided an online platform to connect Internet buyers and sellers. The entrepreneurial Omidyar changed his company's name to eBay in September 1997, and the first item sold on eBay was Omidyar's broken laser pointer for $13.83. eBay's popularity grew quickly by word of mouth, and the company did not need to advertise until the early 2000s. Omidyar had tapped into a huge unmet buyer need, and people flocked to use his software.

eBay generates the revenues that allow it to operate and profit from its electronic auction platform by charging a number of fees to sellers (buyers pay no specific fees). In the original eBay model, sellers paid a fee to list a product on eBay's site and paid a percentage fee of the final price the product was sold at the end of the auction. Indeed, Meg Whitman's biggest problem was to find search engine software that could keep pace with the increasing volume of buyers' inquiries. Initially, small independent suppliers provided this software; then IBM provided this service. But as search technology has advanced in the 2000s, it partnered with Yahoo to use their search to drive buyers to eBay auctions. In fact, because eBay is one of the world's biggest buyers of web search terms, eBay manages a portfolio of 15 million keywords on different search sites, such as Google, Yahoo, and AOL.

From the beginning, eBay's business model and strategies were based on developing and refining Omidyar's auction software to create an easy-to-use online market platform that would allow buyers and sellers to meet and transact easily and inexpensively. eBay's software was created to make it easy for sellers to list and describe their products and easy for buyers to search for, compare, and bid on the products they wanted to purchase. The essence of eBay's software is that the company simply provides the electronic conduit between buyers and sellers; it never takes physical possession of the products that are listed, and their shipping is the responsibility of sellers, and payment, the responsibility of buyers. Thus, eBay does not need to develop all the high-cost functional activities like inventory, shipping, and purchasing to deliver products to customers, unlike Amazon.com, for example, and so, it operates with an extremely low-cost structure given the huge volume of products it sells and the sales revenues it generates. eBay is also low cost since until recently, sellers located outside a buyer's state do not have to collect sales tax on a purchase. This allows buyers to avoid paying state taxes on expensive items such as jewelry and computers, which can save them tens or even hundreds of dollars and makes purchasing on eBay more attractive.

To make transactions between anonymous Internet buyers and sellers possible, however, Omidyar's software had to reduce the risks facing buyers and sellers. In particular, it had to convince buyers that they would receive what they paid for and that sellers would accurately describe their products online. To minimize the ever-present possibility of fraud from sellers misrepresenting their products or from buyers unethically bidding for pleasure and then not paying, eBay's software contains a method for registering feedback, converting it into a trust score that consolidates a buyer's reputation over time. When sellers and buyers consistently act in an honest way in more and more transactions overtime, they are able to build a stronger and stronger positive feedback score that provides them with a good reputation for honesty.

To take advantage of the capabilities of eBay's software, the company expanded the range and categories of the products it offered for sale to increase revenue. Second, it increased the number of retail or selling formats used to bring sellers and buyers together. For example, its original retail format was the 7-day auction format, where the last bidder within this time period won the auction, provided the bid met the seller's reserve or minimum price. Then, it introduced the buy-it-now format where a buyer could make an instant purchase at the seller's specified price, and later a real-time auction format in which online bidders, and bidders at a B&M auction site, compete against each other in real time to purchase the product up for bid. In this format, a live auctioneer, not the eBay auction clock, decides when to close an auction.

Beyond introducing new kinds of retail formats, over time eBay has continuously strived to improve the range and sophistication of the information services it provides its users—to make it easier for sellers to list, describe, present, and ship their products, and for buyers to make better purchasing decisions. For example, software was developed to make it easier for sellers to list their products for sale and upload photographs and add or change information to the listing. Buyers were able to take advantage of the services that are now offered in what is called MyeBay; buyers can now keep a list of watched items so that over the life of a particular auction they can see how the price of a product has changed and how many bidders are interested in it.

By creating and then continually improving its easy-to-use retail platform for sellers and buyers, eBay revolutionized the auction market, bringing together buyers and sellers internationally in a huge, never-ending yard sale. The first-mover advantage eBay gained from Pierre Omidyar's auction software created an unassailable business model that gave eBay effectively a monopoly position in the global online auction market.

15.1.2 Aggregator B-Web

A business web of the *aggregator* type is a digital supermarket; it selects suitable products and services from different producers, decides on the appropriate market segments, sets prices, and supervises the fulfillment of the transaction.

A single company in this B-Web controls several producers in a hierarchical fashion. The aggregator buys products and services according to its own discretion and to a large extent sets the purchase prices. It then determines the selling prices and discounts for the assortment of goods. It also controls the sale and distribution of the goods. Aggregators take on an intermediary function between producers and customers. Normally, they offer a large selection of products and services without or with only minimal value integration.

Using their market volume and market power, aggregators can lower their transaction costs, particularly through the use of Internet technologies and appropriate digital agents. The digital supermarket can be operated to a great extent by intelligent software agents. Simple agents advise the buyers and look for and valuate the desired products in their own supermarket or directly among the providers. Intelligent agents help the customers to clarify their desires and to select an attractive combination from the variety of offers. In individual cases, software agents can themselves negotiate the value mix, quality requirements, price, delivery conditions, and modes of payment.

Aggregator B-Webs have the following advantages:

- Strong negotiation power: The aggregator selects the products and establishes the price.
- Employment of digital advisors: Software agents help with search and comparison procedures and advise the customer.
- Independent product valuation: The advantages and disadvantages of products are understood by the customers and published by the aggregator as a decision-making aid.
- Sale stimulation: In the digital supermarket, products can be bundled and cross-selling measures realized.
- Customers save on shipping costs: The aggregator can create incentives by utilizing scale effects and low transaction costs.

There are aggregators in both the business-to-business (B2B) and the business-to-consumer (B2C) realms. Apart from consumer goods, digital products such as financial and insurance services are also sold with aggregators.

The most well-known aggregator is the online retailer Amazon.

15.1.2.1 Amazon

Amazon was named after the world's largest river in terms of water volume carried, an allusion to its goal of large-volume product delivery. Starting in 1995,

Amazon become the pioneer of online mass retail. It was the first company in its industry to truly harness the power of the Internet. The Internet had a fourfold commercial effect, as an independent sales medium, as a communication medium, as an order and payment medium, as well as a medium for distribution.

In the early 1990s, with its large number of over 20,000 publishers and low concentration in online trade, the book industry appeared to be a suitable starting point for a new internet venture. As today, customers interested in buying books were primarily searching for three attributes: high selection, low prices, and a convenient and fast delivery.

At that time, the landscape of book retail had two main types of competitors:

- Small market players, such as independent bookstores located in city centers, neighborhoods, and at focal points of mass transportation.
- Large corporate groups, which dominated the market: bookstore chains such as Barnes & Noble and Borders, each with about a quarter market share in the United States, together with walk-in chain stores such as Walmart.

Right from its inception, Amazon termed itself "Earth's biggest bookstore." The value proposition involved a 24-hour online book ordering service, offering approximately 1 million titles at an average 2–3 day delivery time. By delivering books directly to the customer, Amazon provided an unprecedented level of convenience. Customers benefited from an array of titles too large for local booksellers to imitate, mainly due to inventory costs.

In addition, the user-friendly design of Amazon's website and, for an online start-up, the particularly good customer service complemented the value proposition. Since the website acted as the sole communication and ordering channel, Amazon's operating costs were massively reduced, compared to brick-and-mortar bookstores. The physical store location became obsolete, and was entirely replaced by a virtual user interface. Amazon not only attempts to build trust and reliability through secure transactions, but also makes use of customized online profiles and recommendation systems. These are designed to provide guidance during the shopping process, and to increase price transparency. In 2013, Amazon bought Goodreads, an online community specializing in book recommendations and ratings, for $150 million.

As regards product sales, Amazon's business logic relies on its long-tail business model, providing not only bestsellers, but also low-volume products. A derived key activity is that the company does not stock all the products it sells, but cooperates with independent vendors for retailing products with low sales volumes. This ensures the manageability of its long-tail business model. By relying on the experience of independent sellers and itself warehousing only the most successful items, Amazon is able to optimize inventory costs.

The Long Tail: Research in the late 1990s revealed power-law distributions in the structure of the Internet and the interconnectedness of the web. A power-law distribution is a curve with a very small number of very high-yield events (like the number of words that have an enormously high probability of appearing in a randomly chosen sentence, like "the" or "to") and a very large number of events that have a very low probability of appearing (like the probability that the word "probability" or "baffel-gab" will appear in a randomly chosen sentence). The number of events with a very low probability creates a heavy or long tail as the probability decreases but never quite reaches zero. In his book *The Long Tail*, *Wired* editor Chris Anderson argued that this distribution is an important property of the Web, in particular because the content and commodities available on the Web are digital. A traditional business, constrained by storage capacity and costs, focuses on the high-frequency end of the power-law distribution in order to reap the greatest profit from every transaction. Anderson uses a music shop as an example. This music shop will focus on providing popular albums because the faster they shift them, the less time the albums remain on the shelves, which in turn means the profit margin is greater. The more difficult-to-sell albums take up space and cost, especially so the longer they idle on the shelves. Such a situation enforces the power-law distribution because it ensures that customers find it harder to buy less popular albums. However, an online music shop has only virtual shelf space and can therefore virtually stock an infinite number of albums, including the least popular. It costs Amazon no more to virtually stock a highly popular album than it does to stock a niche product. As a result, the artificial barrier to users buying less popular albums is lifted and the tail of the distribution grows. Although the number of events under the tail of the distribution is small compared to the high-frequency end, it is still a substantial number considering the total number of users of the Web. Hence, there are significant advantages to businesses in supporting the tastes of those customers who make up the tail. According to Anderson, in traditional retail, new albums account for 63% of sales (in 2005), but online, that percentage is 36%. The long tail is not only important for astute business people; it has significant implications for all the users of the Web. By removing the traditional barriers to content production and storage, the road is open for production by anyone: the Web becomes a read/write space again, but this time on a massively greater scale with infinite room for endless niche markets. This mass producerism creates not only a vast amount of data, but a number of possibilities that arise from the data that are exploited by savvy applications and businesses aware of its potential. In particular, they draw strength from the diversity displayed in the long tail.

As the company did not have any internal logistics capacities, product delivery was outsourced to logistics providers. A second group of key partners was formed by wholesalers and distributors, as Amazon relies heavily on product availability, in order to guarantee rapid and dependable fulfillment to its customers.

A well-scaled IT infrastructure supports the operations of Amazon, allowing customers to efficiently search, evaluate, and order a wide variety of items. Amazon's global fulfillment infrastructure with warehouses, logistics centers, and related personnel allows worldwide product delivery.

Amazon had extremely sleek cost structure, driven by

■ The cost of sales: refers to the inventory value of the products and additional direct labor costs;
■ The cost of fulfilment: refers to the costs of receiving, packaging, and delivering goods;
■ The costs for technology: composed of platform maintenance and R&D costs for platform development;
■ The costs for content: consists of expenses for merchandise selection, editorial content, and product range extension.

The main cost drivers are cost of sales, fulfillment costs, and costs for technology and content, with around 70%, 12%, and 10% of the operating expenses respectively.

Initially, revenues were generated only by book sales; in spite of its risks, this strategy conveyed the benefit of focus. Its retail value proposition has experienced an evolutionary transformation, with a current portfolio largely relying on electronic media devices, household goods, and apparel. The company tremendously extended its offer, doubling the product palette between 2013 and 2015. Simultaneously, it focused on increasing convenience through the Prime service, which allows 1–2-day delivery. Currently, it is most popular retail website in the United States and Europe alike.

The company heavily relies on manufacturers, which form the most relevant partner group. Among these are independent vendors, a heterogeneous group of renowned brands and sellers of no-name products. Since 2000, these partners have the possibility to use the Amazon platform as a channel for online retail and marketing. The second group of partners are logistics service suppliers, such as DHL, UPS, and FedEx, for delivering ordered goods directly to customers. A more traditional delivery model employed by Amazon are the delivery lockers, located for instance in nonstop supermarkets, allowing customers to collect parcels themselves.

During the past decade, Amazon's sales have continuously increased, having reached around $89 billion in 2014 with over 68% of the net sales being generated by electronics and general merchandise.

15.1.3 *Integrator B-Web*

A business web of the *integrator* type is a value-creating chain that includes all of the components desired by the customer, from specification, production, and delivery to support for products and services. An integrator does not itself produce services or product components but rather works as a context provider. As such, it integrates the value contributions of various content providers, such as external developers, parts suppliers, dealers, solution integrators, operators, and other partners. In other words, the integrator controls the organization of the products and the services and directs the steps toward value integration.

Different producers with different capabilities and services are combined into value chains and directed by the integrator. The motivation to implement such a value chain is provided by customers who are striving for an individual and usually complex solution, possibly with a high investment volume. When an individual producer is not able to offer or does not want to offer the optimal solution, the integrator assumes this responsibility; often the integrator takes the role of a general contractor, with the corresponding responsibilities. This again forces the integrator to merge the content providers into an optimized supplier relationship and to competently control the planning, development, installation, and service processes. An integrator's goal is to make the value chain demand oriented. In other words, an offer is only created on demand. A customer need, therefore, triggers the construction of what may be an individually shaped supply network.

Content providers in a B-Web of the integrator type are often spread out and specialized. The success of an integrator therefore depends on the planning and coordination of the different partners. Project management plays an important role in the process, including the use of knowledge resources.

Integrator B-Webs have the following advantages:

- Customer-oriented solutions: The customer order comes first, with initial partial payments being made when the order is placed.
- General contractor: The integrator assumes full responsibility for the customer order.
- Formation of a value chain: The selection of suppliers, the networking, and appropriate negotiations are all realized by the integrator.
- Shop production instead of routine production: All components are custom-made.
- Project and method knowledge: The integrator controls project management and knowledge use.

In the digital economy, the best value chains compete in terms of both cost and differentiation. They must look for customer-oriented solutions and offer individual and service-supported production in place of mass-produced goods.

15.1.3.1 Cisco

Cisco is a $12 billion high-technology company, the fastest growing company of its size in history, faster even than Microsoft, with a market capitalization of $200 billion. Cisco competes in markets where hardware is obsolete in 18 months. How has Cisco managed this startling growth in an industry where technology is constantly changing? Cisco has frequently used acquisitions to obtain new technology (and markets and market share).

Mergers are difficult, maybe more so in the case of Cisco because Cisco's acquisitions are not just to acquire customers, branches, or plants—its mergers are specifically designed to acquire technology and know-how embodied in people, frequently including the founders of the acquired companies. The answer to the mystery of Cisco's ability to grow successfully by acquisition has to do with several complementary values that permeate the company: the importance of cultural fit and shared vision, speed, frugality, and the need and willingness to change continually.

In the early 1990s, fast Ethernet connections were still the LAN technology, but for WAN networking, asynchronous transfer mode (ATM) switches were becoming preferred by customers. ATM was a hardware-based switching technology that transmitted data faster than routers and could be used to connect a finite number of LANs together, with resulting high-speed communication between LANs. Moreover, ATM allows a digital emulation of traditional switch-based phone networks and could bridge between data communications and telephone communications. Thus, Ethernet technology was hooking up computers into LANs, ATM technology was hooking together LANs into WANs, and routers were hooking all into Internet. The IT challenge was in tying LAN nets into WAN nets.

By 1993, an additional growth spurt began in the router market as the Internet continued to expand nationally and globally. New switches were developed for networks using hardware that did what software in routers was doing, but faster. They were also capable of being used to put together larger Ethernet LANs, as switches that could function as better LAN hubs than routers. Cisco's drawback was that it supplied only routers when the market was expecting an end-to-end full service provider. Cisco was eager to find companies that could help them offer increased bandwidth. This would improve a network's ability to move traffic smoothly, without delays. Although routers could expand bandwidth, they were slow, expensive, and hard to manage in larger numbers. Nor did intelligent hubs (devices that make it easier to detect network crashes or faults) increase bandwidth.

The answer came from hardware vendors that began selling LAN switches that switched traffic from point to point and offered huge increases in bandwidth. Boeing had been considering a $10 million router order from Cisco but wished to use new switches from a new firm called Crescendo Communications. John Chambers learned from Boeing that, unless Cisco cooperated with Crescendo, Cisco would not get the Boeing order. Boeing had (and still has) the largest private network in the world. As an early leader in networking, the aircraft maker had a large influence on the networking world as a whole. Its Boeing Computer Services did computer consulting for various customers including the government, managing such projects as Space Station Project Network. Consequently, Cisco decided to buy Crescendo for $97 million in 1990—for a company that had been forecasted to sell only $10 million of equipment the following year. But, in 2000, Cisco's switching business had become a $10 billion business, almost half of its annual revenues. The LAN switch became the core of their enterprise business. This was the first of Cisco's subsequent strategic policy of acquiring competitors to extend and improve technologies to provide advanced and complete customer solutions.

15.1.4 Associator B-Web

A business web of the *associator* type is a loosely coupled and self-organized partner network (also often called a *community*) that pursues a common goal. The individual partners bring their specific know-how to the table and at the same time take part in developing the solution. They remain independent and try to compensate for a lack of competency by producing suitable network partners.

The members of this partner network have dual roles: they are each consumers that have a need and are looking for a solution, and at the same time each participates in solution development as a producer. The word *prosumer* has been created to express this dual producer and consumer role. A B-Web of the associator type is a dynamic creation with equal partners that, upon encountering various challenges, reorganizes itself each time and develops further. In this way, no partner dominates and controls the partner network. Rather, the loosely coupled partner network is held together by a few behavioral rules.

B-Webs of the alliance type develop on a voluntary basis, motivated by a common need. At first, there is a creative idea that needs to be adapted by the partners as a group. Mutual respect, intangible assets, and unconventional ideas are the drivers of such partner networks. Alliances distinguish themselves as being a high-value form of integration; they can be considered *value modules*. In many cases, alliances are temporally limited. They come into being when small companies or individual persons congregate and develop a mutual solution. If the solution is found, it is circulated and passed on, normally free of charge.

The development of the Linux operating system serves as an example of a B-Web of the associator type. After the Finnish student Linus Torvalds developed a simple kernel for a Unix clone for PCs, he made the software available for free on the Internet (i.e., open source) for further development. The users were merely obligated to pass the program and possible extensions on with the source code. In the years that followed, qualified programmers around the world developed innumerable improvements and extensions to this operating system. Today, Linux is a stable and extensive software product that remains available to open source companies and private individuals. It is installed on millions of different servers around the world and fulfills its purpose. Web browsers, e-mail services, and other applications can all be operated on this system.

In their spare time, scientists, self-employed individuals, and employees have voluntarily and without monetary incentives downloaded the source code from Linux and then tested and extended it with ingenious functions. The users of Linux can download the source code over the Internet free of charge, or they can buy a version on CD for a minimal fee from companies such as SuSE or Red Hat and acquire the right to unlimited use. Associators are formed in a variety of ways. Apart from networks for the development of open-source software packages, there are social communities, specific discussion and help forums, networks for freelance artists, expert communities, and so on.

Associator B-Webs have the following advantages:

■ Network formation: Partners in an alliance form a network of equal rights.
■ Self-organization: A few behavioral rules promote collaboration.
■ Prosumers: The partners are simultaneously producers (supplying creative products and services) and consumers (demanding solutions).
■ Value modules: Intangible assets are created together.
■ Idealized objectives: Mutual respect, trust, and common value creation form the basis of the alliance.

An association is a virtual network that aims to develop creative solutions and does so without hierarchical guidance structures. The participants of an alliance form a creative community aligned toward a goal. It therefore remains one of the most transitory and at the same time most innovative types of B-Web.

15.1.5 Distributor B-Web

A business web of the *distributor* type is a distribution network that transfers material products, intangible products, and services from the producer to the user. Distributors fulfill a distribution function, acting, for example, as a transportation company, electricity provider, financial service, courier/postal service, communications network operator, or logistics company.

Integrators and alliances contribute to the value chain by refining raw materials or ideas into products or services. An agora and aggregator selects goods, offers them, and negotiates the price. Distributors, however, in their original form, assist the four previously discussed B-Webs by ensuring that the information, goods, and services are exchanged. The distribution network connects the producer of products and services with the purchaser or customer. It can therefore consist of a physical or digital network and distribution system.

Table 15.1 Comparison of various types of B-Webs

	Agora	Aggregator	Integrator	Alliance	Distributor
Objective	market place for goods and values	digital supermarket	optimized value chain	self-organized value module	exchange of information, goods and services
Characteristics	• market information • negotiation process • dynamic price discovery	• distribution of products • firm price • easy fulfillment	• targeted supplier selection • process optimization • product integration	• innovation • trust building • relinquishment of hierachical control	• network optimization • unlimited use • logistic process
Customer role	market participant	buyer	valur driver	contributor	recipient
Benefits	negotiable market service	comfortable selection and fulfillment	customized product	creative and mutual solution	just-in-time delivery
Examples	eBay auctions. yahoo	etrade amazon	Cisco Dell	Linux Music. download	UPS AT&T Telecom

One special type of digital communications provider is the so-called infomediary. This is a unit that collects, manages, and passes on information from customers. Private consumers and companies make use of infomediaries as buyers of goods and services. Apart from management and distribution functions, they also offer services related to data protection.

15.1.6 Comparison of Commerce Networks

The aims and main characteristics of B-Webs are quite different, and range from open marketplaces with negotiable goods and values (agora type) over tightly organized hierarchical networks (aggregator, integrator, or distributor types) to self-organized and loosely coupled communities (alliance type). In real-world electronic markets, the market participants do not always appear to form clearly definable B-Webs. Rather, a B-Web often exhibits the characteristics of several types of B-Webs.

Table 15.1 shows a comparison of various types of B-Webs.

15.2 Profit Models

Business models for electronic business can be characterized according to positioning, customer benefits, products and services, choice of business web, and profit model. Establishing the sources of profit with which the company refinances itself constitutes a central element of the business model. The profit model describes the financial and intangible benefits from the business activity.

1. Direct profit models:
   a. Price model for products and services: This model is obvious and requires a discussion of price differentiation and the selection of suitable parameters for a price model. An assumption here is that the entire process of procurement to distribution can also be organized economically. With digital products or product parts, costs can be reduced if order procedures, deliveries, and system services are also realized digitally.
   b. Admission model: The customer must pay an admission fee here for the time-limited use of an offer, or rather, for access to content. This profit model is suitable for target groups that need information, know-how, or entertainment.
   c. Subscription model: The sale of content is allowed after a fixed subscription fee that is paid periodically.
   d. Fee model for transactions: Here, a transaction fee is charged to the customer. This can depend on the duration of use (usage fee), the content of the downloaded information (content delivery fee), or the support offered (service fee).
   e. Advertising model: The provider of electronic products and services sells advertising space on its website. This is only possible if the company has a strong market position and has a considerable number of online customers.
2. Indirect profit models:
   a. Fund-raising model: This model is dependent on the external money market.
   b. Credit-borrowing model: This model is also dependent on the external money market.
   c. Sponsoring model: In the sponsoring model, sponsors financially support the presence of the business on the Web for a certain length of time until its services allow it to become self-supporting.
   d. Cost-saving model: This model is based on the premise that investments in Web technologies and in appropriate electronic business processes pays off in the long run and reduces costs.

15.3 Price Fixation

15.3.1 Price Determination

In the usual case of linear price determination, there is a direct correlation between the performance of a product or service and the corresponding price—for instance, the charges for support services based on the number of hours worked. Many consumers evaluate product prices relative to the quantity of the product that they already possess or have consumed. In other words, the margin benefit decreases with the satisfaction that a consumer gets from consuming the products or services (Gossen's law). The first release of a software package brings the user a greater benefit than any of the product versions supplied later. As the product is revised, the buyer's willingness to pay will likewise decrease. Thus, it is essential to impose a nonlinear pricing policy.

In nonlinear price formulation, there is a nonlinear dependency between the product or service and the corresponding price. A nonlinear price consists of multiple price components; the price curve is a combination of a basic charge and a variable usage charge. This price is nonlinear because the basic charge is fixed but distributed across all of the units ordered, and so the basic charge per unit drops as the number of units ordered increases; that is, the greater the sales volume, the lower the average cost per unit.

15.3.2 Price Differentiation

The task of fixing the prices of products and services in a business web is not a simple one because network aspects come into play. The customer evaluates the service of a B-Web as a whole, and also expects an offer. Price differentiation is advantageous for B-Webs or companies since it increases the profit potential of clever pricing policies; it is also attractive from the perspective of the buyer, especially when they draw customers or customer groups that are willing and able to pay.

Price formation represents a special challenge in electronic business, since intangible goods and digital product components must also be included in the calculation. The valuation of intangible product parts is a difficult task, since no generally valid computation method exists for these components. Price differentiation can be flexibly adapted to the changing market conditions.

1. Customer segments–related price differentiation: Customer segments that attract different quotations are formed based on age, sex, or social affiliation. The additional efforts and costs incurred to ascertain the assumed differentiation is compensated by the add-on sales feasible for the identified segment.
2. Time-related price differentiation: It is assumed here that customer groups display a special high or low willingness to pay at a certain time. Thus, a service provider can arrange access to the Internet according to the time of day and offer specific price terms. Purchasable information on market activity is more favorably traded the older the information is.
3. Quantity-related price differentiation: Quantity-related price differentiation means that the quantity ordered in an electronic transaction offers a discount. Thus, an online bookshop delivers books free of charge if a certain quantity of books or a previously declared sum of money is exceeded.
4. Service-related price differentiation: In a digital product with so-called versioning, the range of services differs in terms of user-friendliness, functionality, or service.

15.3.3 Dynamic Price Determination through Auctions

Auctions are regarded as important instruments for dynamic price formation. They provide a standardized sequence of events that make the buying and selling of products and services visible. Auctions make it possible to set up flexible prices based on supply and demand in accordance with market conditions and the terms of competition.

The various types of auctions are as follows:

1. English auction: In the English auction, the bidding process begins with a minimum price. Here, each participant bids several times and can also exceed his previous bid. In electronic auctions, the gathering of bidders in one physical trading place does not take place. Since one does not know how many bidders are participating in the auction, electronic auctions are concluded at a time specified during the run-up. The winner of the auction is the one who submitted the highest bid at that time. In other words, in electronic auctions it is not long until only one bidder remains, and this bidder is then awarded the lot.

2. Japanese auction: This type of auction is equivalent to the English auction, except that the bidder does not call out the price himself. The price rises successively higher until only one bidder remains.

3. Dutch auction: In this auction, events proceed in reverse. At the start of a Dutch auction, a high price is set that is then successively lowered until a bidder is found who accepts that price. In this mechanism of continuous price lowering, the first bidder is awarded the lot. Dutch auctions are proffered with oceangoing ships, whereby remaining storage space is auctioned off in cases of insufficient capacity utilization. Since the unsold transport capacity is worthless when the ship sails, it is worth holding a Dutch auction with a price clock, for instance.

4. First-price sealed-bid auction: In a first-price sealed-bid auction, secret bids are made by the auction participants and simultaneously opened at the end of the auction. The bidder with the highest bid is awarded the lot. The bidders are forbidden to change their bid or to introduce more bids. First-price sealed-bid auctions are seldom found on the Internet; mostly, industrial products or real estate are sold this way.

5. Vickrey auction: This auction is largely equivalent to the first-price sealed-bid auction. The winner is again the bidder with the highest bid. However, in this case the winner does not pay the price of the highest bid but that of the second-highest bid. For this reason, a Vickrey auction is often called a *second-price sealed-bid auction*.

6. Inverse auctions: This type of auction is comparable to an invitation for tenders, where the customers make their preferences known and the providers of products and services must compete.

Auctions on the Web supplement the traditional methods of selling and are often focused on certain particular customer segments and products.

15.4 Electronic Procurement

Electronic procurement (EP) refers to all of the connective processes between companies and suppliers that are enabled by electronic communication networks. EP includes the strategic, tactical, and operational elements of the procurement process.

1. Strategic
   a. Standardizing and specifying the procurement
   b. Selecting the supplies for products and services
2. Tactical
   a. Carrying out contract negotiations
3. Operational
   a. Ordering the products and services
   b. Supervising the delivery
   c. Subscribing to additional services

The products and services to be procured can be classified as follows:

1. Direct goods: Direct goods are commodities or provisions that flow directly into the manufacturing activity. Also included are raw materials and resources, which directly provide basic materials for the product. Enterprise resource planning (ERP) systems primarily support the procurement of direct products.

   The quality, availability, and prices of direct goods are of great importance for the company. Accordingly, a great deal of attention is given to the selection and maintenance of the supplier relationship. To reduce tied-up capital, the principle of just-in-time procurement is often used: the best case is when the company obviates the need for storage and obtains the material directly from the supplier network. Prerequisites for using this approach are a good ability to plan for the need, delivery date reliability, and supplier flexibility.

2. Indirect goods: Indirect goods are products and services that are required and used for the running or operations the company. They are often termed *maintenance, repair,* and *operations* (MRO) goods. These include fuels required for the production process as well as the utility goods and tangible assets needed for the production of the finished product.

   Indirect goods procurement is characterized by
   a. Stock procurement processes for low-value goods or for goods in general (e.g., stationary) involve long delivery periods.
   b. Purchasing expends too much time and routine administrative work on the procurement of indirect goods instead of focusing on more value-adding tasks.

    c. Due to the overburdening of purchasing departments and long procurement times, ad hoc buying is rampant.

    d. For products with short life cycles and dynamic price structuring, printed catalogs are not suitable for ordering.

    e. Orders carried out manually and individually frequently cause wrong deliveries and delays.

Examples of MRO products include

- Preconfigured computers
- PDAs and mobile devices
- Software
- Magazines and newspapers
- Books
- Office furniture and office equipment
- Vehicles
- Work clothes and work equipment
- Advertising material
- Maintenance material
- Office supplies

Examples of MRO services include

- Travel services
- Training courses
- Advertising services
- Consultation and hotlines
- Financial services
- Cafeterias
- Copying services
- Courier services
- Parking lot reservation
- Light entertainment programs
- Cultural programs

15.4.1 Models for Electronic Procurement

The various electronic procurement platforms are controlled either by the provider (sell side), the consumer (buy side), or market organizations, which in turn are provided and controlled by a neutral third-party authority.

Figure 15.1 presents various models for electronic procurement.

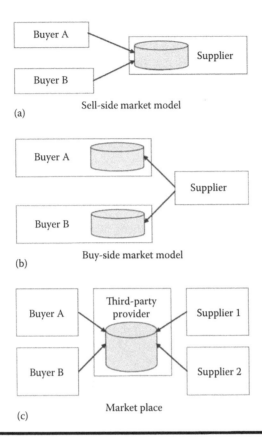

Figure 15.1 **Models for electronic procurement: (a) sell-side market model, (b) buy-side market model, (c) marketplace.**

15.4.1.1 Sell-Side Market Model

In the sell-side market model, the supplier provides the purchase software and an electronic catalog. Some suppliers with sell-side solutions provide extensive functions for personalization, for product configuration, or for compatibility testing. Thus, the buyers can establish rules for the individual customer in the procurement process; the buyer must register with each supplier and familiarize him/herself with different software solutions and navigational aids. Many e-shops used in B2B businesses are based on the sell-side market model. For instance, Amazon can be thought of as a supplier of information (books and other articles)—similarly, Dell, which supplies computers and peripheral devices.

The sell-side approach requires the supplier to provide the entire business logic for the procurement process, including the product catalog in an information system (e.g., purchasing software, e-shop). The supplier performs content management of the electronic catalog entries. He/she maintains the product description and classification and specifies the changing workflow. Ordering processes and settlement processes are likewise supported by software. Search mechanisms for articles and services enable the preparation of a basket of goods as well as the acquisition of orders and commissions. Invoicing takes place with the help of a payment solution. Depending on the operational status of the supplier software, various reports on the buying behavior and the purchasing of products and services are requested.

The user profile of the buyer, as well as his rights and obligations (login, authorization, purchasing limits, and cost center assignment, among other things) must be recorded and maintained by the supplier software. Thus, if the buyer uses several suppliers with sell-side systems, this would entail large amounts of effort and cost.

An e-shop is a classical variant of procurement based on the sell-side principle. It supports the information, agreement, and fulfillment phases with online orders. Such a system facilitates integration with the ERP system of the supplier, depending on the stage of development. The system can then supply additional information such as stock, availability or prices for the individual customer. The repeated issuing of orders to the supplier's ERP system is unnecessary. Depending on the operational status of the e-shop, the buyer can specify complex products using a configurator. For the supplier, this means the automation of consultancy services, a reduction of acquisition expenditure, and the possibility of delegating responsibilities to the procuring company.

It is obvious that a relationship between the procuring company (the buyer) and the supplier must be developed in order to successfully operate a sell-side variant. In particular, the shop system also requires information on the organization of the procuring company. At the same time, changes must be suitably organized. The company is confronted with a multitude of information systems as soon as it procures products with several suppliers. This requires considerably more information and training.

Advantages include the following:

- The configuration of complex products is possible.
- No capital outlays for an ordering system.
- Operating costs for the maintenance of current product lists and prices do not apply.
- Short delivery times through direct input of the order into the supplier's system.
- Querying on current availability and pricing.

Disadvantages include the following:

- Automatic product comparisons are not possible.
- Limited support of the procurement process with the buyer.

- The consumer or requesting customer must use a different information system for each provider.
- Limited integration of the procurement process into the operational information systems of the customer

15.4.1.2 Buy-Side Market Model

In the buy-side market model, the buyer must run and maintain the appropriate software together with extracts from various supplier's product catalog. The procurement process remains largely supplier independent and the process data obtained can be collected and analyzed. Procurement process rules, such as the observance of contract conditions, authority when ordering, or procedures for approval, can be realized for the individual customer.

 Purchasing usually takes place on the supplier's website (sell side); the buy-side market model is only worthwhile with larger companies.

The buy-side option requires the company (the buyer side) to install and maintain the purchasing software, including the product catalog. The supplier is only responsible for the content management, and regularly transmits changes in the product catalog.

User management (with the administration of authorization and access rights) is conducted by the company. The steps in the ordering process with company-specific characteristics (licensing procedure, workflow control, etc.) are likewise determined by the company. The product catalog can be enlarged with offers from additional suppliers and expanded into a purchasing catalog for all MRO goods. Integration into existing software environments and connections to ERP systems are easier to manage.

Procurement applications that are operated by the company are called *desktop purchasing systems* (DPSs). They are established at the workplaces of both the consumer and the solicitor and are aligned with the procuring company's process. They offer a uniform user interface, can take into account company-specific standards, and are usually well integrated into the operational information systems of the company. One prerequisite to the successful operation of such a system is the maintenance of a catalog of the products that can be ordered and negotiated with the suppliers. This catalog is often called the *multisourcing product catalog* because it contains product data from different suppliers.

DPSs on the user side are mostly laid out as Web applications. They support all of the positions within the company involved with procurement. Thus, the consumer can deposit his purchase order request over the Intranet, the cost center manager can grant approval, the buyer can order the product, the consignee can confirm the supply, and the accounts department can pay the invoice. The depth of integration with the supplier determines the extent to which products can be procured without additional interaction and whether the invoice should be delivered electronically to the customer by the supplier.

Advantages include the following:

- The procurement process can be organized in a company-specific manner.
- Internal authorization and licensing procedures are well supported.
- Process turnaround times can be reduced.
- Stocks can be kept small.
- Central administration produced by negotiated products.
- The elimination of maverick shopping.
- Consumers/solicitors can operate the system themselves.
- Systems with uniform menu prompting.

Disadvantages include the following:

- Complex products are not usually supported.
- Advertisements are not planned.
- Capital outlays for information systems are with the procuring company.
- Operating costs for content management are to be supplied.
- Not all suppliers have an electronic product catalog.
- Suppliers sometimes provide poor-quality product data.
- The coordination of the exchange format must be achieved by the procurer and supplier.

15.4.1.2.1 Procurement of MRO Goods

The problems mentioned previously for the procurement of indirect goods and MRO services can be remedied by appropriate information systems—so-called desktop purchasing systems. These systems consolidate the product and service offerings of different suppliers into multisourcing product catalogs. Their browser-based user interfaces support irregular use by employees, who, when required, examine offers for the MRO goods and other material individually. Progressive DPSs offer extensive interfaces with operational information systems and ERP systems and guarantee the integration of the procurement of indirect goods into the company's activities. There are currently various providers of software systems for desktop purchasing.

The search for potential suppliers is already supported by the DPS. Using so-called reverse marketing, the search for and selection of suppliers is simplified. The point of reverse marketing is that the procuring company, aided by the DPS, publishes site-specific information intended for potential suppliers (guidelines for procurement, quality characteristics, points of agreement, etc.) on the Web or announces its need for goods, its delivery terms, and its modes of payment. In other words, the company that wishes to buy takes the initiative and performs the marketing.

The entire ordering process along with settlement and delivery is also supported by the DPS, as the approval process is initiated by company-specific activity and carried out step by step. The tracking functions are interesting. They continually indicate the status of the order with the supplier and the status of the goods in transport on the DPS. Thus, the status of an order is always up to date.

Incoming goods and postage are handled by the DPS and (depending on the depth of integration) are updated directly in the corresponding ERP system. After the commodity has been examined and the date noted, statistics are compiled and (if necessary) complaints are attended to. This means that the procuring company always has up-to-date information on the quality of the supplier.

DPSs can greatly relieve the burden placed on the logistics and purchasing departments of companies. Different services, from the workplace layout and office equipment to services for business trips and company socials, can be efficiently procured and supervised via such systems.

15.4.1.3 Marketplace

When the marketplace option is employed, the platform is operated by an intermediary. This intermediary has the task of bundling information (products) and making it available on the platform. The intermediary consolidates the offers from the providers and supplies comparable product offers to the consumers. He creates contact between providers and consumers and also carries out procurement transactions in the name of the company (the buyer side) according to the requirement. The work of the intermediary essentially consists of providing high-quality information to both providers and consumers and guaranteeing the smooth execution of business transactions.

The intermediary operates the required software solutions and the catalogs. The intermediary can uniformly display and describe the products with their solution. They can provide valuation criteria applicable across the spectrum of suppliers and the functionalities to perform comparisons in order to obtain added value over and above the sell-side and buy-side market models. This platform is used simultaneously by several companies (buyers) as well as by several suppliers.

Various forms of intermediary platform used for procurement exist. They range from trade books (Yellow Pages), advertisement platforms, and auctions to industry-specific platforms. A multitude of price models are also used by the platform operators.

Electronic marketplaces frequently differ according to whether they are vertical or horizontal. Vertical marketplaces focus on specialization or on an industrial solution. One such well-known platform was Covisint, originally put together for the three large American automobile manufacturers Daimler-Chrysler, Ford, and

General Motors, which operated under the name ANX (http://www.anx.com). ANX developed into an exchange platform for automobile manufacturers, aviation, transport, and logistics. Horizontal marketplaces, in contrast to the vertical ones, do not have an industrial focus.

Less than a fifth of all companies buy raw materials over the Internet; this proportion rises to 32% for the manufacturing sector. Almost a third of all companies book business trips (e.g., flights, overnight accommodation, car rentals) online. Thus, like physical products, services are increasingly being bought over the Internet too.

Advantages include the following:

■ The reduction of search time
■ The representation of current and detailed market offerings
■ Efficient transactions
■ The comparability of different offers
■ Anonymous procurement opportunities
■ The bundling of supply and demand in order to achieve better conditions

Disadvantages include the following:

■ A lack of integration into the ERP systems of the procuring company.
■ Intermediaries usually cover only a narrow product range in sufficient depth.
■ Frequently, a large company can negotiate directly with the provider/manufacturer for better prices.
■ Classified directories are frequently not up to date.

Unlike the sell-side and buy-side solutions, comparisons between different providers are made possible by intermediaries. The bringing together of several providers increases the liquidity of the market and ideally results in efficient markets, even in regard to price fixing. Depending on the needs of the providers and consumers, the anonymity of market participants can be guaranteed when products and services are requested.

15.5 Summary

The vision of e-business is that enterprises will have access to a much broader range of trading partners to interact and collaborate with, and not only to buy and sell more efficiently. This chapter began with describing different types of business webs, such as mela (open marketplace), aggregator, integrator, associator, and distributor. This was followed by providing an overview of the applicable profit models. The chapter then presented the process of price formation involving price differentiation, linear, nonlinear, and dynamic price development. The last part of the chapter addressed aspects related to electronic procurement, namely, sell-side and buy-side market models as also the marketplace.

Chapter 16

Platform Networks

What differentiates innovative companies from others is the constancy of generating a stream of strong products. They understand that long-term success does not hinge on any single product; they know that they must generate a continuous stream of value-rich products that target growth markets. Such products form a product family with individual products sharing common technology and addressing related market applications. It is such product families that account for the long-term success of an enterprise. Product families do not emerge one product at a time; they are planned so that a number of derivative products can be efficiently created from the foundation of a common core technology or product platform.

Platforms and families are powerful ways for companies to recoup their high initial investments in research and development (R&D) by deploying the technology across a number of market fields. For example, P&G invested heavily in cyclodextrin development for its original application in detergents, but then was able to use this technology or variants of it in a family of products including odor control (Febreze), soaps and fine fragrances (Olay), off-flavor food control, disinfectants, bleaches, and fabric softening (Tide, Bounce, etc.). They were also able to license out the technology for use in noncompeting areas such as industrial-scale carpet care and in the pharmaceutical industry.

A platform business model is an economic rather than a technical construct. Platform networks solve real business problems by consolidating basic layered functionality in a manner that provides economies of scale. When existing networks are highly fragmented, a system integrator can serve as the glue that holds the networks together. For example, TCP/IP served to integrate several proprietary and heterogeneous networking protocols, including those of Apple and IBM. This may give rise to platform networks. They may also emerge in a niche next to established, slowly evolving industries where there is a broad, unserved market need that may initially be addressed through pioneering but inferior technology. Examples include IP telephony and digital photography that could have been controlled by AT&T and Kodak, respectively, but were missed opportunities.

Mechanisms that facilitate a transition toward platform network markets include

1. Integrating, vertically and horizontally, into markets that exhibit network effects
2. Opening the platform, so as to reduce lock-in and promote adoption
3. Sharing the wealth in order to increase third-party investment

To facilitate the emergence of platform networks, platform sponsors need to manage developers with measures including

1. Opening APIs to allow other systems to interoperate
2. Providing software development kits (SDKs) and integrated development environments (IDEs), as Cisco does for its Unified Communications applications
3. Direct service and support for component suppliers, as in the case of Microsoft.

The ecosystem matters; platform networks can result in 10–15 times more benefits to the ecosystem as a whole.

16.1 Product Platforms

A product platform is a set of subsystems and interfaces that form a common structure from which a stream of derivative products can be efficiently developed and produced. A platform approach to product development dramatically reduces manufacturing costs and provides significant economies in the procurement of components and materials, because so many of these are shared among individual products. The building blocks of product platforms can be integrated with new components to address new market opportunities rapidly.

Greater power in product development can be achieved if these building blocks are leveraged across the product platforms of multiple product lines. For example, Intel's advances in microprocessors are leveraged into new versions of its servers and supercomputers. Many firms fail to leverage their capabilities across product lines; diversified businesses of most large enterprises typically do not share core technologies across their product lines.

A robust product platform is based on a number of building blocks that can be grouped into four areas:

1. Customer insights: Insights into the minds and needs of the customers and the processes of customer and competitive research that uncover and validate those insights. Marketers have many techniques for determining customer needs, perceptions, and preferences. The resulting knowledge gained cannot be a preserve of one function within the enterprise, but should be available enterprise-wide—no function within the enterprise can be allowed to own the customer.

2. Product technologies: Product technologies in materials, components, subsystem interfaces, and development tools. Product technologies can encompass chemistries, material properties, programming languages and algorithms, hardware or logic design, and so forth. One level up from these basic or component technologies are the actual implementations of proprietary knowledge and skills in the form of chemical formulations, material assemblies, software modules, or chips. Rapid platform design, development, and renewal must incorporate the latest advances in the areas of component technologies. Just as derivative products should be rapidly developed through incremental improvements to existing platforms, new platforms should be created by integrating the latest advances in component technologies, either from within or from external suppliers or partners.

3. Manufacturing processes and technologies: Processes and technologies that make it possible for the product to meet competitive requirements for cost, volume, and quality. In many industries such as glass and refining, the firms with the best manufacturing technologies have an edge; for such industries, the manufacturing process is itself the platform. For both assembled and nonassembled products, the tendency is to consider traditional variations in volume or capacity for improvements; but innovation or flexibility improvements in the manufacturing process can result in much better dividends. Flexible manufacturing has enormous implications for the design of plant and equipment, patterns of resource allocation, and the range of product variety that a company can bring to the market.

4. Organizational capabilities: Capabilities that include infrastructures for distribution and customer support, as well as information systems for customer centricity, customer responsiveness, and operational control (including market feedback). Firms must have strong channels through which to distribute their products or services. For many firms, packaging is also a distinct focus of achieving competitive advantage and lies at the confluence between product design and distribution. Likewise, customer support must be available both to help customers realize the full value of the firm's products and as a listening post for gathering customer insights. Remote diagnostics built into industrial and medical equipment can greatly facilitate and improve customer support.

16.1.1 Microsoft's Platform Strategy

Microsoft is a classic example of the successful employment and deployment of platform strategy for extending market ownership. This approach consists of extending advantage while maintaining customer lock-in. Although MS-DOS was only one of three operating systems (OSs) initially offered by IBM, Microsoft priced MS-DOS lower than its competitors. MS-DOS quickly became the de facto OS on the IBM PC. Microsoft transformed this into a platform by treating it as part of a platform of functions tied to the original MS-DOS. While maintaining the MS-DOS OS, Microsoft developed a proprietary GUI that emulated the look and feel of the popular Macintosh computer. Microsoft used Windows to lure customers to stay with MS-DOS and MS-DOS-based applications while they were upgraded progressively. As customers were persuaded to adopt newer products, the MS-DOS-installed base was nurtured and protected; the strategy was always to provide a strong bridge between earlier and later product releases. The next step of Microsoft was built on its applications. Competitors for applications such as WordPerfect dominated word processing, Lotus 1-2-3 dominated spreadsheets, and Harvard Graphics dominated presentation software. But through the linkage of Windows, Microsoft made its word processing (MS Word), spreadsheet (MS Excel), and presentation software (MS PowerPoint) attractively compatible with each other and with Windows. Customers were encouraged to purchase the entire suite of Microsoft applications (MS Office) by highlighting the ease with which customers could interchange documents between any of these applications, which was not possible with the competitor's applications. Microsoft introduced Windows NT for the office PC market.

In the fall of 1995, Microsoft introduced Windows 95, which was a 32-bit OS. It was a vastly improved OS, while maintaining backward compatibility with the early generation MS-DOS OS and applications; it was also cross-platform compatible with Windows NT, bridged again via Windows. Microsoft became the first company to offer high-performance, cross-platform connectivity between the home and office, consolidating the customers from these two markets by promoting third-party applications that worked on both Windows 95 and Windows NT. In order for their product to qualify for Windows 95, third-party developers were required to write applications that would work on both Windows 95 and Windows NT.

With the advent of the Internet, HTML, along with Sun Microsystem's Java, had the potential of becoming an alternate OS for PCs that could also communicate with each other. In response, Microsoft enabled Internet access through their browser Internet Explorer (IE,) which was similar to Netscape's Navigator. However, with the introduction of Windows 98, IE was embedded into Microsoft OS, MS Office, and third-party applications, thus rendering Netscape's browser irrelevant.

16.2 Defining Platform Networks

A platform network is defined by the subset of components used in common across a suite of products that also exhibit network effects. Value is exchanged among a triangular set of relationships including users, component suppliers (co-developers), and platform firms. We focus on platforms where users experience network effects to emphasize the mutually reinforcing interests of participants in the platform ecosystem. In contrast to a traditional linear supply network, a platform network involves interdependent three-way value streams. Various business partners

> Network effects are demand-side economies of scale, such that the value to existing consumers rises with the number of subsequent consumers. They influence user willingness to pay (WTP), user adoption, and thus a platform's value. Network effects are distinct from supply-side economies of scale that come from high fixed/low marginal costs, as in the case of semiconductor manufacture, where average costs decline as production volume increases. Scale economies for both demand and supply commonly occur in the high-tech sector, but must be conceived of and managed differently.

or co-developers associated with the platform transact directly with consumers across the platform, affecting its total value.

Cross-side network effects refer to demand economics of scale from one network group to another (e.g., from users to developers)—for example, the effect of doctors and patients who both want to affiliate via the same HMO. Same-side network effects refer to the effects of one user group on other members of the same group—for example, the positive network effects that PC gamers enjoy from additional users of the same game or the negative effect on drivers of congestion on a highway.

Platforms are not necessarily created and maintained by a single firm. There are three kinds of roles:

1. Provider: Platform providers mediate network users' interactions; they serve as users' primary point of contact with the platform.
2. Component supplier (co-developer): Component suppliers make available essential goods and services that are not offered directly by platform providers. They also provide convenience, customization, and integration, adding value out on the *long tail*.
3. Sponsor: Platform sponsors exercise control rights. They can modify platform technology and determine who may participate in the network. Sponsors may license multiple platform providers to spur innovation or keep this role

for themselves. Despite network effects, sponsors can deliberately limit the number of network users to ensure quality or to extract value by granting exclusive trading rights.

A platform's sponsor and provider roles can be fulfilled by the same company or shared by multiple firms. Examples of platforms with a sole sponsor include Apple's Macintosh and the American Express credit card. Alternatively, multiple parties may jointly sponsor a platform, typically under the auspices of an association (e.g., VISA, which is controlled by 21,000 member banks). At the provider level, platforms are either proprietary or shared. With a proprietary platform, a single firm serves as platform provider (e.g., Monster.com, Xbox). With a shared platform, multiple firms serve as rival providers of a common platform (e.g., VISA's issuing and acquiring banks, who support cardholders and merchants, respectively). Rival providers of a shared platform employ compatible technologies; any network user could switch providers (e.g., from a Dell PC to a Compaq PC, in the case of Microsoft's Windows platform) and still interact with the same partners as before (i.e., all Windows-compatible applications). By contrast, rival platforms employ incompatible technologies (e.g., PlayStation vs. Xbox, VISA vs. American Express). Joint sponsorship usually leads to a shared platform (e.g., Linux, VISA), whereas sole sponsors usually operate proprietary platforms (e.g., eBay, Apple Macintosh). Occasionally, however, a sole sponsor licenses multiple providers. For example, American Express granted third-party banks such as MBNA permission to issue American Express–branded credit cards.

Platforms provide a standardized solution for the problems below the applications layer. Factors that contribute to platform network success include

1. Openness
2. Extensibility
3. Modularity (abstraction and encapsulation)
4. Quality control

Each attribute varies along a continuum and can have nonlinear effects on platform success. For example, more *open* platforms do not uniformly outperform less open platforms. A perfectly open platform—for example, viral free software—offers very little as a basis for building a business. This curbs investments by business stakeholders, a key player in the ecosystem. A perfectly closed network retards third-party innovation, which disqualifies it as a platform.

Successful platforms have extensive mechanisms for quality assurance. The openness that fosters decentralized innovation must also separate the wheat from the chaff. This is as true of open-source projects with peer review as it is for hardware products and routers. For example, the Atari gaming platform failed, in part, because poor-quality games flooded the market and tarnished the brand.

16.3 Salient Characteristics

16.3.1 Fight or Share

If a new market seems likely to be served by a single platform, aspiring intermediaries must decide whether to fight for proprietary control or share the platform with rivals. Even if rival platforms are economically viable over the long term, aspiring intermediaries may still prefer to pool their efforts. Fighting increases the chances of leaving one firm with a Betamax when it could have shared in a VHS. Facing this decision, managers must calculate the impact of each option—fighting versus sharing—on market size, market share, and margins. Of course, the product of market size, share, and margin equals the firm's profit from the new business.

■ Market size: A shared platform is likely to attract more users in both the short and long term. In the short term, some users may delay adoption during a winner-takes-all (WTA) battle for platform dominance. Users will fear being stranded with obsolete investments if they back the loser. This uncertainty hampered the adoption of Blu-Ray and HD-DVD in the beginning, though eventually HD-DVD was discontinued.

In the long term, if a single proprietary platform prevails, then monopoly pricing will reduce the number of network users, compared with a shared platform, for which pricing will be more competitive. Likewise, due to network effects, if rival platforms survive—whether shared or proprietary—then their aggregate market size will be less than the user base would be for a single shared platform.

■ Market share: While jointly developing a platform can build market size, it cuts into each firm's market share. When a shared platform evolves through the consensus-based processes of a standards-setting organization (SSO; e.g., the World Wide Web Consortium), firms will find fewer differentiation opportunities. Market shares are more likely to be determined by firms' relative strengths in manufacturing and distribution. With a WTA battle, market share will tend toward either 100% or 0%, so managers must estimate their realistic odds of winning. This will be determined by cost and differentiation advantages, including access to proprietary technology and/or inimitable scarce resources, and by factors such as the following:

− Firms gain an edge when they have preexisting relationships with prospective users, often in related businesses.
− Users' expectations influence momentum, so a reputation for prowess in past platform wars yields an advantage.
− In a war of attrition, deep pockets matter.

First-mover advantages are often significant in platform battles, but they are not always decisive. When the market evolves slowly, late-mover advantages may be more salient, including the ability to

1. Avoid pioneers' positioning errors
2. Incorporate the latest technology into product designs
3. Reverse engineer pioneers' products and beat them on cost

Platform providers must determine how much of the value created through network interactions they should seek to capture and from which users. A bigger network served by a single platform can create more value in aggregate, but users may worry that a dominant platform provider will extract too much value. Likewise, when the participation of a few large users is crucial for mobilizing a network (e.g., movie studios vis-à-vis new DVD formats), conflict over the division of value between platform providers and "marquee" users is common.

16.3.2 Open or Closed

A market size versus share framework implies a trade-off between improved adoption odds and the reduced appropriability of rents when sharing a platform. Opening the platform encourages value-adding developer investment and user adoption but reduces residual proprietary options for charging. Platform owners sometimes mistakenly assume that maximum control provides maximum value, but this is generally not the case. Be willing to open a platform and reduce one's market share so long as the growth in market size is net profitable.

Openness must be sufficient that third parties can gain the knowledge they need to design for the platform. This provides access to intellectual property. Core intellectual property usually remains protected, but tools for adapting and adding the platform are widespread, not unlike Microsoft's *embrace and extend* approach. An example is the open Session Initiation Protocol (SIP), as implemented by Cisco: anyone can connect a non-Cisco device, but advanced features are only available through licensing the SCCP control protocol, which is proprietary.

Despite the virtues of opening a platform, economic theory suggests that platform development cannot be totally decentralized. Platforms need leaders for at least three reasons:

1. Platform leaders invest in enhancing and promoting the platform.
2. They internalize the network effects that would be mispriced if managed separately.
3. They orchestrate often fractious developers whose competitive instincts can otherwise lead them to advance their individual interests at the expense of overall platform value. Platforms need sponsors; you cannot get order from chaos without a control mechanism.

Confusion sometimes exists over *open* versus *shared*, based on the rapid growth of open-source software (e.g., Linux) and content created through collaborative communities (e.g., Wikipedia). In analyzing platforms, one should not conflate the two simply because platform-mediated networks involve both users and co-developers. Participation within one set may be open, while participation in other sets remains restricted—that is, closed. Consequently, we insist on specificity: open for whom? More importantly, we stress that some platforms are very successful with open/shared models, while others prosper with closed/proprietary models.

Margins can be higher in the long term when the platform is not shared, and the victor in a WTA battle reaps higher rewards. However, in the short term, winning a WTA battle requires a proprietary platform provider to invest heavily to build its user base, either through penetration pricing or aggressive spending on marketing. Likewise, a proprietary platform provider must shoulder the entire cost of inventing platform technologies, whereas shared providers can spread their collective R&D burden. Thus, for growth, adoption, and winning standards battles, it helps to share the wealth.

16.4 Platform Networks: Core Concepts

16.4.1 *Product Life Cycle and the S-Curve*

If you put a pair of rabbits in a meadow, you can watch their population go through an exponential growth pattern at first. As with every multiplication process, one unit brings forth another. But the population growth slows down later as it approaches a ceiling—the capacity of a species' ecological niche. Over time, the rabbit population traces an S-shaped trajectory. The rate of growth traces a bell-shaped curve that peaks when half the niche is filled. The bell-shaped curve for its rate of growth and the S-shaped curve for the total population constitute a pictorial representation of the natural growth process—that is, how a species population grows into a limited space by obeying the laws of survival.

A product's sales follow the same pattern as the product fills its market niche, because competition in the marketplace is intrinsically the same as in the jungle. The product life cycle (PLC) is shown in Figure 16.1, which also shows the cumulative number of units sold each quarter. Table 16.1 lists characteristic PLC times by industry.

The PLC is used to map the life span of a product. There are generally four stages in the life of a product: the introduction stage, the growth stage, the maturity stage, and the decline stage. There is no set time period for the PLC, and the length of each stage may vary. One product's entire life cycle could be over in a few

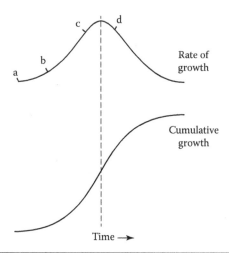

Figure 16.1   PLC and the S-curve.

months; another product could last for years. Also, the introduction stage may last much longer than the growth stage and vice versa.

The four stages of the PLC are as follows:

1. Introduction: The introduction stage is probably the most important stage in the PLC. In fact, most products that fail do so in the introduction stage. This is the stage in which the product is initially promoted; public awareness is very important to the success of a product. If people don't know about the product, they won't go out and buy it. There are two different strategies you can use to introduce your product to consumers. You can use either a penetration strategy or a skimming strategy. If a penetration strategy is used, then prices are set very high initially and then gradually lowered over time. This is a good strategy to use if there are few competitors for your product: profits are high with this strategy, but there is also a great deal of risk. If people don't want to pay high prices, you may lose out. The second pricing strategy is the skimming strategy. In this case, you set your prices very low at the beginning and then gradually increase them. This is a good strategy to use if there are a lot of competitors who control a large portion of the market. Profits are not a concern under this strategy: the most important thing is to make your product known and worry about money at a later time.

2. Growth: The growth stage is where your product starts to grow. In this stage, a very large amount of money is spent on advertising. You want to concentrate on telling the consumer how much better your product is than your competitors' products. There are several ways to advertise your product (e.g., TV and radio commercials and magazine and newspaper ads), or you could get lucky and customers who have bought your product will give good word

Table 16.1   Characteristic PLC Times by Industry

Description	Life Cycle (Years)	Development Cycle (Years)
Financial services	0.2	0.2
Silicon foundries	0.5	0.5
Retailing, entertainment	1.0	1.0
Fashion and textiles	1.5	1.5
Software	2.0	2.0
Electronics	2.5	2.5
Computers	3.0	3.0
Medical and dental	3.5	3.5
Automobiles	4.0	4.0
Metal products	4.5	4.5
Photographic	5.0	5.0
Chemicals, paper	6.0	6.0
Publishing	7.0	2.0
Aircraft	7.0	7.0
Biotechnology	8.0	3.0
Pharmaceuticals	10.0	10.0
Mining	11.0	6.0
Lodging, hotels	11.0	3.0
Foods	11.0	2.0
Tobacco	11.0	1.0
Forestry, oil, and gas reservoirs	12.0	12.0
Military weapons	12.0	2.0
Communication systems	20.0	20.0
Transportation systems	20.5	20.5

of mouth to their family and friends. If you are successful with your advertising strategy, then you will see an increase in sales. Once your sales begin to increase, your share of the market will stabilize. Once you get to this point, you will probably not be able to take any more of the market from your competitors.

3. Maturity: The third stage in the PLC is the maturity stage. If your product completes the introduction and growth stages, then it will spend a great deal of time in the maturity stage. During this stage, sales grow at a very fast rate and then gradually begin to stabilize. The key to surviving this stage is differentiating your product from similar products offered by your competitors. Due to the fact that sales are beginning to stabilize, you must make your product stand out among the rest.

4. Decline: This is the stage in which sales of your product begin to fall. Either everyone that wants to has bought your product or new, more innovative products have been created that replace yours. Many companies decide to withdraw their products from the market due to the downturn: the only way to increase sales during this period is to cut your costs and reduce your spending.

Very few products follow the same life cycle. Many products may not even make it through all four stages; some products may even bypass stages. For example, one product may go straight from the introduction stage to the maturity stage. The corresponding segments in the S-curve are:

1. Introductory stage
2. Ascent stage
3. Maturity stage
4. Decline stage

At the outset of the decline stage, the ideal choice for the incumbent technology is to "leapfrog" to the next S-curve. This means embracing a new disruptive technology solution and using it as the foundation over the incumbent technology solution for its product or service offering in the marketplace. Most firms that attempt it fail miserably because of the investments and commitment in the incumbent solution, coupled with the resulting inertia. The first reaction from the incumbent firm is to ignore the potentially threatening alternative technology, then to dismiss it as irrelevant and low quality, then ferociously engage in process innovation to deliver the existing technology more cost effectively, then to price cut aggressively, and finally to give up.

The pattern can readily be observed in many recent replacement technology solutions, such as e-books vis-à-vis books, digital music distribution vis-à-vis CDs, and voice over Internet vis-à-vis telephones. This is reminiscent of

- The ice harvesting industry when the refrigerator was introduced
- The Pony Express when the telegraph was invented
- Remington typewriters when word processors were first introduced
- Traditional book publishers when e-books first emerged
- How Kodak first responded when its chemical photography business was threatened by digital photography
- Canon's successful digital cameras when smartphones threatened their business

16.4.1.1 Dominant Design

The emergence of the technology solution itself goes through two distinct phases, the shift between which is marked by the emergence of a so-called dominant design. When a technology solution first emerges, multiple firms will enter the fray with competing alternative designs. In the early phases of a platform market, a variety of firms experiment with different types of features, capabilities, and designs to assess the market's response. The predominant design phase is therefore marked by the mass entry of competitors and multiple competing solutions to address the same market needs. As these competing designs continue to improve, at some point one design will eventually become widely accepted—implicitly or explicitly—as the winning standard. This happens when both customers and producers eventually arrive at some consensus about the optimal solution attributes that best meet customers' needs out of all competing designs. This then becomes the industry's dominant design and is usually associated with a mass exit of competitors—a *shakeout*—from the market or switching over to the dominant design. The dominant design does not mean that every competitor will use the same technology per se, but that it defines the expected norms for meeting users' needs. The dominant design is often not necessarily the technologically superior solution. It also invariably involves compromises, because it is designed to appeal to a broad range of users.

16.4.2 Network Effects

Network effects refer to the degree to which every additional user of a platform or app makes it more valuable to every other existing user. The value of adding another user to a platform dramatically increases its potential value to every other user: every additional user dramatically increases the number of other users that he or she can interact with. For example, Facebook's billion users make it much more attractive for the next user after them to join Facebook. The value of the system increases almost exponentially rather than linearly (as the square of the number of users or the number of users times their logarithm, depending on which version of Metcalfe's law one considers); thus, each additional user potentially increases the value of the system to other users dramatically rather than gradually. Once such network effects are triggered, the platform can enter a self-reinforcing cycle.

 While network effects create high barriers to entry into platform markets, they also create a hard-to-assail position once they are in place.

Same-side network effects arise when adding an additional participant (e.g., end user) to one side of the platform changes its value to all other participants on the same side. For example, adding an additional Skype user increases its value to other Skype users (a positive same-side network effect); adding another driver to a busy highway decreases its appeal to other users (a negative, same-side network effect). *Cross-side network* effects arise when adding an additional participant (e.g., end user) to one side of the platform increases or decreases its value to all other participants on the other side. For example, the more people buy iPads, the more developers want to write apps for iPads. This is a positive cross-side network effect.

Network effects of a second kind arise when the demand for one platform complement with strong network effects increases the demand for the platform itself. Independent of whether the positive network effects are same-side or cross-side at the platform level or even at the app level, the platform stands to gain from them. For example, the presence on a platform of a popular app with strong network effects (e.g., Skype) increases the demand for the platform as well (e.g., iOS devices).

16.4.3 Multisidedness

Multisidedness is a distinguishable characteristic of platform networks, where each "side" refers to a distinct group of stakeholders that the platform brings together. For example, the iOS platform brings together app developers (one side) and end users (the other side). These two sides would ordinarily face much higher costs in finding and transacting with each other without the platform than with it. The platform creates value by facilitating participants on one side finding those on the other side or mediating their interactions. In theory, both sides can find and trade with each other directly and without the platform, and this must be costlier for a platform to be viable. The platform is therefore valuable to either side when interacting.

In two-sided platform networks, two distinct groups of participants exist (Table 16.2). Examples include

- Credit cards (cardholders and merchants)
- Video gaming (gamers and game producers)
- Movie theaters (studios and moviegoers)

Table 16.2   Multisided Market Makers

Two-Sided Market-Maker	First Side	Second Side
Credit cards	Cardholders	Merchants
HMOs	Patients	Physicians
Operating systems	End users	Application developers
Travel sites	Travelers	Airlines
e-healthcare	Physicians	Medical services firms
Cable television networks	Subscribers	Content providers and studios
Professional services firms	Professional specialists	Clients

Three-sided platforms connect three distinct types of groups. For example, Apple increasingly connects three distinct types of groups with the free apps distributed in the iOS App Store: end users, app developers, and advertisers.

16.4.4 Multihoming

Multihoming in platforms refers to when a platform participant participates in more than one platform ecosystem. An app developer who simultaneously develops his/her app for Android and iOS is multihoming on those platforms. An end user who owns both an American Express and an VISA card is multihoming on these platforms. Similarly, an end user who owns both a Blackberry and an iPhone is similarly multihoming on these platforms. An adopter can multihome in ownership, usage, or both.

For end users, the ongoing costs of establishing and maintaining multiple platform affiliations is usually a deterrent to multihoming. The higher these costs, the lower the likelihood that an app developer or end user will multihome. Platform owners can discourage multihoming by decreasing the costs of homing on their platform vis-à-vis rival platforms. The costs of multihoming are therefore distinct from the switching costs associated with platform lock-ins.

The software industry has historically relied on exclusivity contracts and intentional incompatibility to coerce developers to single-home. However, intense market competition, particularly in platform markets where a clear winner is yet to emerge, increases the likelihood that developers will multihome. It is also a rational approach because they can place their bets on multiple competing platforms and avoid the downsides of being stranded on a losing platform.

16.4.5 Tipping

Network effects kick in only after a minimum number of users have adopted the technology solution. This minimum number of adopters after which network effects are manifested is known as the platform's *critical mass* or *tipping point*. Once a platform reaches this critical mass, network effects become noticeable and a potentially self-reinforcing positive feedback loop begins. For new platforms, reaching this critical mass with the first distinct set of adopters is perhaps the biggest hurdle that platform owners face. For existing platforms, harnessing them to nudge the platform's evolutionary trajectory is the key challenge. Therefore, a platform requires vastly different strategies before and after it reaches a tipping point.

16.4.6 Lock-In

A successful platform is therefore likely to face intense competition both from copycat platforms as well as truly differentiated platforms. While this competition increases the variety of alternatives available and is usually good for consumers, it can often create the conditions of a zero-profit industry for platform owners and app developers. Severe price competition means that the pricing of rival platforms can devolve into a race to the bottom. The challenge, then, is retaining both users and app developers who might be tempted to switch to a competing platform. The ways in which a platform can make it more desirable for existing users to stay put and not jump ship to a rival platform are broadly referred to as *lock-in*.

Lock-in can be of two types:

1. *Coercive lock-in* makes it costly or impossible for existing users to switch to a competing platform, a heavy-handed approach that eventually fails. Coercive lock-in is potentially breakable (using technologies such as middleware, adapters, and protocol translators). This approach relies on creating high switching costs: the costs associated with terminating the existing use of a technology solution to migrate to a rival one.
2. *Value-driven lock-in* makes the platform increasingly more valuable to its users, so that the choice to switch to a competing platform simply becomes unappealing vis-à-vis staying with the incumbent platform. The strategies for creating such platform lock-ins are potentially more bountiful in software-based platforms relative to non-software-based platforms. The effective strategies for value-driven lock-in that platform owners can use over end users and app developers also vary based on the stage of the platform's life cycle.

16.5 Platform Network Enterprises Examples

16.5.1 Uber

Uber is one of the leading transportation services in the world, with a market value over $20 billion. The cofounders Travis Kalanick and Garrett Camp were attending a conference in Paris in 2008. They were complaining about finding a cab, especially while carrying luggage and under the rain. When they started to brainstorm the next day, they came up with three main requirements:

■ The solution had to be Internet-based (i.e., request and track service from mobile device).
■ It had to provide the service fast.
■ The rides had to be picked up from any location.

The key component of Uber's solution is the Internet-based platform connecting customers (passengers) with the service providers (car drivers). Because the consumers are not Uber's employees, and because there are practically an infinite number of cars that could potentially join Uber, Uber has the requirement to scale at an incredibly fast rate at zero marginal cost.

Uber uses sensor technologies in driver's smartphones to track their behaviors. If you ride with Uber and your driver speeds, brakes too hard, or takes you on a wildly lengthy route to your destination, it is no longer your word against theirs. Uber is using gyrometer and GPS data to track the behavior of its drivers. Gyrometers in smartphones measure small movements, while GPS combined with accelerometers show how often a vehicle starts and stops and the overall speed.

16.5.2 Airbnb

Airbnb is one of the leading hotel services in the world with a market value close to $20 billion. Like Uber, Airbnb built a multibillion-dollar business based on an Internet platform connecting people and places together that competently disrupted the traditional hotel business model. These linear businesses have to invest millions into building new hotels, while Airbnb bypasses these issues altogether.

Airbnb is an Internet-based service for people to list, find, and rent lodging. It was founded in 2008 in San Francisco, California, by Brian Check and Joe Gebbia shortly after creating airbed and breakfast during a conference. The original site offered rooms, breakfast, and a business networking opportunity for the conference attendees who were unable to find a hotel. In February 2008, technical architect Nathan Belcharczyk joined Airbnb as the third cofounder. Shortly thereafter, the newly created company focused on high-profile events where alternative lodging was very limited.

Incredibly similar to the Uber model, Airbnb utilizes a platform business model. This means they facilitate the exchange between consumers (travelers) and service providers (homeowners). Airbnb also required a scalable Internet-based platform supporting from a few customers to hundreds of thousands during major events.

16.6 Summary

Product families do not emerge one product at a time; they are planned so that a number of derivative products can be efficiently created from the foundation of a common core technology or product platform. Platforms and families are powerful ways for companies to recoup their high initial investments in research and development (R&D) by deploying the technology across a number of market fields. After introducing the concept of product platforms, this chapter defined platform network enterprises. The latter part of the chapter addressed core concepts of platform network enterprises, namely, network effects, multisidedness, multihoming, tipping, and lock-in. The chapter ended with an overview of prime examples of platform network enterprises, namely, Uber and Airbnb.

Chapter 17

Social Networks

Social networking is the use of social software, which is based on creating or re-creating online social conversations and social contexts through the use of software and technology. An example of a social network is the use of email for maintaining social relationships. Social networks (SN) are social structures made up of nodes and ties; they indicate the relationships between individuals or organizations and how they are connected through social contexts. SN operate on many levels and play an important role in solving problems, on how organizations are run, and they help individuals succeed in achieving their targets and goals. Computer-based social networks enable people in different locations to interact with each other socially (e.g., chat, viewable photos, etc.) over a network. SN are very useful for visualizing patterns: a social network structure is made up of nodes and ties; there may be few or many nodes in the networks, or one or more different types of relations between the nodes. Building a useful understanding of a social network is to sketch a pattern of social relationships, kinships, community structure, and so forth. The use of mathematical and graphical techniques in social network analysis is important to represent the descriptions of networks compactly and more efficiently.

Social networks operate on many different levels, from families up to nations, and play a critical role in determining the way problems are solved, organizations are run and the degree to which people succeed in achieving their goals.

17.1 Social Networks

The study of social networks really began to take off as an interdisciplinary specialty only after 1970, when modern discrete combinatorics (particularly graph theory) experienced rapid development and relatively powerful computers became readily available. Since then, it has found important applications in organizational behavior, interorganizational relations, the spread of contagious diseases, mental health, social support, the diffusion of information, and animal social organization.

Social groups can exist as personal and direct social ties between individuals or as impersonal, formal, and instrumental social links. German sociologist Ferdinand Tönnies was a major contributor to sociological theory and it was he who initially highlighted that social groups exist by containing individuals who are linked together through shared beliefs and values. Émile Durkheim gave a nonindividualistic explanation of social facts, arguing that social phenomena arise when interacting individuals constitute a reality that can no longer be accounted for in terms of the properties of individual actors. He distinguished between traditional society—*mechanical solidarity*—which prevails if individual differences are minimized, and modern society—*organic solidarity*—which develops out of cooperation between differentiated individuals with independent roles. By the turn of the twentieth century, another major German sociologist, Georg Simmel, became the first scholar to think appropriately in social network terms, producing a series of essays that pinpointed the nature of network size. He displayed a further understanding of social networking with his writings, highlighting that social interaction existed within loosely knit networks as opposed to groups. The next real significant growth of social networking theory didn't commence until the 1930s, when three main social networking traditions emerged. The first to emerge was pioneered by Jacob Levy Moreno, who was recognized as one of the leading social scientists. Moreno began the systematic recording and analysis of social interaction in smaller groups such as work groups and classrooms. The second tradition was founded by a Harvard group that began to focus specifically on interpersonal relations at work. The third tradition originated from Alfred Radcliffe-Brown, an English social anthropologist. Social network analysis has emerged as a key technique in modern sociology, and has also gained a following in anthropology, biology, communication studies, economics, geography, information science, organizational studies, social psychology, and sociolinguistics.

Efforts to support social networks via computer-mediated communication were made in many early online services, including Usenet, Arpanet, listserv, and bulletin board services (BBS). Many prototypical features of social networking sites were also present in online services such as America Online, Prodigy, and CompuServe. Early social networking on the World Wide Web began in the form of generalized online communities such as TheGlobe.com (1995), Geocities (1994), and Tripod. com (1995). Many of these early communities focused on bringing people together to interact with each other through chat rooms, and encouraged users to share personal information and ideas via personal Web pages by providing easy-to-use publishing tools and free or inexpensive Web space. Some communities, such as Classmates.com, took a different approach by simply having people link to each other via e-mail addresses. In the late 1990s, user profiles became a central feature of social networking sites, allowing users to compile lists of "friends" and search for other users with similar interests.

New social networking methods were developed by the end of the 1990s, and many sites began to develop more advanced features for users to find and manage friends. Web-based social networking services make it possible to connect people who share interests and activities across political, economic, and geographic borders. Through e-mail and instant messaging, online communities are created where a gift economy and mutual unselfishness are encouraged through collaboration. Information is particularly suited to gift economy, as information is a nonrival good and can be gifted at practically no cost. The newer generation of social networking sites began to flourish with the emergence of Makeoutclub in 2000, followed by Friendster in 2002, and soon became part of the Internet mainstream. Friendster was followed by MySpace and LinkedIn a year later, and finally Bebo and Facebook in 2004. Attesting to the rapid increase in social networking sites' popularity, by 2005, MySpace was reportedly receiving more page views than Google. Facebook launched in 2004 and has since become the largest social networking site in the world. As of the publication of this book, it is estimated that there are now over 200 active sites using a wide variety of social networking models.

Social networks differ from most other types of networks, including technological and biological networks, in two important ways. First, they have nontrivial clustering or network transitivity, and second, they show positive correlations between the degrees of adjacent vertices. Social networks are often divided into groups or communities, and it has recently been suggested that this division could account for the observed clustering. Furthermore, group structure in networks can also account for degree correlations. Hence, assortative mixing in such networks with variations in the sizes of the groups provides the predicted level and compares well with that observed in real-world networks.

A definition of social networks that is merely based on their structure is as follows: *A social network is an organized set of people that consists of two kinds of elements: human beings and the connections between them.* Online social networks, in that case, are tools or platforms that facilitate the development and maintenance of this relationship, which may stem from the different needs of the participants.

17.1.1 Social Networks Metrics

The current metrics for social network analysis are as follows:

- *Bridge*: An edge is said to be a bridge if deleting it would cause its endpoints to lie in different components of a graph.
- *Centrality*: This measure gives a rough indication of the social power of a node based on how well it "connects" the network. *Betweenness*, *closeness*, and *degree* are all measures of centrality.

- *Betweenness*: The extent to which a node lies between other nodes in the network. This measure takes into account the connectivity of the node's neighbors, giving a higher value for nodes that bridge clusters. The measure reflects the number of people a person is connecting indirectly through their direct links.

- *Closeness*: The degree to which an individual is near all other individuals in a network (directly or indirectly). It reflects the ability to access information through the "grapevine" of network members. Thus, closeness is the inverse of the sum of the shortest distances between each individual and every other person in the network. The shortest path may also be known as the *geodesic distance*.

- *Centralization*: The difference between the number of links for each node divided by the maximum possible sum of differences. A centralized network will have many of its links dispersed around one or a few nodes, while a decentralized network is one in which there is little variation between the number of links each node possesses.

- *Clustering coefficient*: A measure of the likelihood that two associates of a node are associates. A higher clustering coefficient indicates a greater "cliquishness."

- *Density*: The degree to which a respondent's ties know one another/the proportion of ties among an individual's nominees. Network- or global-level density is the proportion of ties in a network relative to the total number possible (sparse vs. dense networks).

- *Degree*: The number of ties to other actors in the network.

- *Cohesion*: The degree to which actors are connected directly to each other by cohesive bonds. Groups are identified as *cliques* if every individual is directly tied to every other individual, *social circles* if there is less stringency of direct contact, which is imprecise, or as *structurally cohesive blocks* if precision is wanted.

- *Eigenvector centrality*: A measure of the importance of a node in a network. It assigns relative scores to all nodes in the network based on the principle that connections to nodes having a high score contribute more to the score of the node in question.

- *Prestige*: In a directed graph, prestige is the term used to describe a node's centrality. *Degree prestige*, *proximity prestige*, and *status prestige* are all measures of prestige.

- *Reach*: The degree to which any member of a network can reach other members of the network.

- *Structural hole*: Static holes that can be strategically filled by connecting one or more links to link together other points. This is related to the idea of social capital: if you link to two people who are not linked, you can control their communication.

The most important centrality measures are *degree centrality, closeness centrality*, and *betweenness centrality*.

1. Degree centrality: The degree of a node is the number of direct connections a node has. Degree centrality is the sum of all other actors who are directly connected to the *ego*. It signifies activity or popularity. Lots of ties coming in and lots of ties coming out of an actor would increase degree centrality.

2. Betweenness centrality: This type of centrality is the number of times a node connects pairs of other nodes, who otherwise would not be able to reach one another. It is a measure of the potential for control, as an actor who is high in *betweenness* is able to act as a gatekeeper, controlling the flow of resources (e.g., information, money, power) between the *alters* that he or she connects. This measurement of centrality is a purely structural measure of popularity, efficiency, and power in a network; in other words, more connected or centralized actors are more popular, efficient, or powerful.

3. Closeness centrality: Closeness centrality is based on the notion of distance. If an node or actor is close to all others in the network, by a distance of no more than one, then it is not dependent on any other to reach everyone in the network. Closeness measures independence or efficiency. With disconnected networks, closeness centrality must be calculated for each component.

As indicated earlier, the two basic elements of social networks are links and nodes. Links are connections, or ties, between individuals or groups, and nodes are the individuals or groups involved in the network. A node's importance in a social network refers to its centrality. Central nodes have the potential to exert influence over less central nodes. A network that possesses just a few or perhaps even one node with high centrality is a centralized network. In this type of network, all nodes are directly connected to each other. Subordinate nodes direct information to the central node and the central node distributes it to all other nodes. Centralized networks are susceptible to disruption because they have few central nodes and damage to a central node could be devastating to the entire network.

Decentralized networks are those that do not possess one central hub but rather possess several important hubs. Each node is indirectly tied to all others and therefore the network has more elasticity. Consequently, these networks are more difficult to disrupt due to their loose connections and ability to replace damaged nodes. Consequently, terror networks choose this type of structure whenever possible.

The term *degrees* is used in reference to the number of direct connections that a node enjoys. The node that possesses the largest number of connections is the hub of the network. The term *betweenness* refers to the number of groups that a node is indirectly tied to through the direct links that it possesses. Therefore, nodes with high a degree of betweenness act as liaisons or bridges to other nodes in the structure. These nodes are known as *brokers* because of the power that they wield. However, these brokers represent a single point of failure because if their communication flows are disrupted, then they will be cut off to the nodes that it connects. Closeness measures the trail that a node would take in order to reach all other nodes in a network. A node with high closeness does not necessarily have the most direct connections; but because they are "close" to many members, they maintain rapid access to most other nodes through both direct and indirect ties.

17.2 Popular Social Networks

This section briefly describes popular social networks such as LinkedIn, Facebook, Twitter, and Google+.

17.2.1 LinkedIn

LinkedIn is currently considered the de facto source of professional networking. Launched in 2003, it is the largest business-oriented social network, with more than 260 million users. This network allows users to find the key people they may need to make introductions into the office of the job they may desire. Users can also track friends and colleagues during times of promotion and hiring to congratulate them if they choose; this results in a complex social web of business connections. In 2008, LinkedIn introduced their mobile app as well as the ability for users to not only endorse each other, but also to specifically attest to individual skills that they may hold and have listed on the site. LinkedIn now supports more than 20 languages.

Users cannot upload their resumes directly to LinkedIn. Instead, users add their skills and work histories to their profiles. Other users inside that social network can verify and endorse each attribute. This essentially makes a user's presence on LinkedIn only as believable as the people they connect with.

17.2.2 Facebook

Facebook was created by Mark Zuckerberg at Harvard College. Launched in 2004, it grew rapidly and now has more than 1.5 billion users. In 2011, Facebook introduced personal timelines to complement a user's profile; timelines show the chronological placement of photos, videos, links, and other updates made by a user and his or her friends. Though a user can customize their timeline as well as the kind of content and profile information that can be shared with individual users, Facebook networks rely heavily on people posting comments publically and also tagging people in photos. Tagging is a very common practice that places people and events together, though, if required, a user can always untag him/herself.

Conceptually, a timeline is a chronological representation of a person's life from birth until his or her death, or the present day if you are still using Facebook. A user's life can be broken up into pieces or categories that can be more meaningfully analyzed by the algorithms run by Facebook. These categories include Work and Education, Family and Relationships, Living, Health and Wellness, and Milestones and Experiences. Each category contains four to seven subcategories. Users have granular control over who sees what content related to them but less over what they see in relation to other people.

Facebook is often accused of selling user information and not fully deleting accounts after users choose to remove them. Because Facebook has such a generalized privacy policy, they can get away with handling user information in almost any way that they see fit. Facebook has done many things to improve security in recent years.

Facebook has provided users with a detailed list of open sessions under their account name and given them the ability to revoke them at will. This is to say that, if an unauthorized person accesses a user's account or the user forgets to log out of a computer, they can force that particular connection to close. The location and time of access are listed for each open session, so a user can easily determine if their account is being accessed from somewhere unexpected.

When viewed through a Web browser, Facebook supports HTTPS. This protocol is considered secure; however, it is not supported by mobile devices. Data transmitted by Facebook to mobile devices have been proven to be in plain text, meaning that if it is intercepted, it is easily human readable. However, global positioning system (GPS) coordinates and information about your friends require special permission. Default access granted to any Facebook app includes user ID, name, profile picture, gender, age range, locale, networks, list of friends, and any information set as public. Any of this information can be transmitted between devices at any time without a user's express permission, and, in the case of mobile devices, in plain, unencrypted text.

> Facebook has partially solved this problem by releasing a separate app for messaging. It provides more granular control for mobile device permissions, such as contact syncing and specific profile information.
> The only problem with this solution is that it relies on every user to not only know about and download the separate app but to also carefully take the considerable amount of time to properly read through and set all the new permissions properly.

17.2.3 Twitter

Twitter's original idea was to design a system for individuals to share short messages with a small group of people. Hence, tweets were designed to be short and led to the limit of 140 characters per tweet. By 2013, Twitter had 200 million users sending 500 million tweets a day.

Twitter was originally designed to work with text messages. This is why the 140 character limit was put into the original design, to comply with text message rates. Twitter's original design was to create a service that a person could send a text to, and that text would not only be available online but it would then be available to resend to other people using the service. Subsequently, Twitter has incorporated many different sources of media. In 2010, Twitter added facilities for online video and photo viewing without redirection to third-party sites. In 2013, Twitter added its own music service as an iPhone app. Despite Twitter's continued expansion of supported content, the language used in modern tweets along with some other helpful additions has continued to adhere to the 140 character limit.

> When Twitter was first implemented, tweets were handled by a server running Ruby on Rails and stored tweets in a shared MySQL database. As the number of Twitter users grew rapidly and the number of tweets being made skyrocketed past the throughput capacity of the system, the MySQL database could not keep up, resulting in read and write errors that prevented tweets from being handled properly. Eventually, Rails components were replaced with the corresponding Scala implementations, leading to improvement of throughput by more than 50 times.

17.2.4 Google+

Google+ is the only social network to rival Facebook's user base, with more than a billion users. The main feature of Google+ is *circles*; by being part of the same circle, people create focused social networks. Circles allow networks to center around ideas and products; circles are also the way that streaming content is shared between people. Circles generate content for users and help organize and segregate with whom information is shared. A user makes circles by placing other Google+ users into them. This is done through an interface built very similar to Gmail and Google maps.

When circles create content for a user, it is accumulated and displayed on their *stream*. A user's stream is a prioritized list of any content from that user's circles that they have decided to display. A user can control how much of a circle's content is included in their stream. Circles can also be shared, either with individual users or other circles. This action being a one-time share means that there is no subsequent syncing after the share takes place. The lack of synchronous updates without sharing a circle again means that it is simply very easy for others to have incorrect information about circles that change on a regular basis. If frequent updates are made and a user wants his or her network to stay up to date, a user may have to share a circle quite frequently.

Google+ *pages* are essentially profiles for businesses, organizations, publications, or other entities that are not related to a single individual. They can be added to circles like normal users and share updates to user streams in the same way. The real distinction is that pages do not require a legal name to be attached to the associated Google account.

Google+ has a large amount of additional services and support owing to its high level of integration with Google accounts, including games, messenger, photo editing and saving, mobile uploads and diagnostics, apps, calendars, and video streaming. Hangouts, which is Google's video-streaming application, is available to use for free and supports up to 10 simultaneous users in a session. Hangouts can be used as a conference call solution or to create instant webcasts. Functionally, Hangouts is similar to programs such as Skype.

17.2.5 Other Social Networks

Here are some of the other notable social networks:

1. Classmates.com was established in 1995 by Randy Conrads as a means for class reunions, and has more than 50 million registered users. By linking together people from the same school and class year, Classmates.com provides individuals with a chance to "walk down memory lane" and get reacquainted with old classmates that have also registered with the site. With a minimum age limit of 18 years, registration is free and anyone may search the site for classmates that they may know. Purchasing a gold membership is required to communicate with other members through the site's e-mail system. User e-mail addresses are private, and communication for paying members is handled through a double-blind e-mail system, which ensures that only paying members can make full use of the site, allowing unlimited communication and orchestration of activities for events, such as reunions.
2. Friendster was launched in 2002 by Jonathan Abrams as a generic social network in Malaysia. Friendster is a social network made primarily of Asian users. Friendster was redesigned and relaunched as a gaming platform in 2011, where it would grow to its current user base of more than 115 million. Friendster filed many of the fundamental patents related to social networks. Eighteen of these patents were acquired by Facebook in 2011.
3. hi5 is a social network developed by Ramu Yalamanchi in 2003 in San Francisco, California, and was acquired by Tagged in 2011. All of the normal social network features were included such as friend networks, photo sharing, profile information, and groups. In 2009, hi5 was redesigned as a purely

social gaming network with a required age of 18 years for all new and existing users. Several hundred games were added, and application programming interfaces (APIs) were created that include support for Facebook games. This popular change boosted hi5's user base, and at the time of acquisition its user base was more than 80 million.

4. Orkut was a social network almost identical to Facebook that was launched in 2004 and shut down by the end of September 2014. Orkut obtained more than 100 million users, most of which were located in India and Brazil.

5. Flickr is a photo-sharing website that was created in 2004 and acquired by Yahoo in 2005; videos can also be accessed via Flickr. It has tens of millions of members sharing billions of images.

6. YouTube is a video-sharing website created in 2005 and acquired by Google in 2006. Members, including corporations and organizations, post videos of themselves as well as various events and talks. Movies and songs are also posted on this website.

17.3 Social Networks Analysis (SNA)

In social science, the structural approach to the study of interactions among social actors is called *social network analysis*. The relationships that social network analysts study are usually those that link individual human beings, since these social scientists believe that besides individual characteristics, relational links and social structures are necessary and indispensable to fully understanding social phenomena.

Social network analysis is used to understand the social structure that exists among entities in an organization. The defining feature of SNA is its focus on the structure of relationships, ranging from causal acquaintances to close bonds. This is in contrast to other areas of the social sciences, where the focus is often on the attributes of agents rather than on the relations between them. SNA maps and measures formal and informal relationships to understand what facilitates or impedes the knowledge flows that bind the interacting units—that is, who knows whom, and who shares what information and how. Social network analysis is focused on uncovering the patterning of people's interactions. SNA is based on the intuition that these patterns are important features of the lives of the individuals who display them. Network analysts believe that how an individual lives depends chiefly on how that individual is tied into a larger web of social connections. Moreover, many believe that the success or failure of societies and organizations often depends on the patterning of their internal structure, which is guided by formal concept analysis, which is grounded in the systematic analysis of empirical data. With the availability of powerful computers and discrete combinatorics (especially graph theory) after 1970, the study of SNA took off as an interdisciplinary specialty, the applications of which are found in many fields including organizational behavior, interorganizational relations, the spread of contagious diseases, mental health, social support, the diffusion of information, and animal social organization. SNA software provides the researcher with data that can be analyzed to determine the centrality, betweenness, degree, and closeness of each node.

An individual's social network influences his/her social attitude and behavior. Before collecting network data, typically through interviews, it must first be decided as to the kinds of networks and kinds of relations that will be studied.

1. One-mode versus two-mode networks: The former involve relations among a single set of similar actors, while the latter involve relations among two different sets of actors. An example of a two-mode network would be one consisting of private, for-profit organizations and their links to nonprofit agencies in a community. Two-mode networks are also used to investigate the relationship between a set of actors and a series of events. For example, although people may not have direct ties to each other, they may attend similar events or activities in a community, and in doing so, this sets up opportunities for the formation of *weak ties*.

2. Complete/whole versus ego networks: Complete/whole or sociocentric networks consist of the connections among members of a single, bounded community. Relational ties among all of the teachers in a high school is an example of a whole network. Ego/egocentric or personal networks refer to the ties directly connecting the focal actor (*ego*) to others (the ego's *alters*) in the network, plus the ego's views on the ties among his or her alters. If we asked a teacher to nominate the people he/she socializes with outside of school, and then asked that teacher to indicate who in that network socializes with the others nominated, it is a typical ego network.

   a. Egocentric network data focus on the network surrounding one node—in other words, a single social actor. Data are on nodes that share the chosen relation(s) with the ego and on relations between those nodes. Ego network data can be extracted from whole network data by choosing a focal node and examining only nodes connected to this ego. Ego network data, like whole network data, can also include multiple relations; these relations can be collapsed into single networks, as when ties to people who provide companionship and emotional aid are collapsed into a single support network. Unlike whole network analyses, which commonly focus on one or a small number of networks, ego network analyses typically sample large numbers of egos and their networks.

   b. Complete/whole networks focus on all social actors rather than focusing on the network surrounding any particular actor. These networks begin from a list of included actors and include data on the presence or absence of relations between every pair of actors. When a researcher adopts the whole network perspective, he/she will consult each social actor and all other individuals to collect relational data.

> Using a network perspective, Mark Granovetter put forward the theory of the *strength of weak ties*. Granovetter found in one study that more numerous weak ties can be important in seeking information and innovation. Because cliques have a tendency to have more homogeneous opinions and common traits, individuals in the same cliques would also know more or less what the other members know. To gain new information and opinion, people often look beyond the clique to their other friends and acquaintances.

17.4 Social Network Performance

Once the network analysis is completed, the network dynamics predict the performance of the network, which can be evaluated as a combination of

1. The network's robustness to the removal of ties and/or nodes
2. Network efficiency, in terms of the distance to traverse from one node to another and its nonredundant size
3. The effectiveness of the network, in terms of information benefits allocated to central nodes
4. Network diversity, in terms of the history of each of the nodes

17.4.1 Robustness

Social network analysts have highlighted the importance of network structure with relation to the network's robustness. The robustness can be evaluated based on how it becomes fragmented when an increasing fraction of nodes is removed. Robustness is measured as an estimate of the tendency of individuals in networks to form local groups or clusters of individuals with whom they share similar characteristics—that is, clustering. For example, if individuals X, Y, and Z are all computer experts and if X knows Y and Y knows Z, then it is highly likely that X knows Z using the so-called chain rule. If the measure of the clustering of individuals is high for a given network, then the robustness of that network increases—within the cluster/group.

17.4.2 Efficiency

Network efficiency can be measured by considering the number of nodes that can instantly access a large number of different nodes—sources of knowledge, status, and so on—through a relatively small number of ties. These nodes are treated as nonredundant contacts. For example, with two networks of equal size, the one with more nonredundant contacts provides more benefits than the others. Also, it is quite evident that the gain from a new contact redundant with existing contacts will be minimal. However, it is wise to consume time and energy in cultivating a new contact to unreached people. Hence, social network analysts measure efficiency by the number of nonredundant contacts and the average number of ties an ego has to traverse to reach any alter; this number is referred to as the average path length. The shorter the average path length relative to the size of the network and the lower the number of redundant contacts, the more efficient is the network.

17.4.3 Effectiveness

Effectiveness targets the cluster of nodes that can be reached through nonredundant contacts. In contrast, efficiency aims at the reduction of the time and energy spent on redundant contacts. Each cluster of contacts is an independent source of information. One cluster around this nonredundant node, no matter how numerous its members are, is only one source of information, because people connected to one another tend to know about the same things at about the same time. For example, a network is more effective when the information benefit provided by multiple clusters of contacts is broader, providing better assurance that the central node will be informed. Moreover, because nonredundant contacts are only connected through the central node, the central node is assured of being the first to see new opportunities created by needs in one group that could be served by skills in another group.

17.4.4 Diversity

While efficiency is about gaining a large number of (nonredundant) nodes, a node's diversity, conversely, suggests a critical performance point of view where those nodes are diverse in nature; that is, the history of each individual node within the network is important. It is particularly this aspect that can be explored through case studies, which is a matter of intense discussion among social network analysts. It seems to suggest that social scientists should prefer and use network analysis according to the first strand of thought developed by social network analysts instead of actor attribute–oriented accounts based on the diversity of each the nodes.

17.5 Summary

This chapter discussed the social networks. It started with an introduction to the concept of social networks and real world example social networks, like LinkedIn, Facebook, Twitter, and Google+. The chapter then discussed the characteristics of social network analysis. The end part of the chapter presented social network performance in terms of aspects like robustness, efficiency, effectiveness, and diversity.

Chapter 18

Wireless Sensor Networks

A sensor network consists of a large number of sensor nodes that are densely deployed in a sensing region and collaborate to accomplish a sensing task. It requires a suite of network protocols to implement various network control and management functions—for example, synchronization, self-configuration, medium access control (MAC), routing, data aggregation, node localization, and network security. However, existing network protocols for traditional wireless networks—for example, cellular systems and mobile ad hoc networks (MANETs)—cannot be applied directly to sensor networks because they do not consider the energy, computation, and storage constraints in sensor nodes. On the other hand, most sensor networks are application specific and have different application requirements. For these reasons, a new suite of network protocols is required, which take into account not only the resource constraints in sensor nodes but also the requirements of different network applications. For this reason, it is important to define a protocol stack to facilitate the protocol design for WSNs.

18.1 Wireless Sensor Networks

Wireless sensor networks (WSNs) are widely considered one of the most important technologies for the twenty-first century. Enabled by recent advances in micro-electronic mechanical systems (MEMS) and wireless communication technologies, tiny, cheap, smart sensors deployed in a physical area and networked through wireless links and the Internet provide unprecedented opportunities for a variety of applications, such as environmental monitoring and industry process control. In contrast with traditional wireless communication networks such as cellular systems and mobile ad hoc networks (MANET), there are many challenges in the development and application of WSNs, which often have unique characteristics such as a denser level of node deployment, less reliable sensor nodes, and severe energy, computation, and storage constraints.

18.1.1 WSN Characteristics

A WSN typically consists of a large number of low-cost, low-power, and multifunctional sensor nodes that are deployed in a region of interest. These sensor nodes are small in size but are equipped with sensors, embedded microprocessors, and radio transceivers, and therefore have not only sensing capabilities but also data-processing and communicating capabilities. WSNs communicate over a short distance via a wireless medium and collaborate to accomplish a common task. The characteristic features of WSNs are:

1. Application specific: Sensor networks are application specific. A network is usually designed and deployed for a specific application. The design requirements of a network change with its application.
2. No global identification: Due to the large number of sensor nodes, it is usually not possible to build a global addressing scheme for a sensor network because it would introduce a high overhead for the identification maintenance.
3. Dense node deployment: Sensor nodes are usually densely deployed in a field of interest. The number of sensor nodes in a sensor network can be several orders of magnitude higher than that in a MANET.
4. Frequent topology change: Network topology changes frequently due to node failure, damage, addition, energy depletion, or channel fading.
5. Many-to-one traffic patterns: In most sensor network applications, the data sensed by sensor nodes flow from multiple source sensor nodes to a particular sink, exhibiting a many-to-one traffic pattern.
6. Battery-powered sensor nodes: Sensor nodes are usually powered by battery. In most situations, they are deployed in a harsh or hostile environment where it is very difficult or even impossible to change or recharge the batteries.
7. Severe energy, computation, and storage constraints: Sensor nodes are highly limited in energy, computation, and storage capacities.
8. Self-configurable: Sensor nodes are usually randomly deployed without careful planning and engineering. Once deployed, sensor nodes have to autonomously configure themselves into a communication network.
9. Unreliable sensor nodes: Sensor nodes are usually deployed in harsh or hostile environments and operate without attendance. They are prone to physical damages or failures.

10. Data redundancy: In most sensor network applications, sensor nodes are densely deployed in a region of interest and collaborate to accomplish a common sensing task. Thus, the data sensed by multiple sensor nodes typically have a certain level of correlation or redundancy.

18.1.2 WSN Design Challenges

The unique network characteristics present many challenges in the design of sensor networks, which involve the following main aspects:

1. Limited energy capacity: Sensor nodes are battery powered and thus have very limited energy capacity. This constraint presents many new challenges in the development of hardware and software and the design of network architectures and protocols for sensor networks.

 To prolong the operational lifetime of a sensor network, energy efficiency should be considered in every aspect of sensor network design, not only hardware and software but also network architectures and protocols.

2. Limited hardware resources: Sensor nodes have limited processing and storage capacities, and thus can only perform limited computational functionalities. These hardware constraints present many challenges in network protocol design for sensor networks, which must consider not only the energy constraint in sensor nodes but also the processing and storage capacities of sensor nodes.
3. Massive and random deployment: Most sensor networks consist of hundreds to thousands of sensor nodes; node deployment can be either manual or random. In most applications, sensor nodes can be scattered randomly in an intended area or dropped massively over an inaccessible or hostile region. The sensor nodes must autonomously organize themselves into a communication network before they start to perform a sensing task.
4. Dynamic and unreliable environment: A sensor network usually operates in a dynamic and unreliable environment. On one hand, the topology of a sensor network may change frequently due to node failures, damages, additions, or energy depletion. On the other hand, sensor nodes are linked by a wireless medium, which is noisy, error prone, and time varying. The connectivity of the network may be frequently disrupted because of channel fading or signal attenuation.
5. Diverse applications: Sensor networks have a wide range of diverse applications. The requirements for different applications may vary significantly. No network protocol can meet the requirements of all applications. The design of sensor networks is application specific.

18.1.3 WSN Design Objectives

It is almost impractical to implement all the design objectives in a single network. Instead, only a part of these networks are application specific and consequently have different application requirements.

The main design objectives for sensor networks include the following:

1. Small node size: Reducing node size is one of the primary design objectives of sensor networks. Sensor nodes are usually deployed in a harsh or hostile environment in large numbers. Reducing node size can facilitate node deployment and also reduce the cost and power consumption of sensor nodes.

2. Low node cost: Since sensor nodes are usually deployed in a harsh or hostile environment in large numbers and cannot be reused, it is important to reduce the cost of sensor nodes so that the cost of the whole network is reduced.

3. Low power consumption: Reducing power consumption is the most important objective in the design of a sensor network. Since sensor nodes are powered by battery and it is often very difficult or even impossible to change or recharge their batteries, it is crucial to reduce the power consumption of sensor nodes so that the lifetime of the sensor nodes, as well as of the whole network, is prolonged.

4. Self-configurability: In sensor networks, sensor nodes are usually deployed in a region of interest without careful planning and engineering. Once deployed, sensor nodes should be able to autonomously organize themselves into a communication network and reconfigure their connectivity in the event of topology changes and node failures.

5. Scalability: In sensor networks, the number of sensor nodes may be on the order of tens, hundreds, or thousands. Thus, network protocols designed for sensor networks should be scalable to different network sizes.

6. Adaptability: In sensor networks, a node may fail, join, or move, which results in changes in node density and network topology. Thus, network protocols designed for sensor networks should be adaptive to such density and topology changes.

7. Reliability: For many sensor network applications, it is required that data be reliably delivered over noisy, error-prone, and time-varying wireless channels. To meet this requirement, network protocols designed for sensor networks must provide error control and correction mechanisms to ensure reliable data delivery.

8. Fault tolerance: Sensor nodes are prone to failures due to harsh deployment environments and unattended operations. Thus, sensor nodes should be fault

tolerant and have the abilities of self-testing, self-calibrating, self-repairing, and self-recovering.

9. Security: In many military or security applications, sensor nodes are deployed in a hostile environment and thus are vulnerable to adversaries. In such situations, a sensor network should introduce effective security mechanisms to prevent the data information in the network or a sensor node from unauthorized access or malicious attacks.

10. Channel utilization: Sensor networks have limited bandwidth resources. Thus, communication protocols designed for sensor networks should efficiently make use of the bandwidth to improve channel utilization.

11. Quality-of-service (QoS) support: In sensor networks, different applications may have different QoS requirements in terms of delivery latency and packet loss. For example, some applications, such as fire monitoring, are delay sensitive and thus require timely data delivery. Some applications, such as data collection for scientific exploration, are delay tolerant but cannot stand packet loss. Thus, network protocol design should consider the applicable or relevant QoS requirements of the specific applications.

18.1.4 WSN Architecture

A sensor network typically consists of a large number of sensor nodes densely deployed in a region of interest and one or more data sinks or base stations that are located close to or inside the sensing region, as shown in Figure 18.1a. The sink(s) sends queries or commands to the sensor nodes in the sensing region, while the sensor nodes collaborate to accomplish the sensing task and send the sensed data to the sink(s). Meanwhile, the sink(s) also serves as a gateway to outside networks—for example, the Internet. It collects data from the sensor nodes, performs simple processing on the collected data, and then sends relevant information (or the processed data) via the Internet to the users who requested it or use the information.

To send data to the sink, each sensor node can use single-hop long-distance transmission, which leads to single-hop network architecture, as shown in Figure 18.1b. However, long-distance transmission is costly in terms of energy consumption; in sensor networks, the energy consumed for communication is much higher than that for sensing and computation. Additionally, the energy consumed for transmission dominates the total energy consumed for communication, and the required transmission power grows exponentially with the increase of transmission distance. In order to reduce the amount of traffic and transmission distance and, consequently, increase energy savings and prolong network lifetime, multihop short-distance communication is highly preferred.

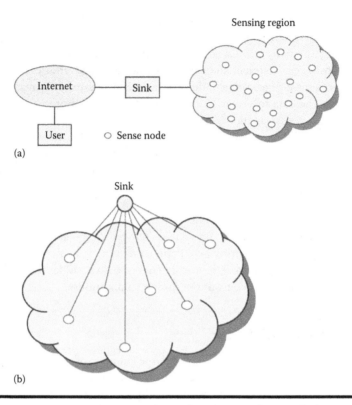

Figure 18.1 (a) Sensor network architecture, (b) single-hop network architecture.

 The basic organization of a sensor network can be of two types:

1. Flat architecture: In a flat network, each node plays the same role in performing a sensing task and all sensor nodes are peers. Due to the large number of sensor nodes, it is not feasible to assign a global identifier to each node in a sensor network. For this reason, data gathering is usually accomplished by using data-centric routing, where the data sink transmits a query to all nodes in the sensing region via flooding and only the sensor nodes that have the data matching the query will respond to the sink. Each sensor node communicates with the sink via a multihop path and uses its peer nodes as relays.

2. Hierarchical architecture: In a hierarchical network, sensor nodes are organized into clusters, where a node with

lower energy can be used to perform the sensing task and send the sensed data to its cluster head at short distance, while a node with higher energy can be selected as a cluster head to process the data from its cluster members and transmit the processed data to the sink. This process can not only reduce the energy consumption for communication but also balance traffic load and improve scalability when the network size grows. Since all sensor nodes have the same transmission capability, clustering must be periodically performed in order to balance the traffic load among all sensor nodes. Moreover, data aggregation can also be performed at cluster heads to reduce the amount of data transmitted to the sink and improve the energy efficiency of the network even further.

A sensor network can be organized into a single-hop clustering architecture or a multihop clustering architecture, depending on the distance between the cluster members and their cluster heads. Similarly, a sensor network can be organized into a single-tier clustering architecture or a multitier clustering architecture, depending on the number of tiers in the clustering hierarchy envisaged for the network. Figures 18.2a,b,c show single-hop, multihop, and multitier clustering architecture, respectively.

18.1.4.1 Sensor Node Structure

A sensor node typically consists of four basic components: a sensing unit, a processing unit, a communication unit, and a power unit, as shown in Figure 18.3.

1. The sensing unit usually consists of one or more sensors and analog-to-digital converters (ADCs). The sensors observe the physical phenomenon and generate analog signals based on the observed phenomenon. The ADCs convert the analog signals into digital signals, which are then fed to the processing unit.

2. The processing unit usually consists of a microcontroller or microprocessor with memory (e.g., Intel's StrongARM microprocessor or Atmel's AVR microprocessor), which provides intelligent control to the sensor node.

3. The communication unit consists of a short-range radio for performing data transmission and reception over a radio channel.

4. The power unit consists of a battery for supplying power to drive all other components in the system.

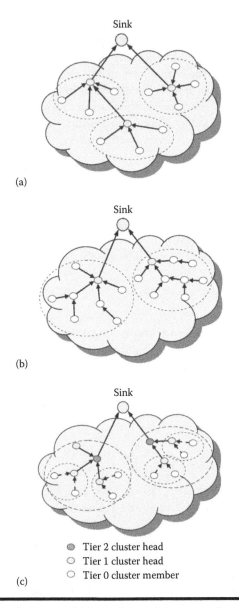

(a)

(b)

(c)

- Tier 2 cluster head
- Tier 1 cluster head
- Tier 0 cluster member

Figure 18.2   (a) Single-hop multiclustering architecture, (b) multihop clustering architecture, and (c) multitier clustering architectures.

In addition, a sensor node can also be equipped with other units, depending on specific applications. For example, a motor may be needed to move sensor nodes in some sensing tasks. A global positioning system (GPS) may be needed in some applications that require location information for network operation. All these units should be built into a small module with low power consumption and low production cost.

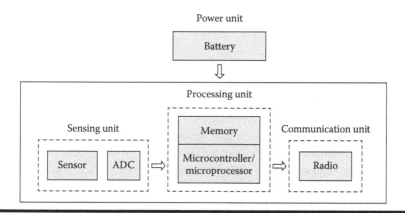

Figure 18.3   Sensor node structure.

18.1.4.2 WSN Protocol Stack

Figure 18.4 shows the generic WSN protocol stack. The application layer contains a variety of application layer protocols to generate various sensor network applications. The transport layer is responsible for reliable data delivery, as required by the application layer. The network layer is responsible for routing the data from the transport layer. The data link layer is primarily responsible for data stream multiplexing, data frame transmission and reception, medium access, and error control. The physical layer is responsible for signal transmission and reception over a physical communication medium, including frequency generation, signal modulation, transmission and reception, data encryption, and so on.

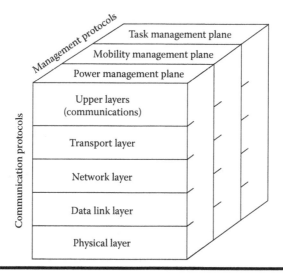

Figure 18.4   Generic WSN protocol stack.

Tables 18.1 and 18.2 present a possible protocol stack and possible lower-layer protocols, respectively.

18.1.4.2.1 Application Layer

The application layer includes a variety of application layer protocols that perform various sensor network applications, such as query dissemination, node localization, time synchronization, and network security. For example, the Sensor Management Protocol (SMP) is an application layer management protocol that provides software operations to perform a variety of tasks—for example, exchanging location-related data, synchronizing sensor nodes, moving sensor nodes, scheduling sensor nodes, and querying the status of sensor nodes. The Sensor Query and Data Dissemination Protocol (SQDDP) provides user applications with interfaces to issue queries, respond to queries, and collect responses. The Sensor Query and Tasking Language (SQTL) is a sensor-programming language used to implement middleware in WSNs. Although many sensor network applications have been proposed, their corresponding application layer protocols still need to be developed.

18.1.4.2.2 Transport Layer

The transport layer is responsible for reliable end-to-end data delivery between the sensor nodes and the sink(s). Due to the energy, computation, and storage constraints of sensor nodes, traditional transport protocols—such as the conventional end-to-end retransmission-based error control and window-based congestion control mechanisms used in the Transport Control Protocol (TCP)—cannot be applied directly to sensor networks without modification.

Table 18.1   Possible WSN Protocol Stack

Upper layers	In-network applications, including application processing, data aggregation, external querying query processing, and external database
Layer 4	Transport, including data dissemination and accumulation, caching, and storage
Layer 3	Networking, including adaptive topology management and topological routing
Layer 2	Link layer (contention): Channel sharing (MAC), timing, and locality
Layer 1	Physical medium: Communication channel, sensing, actuation, and signal processing

Table 18.2 Possible Lower-Layer WSN Protocols

	GPRS/GSM 1xRTT/CDMA	IEEE 802.11b/g	IEEE 802.15.1	IEEE 802.15.4
Market name for standard	2.5G/3G	Wi-Fi	Bluetooth	ZigBee
Network target	WAN/MAN	WLAN and hotspot	PAN and DAN (desk area network)	WSN
Application focus	Wide area voice and data	Enterprise applications (data and VoIP)	Cable replacement	Monitoring and control
Bandwidth (Mbps)	0.064–0.128+	11–54	0.7	0.020–0.25
Transmission range (ft)	3000+	1–300+	1–30+	1–300+
Design factors	Reach and transmission quality	Enterprise support, scalability, and cost	Cost, ease of use	Reliability, power, and cost

18.1.4.2.3 Network Layer

The network layer is responsible for routing the data sensed by source sensor nodes to the data sink(s). In a sensor network, sensor nodes are deployed in a sensing region to observe a phenomenon of interest; the observed phenomenon or data need to be transmitted to the data sink. Sensor nodes are densely deployed and neighboring nodes are close to each other, which makes it feasible to use short-distance communication. In multihop communication, a sensor node transmits its sensed data toward the sink via one or more intermediate nodes, which can not only reduce the energy consumption for communication but also effectively reduce the signal propagation and channel-fading effects inherent in long-range wireless communication, and is therefore preferred.

However, routing protocols for traditional wireless networks are not suitable for sensor networks because they do not consider energy efficiency as the primary concern. Also, data from the sensing region toward the sink exhibit a unique many-to-one traffic pattern in sensor networks. The combination of multihop and many-to-one communications results in a significant increase in transit traffic intensity and thus packet congestion, collision, loss, delay, and energy consumption as data move closer toward the sink. Therefore, it is important to take into account the energy constraint of sensor nodes as well as the unique traffic pattern in the design of the network layer and routing protocols.

18.1.4.2.4 Data Link Layer

The data link layer is responsible for data stream multiplexing, data frame creation and detection, medium access, and error control in order to provide reliable point-to-point and point-to-multipoint transmissions. One of the most important functions of the data link layer is medium access control (MAC), whose primary objective is to fairly and efficiently share the shared communication resources or medium among multiple sensor nodes in order to achieve good network performance in terms of energy consumption, network throughput, and delivery latency. However, MAC protocols for traditional wireless networks cannot be applied directly to sensor networks without modifications because they do not take into account the unique characteristics of sensor networks—in particular, the energy constraint. For example, the primary concern in a cellular system is to provide quality of service (QoS) to users. Energy efficiency is only of secondary importance because there is no power limit with the base stations, and mobile users can replenish the batteries in their handsets. In MANETs, mobile nodes are equipped with portable devices powered by battery, which is also replaceable. In contrast, the primary concern in sensor networks is energy conservation for prolonging network lifetime, which makes traditional MAC protocols unsuitable for sensor networks.

In many applications, a sensor network is deployed in a harsh environment where wireless communication is error prone. In this case, error control becomes indispensable and critical for achieving link reliability or reliable data transmission. In general, there are two main error control mechanisms: Forward Error Correction (FEC) and Automatic Repeat reQuest (ARQ). ARQ achieves reliable data transmission by retransmitting lost data packets or frames. Obviously, this incurs significant retransmission overheads and additional energy consumption, and is therefore not suitable for sensor networks. FEC achieves link reliability by using error control codes in data transmission, which introduces additional encoding and decoding complexities that require additional processing resources in sensor nodes. Therefore, a trade-off should be optimized between the additional processing power and the corresponding coding gain in order to have a powerful, energy-efficient, and low-complexity FEC mechanism.

18.1.4.2.5 Physical Layer

The physical layer is responsible for converting bit streams from the data link layer to signals that are suitable for transmission over the communication medium. It must deal with various related issues, such as

- Transmission medium and frequency selection, carrier frequency generation, signal modulation and detection, and data encryption
- The design of the underlying hardware
- Electrical and mechanical interfaces

Medium and frequency selection is an important problem for communication between sensor nodes. One option is to use radio and the industrial, scientific, and medical (ISM) bands that are license-free in most countries. The main advantages of using the ISM bands include free use, large spectrums, and global availability. However, the ISM bands have already been used for communication systems such as cordless phone systems and wireless local area networks (WLANs). On the other hand, sensor networks require a tiny, low-cost, and ultra-low-power transceiver. For these reasons, the 433 MHz ISM band and the 917 MHz ISM band have been recommended for use in Europe and North America, respectively.

Across each layer, the protocol stack can be divided into a group of management planes:

1. The *power management* plane is responsible for managing the power level of a sensor node for sensing, processing, and transmission and reception, which can be implemented by employing efficient power management mechanisms at different protocol layers. For example, at the MAC layer, a sensor node can turn off its transceiver when there are no data to transmit and receive. At the network layer, a sensor node may select a neighbor node with the most residual energy as its next hop to the sink.
2. The *connection management* plane is responsible for the configuration and reconfiguration of sensor nodes to establish and maintain the connectivity of a network in the case of node deployment and topology change due to node addition, node failure, node movement, and so on.
3. The *task management* plane is responsible for task distribution among sensor nodes in a sensing region in order to improve energy efficiency and prolong network lifetime. Since sensor nodes are usually densely deployed in a sensing region and are redundant for performing a sensing task, not all sensor nodes in the sensing region are required to perform the same sensing task. Therefore, a task management mechanism can be used to perform task distribution among multiple sensors.

18.2 Sensor Data Processing

18.2.1 Sensor Data-Gathering and Data Dissemination Mechanisms

Two major factors that determine the system architecture and design methodology are

1. The number of sources and sinks within the sensor network: Sensor network applications can be classified into three categories:
   - One sink, multiple sources
   - One source, multiple sinks
   - Multiple sinks, multiple sources

   An application wherein the interaction between the sensor network and the subscribers is typically through a single gateway (sink) node falls into the *multiple sources–one sink* category. On the other hand, a traffic-reporting system that disseminates traffic conditions (e.g., an accident) at a certain location to many drivers (sinks) falls in the *one source–multiple sinks* category.

2. The trade-offs between energy, bandwidth, latency, and information accuracy: An approach cannot usually optimize its performance in all aspects. Instead, based on the relative importance of its requirements, an application usually trades less important criteria for optimizing the performance with respect to the most important attribute. For instance, for mission-critical applications, the end-to-end latency is perhaps the most important attribute and needs to be kept below a certain threshold, even at the expense of additional energy consumption.

   Data-gathering and dissemination mechanisms are based on the following three factors:
   - Storage location
   - The direction of diffusion
   - The structure of devices

18.2.1.1 Mechanisms Based on Storage Location

In order to process historical queries, data collected at different sensors have to be properly stored in a database system for future query processing. The three scenarios of placing storage at different locations are

1. External storage (ES): All the data collected at sensors in a sensor network are relayed to the sink and stored at its storage for further processing. For a sensor network with n sensor nodes, the cost of transmitting data to the external storage is $O(\sqrt{n})$. There is no cost for external queries, while the cost of a query within the network incurs a cost of $O(\sqrt{n})$.

2. Local storage (LS): Data are stored at each sensor's local storage and, thus, no communication cost for data storage is incurred. However, each sensor needs to process all queries and a query is flooded to all sensors. The cost of flooding a query is $O(\sqrt{n})$.

3. Data-centric storage (DCS): DCS stores the data at a sensor (or a location) in the sensor network based on the content of the data. Data storage in a DCS system consists of two steps: first, the sensor maps an event it detects

to a label via a consensus hash function; then, it routes the data to a node according to the label. The label can be a location and the sensor can route the data via geographic routing. We will introduce two of the representative approaches relying on geographic information—namely, geographic hash table (GHT) and distributed index for multidimensional (DIM) data. Both data and query communication costs are $O(\sqrt{n})$.

18.2.1.1.1 Database with Geographic Information

One of the common hash functions in sensor database systems is to map the data to a location and then send the data via geographic routing to the sensor node that is closest to the mapped location for storage. If all of the sensors have the same hash function, a query with a specific content can be converted to a location where the data were stored for future retrieval.

Adopting greedy perimeter stateless routing (GPSR) as the underlying routing protocol, two differing hash functions can be employed.

1. Geographic hash table (GHT): In GHT, the input to the hash function is a reading of a single attribute or a specific type of event, and the hash result is a point in the two-dimensional space. If no sensor node is located at the precise coordinates of the hash result, the data are stored at the node closest to the hash result. With the use of the perimeter mode of GPSR, the data packet traverses the entire perimeter, enclosing the location of the hash result, and the closest location can be identified.
2. Distributed index for multidimensional (DIM) data: DIM is designed especially for multidimensional range queries. DIM maps a vector of readings with multiple attributes to a two-dimensional geographic zone. Assuming that the sensors are static and are aware of their own locations and field boundaries, the entire field is divided recursively into zones. The sequence of divisions is vertical, horizontal, and so on. Each zone is encoded with a unique code based on, say, the following rule: For a vertical division (the ith division where i is an odd number), the ith bit code of the zone is encoded as 1 if it is in the right region and 0 otherwise. Similarly, the even bit of the code word is determined by whether the zone is above (1) or below (0) the divided line.

Due to the fact that sensors may not be uniformly deployed in an area, every zone just defined may not contain a sensor. In other words, a sensor needs to determine the zone(s) it owns where no other sensors reside. This can be easily achieved when a node is aware of its neighbors' locations. With the encoding rules for both zones and events, the next task is to route the event to the node that owns the zone (code word) of the event.

18.2.1.2 Mechanisms Based on the Direction of Diffusion

The data-gathering process usually consists of two steps: query and reply. A sink (or user) sends a query to a sensor network, and sensors that detect events matching the query send replies to the sink. Applications with different requirements opt for different communication paradigms:

1. One-phase pull diffusion: The overheads of flooding of both queries and replies are high in cases where
   a. There exist a large number of sinks or sources.
   b. The rate of queries for different events is high.
   One-phase pull diffusion skips the flooding process of data diffusion. Instead, replies are sent back to neighbors that first send the matching queries. In other words, the reverse path is the route with the least latency. One-phase pull diffusion is well suited to scenarios in which a large number of disparate events are being queried.
2. Two-phase pull diffusion: The most representative approach in this category is directed diffusion. Both the queries for events of interest and the replies are initially disseminated via flooding, and multiple routes may be established from a source to the sink. In the second pull phase, the sink reinforces the best route (usually with the lowest latency) by increasing its data rate (i.e., gradient). Data are then sent to the sink along this route. Two-phase pull diffusion is especially well suited to applications with many sources and only a few sinks.
3. Push diffusion: In the push diffusion mechanism, a source actively floods the information collected when it detects an event and sinks subscribe to events of interest via positive enforcements. Push diffusion is well suited to
   a. Applications in which there exist many sinks and only a few sources, and sources generate data only occasionally.
   b. Target-tracking applications in which data sources constantly change with time, and hence data routes cannot be established effectively via reinforcement. Sensor Protocol for Information via Negotiation (SPIN) can be classified as a protocol built on the push diffusion mechanism.

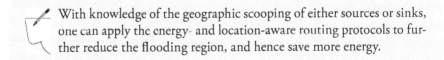 With knowledge of the geographic scooping of either sources or sinks, one can apply the energy- and location-aware routing protocols to further reduce the flooding region, and hence save more energy.

18.2.1.2.1 Directed Diffusion

Directed diffusion is a two-phase pull routing mechanism in which data consumers (sinks) search for data sources matching their interests and the sources

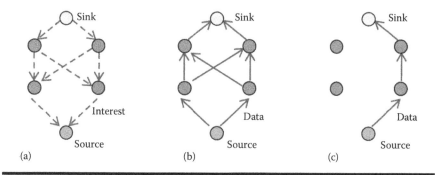

Figure 18.5 **Three phases in directed diffusion: (a) interest propagation, (b) data propagation, (c) data delivery along reinforced path.**

find the best routes to route their data back to the subscribers. Directed diffusion consists of three phases: interest propagation, data propagation, and reinforcement (Figure 18.5). Sinks first broadcast interest packets to their neighbors. When a node receives an interest packet, the packet is cached and rebroadcast to other neighbors if it is new to this node. The propagation of interest packets also sets up the gradient in the network to facilitate data delivery to the sink. A gradient specifies both a data rate and a direction to relay data. The initial data rate of the gradient is set to be a small value and will be increased if the gradient along the path is enforced.

When a node matches an interest (e.g., it is in the vicinity of the event in the target-tracking application), it generates a data packet with the data rate specified in the gradient. The data packet is unicast individually to the neighbors from which the interest packet is received. When a node receives a data packet matching a query in its interest cache, the data packet is relayed to the next hop toward the sink. Both interest and data propagation are exploratory, but the initial data rate is low.

When a sink receives data packets from some neighbors, it reinforces one of the neighbors by increasing the data rate in the interest packet. Usually, this neighbor is the one on the least-delay path. If a node receives an interest packet with a higher data rate, it also reinforces the path in the interest cache. Since the entries in the interest cache are kept as soft state, eventually only one path remains, while other paths are torn down.

18.2.1.2.2 Sensor Protocol for Information via Negotiation (SPIN)

SPIN is a push diffusion mechanism in which data sources initiate the data-sending activities. SPIN consists of three-stage handshaking operations (Figure 18.6), including *ADV* (advertisement), *REQ* (request for data), and *DATA* (data message). Instead of directly flooding new data, its metadata are exchanged in the

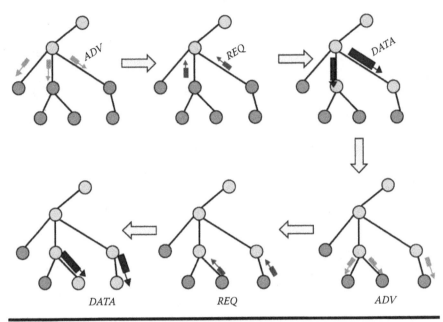

Figure 18.6 Three-phase handshaking protocols in SPIN.

first two advertisement subscription phases to reduce message overhead. If a node receives an advertisement with new information that is of interest to it, it replies with a request packet. The real data are then transmitted in the third phase upon receipt of such a request. The propagation of new information is executed hop by hop throughout the entire network.

18.2.1.3 Mechanisms Based on the Structure of Dissemination

The number of sources and sinks in sensor network applications not only determines the direction of diffusion but also plays a crucial role in laying the structure of dissemination in the system, especially when it is considered in conjunction with data fusion.

18.2.1.3.1 Tree

One of the most common dissemination structures used in sensor networks is a tree that is rooted at the sink and spans the set of sources from which the sink will receive information. It is usually constructed in the reverse multicast fashion. TAG and TinyDB use sink trees for data dissemination. At the other extreme, in the scenario of a single source and multiple sinks, a tree is rooted at a source and constructed in the usual multicast fashion. The sinks broadcast their interest packets for certain events. Upon receipt of an interest packet, each sensor updates its distance to the sink and forwards the packet if it is new to the sensor. Each of the interest packets that record a minimum distance from some sink will be used by the source to construct the shortest path tree. The tree grows from the root and follows the reverse paths to reach sinks. A sensor node with a new stimulus joins the tree at the on-tree sensor that is closest to it, thus creating a new branch of the tree.

In the Scalable Energy-efficient Asynchronous Dissemination (SEAD) protocol, a dissemination tree is built to deliver data from a source (root) to multiple mobile sinks (leaves). The tree is built on an underlying geographical routing protocol. When a mobile sink would like to receive data from a source, it connects to the dissemination tree through one of its neighboring sensors, called an *access node*. Similar to the home agent in Mobile Internet Protocol (Mobile IP), the access node acts as an anchor node to relay data to the sink. When the sink moves out of the transmission range of its access node, it informs the access node of its new whereabouts by sending a *PathSetup* message. The latter will then forward all the data packets that are of interest to the node.

When the distance to the original access node exceeds a predetermined threshold, the mobile sink joins a new access node. In order to reduce the number of messages transmitted over the tree, a source node duplicates its data at several replicas. The criterion for placing a replica on the tree is to minimize the extra cost of constructing a branch for a new join request.

18.2.1.3.2 Cluster

When data fusion is integrated with data dissemination, data generated by sensors are first processed locally to produce a concise digest, which is then delivered to a sink. A hierarchical cluster structure is better suited for this purpose. The low-energy adaptation clustering hierarchy (LEACH), which aims to balance the load of sensors with the achievement of energy efficiency, is a two-level clustering mechanism in which sensors are partitioned into clusters. Each sensor volunteers to become a *clusterhead* (CH) with a certain probability, such that the task of being CHs is evenly distributed and rotated among all sensors. Once a sensor elects itself as the CH, it broadcasts a message to notify other nearby sensor nodes of the fact that it is willing to be a CH. The remaining sensors then select a minimum transmission power to join their closest CHs. Within the cluster, a CH uses time division multiple access (TDMA) to allocate time slots to cluster members (so that the latter can relay their readings to the CH), compresses received data, and transmits a digested report directly to the base station (i.e., sink).

18.2.1.3.3 Grid

Similar to SEAD, two-tier data dissemination (TTDD) is designed for scenarios with a single source and multiple mobile sinks; however, unlike SEAD, a grid structure is adopted as the dissemination structure in TTDD. In the higher tier, a source that detects an event proactively constructs a grid structure where sensors close to the grid points are elected as dissemination nodes. In the lower tier, a mobile sink sends a query to, and receives data from, its nearest point on the local grid. When a sink moves to another grid, it can quickly connect to the grid structure and the information access delay thus incurred is reduced. One of the applications for which TTDD is particularly well suited is target tracking in the battlefield.

18.2.1.3.4 Chain

If the energy efficiency and bandwidth usage requirement is more important than the latency requirement, the chain structure that allows the aggregation of data along a path ending at a sink is a competitive solution. Power-Efficient Gathering in Sensor Information Systems (PEGASIS) is designed to aggregate data collected by all sensors in the entire network. Only one leader is elected each time, and the leadership is rotated among all the sensors. Under the assumption that the network topology is a complete graph, the leader is able to connect all the sensors with the chain structure. Starting from the sensor at one end of the chain, data are propagated and aggregated along the chain toward the leader. Then the data dissemination and aggregation processes continue from the other end. The aggregations from both ends arrive at the leader, which directly transmits the aggregation result to the sink.

18.3 Sensor Database

The main purpose of a sensor database system is to facilitate the data collection process. Users specify their interests via simple, declarative Structured Query Language (SQL)-like queries. Upon receipt of a request, the sensor database system efficiently collects and processes data within the sensor network, and disseminates the result to users. A query-processing layer between the application layer and the network layer provides an interface for users to interact with the sensor network. The layer should also be responsible for managing the resources (especially the available power).

Sensor networks can be envisioned as a distributed database for users to query the physical world. In most sensor network applications, sensors extract useful information from the environment, and either respond to queries made by users or take an active role to disseminate the information to one or more sinks. The information is then exploited by subscribers and/or users for their decision making.

Consider an environment monitoring and alert system that uses several types of sensors, including rainfall sensors, water-level sensors, weather sensors, and chemical sensors, to record the precipitation and water level regularly, to report the current weather conditions, and to issue flood or chemical pollution warnings.

A complete (four-tier) hierarchical architecture of sensor database systems for such a monitoring application is shown in Figure 18.7a. The lowest level is a group of sensor nodes that perform sensing, computing, and in-network processing in a field. The data collected within the sensor network are first propagated to its gateway node (second level). Next, the gateway node relays the data through a transit network to a remote base station (third level). Finally, the base station connects to a database replica across the Internet. Among the four tiers, the resource within the sensor networks is the most constrained. In most of the applications, the sensor network is composed of sensors and a gateway node (sink), as shown in Figure 18.7b, although the number of sinks or sources might vary from application to application.

TinyDB evolved from Tiny Aggregation (TAG), and is built on top of the TinyOS operating system. The sink and sensors are connected in a routing tree, shown in Figure 18.7b. A sensor chooses its parent node, which is one hop closer to the root (sink). The sink accepts queries from users outside the sensor network. Query processing can be performed in four steps:

1. Query optimization
2. Query dissemination
3. Query execution
4. Data dissemination

For the monitoring application under consideration, there are five types of queries that users typically make.

1. Historical queries: These queries are concerned with aggregate, historical information gathered over time and stored in a database system—for example, "What was the average level of rainfall of Thane District in May 2010?"
2. Snapshot queries: These queries are concerned with the information gathered from the network at a specific (current or future) time point—for example, "Retrieve the current readings of temperature sensors in Thane District."
3. Long-running queries: These queries ask for information over a period of time—for example, "Retrieve every 30 minutes the highest temperature sensor reading in Thane District from 6:00 p.m. to 10:00 p.m. tonight."
4. Event-triggered queries: These queries prespecify the conditions that trigger queries—for example, "If the water level exceeds 10 m in Thane District, query the rainfall sensors about the amount of precipitation during the past hour. If the amount of precipitation exceeds 100 mm, send an emergency message to the base station to issue a flood warning."

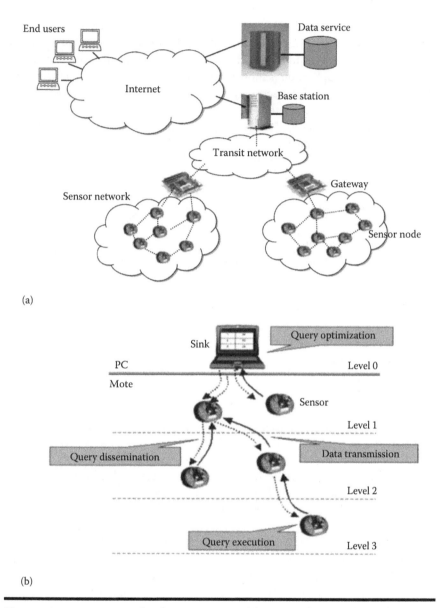

(a)

(b)

Figure 18.7   (a) Sensor database system architecture, (b) procedures for query and data extraction in TinyDB.

5. Multidimensional range queries: These queries involve more than one attribute of sensor data and specify the desired search range as well—for example, "In Thane District, list the positions of all sensors that detect water levels of 5–8 m and have temperatures of 50°F–60°F.

TinyDB provides a declarative SQL-like query interface for users to specify the data to be extracted. Similar to SQL, the acquisitional query language used in TinyDB, TinySQL consists of a *select-from-where* clause that supports selection, join, projection, and aggregation. The data within sensor networks can be considered a table, each column of which corresponds to an attribute and each row of which corresponds to a sample measured at a specific location and time. The query language in the sensor database differs from SQL mainly in that its queries are continuous and periodic.

Upon reception of a query, the sink performs query optimization to reduce the energy incurred in the pending query process.

- Ordering sampling operations: Since the energy incurred in retrieving readings from different types of sensors is different, the sampling operations should be reduced for sensors that consume high energy.
- Query aggregation: By combining multiple queries for the same event into a single query, only one query needs to be sent.

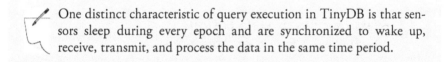 One distinct characteristic of query execution in TinyDB is that sensors sleep during every epoch and are synchronized to wake up, receive, transmit, and process the data in the same time period.

After a query is optimized at the sink, it is broadcast by the sink and disseminated to the sensor network. When a sensor receives a query, it has to decide whether to process the query locally and/or rebroadcasts it to its children. A sensor only needs to forward the query to those child nodes that may have the matched result. To this end, a sensor has to maintain information on its children's attribute values. In TinyDB, a semantic routing tree (SRT) containing the range of the attributes of its children is constructed at each sensor. The attributes can be static information (e.g., location) or dynamic information (e.g., light readings). For attributes that are highly correlated among neighbors in the tree, the SRT can reduce the number of disseminated queries.

18.4 Data Fusion Mechanisms

In most sensor network applications, sensors are deployed over a region to extract environmental data. Once data are gathered by multiple sources (e.g., sensors in the vicinity of the event of interest), they are forwarded perhaps through multiple hops to a single destination (sink). This, coupled with the facts that the information gathered by neighboring sensors is often redundant and highly correlated, and that the energy is much more constrained (because once deployed, most sensor networks operate in the unattended mode), necessitates the need for data fusion. Instead of transmitting all the data to a centralized node for processing, data are processed locally and a concise digest is forwarded (perhaps through multiple hops) to sinks. Data fusion reduces the number of packets to be transmitted among sensors and, thus, the usage in bandwidth and energy. Its benefits become manifest especially in a large-scale network: for a network with n sensors, the centralized approach takes $O(\sqrt{n^{3/2}})$ bit-hops, while data fusion takes only $O(\sqrt{n})$ bit-hops to transmit data.

When data fusion is considered in conjunction with data gathering and dissemination, the conventional address-centric routing, which finds the shortest routes from sources to the sink, is no longer optimal. Instead, data-centric routing, which considers in-network aggregation along the routes from multiple sources to a sink, achieves better energy and bandwidth efficiency, especially when the number of sources is large and/or when the sources are located closely to one another and far from the sink. Figure 18.8 gives a simple illustration of data-centric routing versus address-centric routing. Source 1 chooses node A as the relaying node in address-centric routing, but chooses node C as the relaying and data aggregation node in data-centric routing. As a result, a smaller number of packets are transmitted in data-centric routing.

18.4.1 Classification of Data Fusion Mechanisms Based on Functions

The major purpose of incorporating data fusion into the data-gathering and dissemination process is to reduce the number of packets to be transmitted and, hence, the energy incurred in transmission. There are two types of data aggregation: *snapshot aggregation* is data fusion for a single event, such as tracking a target,

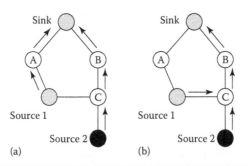

Figure 18.8   Address-centric routing vs. data-centric routing.

while *periodic aggregation* periodically executes the data fusion function, such as monitoring an environment parameter periodically.

Depending on the application requirements, three types of data fusion functions can be used.

1. Basic operations: The most basic operations for data fusion include: COUNT, MIN, MAX, SUM, and AVERAGE.
2. Redundancy suppression: Data fusion, in this case, is equivalent to data compression. Due to the fact that correlations exist in sensor data both in the spatial and temporal domains, one of the most important data fusion functions is to eliminate data redundancy, or in a more concrete term, to exploit the correlation structure that exists in sensor data via distributed source coding.
3. Estimation of a system parameter: Based on the observations from several pieces of sensor data, the data fusion function aims to solve an optimization problem to minimize the estimation error of a system parameter. An example of such an optimization problem is to average all the temperature readings of sensors within a room to estimate the temperature. The estimation is optimal with respect to the minimum square error (MSE) criterion. Another example is to track targets to minimize the estimation error of the target's location.

18.4.2 System Architectures of Data Fusion

Besides the sources and sinks, a sensor network that considers data fusion has an additional component: the data aggregator. There exist a wide variety of ways to determine the location of the data aggregator.

Data funneling is intrinsically an energy-efficient routing protocol integrated with data aggregation and compression techniques. The basic idea of data funneling is to build a cost field with the funnel shape to pull the data from sources to the sink. The sink initials directional flooding to send an interest packet toward a target region. During the process of forwarding interest packets, a forwarder computes its (energy) cost for communicating back to the sink and updates the cost field in the interest packet.

When a node within the target region receives an interest packet from the nodes outside the region, it designates itself a border node. The cost required to reach the sink (i.e., the cost in the interest packet) is recorded, and a field that is used to keep track of the cost to reach the border node is also included. Since there could be multiple *entries* (i.e., border nodes) to the target region, a node within the target region might receive multiple interest packets from border nodes. Instead of requesting all the nodes to send individual reports back to the sink, one of the border nodes is responsible for the task of collecting and aggregating all reports in the region and sending a single packet to the sink. All the sensors within the region share a common schedule of which border node will be the data aggregator during each round of reporting. The schedule is determined by a deterministic function of the costs to reach the sink from all border nodes. Sensors with a longer distance to the designated aggregator send their reports earlier and the readings are concatenated in a single packet to eliminate redundant headers. After receiving reports from all the sensors within the region, the designated border node further compresses the data by applying a coding technique based on ordering.

18.4.3 Trade-Offs of Resources

Depending on the resource constraints in a sensor network, there exist the following trade-offs: energy versus estimation accuracy, energy versus aggregation latency, and bandwidth versus aggregation latency.

18.4.3.1 Trade-Off between Energy and Accuracy

The requirement of higher accuracy demands more message exchanges and leads to higher energy consumption. A distributed periodic aggregation approach to estimate the maximum sensor data in a field entails the fact that the maximum sensor data are modeled to be Gaussian distributed. Compared with multiple *snapshot aggregations*, the proposed approach exploits the energy–accuracy trade-off and provides users with a system-level knob to control the desired accuracy and energy consumption. The distributed optimization approach shows that $O(\varepsilon^{-2})$ iterations of aggregation are required to achieve the desired accuracy ε.

18.4.3.2 Trade-Off between Energy and Latency

This deals with the trade-off between energy consumption and propagation latency from data sources to a sink. Energy is saved via directly turning off the radio circuitry when a sensor is not transmitting or receiving data. While the low duty cycle reduces power consumption, it increases the propagation latency from a data source to the sink. The Sparse Topology and Energy Management (STEM) protocol is proposed to deal with the problem. STEM utilizes dual bands for data transmission and wake-up signaling. The channel for wake-up signaling is operated in a low duty cycle. Each node periodically turns on the radio circuitry for the wake-up channel to hear whether any other node has attempted to communicate with it. Once a node detects such an activity in the wake-up signaling channel, it turns on its radio circuitry for the data channel. The increased latency due to the sleep state is thus bounded by the sleep–listen period in the wake-up channel. STEM is especially well suited for applications with most operations in the monitoring state. For instance, in a fire alarm system, the network only senses the environment in an energy-efficient way, and the system stays in the monitoring state most of the time. Once an event takes place, the system quickly changes to the transfer state and reports the event to the data sink in a timely manner.

18.5 Summary

The creation and optimization of sensor networks goes beyond robust and low-cost platforms, since the node distribution, communication, and dissemination strategies, as well as the cooperative processing capabilities of hundreds or even thousands of small devices are critical aspects to assure the actual performance and reliability of the planned application. The chapter first introduced the wireless sensor networks (WSN) in terms of aspects like characteristics, design challenges, and consequent objectives and application architecture. The chapter then presented sensor data mechanisms and storage. The chapter ended with the description of several data fusion mechanisms.

Epilogue

Organizations as a Network of Projects

Organizations can be treated as an *ensemble* of projects—thus, rendering projects as the smallest addressable entities within an organization. Projects have identified objectives, are dynamic, have a finite lifecycle, and consume resources (money, material, manpower, time, information, etc.) while constantly interacting with the environment and interfacing with other project(s). In parallel with the network/hierarchy of objectives, organization can be envisaged as a network/hierarchy of projects; projects can be of all types: business, strategy, financial, technical, or technology types; projects can be of all sizes and also evolve. Projects can be fully internal or allied with other appropriate organizations or joint ventures or even fully outsourced external organizations.

Conventional approaches to management tend to have a static view of its operations. In contrast, management by projects inherently reflects the dynamic nature of organization; it also emphasizes the executional aspects of businesses that is often lacking.

Organizations, when examined in the light of network theory, can be seen to inherently possess a network-like nature, and we can analyze their behavior and development with this new understanding. More importantly, this knowledge enables us to consciously design, manage, operate, and improve the organization with a much higher level of optimization.

On the lines of how Peter Drucker conceived of management by objectives (MBO), one can state that if organizations are a network of projects, then managing them as such would effectively mean *management by projects* (MBP).

Bibliography

R. Anupindi, S. Chopra, S. D. Deshmukh, J. A. Van Mieghem, and E. Zemel, *Managing Business Process Flows: Principles of Operations Management* (Prentice-Hall, 3rd Ed, 2012)

Albert-Laszlo Barabasi, *Linked: The New Science of Networks* (Perseus Publishers, 2002)

Joel A. C. Baum and Timothy J. Rowley (Eds.), *Network Strategy* (Emerald Group Publishers, 2008)

R. E. Baxter, *The Membership Economy: Find Your Superusers, Master the Forever Transaction and Build Recurring Revenue* (McGraw-Hill, 2015)

Stefan Bornholdt and Heinz Georg Schuster (Eds.), *Handbook of Graphs and Networks: From the Genome to the Internet* (Wiley, 2003)

J. L. Bradach, *Franchise Organizations* (Harvard Business Review Press, 1998)

Tom Brughmans, Anna Collar, and Fiona Cowards (Eds.), *The Connected Past: Challenges to Network Studies in Archaeology and History* (Oxford University Press, 2016)

Hans de Bruijn and Ernst ten Heuvelhof, *Management in Networks: On Multi-Actor Decision Making* (Routledge, 2008)

M. Burgess, *In Search of Certainty: The Science of Our Information Infrastructure* (CreateSpace, 2013)

L. M. Camarinha-Matos and H. Afsarmanesh (Eds.), *Collaborative Networks: Reference Modeling* (Springer, 2010)

L. M. Camarinha-Matos, H. Afsarmanesh, and M. Ollus (Eds.), *Virtual Organizations: Systems and Practices* (Springer, 2010)

Otto Carlos, M.B. Duarte, and Guy Pujolle, *Virtual Networks: Pluralistic Approach for the Next Generation of Internet* (Wiley, 2013)

M. Castells, *The Information Age: Economy, Society and, Culture-Volume I The Rise of the Network Society* (Wiley-Blackwell, 2nd Ed. 2010)

C. Cioffi-Revilla, *Introduction to Computational Social Science: Principles and Applications* (Springer, 2014)

G. Coulouris, J. Dollimore, T. Kindberg, and G. Blair. *Distributed Systems: Concept and Design* (Boston, MA: Addison-Wesley, 2011)

M. M. Cunha and G. D. Putnik, *Agile Virtual Enterprises: Implementation and Management Support* (Idea Group Publishing, 2006)

M. Dehmer (Ed.), *Structural Analysis of Complex Networks* (Birkhauser, 2011)

N. Deo, *Graph Theory with Applications to Engineering & Computer Science* (Dover, 2016)

Jerzy Domżał, Robert Wójcik, and Andrzej Jajszczyk, *Guide to Flow-Aware Networking: Quality-of-Service Architectures and Techniques for Traffic Management* (Springer, 2015)

D. Easley and J. Klienberg, *Networks, Crowds and Markets: Reasoning about a Highly Connected World* (Cambridge University Press, 2010)

Chris Fill and Karen E. Fill, *Business-to-Business Marketing: Relationships, Systems and Communications* (Pearson Educational, 2005)

A. Gegov, *Fuzzy Networks for Complex Systems: A Modular Rule Base Approach* (Springer, 2010)

B. George and S. Kim, *Spatio-Temporal Networks: Modeling and Algorithms* (Springer, 2013)

Ian Graham and P. L. Jones, *Expert Systems: Knowledge, Uncertainty and Decision* (Chapman & Hall, 1988)

D. S. Grewal, *Network Power: The Social Dynamics of Globalization* (Yale University Press, 2009)

I. Goldin and M. Mariathasan, *The Butterfly Defect: How Globalization Creates Systemic Risks, and What to Do About It* (Princeton University, 2014)

Tor Guimaraes, *Enabling the Virtual Organizations with Agent Technology* in C. Camison, D. Palacios, F. Garrigos and C. Devece, *Connectivity and Knowledge Management in Virtual Organizations: Networking and Developing Interactive Communications* (IGI Global, 2009)

A. Gunasekaran, *Agile Manufacturing: The 21st Century Competitive Strategy* (Elsevier, 2001)

John Hagel III, *Out of the Box: Strategies for Achieving Profits Today and Growth Tomorrow through Web Services* (Harvard Business Review Press, 2005)

N. J. A. Hastings and J. M. C. Mello, *Decision Networks* (Wiley, 1978)

C. Heinrich, *Adapt or Die: Transforming Your Supply Chain into an Adaptive Business Network* (Wiley, 2003)

K. Hwang, J. Dongarra, and G. Fox, *Distributed and Cloud Computing: From Parallel Processing to the Internet of Things* (Morgan-Kaufmann, 2011)

B. H. Junker and F. Schreiber (Eds.), *Analysis of Biological Networks* (Wiley, 2008)

Vivek Kale, *Guide to Cloud Computing for Business and Technology Managers: From Distributed Computing to Cloudware Applications* (London: Auerbach Publications, 2015)

Vivek Kale, *Big Data Computing: A Guide for Business and Technology Managers* (Chapman & Hall, 2016)

Parag Khanna, *Connectography: Mapping the Future for Global Civilization* (Random House, 2016)

P. R. Kliendorfer and Yoram (Jerry) Wind, *The Network Challenge: Strategy, Profit, and Risk in an Interlinked World* (Pearson, 2009)

Paul R. Kleindorfer and Yoram (Jerry) Wind, *The Network Challenge: Strategy, Profit, and Risk in an Interlinked World* (Wharton School Publishing, 2009)

Daphne Koller and Nir Friedman, *Probabilistic Graphical Models: Principles and Techniques* (MIT Press, 2009)

D. Lepore, A. Montgomery, and G. Siepe, *Quality Involvement Flow: The Systemic Organization* (CRC Press, 2017)

Alain Martel and Walid Klibi, *Designing Value-Creating Supply Chain Networks* (Springer, 2016)

A. Meier and H. Stormer, *eBusiness & eCommerce: Managing the Digital Value Chain* (Springer, 2009)

A. Nagumay and S. Siokos, *Financial Networks: Statics and Dynamics* (Springer, 1997)

A. Nagumay and J. Dong, *Supernetworks: Decision-Making for the Information Age* (Edward Elgar, 2002)

R. E. Neapolitan, *Probabilistic Reasoning in Expert Systems: Theory and Algorithms* (CreateSpace, 2012)

N. E. J. Newman, *Networks: An Introduction* (Oxford University Press, 2010)

H. Osterle, E. Fleisch, and R. Alt, *Business Networking: Shaping Collaboration Between Enterprises* (Springer, 2nd Ed., 2001)

M. P. Papazoglou and Pieter M.A. Ribbers, *e-Business Organizational and Technical Foundations* (Wiley, 2006)

G. Passiante (Ed.), *Evolving Towards the Internetworked Enterprise: Technological and Organizational Perspective* (Springer, 2010)

A. Prencipe, A. Davies, and M. Hobday, *The Business of Systems Integration* (Oxford University Press, 2008)

J. Pearl, *Probabilistic Reasoning in Intelligent Systems: Networks of Plausible Inference* (Morgan Kaufmann Publishers, 1988)

Edward S. Pound, Jeffrey H. Bell, and Mark L. Spearman, *Factory Physics for Managers-How Leaders Improve Performance in a Post-Lean Six Sigma World* (McGraw-Hill, 2014)

Lee Rainie and Barry Wellman, *Networked: The New Social Operating System* (MIT Press, 2012)

G. Ritzer, *Globalization: The Essentials* (Wiley, 2011)

Luiz A.O. Rocha, Sylvie Lorente, and Adrian Bejan (Eds.), *Constructal Law and the Unifying Principle of Design* (Springer, 2013)

D. L. Rogers, *The Network is Your Customer: Five Strategies to Thrive in a Digital Age* (Yale University Press, 2010)

Thomas L. Saaty and Luis G. Vargas, *Decision Making with the Analytic Network Process: Economic, Political, Social and Technological Applications with Benefits, Opportunities, Costs and Risks* (Springer, 2013)

Sherif Sakr, F. M. Orakzai, I. Abdelaziz, and Z. Khayyat, *Large Scale Graph Processing using Apache Giraph* (Springer, 2016)

Sebastian Seung, *Connectome: How the Brain's Wiring Makes Us Who We Are* (Houghton Mifflin Harcourt, 2012)

J. N. Sheth and A. Parvatiyar, *Relationship Marketing* (Sage Publishing, 1999)

Oz Shy, *Industrial Organization: Theory and Applications* (The MIT Press, 1995)

Włodzimierz Sroka and Stefan Hittmar, *Management of Network Organizations: Theoretical Problems and the Dilemmas in Practice* (Springer, 2015)

R. Stocker and T. Bossomaier. *Networks in Society: Links and Language* (Pan Stanford Publishing, 2013)

Don Tapscott, David Ticoll, and Alex Lowy, *Digital Capital: Harnessing the Power of Business Webs* (Havard Business School Press, 2000)

E. Todeva, *Business Networks: Strategy and Structure* (Routledge, 2006)

Peter H.M. Vervest, Diederik W. van Liere, and Li Zheng, *The Network Experience: New Value from Smart Business Networks* (Springer, 2009)

T. W. Walker, *Supply Chain Construction: The Basics for Networking the Flow of the Material, Information, and Cash* (CRC Press, 2015)

J. Warrillow, *Automatic Customer: Creating a Subscription Business in Any Industry* (Portfolio, 2015)

D. J. Watts, *Six Degrees: The Science of Connected Age* (W. W. Norton, 2004)

J. Word (Ed.), *Business Network Transformation: Strategies to Reconfigure Your Business Relationships for Competitive Advantage* (Jossey-Bass, 2009)

E. Yücesan, *Competitive Supply Chains: A Value-Based Management Perspective* (Palgrave Macmillan, 2007)

Index